The Guantánamo Lawyers

The Guantánamo Lawyers

Inside a Prison Outside the Law

EDITED BY

Mark P. Denbeaux and Jonathan Hafetz

WITH

Grace A. Brown, Michelle Fish,
Jillian Gautier, and Mark Muoio

Central Islip Public Library
33 Hawthorne Avenue
central Islip, NY 11722-2496

NEW YORK UNIVERSITY PRESS
New York and London

3 1800 00265 3547

To all lawyers fighting against illegal detention.

NEW YORK UNIVERSITY PRESS
New York and London
www.nyupress.org

© 2009 by New York University
All rights reserved

Library of Congress Cataloging-in-Publication Data

The Guantánamo lawyers : inside a prison outside the law /
edited by Mark P. Denbeaux and Jonathan Hafetz ; with Grace A. Brown . . . [et al.].
p. cm.
Includes index.
ISBN-13: 978-0-8147-3736-1 (cl : alk. paper)
ISBN-10: 0-8147-3736-6 (cl : alk. paper)
1. Prisoners of war—Legal status, laws, etc.—Cuba—Guantánamo Bay Naval Base.
2. Detention of persons—Cuba—Guantánamo Bay Naval Base. 3. Lawyers—Cuba—
Guantánamo Bay Naval Base. 4. Guantánamo Bay Detention Camp. 5. Prisoners of
war—Legal status, laws, etc.—Afghanistan—Kapisa (Extinct city) 6. Detention of
persons—Afghanistan—Kapisa (Extinct city) I. Denbeaux, Mark P. II. Hafetz, Jonathan.
III. Brown, Grace A.
KZ6495.G83   2009
343.73'0143—dc22   2009023488

New York University Press books are printed on acid-free paper,
and their binding materials are chosen for strength and durability.
We strive to use environmentally responsible suppliers and materials
to the greatest extent possible in publishing our books.

Manufactured in the United States of America

10 9 8 7 6 5 4 3 2 1

Contents

Introduction

Mark P. Denbeaux and Jonathan Hafetz

Following the terrorist attacks of September 11, 2001, the United States imprisoned more than 750 men at its naval base at Guantánamo Bay, Cuba. The prisoners ranged in age from teenage boys to elderly men. They were seized from more than forty countries around the world: some from Afghanistan, others from places as far flung as Bosnia and the Gambia. Many had wives and children. And the prisoners had some other things in common. They were all detained for years without charges, without trial, and without a fair hearing. They were all denied any legal status or protection because President Bush had unilaterally declared them "unlawful combatants." They were all held in secret and denied communication with their families and loved ones. Most, if not all, were subjected to extreme isolation, physical and mental abuse, and, in some instances, torture. Many were innocent; none was provided an opportunity to prove it.

These are their stories. The stories are told by their lawyers because the prisoners themselves were silenced. From the moment the first prisoners arrived at Guantánamo shackled and hooded in January 2002, the U.S. government prevented them from communicating with the outside world. The United States initially refused even to reveal the prisoners' names. No one knew who was at Guantánamo, why they had been imprisoned there, or how they were being treated. The public knew only what the Bush administration told it: that the detainees there were all hardened terrorists, "the worst of the worst."

It took lawyers more than two years—and a ruling from the U.S. Supreme Court—to finally gain the right to visit and talk to the men at Guantánamo. Even then, lawyers were forced to operate under severe restrictions designed to inhibit communication and envelop the prison in secrecy. In time, however, lawyers were able to meet with their clients, observe their suffering, and begin to describe to the world the truth about

Guantánamo. To date, lawyers remain the only people other than government officials and representatives from the International Committee for the Red Cross (who are bound to confidentiality) to see or speak to the Guantánamo detainees. Lawyers have remained on the front lines in the long-running struggle to bring justice to Guantánamo, a battle that has been waged both inside and outside courtrooms, at home and abroad, for more than seven years.

Ironically, lawyers were never meant to go to Guantánamo. After September 11, the Bush administration was looking for a place to bring prisoners captured during the U.S.-led military invasion of Afghanistan (many of whom were sold to the United States for a bounty), as well as prisoners seized elsewhere in connection with the so-called global "war on terror." The administration believed it had captured many dangerous people and wanted to find a place where it could detain and interrogate them without restriction or interference. It also wanted a place that would be beyond the reach of the courts. So it chose the U.S. naval base at Guantánamo Bay, an approximately forty-five-square-mile area at the eastern end of Cuba.

Although Guantánamo Bay still formally belongs to Cuba, the United States has for more than a century maintained total and exclusive control over the territory through a series of lease agreements. Under the agreements, that control is effectively permanent, lasting as long as the United States wishes to occupy the territory. Bush administration officials thus saw in Guantánamo the possibility of creating an enclave over which the United States exercised complete dominion but whose formal status as "Cuban territory" would place it beyond the reach of any court. Administration officials also believed that by labeling Guantánamo detainees "enemy combatants," it could hold them at Guantánamo indefinitely, potentially for life, without charges or trial. At the same time, the Bush administration made a series of determinations that the prisoners at Guantánamo, as well as others held as "enemy combatants" in the global "war on terror," were not entitled to any protections under American or international law, including under the Geneva Conventions, which were intended to ensure that no prisoner is outside the law.

The fact that over time Guantánamo was brought—at least partially— within the rule of law had nothing to do with the Bush administration, which resisted affording detainees any protections and sought to undermine court decisions at every step. Nor can credit be given to Congress, which initially stood silently by and then twice tried to strip detainees of meaningful access to U.S. courts. Rather, it had to do with the resilience of habeas corpus. For centuries, the writ of habeas corpus has served as the preeminent safeguard of individual liberty and check against arbitrary government power, mandating that the state justify a prisoner's detention before a judge. After September 11, habeas corpus resumed its historical function as a remedy against executive imprisonment and became the main vehicle in challenging the detention and mistreatment of prisoners held in the "war on terror."

In June 2004, the U.S. Supreme Court ruled that the federal habeas corpus statute extended to detainees at Guantánamo and rejected the Bush administration's claim that it could operate a prison without any judicial oversight. "Executive imprisonment," wrote Justice John Paul Stevens in rendering the decision, "has been considered oppressive and lawless" since Magna Carta. Yet, in many ways, the struggle had only begun. The administration quickly sought to block judicial hearings by creating military boards—known as Combatant Status Review Tribunals—that lacked the most basic elements of due process, denying detainees an opportunity to see and respond to the evidence against them and laundering information gained through torture. The administration then twice persuaded Congress (first in 2005 and again in 2006) to amend the habeas corpus statute, which had provided a remedy for federal prisoners since the nation's founding, to eliminate access to the writ for any foreign national the executive designated an "enemy combatant." No hearings occurred as legal battles over the legislation played out. Meanwhile, detainees at Guantánamo continued to languish, day after day, month after month, year after year.

Finally, in 2008, the Supreme Court decisively rejected the Bush administration's continued effort to deny Guantánamo detainees habeas corpus. This time, the Court made clear that the right to habeas corpus was grounded in the Constitution, not merely in a federal statute, which could be amended by Congress. The Court also did not limit its ruling to Guantánamo but instead held that habeas corpus could potentially reach anywhere the United States deprived a person of liberty. Treating detention as a shell game, where a prisoner's location could be shifted to evade habeas review, the Court explained, would make the scope of the Constitution "subject to manipulation by those [Executive branch officials] whose power it is designed to restrain." The Supreme Court thus dealt a significant blow not only to Guantánamo but also to the concept of a lawless enclave on which it was based. Following the Court's decision, district court judges began holding the first hearings for Guantánamo detainees since their imprisonment—a wait that in some cases had stretched more than seven years.

An important legal principle had been vindicated: the right of individuals detained by the United States to seek review before a judge. But the human, moral, and reputational price of this victory was staggering. Hundreds of individuals had been held for years without a fair hearing and subjected to torture and other abuse. The prisoners had largely been kept in isolation and denied all meaningful contact with their families and the outside world. None had been charged with a crime in a court of law.

Guantánamo, meanwhile, had become the source of universal criticism, including from the United States' closest allies. The attorney general of the United Kingdom perhaps best symbolized the broad opposition, remarking that the prison had become a symbol of injustice throughout the world. Calls came from across the political spectrum to close it. Military and diplomatic officials became some of Guantánamo's fiercest critics, maintaining that the prison undermined the United States' credibility and security and diminished its ability to fight terrorism worldwide.

To be sure, Guantánamo had changed over the years. Prisoners no longer were held in the makeshift open-air cells that one former government official compared to "an outdoor cattle stable." By the end of the Bush administration, most of the remaining 250 detainees were being held in modern facilities built to resemble state-of-the-art maximum-security prisons in the United States. But the underlying reality of Guantánamo— one of indefinite detention outside the ordinary judicial system—had not changed; it had become institutionalized.

On Barack Obama's inauguration on January 20, 2009, the new president told the nation, "As for our common defense, we reject as false the choice between our safety and our ideals." In the first hours of his presidency, President Obama ordered that the prison at Guantánamo be closed within a year. The announcement stirred hopes for an end to an ignominious chapter in the country's history and for the restoration of the rule of law in the United States.

Yet important questions remained. What would happen to the remaining prisoners? Would they simply be moved onshore and held under the same failed regime without charges or trial? Would the United States continue to deny prisoners held elsewhere the right to habeas corpus? In short, would Guantánamo simply be modified, or was the Guantánamo system at an end? Those questions have yet to be answered. And despite President Obama's positive first steps, his administration subsequently showed troubling signs of adhering to failed Bush-era national security policies, from reviving military commission trials to maintaining over-broad claims of secrecy and detention power in ongoing litigation.

It is impossible to capture Guantánamo fully in one book. This book is no exception, but as a collection of stories meant to reflect the experience of habeas attorneys and their clients, the detainees, through the process of the Guantánamo litigation, the book's cumulative perspective offers an exceptional point of view. What is ultimately most striking is the passion of the stories' individual expression—poetic, ironic, somber, and occasionally dryly amusing.

These stories constitute only a fraction of the experiences of the men who have been imprisoned at Guantánamo. Yet through these accounts we hope to provide a fuller picture of some important events during the struggle to bring justice to Guantánamo and to give voice to the experiences of the detainees. The book's goal is to create a historical record of Guantánamo's legal, human, and moral failings and provide a window into the United States' catastrophic effort to create a prison beyond the law, disdainful of its own best traditions and world opinion, a failure that will take many years to repair even after the doors of the prison are finally shuttered.

The stories are organized to take the reader on a roughly chronological journey of the Guantánamo detainee litigation through the eyes of the attorneys. The chapters consist of accounts written mostly by lawyers about their experiences and the experiences of their clients. More than 100 lawyers contributed to this book. Their stories have been edited, and sometimes pieces of the same narrative appear in different chapters. The full and unedited stories of the lawyers are collected and preserved in an electronic archive through the Seton Hall Law School and the New York University Libraries. The editors' text is interwoven throughout the book to help provide context and is demarcated by italics. All quotations without citation in the book have been obtained from sources in the public domain and personal interviews. The pieces were all completed by or before June 2009.

Chapter 1 describes how and why attorneys from a variety of backgrounds decided to get involved in the litigation. Chapter 2 describes the landmark U.S. Supreme Court decision, *Rasul v. Bush*, that first granted attorneys access to the detainees. It also discusses the process of getting to Guantánamo and what the attorneys encountered there. Chapter 3 describes what it was like for attorneys finally to meet their clients and to learn about their lives and experiences at Guantánamo. Attorneys faced many legal challenges in trying to secure rights for their clients. These barriers are described in chapter 4. This chapter also describes the legal battles to vindicate the detainees' rights to habeas corpus and their day in court. Chapter 5 focuses on the torture and mistreatment of the detainees while at Guantánamo. It also describes the reactions of detainees, including their frustration and despair. Blocked by the lack of legal process, many attorneys discovered alternative routes to advocate for their clients, as portrayed in chapter 6. After years of imprisonment, some detainees were finally released. Yet many remained at Guantánamo, despite the government's admission that they were no longer "enemy combatants." Attorneys describe the devastating effects of this prolonged and arbitrary detention in chapter 7. Finally, chapter 8 describes the treatment of detainees held as "enemy combatants" in the United States and at secret CIA-run "black sites" abroad, which together illustrate that Guantánamo was not simply a prison but part of a larger, global detention system.

Prelude

P. Sabin Willett: Who's at Guantánamo Anyway?

That's what I was wondering one hot day last July when I walked across a prison yard so silent and sterile as to be a little eerie. Nothing grew in the yard: no grass or flower or tree or even weed. We approached a hut. Inside was a man chained to the floor. His name was Adel. My firm had filed a habeas case for him the previous March, but I'd never seen him or spoken to him before. Was he a terrorist? One of the worst of the worst?

Three weeks before I got to Guantánamo, Vice President Cheney said, "The people that are there are people we picked up on the battlefield, primarily in Afghanistan. They're terrorists. They're bomb makers. They're facilitators of terror. They're members of al Qaeda and the Taliban."

Something was off, right from the first minute. Something about the young man's gentle smile; his calm didn't fit. On that day last July, I discovered what President Bush, and his lawyers at the Justice Department, had kept secret from the public, and even from the court: the military had concluded that Adel was innocent. Not a terrorist. Not an enemy soldier. Not a criminal. Never been on a battlefield. He'd been sold to U.S. forces from the soil of Pakistan, a nation with whom we have never been at war.

Vice President Cheney says that Adel and men like him were picked up on the battlefield, but according to a 2005 study conducted by Seton Hall School of Law, five percent were picked up on the battlefield. Ninety-five percent were not.

How did we get the rest? We distributed leaflets, with smiling Afghans declaring, "Get wealth and power beyond your dreams. . . . You can receive millions of dollars helping the anti-Taliban forces catch al-Qaida and Taliban murderers. This is enough money to take care of your family, your village, your tribe for the rest of your life. Pay for livestock and doctors and school books and housing for all your people."

P. Sabin Willett's comments are based on a speech he gave at Princeton University in February 2006.

7

Eighty-six percent of the Guantánamo detainees were sold to the United States by people who got the flyers. Vice President Cheney says that these men are al Qaeda fighters. What do the data show? Eight percent are al Qaeda fighters. Ninety-two percent are not.

Vice President Cheney says they committed hostile acts against Americans or their allies. What do the data say? Fifty-five percent of the detainees committed no hostile act against the United States or its allies or anyone else. By the way, Cheney and other Bush administration officials construed "hostile act" extremely broadly. Fleeing from bombing by U.S. forces is a hostile act. Being sold to U.S. forces is a hostile act. Possessing a Kalashnikov rifle is a hostile act. It has been estimated that there were upwards of ten million Kalashnikovs in Afghanistan in 2001 and only eight million adult males. An adult Afghan male who hadn't possessed a Kalashnikov was harder to find than an adult Texan male who hadn't possessed a hunting rifle. If you walked into a restaurant in Kabul, you found Kalashnikovs hanging on the coat rack.

For sixty percent of the detainees, the only hook by which they are deemed enemy combatants is that they were "associated with" the Taliban. But you have to understand that in 2001 in Afghanistan, the Taliban was pervasive. Except in a few strongholds of the Northern Alliance, they controlled every village, every town, every guesthouse. If you traveled to Kabul and stayed in a guesthouse, you associated with the Taliban. If you were conscripted against your will into a Taliban militia, you "associated with" the Taliban. For two Saudis held at Guantánamo, their association with the Taliban is that the Taliban held them in prison as enemies of its regime.

I'm not making this up.

Who's at Guantánamo? Privates, orphans, the poor, conscripts, cooks, drivers. The mayors, the ministers, the Taliban generals—they're not there. Take Sayed Rahmutullah Hashemi. He joined the Taliban as a young man. He became a party spokesman. Osama bin Laden came to his office. Is Rahmutullah at Guantánamo? No. He is a freshman at Yale. Some of his former Taliban colleagues are now in the Afghan parliament that the United States helped create. The desperately poor kids they employed as drivers and cooks sit in Guantánamo.

The last lie, the whopper, the huge one, is that Guantánamo holds terrorists. President Bush, Vice President Cheney, their amen chorus in the Senate, they all tell you relentlessly that these people are terrorists. I don't say that there is no terrorist there. But when you review the data, when you search it for anything remotely like a terrorist act—an act of violence against persons or property, for bombing or bomb making or the teaching of bomb making or the fundraising for it—you find that that is, most of all, who *isn't* at Guantánamo.

If there is anyone in Guantánamo who conspired in the 9/11 murders, then I would like to see him tried. If he is guilty, I hope he is convicted. If he is tried and convicted by a federal court or military court martial duly constituted under the Uniform Code or Military Justice, I would shed no tear for the ultimate sentence. All that we lawyers have been asking for, since the beginning, is a hearing, a chance to show whether someone really is an "enemy combatant" or not. And when Guantánamo cases have come up for an actual hearing, like Shafiq Rasul's, what happened after his case came under Supreme Court scrutiny?

They released him.

What happened to Moazzem Begg, another "worst of the worst"?

They released him.

Mamdouh Habib?

When the story of his torture in Egypt surfaced, they released him.

They told us these people were the worst of the worst, and yet rather than prove it, rather than protect you and me from them, they released them before a judge could see any facts. The Nazi war criminals were tried in the sunlight, and the world has never doubted the judgment at Nuremberg. But in no Guantánamo habeas case has President Bush been willing to let a federal judge hear a single fact about the worst of the worst. Instead, in the name of the global "war on terror," the president can seize anyone, anywhere in the world, and transport him to Guantánamo Bay, where he may be held without criminal charge or process. The president may do so even after he has determined that the person was taken by mistake, as in Adel's case, and hold him as long as the war on terror lasts.

So I want you to ask a question. How long will the war on terror last?

We need to acknowledge, if we are thoughtful people, that terror is everywhere and has been with us always and involves all kinds of people who later get called "men of peace." My point is not that we should cease to fight terrorism. It is to ask, does anyone think he or she will live to see the *end* of terrorism? And thus the end of the global war against it? Do you think you'll watch on TV as the Emperor of Terror comes aboard a navy warship to sign the instrument of surrender?

When we say the president has special powers during the global war on terror, we are saying he has them forever. Always and forever can the president lock people up at Guantánamo without meaningful judicial review. Always and forever he can ignore the Congress's ban against torture, as he vowed to do. Always and forever he can tap your phone, download from your iMac, and go snuffling through your trash. Always and forever he can ignore the writ of habeas corpus.

Now you might ask, why care about this? Why volunteer your time to represent these men? It's the war on terror, isn't it? So what if somebody is roughed up a little in Kandahar or Bagram? There are horrors in Darfur and New Orleans. So what if a few Uighurs pay the price? We have reservists from Vermont losing mortgages. Injustices abound in the world. Why care about this particular one?

I want my flag back. My country has been hijacked, and I want it back. If we care about being a civilized people, then it is precisely in times of fear that we have to hold fastest to our rule of law. We already have the tools to deal with fanatics who blow up buildings and murder the innocent. We knew how to deal with Timothy McVeigh and not surrender our souls.

During the Vietnam War, a protestor stood outside the White House with a candle. Every night for weeks. He stood in the cold, in the rain. One day a reporter came up to him and asked, "Do you really think, with your candle, you're going to change White House policy?"

"No," he said, "I'm sure I won't change White House policy. But that's not why I'm doing this."

"Then why are you doing this?" the reporter asked.

"So that White House policy doesn't change me."

Can I bring you any good news? Only a little. Adel's story made its way to the press and thence to Sweden, where a Uighur woman was living as a refugee. On July 28, 2005, I listened on a telephone as she wept. She is Adel's sister, and for four long years she thought he was dead. You see, no one knows who is in Guantánamo. A few weeks later, with the help of some judicial pressure, we organized a very unusual event at GTMO. A phone call between these two people, Adel and his sister. I saw Adel again late in August, after that call. The sleepy-eyed man had come to life. Before, he told me, "It was as though I had evaporated from the earth." A phone call—so small a thing.

The rule of law is not coming back on its own. It will come back only when you go out and grab hold of it by the ears and drag it back. In the ballot box and the courtroom and the newspaper and the classroom and the public street. Can you remember where you were in January 2002? Think back. Now reflect for a moment on what has happened in your life since then. Where you've been. What you've done. Whom you've loved. Who has loved you. Now imagine that none of those things in your life happened because, like Adel, every single one of those days since January 2002 you had been cut off in a prison, just outside the map of the world. Even though the military determined there was no basis to hold you. And imagine the Congress of the United States voted to deny you the chance to ask a judge to make it right. So who's at Guantánamo? The truth is, the answer to the question is . . . You. And me. Until we shut it down, it imprisons all of us.

Thomas P. Sullivan: A Day in Court

Times of real or perceived national crisis test our commitment to the principles that we teach in our schools, announce in the Declaration of Independence and in our federal and state constitutions, and parade on the Fourth of July. Sad to say, as a nation we often slip our moorings, as we did by incarcerating Japanese American citizens during World War II and by spreading the fear of Communist infiltration during the McCarthy era. It is happening again as a result of the September 11, 2001, terrorist attacks.

My impression of the prisoners I've encountered at Guantánamo is shared by my partners who have visited our clients at the prison, as well as by the other fine lawyers for prisoners with whom we've spoken. We believe most of these men are not and never were criminals or terrorists, were not connected with al Qaeda, should not have been imprisoned in the first place, and if sent home would resume peaceful, productive lives, albeit damaged by the awful experiences they have endured during the past seven years. But be they good or evil, these men are entitled to have their captor—the U.S. government—establish before a fair tribunal a valid reason why they should be imprisoned.

"Detainee" is a euphemism used by the government to suggest temporary confinement. It is an inappropriate description of the status of these men. Their "housing" resembles the cellblocks reserved for the most hardened and unruly felons in our state and federal prisons, and their isolation is patterned on how we isolate convicted murderers on death row. The way we are treating them, and the conditions of their confinement, are demeaning, cruel, and unnecessary.

So far as I am able to discern, what keeps these men from sinking into madness is a deep-seated faith and a passionate belief in their religion: Allah has willed their imprisonment, and when He wills otherwise, pursuant to His divine purposes, He will set them free. In the meantime, they take it day by day.

There is ominous potential for future danger flowing from our conduct. Bear in mind one of President Bush's justifications for invading Afghanistan in 2001: that Taliban leaders had not submitted to his demand that they "return all foreign nationals, including American citizens, unjustly detained in their country." If dedication to the rule of law and fair play does not motivate our leaders, they ought to consider the standard we have established for redressing unjust imprisonment of other nations' citizens.

In the past, I have described this state of affairs as a national disgrace, but those words grossly understate my feelings and concerns. The prison at Guantánamo Bay is perceived throughout the globe to be an example of the wretched way Americans treat people of the Islamic faith. As a result, we have brought ourselves into disrepute in many parts of the world. We have become an international bully, treating international rules and our treaty obligations as one-sided, applicable to other countries but not to our own. We are committed as a nation to affording all persons fair hearings and due process of law, regardless of religious belief, skin color, or national origin and without regard to the nature or seriousness of the crimes of which they are accused. Our actions with regard to the men at Guantánamo Bay have violated and continue to this day to violate these basic American principles.

1

Representing the "Worst of the Worst"

How and Why the Lawyers Started Representing Detainees

Initially, only a small number of attorneys came to the defense of the detainees at Guantánamo. In the immediate aftermath of September 11, most people did not question the actions of the U.S. government, and little was known about the new detention center. Over time, however, it became clear that the United States was denying prisoners basic due process and was engaging in abuse. The legal profession rose to the occasion, and lawyers from all types of backgrounds, practices, and locations joined together to provide representation to the detainees and to demand justice. Here is how some explain their involvement.

Kristine A. Huskey: An Inquiry from Abroad

On the morning of September 11, 2001, I was sitting in a conference room at the Waldorf-Astoria in New York City waiting to examine an expert witness in a $40 million reinsurance arbitration. Instead, we watched the Twin Towers collapse on TV, knowing that as people jumped to their death on the small screen, they were jumping to their death in real life just a few miles down Broadway.

That afternoon I walked out to the quiet streets of midtown Manhattan. Streets were devoid of traffic and sparsely littered with people in panic and disbelief. Everyone was speaking in quiet voices, but the fear was full volume. I felt full of fear too, yet within weeks and with little effort, I moved from fear to a low level of uneasiness to getting on with my life and my busy corporate litigation practice at Shearman & Sterling, a large private firm.

Less than six months after 9/11, Tom Wilner, a partner at Shearman and my mentor, colleague, and good friend, received a call, an inquiry from abroad: Would we take on a matter regarding Kuwaiti citizens who had gone abroad to do humanitarian work and who now *might be* in the custody of the United States? The project was investigatory in nature: talk to some friends at the Department of Justice (DOJ), maybe file a Freedom of Information Act (FOIA) request that would require the government to provide information to the public, track down the Kuwaiti do-gooders, and just give the information to their families so they could connect. Then maybe we would continue to represent them if there was a need. What that "need" might be was very unclear at the time. Indeed at that time, it wasn't at all clear that they were at Guantánamo or even in Afghanistan. And it certainly wasn't readily apparent that the project would be so difficult.

Our first meeting was in a conference room in the Sheraton in Kuwait City, the same hotel that had been devastated by Iraqi soldiers in the Gulf War in the early 1990s. Tom and I were met by the Kuwaiti lawyer, an American lawyer, and Mr. Khalid al Odah, the father of one of the missing Kuwaiti individuals and a former Kuwaiti Air Force pilot who had flown with Americans in the first Gulf War. Khalid had fought alongside American soldiers, and when our tanks rolled in to Kuwait City signaling the country's liberation, his son, Fawzi, ran to greet them, waving an American flag.

Introductions and niceties took up most of the morning. By the afternoon, we had learned some general information, that the missing Kuwaitis had gone abroad to do humanitarian work (dig wells, teach the Quran, help refugees), had gotten caught up in the conflict, and now were most likely in Guantánamo. Though some articles touched on Guantánamo, there really wasn't that much information about it and the individuals that were being transferred there. In 2002, the Bush administration wasn't talking, and the public wasn't asking. It was becoming clear that the Kuwaitis had gotten lost in that big secret, and it was our job to find them.

We spent the next two days meeting with the families, one by one, essentially doing intake. Who is missing? What is your relationship to him? Why did he travel abroad and where to? When did you last hear from him? Most families had put together a packet of information on their missing person: personal stats such as date of birth, wife, children, job, etc., copies of certificates of charitable works from the past, and other miscellaneous information. Some even had copies of letters from their missing loved one that appeared to have been transmitted through the Red Cross from Guantánamo. The families had found one another somehow through the community and joined together to try to find their sons and brothers. Many of the Kuwaiti men could speak English, and for those who couldn't, either Khalid or another relative translated.

While in Kuwait, we also met with the people in the Foreign Ministry who were exceptionally helpful, sharing with us a fax from the U.S.

embassy in Kuwait that indicated in the briefest of words that six of the missing Kuwaiti citizens were in Guantánamo. The United States offered no explanation of how they got there or why they were there. The Kuwait government had no additional information to tell us.

Additionally, we spent one afternoon visiting a couple of well-known Kuwaiti relief organizations to find out more information about the kind of charity work they did. We learned that Kuwaitis are taught at a very young age to give to charity, to donate both their money and time. It is not unusual for a Kuwaiti citizen to spend half his vacation time in a location overseas doing charitable works. Indeed, Kuwait often led the region in the amount of aid donated to poor countries. The fact that the Kuwaiti individuals had been abroad doing humanitarian work was not unbelievable then, nor was it inconceivable to me that many of them had gone to conflict areas. This issue arose again and again when people asked me with suspicion just exactly what they were doing in the Afghanistan-Pakistan region if they were not in fact joining the Taliban or al Qaeda. Wasn't that the only reason one would go to a war zone? Many Americans didn't believe that the Kuwaitis or any other Guantánamo detainee had gone to a conflict area to help others. Generally speaking, Americans do not travel overseas, they do not travel overseas to volunteer, and they certainly do not travel overseas to conflict zones to volunteer. Many Americans simply cannot understand why anybody would travel to a conflict zone unless he was fighting in the conflict.

Michael Ratner: Guantánamo: The Ninth Circle of Hell

On November 14, 2001, I awoke to read in the morning paper that President Bush, under his authority as commander in chief, had issued a military order for the detention and trial of noncitizens in the "war on terrorism." As president of the Center for Constitutional Rights (CCR), I recall my shock. I remember thinking that there had just been a coup d'etat in the United States, perhaps an exaggerated reaction but a watershed moment for me in a country that I still thought had some semblance of a democracy and some adherence to the principle that presidential authority remain under law.

The order had three key provisions. First, President Bush claimed the authority to capture, kidnap, or otherwise arrest any noncitizen (the claim was later extended to citizens) anywhere in the world, including the United States, who the president believed was involved in international terrorism. The president could then hold that person forever without any charges, proceedings, or trial. Second, the order provided that if, and *if* is the crucial word here, the person was tried (there never needed to be a trial), such trials were to be held by special ad hoc courts called military commissions. These commissions bore no resemblance to regular trial courts. The entire proceeding could take place in secret, with evidence garnered from torture; those found guilty could be executed; and the executions could be held in secret. Third, no court could hear the case of anyone detained under the order. The president did not need to demonstrate in any court a legal reason for a person's imprisonment. In other words, the writ of habeas corpus was abolished.

Of course, we had no clients. But we did not need to wait long. On December 13, 2001, it was announced that David Hicks, an Australian, had been captured in Afghanistan by the Northern Alliance and turned over to the United States. A few days later it was revealed that the United States would be using Guantánamo as its offshore prison, where presumably Hicks would be sent and where he could remain forever without any court hearing or access to a lawyer. He was detained solely because the president thought he should be detained. It was in the newspaper that I found the name of Hicks's lawyer, Steven Kenny, in Australia. More accurately, I found the name of the lawyer for Hicks's father, as David Hicks could have no contact with his family or lawyers. I called Kenny immediately. We began the discussion of our representation of David Hicks, and after a week or so, it was agreed. CCR and the lawyers we were working with would file a petition for a writ of habeas corpus on David Hicks's behalf. However, David Hicks would not know about our lawsuit, nor would we be able to consult with him. All communications with Hicks were barred, whether from Kenny, us, or his parents. We would file the habeas case as Hicks's "next friend"—a provision in U.S. law that allows close relatives or others to act on behalf of those who cannot act themselves. Traditionally, this device had been used only for people who are mentally incompetent or physically incapacitated. Here, it was used because the prisoners were being held incommunicado.

I was quite shocked that the United States was planning to use Guantánamo as its offshore prison—*again*. I say "again" because I had been one of the attorneys who had worked on an earlier Guantánamo case: when the administrations of George H. W. Bush and Bill Clinton had used the military base as an offshore "refugee camp" for Haitians who were entitled to asylum in the United States but who were prohibited from entering the country because they were HIV-positive. I had learned important lessons from that litigation. First, I learned that Guantánamo was a really bad place to be imprisoned. I compared the refugee camp to Dante's Ninth Circle of Hell, with its extreme heat, barbed wire, scorpions, hardscrabble ground, arbitrary beatings, hunger strikes, and appalling detention facilities. Second, and of critical importance, the two prior administrations had argued, and somewhat successfully, that Guantánamo was a lawfree zone, that the refugees were not protected by the Constitution, and that no court could protect their rights.

So we knew what to expect: horrendous conditions and arguments that no court could undertake to hear a case about Guantánamo and that even if it did, David Hicks and others were not protected by law. We knew it would be a major uphill battle to get a court even to hear the case. We suspected at the time that Guantánamo was chosen by the Bush administration precisely because of the argument that the Constitution and habeas corpus did not apply there. Subsequently, we learned we were right: a memo was written on December 28, 2001, from Deputy Attorney General Patrick F. Philbin to Deputy Assistant Attorney General John Yoo entitled "Possible Habeas Jurisdiction over Aliens Held in Guantánamo Bay, Cuba." It concluded "that a district court cannot properly entertain an application for a writ of habeas corpus by an enemy alien detained at Guantánamo Bay Naval Base, Cuba." But the memo also cautioned that the question has not been definitively decided and that "there is some possibility that a district court would entertain such an application."

President Bush's November 13 military order was the latest in a succession of laws, executive orders, and actions since 9/11 that had alarmed me and my colleagues. We saw fundamental constitutional rights under attack, and we saw the president, often with congressional collaboration, grabbing almost unchecked powers. In the two months since 9/11, there had been roundups of hundreds and eventually thousands of Muslim men; the passage of the Patriot Act, with its grant of broad power to spy on Americans; and the passage of the Authorization for Use of Military Force, which arguably gave the government power to use military force anywhere in the world, even in the United States, against those nations, organizations, or persons involved in 9/11.

The Bush administration claimed that the attacks were an act of war, that the United States was fighting a "war on terror," and that the war would continue for a very long time, possibly for generations. Under this theory, President Bush claimed highly exaggerated wartime powers to override treaties, statutes, Congress, and the courts. The Bush administration could also then look to the laws of war to assert the right to detain those it termed "enemy combatants" until the war was over. Yet, at the same time, because this war was clearly not a conventional war, the administration claimed it could pick and choose among the laws of war most applicable to what it asserted was a "new paradigm." The result: virtually limitless power for the president and no protections for the detainees.

The November 13 order pushed CCR into action. It was this document that made us begin the historic fight for the rights of those who a few months later would be imprisoned at Guantánamo. It was not automatic that CCR would take on the cases of those jailed under this order, and it was not immediately clear what those cases would be about. At first, most of the focus of CCR, the media, and experts was on the draconian, ad hoc trial provisions and on the death penalty aspects of the president's order. Few of us paid much attention to its indefinite detention aspects.

We began a discussion about representing the first people detained or tried under the order. It was not the easiest of discussions. Our office in Manhattan is close to the World Trade Center. I had actually witnessed the attacks. For months New York was like a massive funeral. We were all frightened; the anthrax scare came immediately on the heels of the attacks. Did we really want to be representing those who may have been directly involved? Some of us were uncomfortable doing so. Others were worried about funding, as CCR depends on private donations and foundations. Would it be personally dangerous to represent those accused of the attacks?

Of course, it was possible that those accused were innocent, but at the time we took the cases, we had to assume our clients might not be. We decided that the military order was so contrary to law and represented such a threat to fundamental liberties that we needed to challenge it, particularly its denial of habeas corpus. Habeas corpus is the hallmark of a state in which authority is under law. This principle is so important that we were willing to put aside our concerns regarding funding and the angry, vengeful mood in much of the country.

Once we made the commitment to challenge the November 13 order, we went public with our decision as a means of putting the administration on notice that its overreaching would not go unchallenged and to encourage those critics who might be more timid to fight back. Our next step was to try to round up a legal team for what we knew would be major cases. We found some attorneys from the law firm Shearman & Sterling. We had difficulty finding others to work on a possible case for all the reasons I have mentioned: fear of the public reaction, loss of financial support, and the creation of bad precedent. However, by this time, early December

2001, we had attracted some lawyers from outside CCR. I do not know all their motivations, but the fact that their experience was in the areas of death penalty and habeas corpus litigation is a clue as to their interest. The earliest members of the team were Joe Margulies, a civil rights and death penalty lawyer from Minneapolis; Clive Stafford Smith, a death penalty lawyer from New Orleans; Eric Freedman, a professor at Hofstra and an expert in habeas corpus; and me. All of us, more than seven years later, remain deeply involved with these cases.

Richard Grigg: A Human Face

I first heard about the request for attorneys to volunteer to represent Guantánamo detainees at an International Academy of Trial Lawyers meeting in June 2005. Being a "car wreck and sore back" lawyer, I had never been involved in anything remotely related to these cases. However, I strongly disagreed with the Bush administration's contempt for the rule of law and decided that this was a chance to put my money where my mouth was. I volunteered.

In August 2005, I attended a two-day training session conducted by CCR in Washington, D.C. I was very surprised at my "classmates." I was expecting a bunch of hippie civil rights lawyers out of the 1960s but found instead that the majority of the volunteer attorneys were from large, national, conservative law firms. It was a group of extremely bright, dedicated attorneys who strongly believed that much more was at stake here than the fate of the detainees. I was proud to be a part of the "Guantánamo Bar" and of this effort by so many lawyers to stand up for the principles that have made the American legal system the envy of the world.

After attending the training session, I was assigned a client—Mohammad Akhtiar, an Afghan. I then filed a petition of habeas corpus. Because I am primarily a plaintiff personal injury lawyer, it was a first for me. It was definitely a Clint Eastwood experience. It made my day to sue President Bush and Donald Rumsfeld.

I can honestly say that meeting my client, Mohammad Akhtiar, at the Guantánamo prison was the most moving experience of my thirty-four years as a lawyer. It put a human face on what had previously been a legal issue. No longer was I representing a detainee on a habeas corpus petition. I was representing a human being, a man about my age who had been up-rooted from his family, flown 10,000 miles from his home, and placed in a dog cage. Here was a human being who had never been charged with any crime, a man with very little hope.

Buz Eisenberg: An Oath

I've been asked the question more times than I can remember: "Why did you want to represent Guantánamo detainees?" My answer never changes: "Because I took an oath." Of all the complex reasons and rhetoric and lofty answers I could summon, more than any, it really comes down to that moment you stood there with your right arm raised and made a promise to yourself and your society. Amid an active law practice, it's easy to forget you took that oath so many years ago. But in every jurisdiction, every attorney is deemed qualified for that license to practice only after subscribing to an oath. And since 1789, that oath has included a promise to support the Constitution of the United States. I had a small practice in rural western Massachusetts, and for twenty-five years I'd tried to fulfill that promise.

Then I found myself watching as my country was holding men without charges and without fair process. I observed all three branches of government seemingly conspire to block the federal courts from so much as hearing a single claim that these detentions were contrary to our constitutional guarantees. And no matter how horrific the reports of cruel, inhumane, and degrading conditions under which they were held, nothing was being done. There I sat, license in my wallet . . . and I'd taken that oath.

Tina Monshipour Foster: My Sabbatical

"I'd like to take a sabbatical from the firm," I said, trying as hard as I could to make it sound like a nonevent. Across from me sat my boss, leaning back in his office chair with his hands clasped behind his head. "Really?" He raised his eyebrows, surprised.

Through the tinted glass wall behind him I saw it raining, a dreary midtown-Manhattan afternoon.

"It's not that I'm unhappy here," I said a little worriedly. "I really do love Clifford Chance, and if I am going to be working at a firm, it would be here. I just want to spend six months doing something else."

"What's that?" he asked.

"Working full-time on the Guantánamo Bay detainee cases."

He unclasped his hands and sat up straight. "*Really?*" He seemed both shocked and fascinated.

"Yes." I must have started to look really worried then.

"No, no, I think that's great," he said. "I wasn't expecting you to say that. I'm not exactly sure what I was thinking you were going to say.

Maybe that you were taking a break to write a novel or go hiking in South America or tour with a rock band or something. I expected almost anything except that."

It might seem hard to understand why I would want to upset my life in order to work, without pay, on behalf of people popularly thought of at the time as "the worst of the worst." For someone who hadn't been involved with the litigation it was hard to understand its appeal. Yet after some initial surprise, everyone at Clifford Chance was as supportive as they had always been of involvement in the Guantánamo cases. I was lucky to have had the opportunity to work on the cases in the first place.

When the Center for Constitutional Rights began to look for additional *pro bono* assistance on the cases and for firms that would be willing to take on additional clients, it had asked organizations with which it had established relationships to help recruit. When one of those organizations, the International Senior Lawyer's Project, sent out an e-mail asking more firms to take on clients, Clifford Chance responded.

Clifford Chance had been one of first to represent a client at Guantánamo in the early days, when only a handful of private law firms entertained the thought of taking on clients such as the three young men from France detained at GTMO. At the time, there was virtually no evidence about who the detainees really were or what they had done. All the public knew was that they had been labeled "terrorists." In the case of many of the detainees, getting a lawyer meant getting out—if only because the detainee was finally on someone's radar.

On September 11, 2001, I was living right next to the World Trade Center. My law-firm salary allowed me to rent out a beautiful new apartment on the twenty-seventh floor of a building overlooking Wall Street, the Statue of Liberty, and New York Harbor, so close to the Twin Towers that it was badly damaged by the smoke and debris from their collapse. All the tenants had been evacuated, and we weren't allowed to move back until several months later, when it was "safe" again.

I didn't go out looking to save the world. The problem came to me, outside my window and into my office. Righting my furniture and unpacking my clothes didn't address the need that seemed increasingly urgent—to ensure that the U.S. government didn't begin to threaten our freedom in the name of protecting it. To argue for basic rights on behalf of Guantánamo detainees was also a way to defend our Constitution and legal system not against some unclear, foreign predator but against the powers that be, which were miscarrying justice much closer to home.

David M. Brahms: Thank You, *Zeyde*

"GTMO"—that's the sobriquet that we Marines use for the naval base at Guantánamo, Cuba. A godforsaken place that spawned the events portrayed in the movie *A Few Good Men*. GTMO is a long distance from Carlsbad, California, where I chose to hang my hat after retiring from the Corps. Then I get a call from Rear Admiral John Hutson urging me to sign on to an amicus (or "friend of the court") brief pertaining to someone confined at the godforsaken place.

The admiral wants me to speak up on behalf of a detainee who has been labeled an enemy of our country. It would be crazy to get involved with this. I live in a red area; liberals meet in telephone booths. My reputation, grounded in my long service to country and Corps, could be at stake, and my work, defending accused military personnel before courts-martial, could be placed at risk. I would be violating a fundamental tenet taught by my mother: don't become controversial. There was no reason to sign on to this damned fool cause.

The admiral was insistent and a civilian attorney from a highfalutin Chicago law firm, Gary Isaac, added his voice to the chorus. I surprised myself by saying yes. If you asked me at the time, I couldn't tell you why I did so. The best that I could have done is to say, "It feels right." Now I can articulate why.

My *zeyde* (Yiddish for "grandfather") was a Latvian Jew who came to the United States shortly after the turn of the twentieth century. He came for the dream. Unlike in his country of birth, the American rule of law kept at bay those who would prey on him out of hate, and it gave him a chance to live that dream. The rule of law is what distinguishes our country. It applies to all: minorities, the downtrodden, and even those who are alleged to be bad men.

I said yes because the voice of my *zeyde* told me to. I did his bidding and became a part of defending the American way against those who would sully it for parochial ends.

Once I joined the fray, my angst did not go away. Was I helping enemies of my country? Was there an imperative for the government to act in ways that only seemed to be unlawful but weren't? Shouldn't the president have a free hand to do whatever he believed was necessary to protect us against attack, to preserve the well-being of the nation? Maybe I didn't have all the information I needed to make an informed choice.

Invited to be an expert witness on behalf of one of the GTMO detainees, I said no. I can't help someone who was suspected of acting against our nation. Shortly after communicating that decision, I had a "huh moment." There is no distinction between helping the detainees by speaking out against the manner in which they were being treated generically and testifying to that very matter in an individual case. Have I become a partisan intellectual dilettante, playing a game grounded in political distaste for the Bush administration, rather than speaking as a matter of conscience?

Notwithstanding all this angst, I stayed the course. The insistent voice of my grandfather was the constant. Thank you, *zeyde*, for helping me see what was right.

Julia Tarver Mason: Nerdy Patriotism

I am one of the habeas lawyers—a proud member of the self-proclaimed "Guantánamo Bay Bar Association." I am an American. I am a New Yorker, who felt very painfully, and personally, what happened on 9/11. I am a woman, educated by public schools, who believes passionately in all the advantages and opportunities this great nation has to offer. My friends have mocked me at times for what they call my "nerdy patriotism." To this day, I still get chill bumps when I put my hand over my heart and sing the national anthem at baseball games. To put it simply, I *believe* in the United States of America. I *believe* in everything this special country stands for. And I believe it is my duty as a citizen, as a lawyer, and as a patriot to fight to uphold those values that define us as a nation.

If you had told me ten years ago that our government would be deliberately holding people in captivity on a naval base outside the U.S. mainland so that we could do whatever we wanted to them without the intervention of U.S. courts, I would have told you that you had watched one too many miniseries on TV. If you had told me that the government would have refused to release even the names of those human beings so their families would know where they were, I would have told you to stop reading all those Tom Clancy novels. Sadly, though, this isn't fiction. This is what is happening *today*, in the country I love so much.

Hannah Tennant-Moore: Habeas Will Be There in Ten Minutes

In the middle of the night on June 9, 2006, three men imprisoned at Guantánamo Bay reportedly hanged themselves with clothing and sheets. One of these men had been cleared for release but had not yet been told.

The following Monday, my mother, Doris Tennant, and Ellen Lubell arrived at their small law office in Newtonville, a suburb of Boston. Before they'd put away their homemade lunches or removed their coats, they sat down on the couch in their shared reception area, already knowing what the weekend's news meant for both of them: as lawyers, they had to do something. The force of this decision was fueled by the government's reaction to the deaths: they were immediately termed acts of "asymmetrical warfare," just as suicide attempts preceding them had been labeled "manipulative self-injurious behavior." Guantánamo detainees commit self-injurious behavior about twice as often as they commit disciplinary violations.

Meanwhile, Ellen and Doris gave themselves a crash course in constitutional law, which they were rash enough to believe had some relevance to their client's confinement. Doris is a divorce attorney specializing in mediation and collaborative law, both of which spare her clients the expense and anguish of litigation. Ellen's expertise is in nonprofits and intellectual property. They also embarked on an aggressive fundraising campaign to raise the $20,000 or more a year needed to represent Aziz, a prohibitive sum for a firm consisting solely of Ellen and Doris. But within six months, they'd raised enough money to finance their first year of *pro bono* work. For the many Americans who feel like powerless bystanders to the constitutional desecration of the past eight years, the Tennant-Lubell fundraising letter represented a simple, concrete act that felt a little like fighting back.

Hanna F. Madbak: A Question of Humanity

It appears to me that, in general, the arguments made for and against the Guantánamo prison correlate highly with conservative and liberal politics, respectively. However, the reasons for my involvement in this legal battle are apolitical. In my mind, humanity transcends politics, and human rights should never be compromised for political reasons. I represent Guantánamo detainees to preserve their human rights, regardless of their guilt or innocence.

My habeas work with Guantánamo detainees started in 2005 when I was a member of a team representing various detainees. One of those detainees was a Yemeni national who tragically died in Guantánamo in June 2006, before he had any opportunity to meet with counsel. At that time, the question of the detainees' access to counsel, which I consider to be a fundamental human right, was unfortunately still being debated in court.

The haunting question is whether the deaths of this and other detainees could have been prevented had they had access to a lawyer or a means of challenging their detention. I was overwhelmed by a sense of loss even though I had never met my deceased client. As the only Arabic speaker on the team, I was extremely anxious about delivering the tragic news to his father. The circumstances surrounding the deaths of detainees at Guantánamo are shrouded in mystery for various reasons, the least of which is the unwillingness of the government to have an unbiased third party conduct an independent autopsy. Regardless of how you interpret them, the circumstances surrounding the deaths of these prisoners are deeply troubling. And the purpose of my continued involvement is to ensure that these circumstances never arise again.

Eric M. Freedman: Death Penalty Lawyers

Many of the lawyers involved in the Guantánamo cases had prior experience in death penalty litigation. One characteristic of the capital defense field is that the same individuals tend to stay involved over the course of their careers, notwithstanding changes in their institutional affiliations. Familiar colleagues may from one day to the next be housed in public defender offices, large or small firms, universities, human rights groups, bar organizations, the military, and various other practice settings. To the great credit of the American bar, just such an array of advocates stepped forward to do the Guantánamo work, and death penalty lawyers were particularly well suited for working in that environment.

In addition, death penalty practice starkly presents the lawyer on a daily basis with the need to pursue every possible avenue of relief for the individual facing execution, while at the same time the lawyer must remain aware that the client's cause will be best served by the success of coordinated efforts by the capital defense community as a whole. That is precisely the situation in the Guantánamo cases. Each individual client needs to have his case handled by a lawyer taking whatever route is in the client's best interest. But that lawyer needs to act in keen awareness that the client's fate will depend critically on overall political and legal developments and needs to make tactical decisions in the context of the larger collective strategy. The lawyers with prior death penalty experience were in a particularly good position to communicate to their co-counsel the message that unless we all hung together, we would all hang separately.

There were also some purely practical factors. Death penalty lawyers know a good deal about habeas corpus and rapid-fire litigation practice involving fairly arcane emergency procedures. They have been pioneers in the use of computer technology to coordinate the efforts of teams whose members are based in a variety of institutions around the world. And they regularly face many of the same client-relationship issues that have arisen in the Guantánamo detainee cases. From the earliest day, it made sense that death penalty practitioners would be a good source of assistance to the Guantánamo efforts.

Elizabeth Wilson: We Are All Americans Now

I became a lawyer mainly to create a more secure economic future for myself and planned originally to take a corporate job in Boston. When I went to law school at age forty-two, I was broke, a former Yale professor of English whose career had been "downsized" in the 1990s. But after 9/11, my goals changed, and I decided at the last moment to move to Washington, D.C., planning to spend a couple years at a corporate law firm and then move into the government, preferably doing counterterrorism work. I didn't anticipate that while working at a corporate law firm I would have the opportunity to become involved with what I came to regard as the most important litigation in the "war on terrorism."

It has never been possible for me to regard my Guantánamo work as professional "service"—the *pro bono* work that we as lawyers have a professional responsibility to provide. My Guantánamo work has become a passion, work I have done because I totally loved it and believed in it. I once heard another GTMO lawyer say of this work, "It's like a drug," and I agree. It has an addictive quality, and it is the work I have been most proud of in my career as a lawyer.

But like most drugs, it has had its costs. I was not with my mother when she died, in part because I was working on GTMO matters. The work has caused me grief, as well as providing solace from grief. It has been the occasion for great professional experiences—and for terrible ones. It kept me working in a corporate environment longer than was good for my physical, mental, and spiritual health, though it eventually led me to full-time work in the human rights field. In spite of all that, I don't regret anything about doing it, except that I didn't get to do more of it—and that, despite winning three times in the Supreme Court, we were not able to force a reckoning in a court of law and get past the roadblocks that the Bush administration's lawyers threw up in our path. When I had started law school, I once jokingly told a friend that I wouldn't mind being single for the rest of my life if I got to prosecute war criminals. It just never occurred to me that they would be *American* war criminals.

Because the patriotism of Guantánamo lawyers is sometimes impugned, it is important to add that I also felt intensely patriotic after 9/11. I was incredibly moved by the outpouring of feeling around the world. I felt that the United States *meant* something to people. A German friend wrote me a moving e-mail after 9/11. He described the day before 9/11 as "a world that now seemed very far away, about which nothing much mattered anymore." I knew why Americans felt that way, but why did *Germans* feel that way? What did it mean that *Le Monde* said, "We are all Americans now"? I wanted the United States to be deserving of this goodwill. And so when I saw the course that the United States was embarking on after 9/11—beyond the war in Afghanistan—I felt that I needed to fight for the soul of my country. That is why I joined the GTMO litigation.

David J. Cynamon: Rule of Law

I have been representing Kuwaiti detainees at Guantánamo since May 2006. Although I have been a civil litigator for more than thirty-five years and have argued many civil rights cases, Guantánamo has been a unique experience, both depressing and exhilarating.

The best thing about Guantánamo has been meeting and working with the wide variety of lawyers who have been involved in these cases—big-firm partners and associates, sole practitioners, federal public defenders, lawyers for public-interest organizations, law professors, lawyers with extensive experience in criminal and civil rights litigation, lawyers with no prior experience in those fields, young lawyers, old lawyers, lawyers who are Democrats, lawyers who are Republicans, and lawyers who are independents (maybe even a few Naderites!). The common thread is that all of them are enthusiastic about what they are doing, all of them are deeply committed to the concept that the rule of law means something, and all of them are deeply angered and ashamed of how the Bush administration tried to destroy it. The Guantánamo litigation brings to mind the oft-misunderstood quotation from Shakespeare's *Henry VI*: "The first thing we do, let's kill all the lawyers"—not because lawyers are annoying pests who make people's lives miserable but because without lawyers there would be no laws, and a tyrant could rule unrestrained. Although the Bush administration came pretty close to killing the rule of law, I am proud to be a small part of the large group of lawyers who prevented that from happening.

2

Getting behind the Wire

Rasul/Al Odah: The Right to Representation

The first step in challenging the detentions at Guantánamo was gaining access to the prisoners who were being held in secret and without legal process. It took more than two years and a decision by the U.S. Supreme Court to achieve this first, but critical, step in the habeas corpus litigation.

Kristine A. Huskey: The First Habeas Cases: *Al Odah v. United States*

In 2002, after we were retained by the families in Kuwait concerned about their disappeared children, we sought information from the U.S. government. My colleague Neil Koslowe, a longtime DOJ lawyer, sought to get some information from his former employer and colleagues. Years of service in the DOJ, however, apparently were not enough to get anything other than unreturned phone messages or a change in the conversation. Neil was told that the Bush administration and the Department of Defense (DOD) were handling "it"; he was told we should leave "it" alone. Neil also inquired into making Freedom of Information Act (FOIA) requests, that is, requests for documents containing basic information, such as where the Kuwaiti citizens were and in whose custody or control they were. We still thought that all we had to do was find out what agency and which officials were in charge and then put the Kuwaiti families in touch with the right officials, and they would then be able to make contact with their "missing" son or brother. The men might be locked up, but we never imagined that they would be locked up incommunicado, without access to a lawyer. I mean, it was the United States for god's sake. Five years ago, a "prisoner" didn't vanish into U.S. custody unless a mistake had been made. But the response to Neil's casual inquiries was, "Guantánamo? Don't bother asking, you won't get anything. Nothing's coming out."

After a brief internal discussion, we decided that we had no choice but to file suit on behalf of the Kuwaiti citizens. The issues—arbitrary detention being the primary one—were going before a court in another case, on behalf of detainees from England and Australia, which had been filed by the Center for Constitutional Rights and an experienced civil rights and death penalty attorney, Joseph Margulies. Although perhaps we were arrogant to believe that we could contribute something of value to the litigation, it would have been remiss to remain mere observers. On the other hand, we were getting some pushback from the firm. Our colleagues at Shearman were split on whether we should even be representing individuals at Guantánamo. In the end, Tom Wilner, the partner leading our litigation, convinced our colleagues—as he adeptly went on to convince many more people—that we were both right and righteous to stand up for what we believed were fundamental principles of American justice.

In an attempt to appear to the court more modest and less like we were demanding release, we chose not to file a habeas corpus petition, as was done in the other cases. Rather, we filed a traditional civil complaint, which merely "complains" that the entity being sued is doing something against the law. Our complaint alleged that the Kuwaiti citizens were being detained unlawfully and that they were entitled to due process and access to counsel and their families. We believed that we were requesting the most minimal of rights. Of course, we understood there was a "war" in Afghanistan. We knew that the Bush administration was not giving individuals allegedly "captured on the battlefield" prisoner-of-war rights, but we assumed that they had *some* rights, at least those we consider fundamental. In the complaint, we were deliberate in our words, trying not to reach too far. We didn't have an organizational position to maintain. And we were lawyering in a large, conservative, international law firm that didn't even want us to sue President Bush, as if he might take personal affront. In a compromise, we listed the United States as the first defendant so that the case would be known as *Al Odah v. United States*, rather than *Al Odah v. Bush*. Once filed in the District Court for the District of Columbia, our case was joined with *Rasul v. Bush*, and thereafter the two captions were often used interchangeably, much to the firm's chagrin.

Not surprisingly, the government responded to both the *Al Odah* complaint and the *Rasul* habeas petitions with a motion to dismiss. More surprising to us was the government's reasoning. It was not that we were in a war and there was a need for unrestrained executive command authority, though this theory was certainly put forth. The government's primary argument was that, regardless of whether there was an ongoing war, the courts did not have the jurisdiction or the authority even to hear the claims of the Guantánamo detainees *solely* because they were foreign citizens and Guantánamo was not in the sovereign territory of the United States, despite the fact that the United States had exclusive control and jurisdiction over the naval base there. We were taken aback by this stark position. In our reply, we decried the government's expansive grasp of power, emphasizing that under such a theory the United States could pick a person up off the streets of Rome, detain him, torture him, and summarily execute him, and the U.S. courts would have no authority to hear his claims. Notwithstanding what we thought was a compelling analogy, the court dismissed the cases.

This early time period in the Guantánamo detainee litigation is one of my prouder moments in my law career thus far. You know you're making an impression when you get hate mail, and we received our share of it: "You should be locked up in Guantánamo with the terrorists." Before our cases reached the Supreme Court in 2004, not too many people would touch Guantánamo—not other law firms, not even the media, who told us confidentially that if they asked questions about Guantánamo at White House press conferences, they would be blacklisted. So much for the fourth branch.

At that time, Congress was completely acquiescent in the whole matter. In the first year or so after 9/11, I don't recall a single amendment or legislative proposal that was raised on the Hill, or even a formal hearing to inquire into the detentions at Guantánamo. Sometime in 2002, Tom and I met with staffers on the House Judiciary Committee at our request. It was my first trip to the Hill as a lawyer. I was excited, nervous, and very optimistic. Oh, how naive I was! The two staffers, both lawyers, were polite and even seemed deeply interested in what we were saying: "arbitrary detentions, no charges, no hearings, no judicial oversight . . ." They nodded and clucked. They promised to look into it. We left our cards and never heard from them.

After losing in the D.C. District Court, we also appealed the dismissal to the D.C. Circuit Court. The panel affirmed the lower court's ruling and dismissed our cases. We were headed for the Supreme Court. I should say, *we* thought we were going to the Supreme Court. Many others thought that though we were headed that way, we would never get there. But by then, the fall of 2003, Guantánamo had picked up some speed in the press and the public's consciousness. More and more people agreed with our position, or at least found the Bush administration's assertion of unchecked executive power unacceptable.

The Supreme Court not only agreed to hear the case, but on June 28, 2004, it decided the case in our favor, holding in *Rasul v. Bush* that the Guantánamo detainees had the right to challenge the legality of their detention in U.S. courts through the writ of habeas corpus. We immediately started making plans to go to Guantánamo to visit clients with whom we had never met or even spoken but had been representing for the past two years. Wait. Not so fast. What was I thinking? That the government would just roll out the welcome mat to the detainees' counsel simply because the Supreme Court ruled that the detainees had habeas rights? Despite the ruling, the government refused to concede that the detainees had a right to counsel, saying only that through its grace, it would now allow counsel down to Guantánamo to meet with clients. The government, meanwhile, would continue to try to restrict attorney access and to pry into confidential attorney-client communications. After months of litigating exactly how the visits and communications would proceed, taking into consideration the protection of national security and attorney-client confidentiality, we finally took our first trip to Guantánamo on December 26, 2004.

Michael Ratner: The First Habeas Cases: *Rasul v. Bush*

When CCR filed its first habeas corpus case in the District Court in Washington, D.C., there was a lot of debate on what should go in our legal papers. We filed for habeas corpus relief, even though we knew that the court might well dismiss it on the basis of *Johnson v. Eisentrager*, a World War II–era Supreme Court decision limiting access of enemy aliens to U.S. courts during wartime. As an alternative we filed under a federal statute that CCR had pioneered, the Alien Tort Statute, which permitted suits by aliens for violations of fundamental rights protected by international law. The international law we relied on was the prohibition regarding arbitrary detention and the Geneva Conventions. We wanted to take this route in part because even if the Constitution might not apply at Guantánamo, international law did. In addition, the Alien Tort Statute gave us a separate basis for the court to assert jurisdiction besides habeas corpus. On February 19, 2002, we filed *Rasul v. Bush,* one of the cases that ultimately led to the Supreme Court victory in June 2004. We asked the federal district court to give our clients an immediate hearing, and we asked for a declaration that their imprisonment was illegal.

In addition to the habeas corpus charge filed in federal court, on February 12, 2002, we sought a ruling in the Inter-American Commission on Human Rights that the men we represented at Guantánamo were entitled to a hearing in which their status could be determined by a competent court. The Inter-American Commission is a human rights commission that has jurisdiction over violations of the American Declaration of Human Rights, questions of compliance with the Geneva Conventions, and other international treaties protecting human rights. Unfortunately, the commission has no enforcement power; its rulings need to go to the Inter-American Court if a country refuses to comply. The United States has not signed the treaty that grants jurisdiction to the court, so rulings of the commission cannot be enforced. However, a victory at the commission would send an important message regarding the illegality of the Bush administration's imprisonment of the Guantánamo detainees and might favorably affect the court cases.

Within days of filing our petition to the Inter-American Commission, we won a significant and well-reasoned victory. The commission, on an emergency basis, decided exactly what the law required: that every human being had a status under law to which rights attached, and that hearings needed to be held immediately to determine the status of those held at Guantánamo. As the commission stated,

> [A] competent court or tribunal, as opposed to a political authority, must be charged with ensuring respect for the legal status and rights of persons falling under the authority and control of a state. . . . To the contrary, the information available suggests that the detainees remain entirely at the unfettered discretion of the United States government. . . . On this basis, the Commission hereby requests that the United States take the urgent measures necessary to have the legal status of the detainees at Guantánamo Bay determined by a competent tribunal.

The commission got it exactly right: a court or tribunal must be used to determine status and rights; it cannot be left up to the executive. Sadly, it would take several years and three Supreme Court decisions for the United States even to begin to comply with this ruling.

John J. Gibbons: Checking the Executive

On the morning of September 11, 2001, along with two other lawyers from our firm, Gibbons, P.C., I was in the Trenton courtroom of the New Jersey Supreme Court awaiting argument in a death penalty case. Shortly after the court's usual starting time, a court attendant advised us that there would be no arguments that day because an aircraft had struck the World Trade Center. We returned to our car and learned from the car radio that we would not be able to return to our Newark office by the usual route and would have to find another. By the time we made our way to my home in Short Hills, New Jersey, we were aware that a massive coordinated attack had occurred in New York, in Washington, D.C., and elsewhere. The three of us knew, even while driving home, that this coordinated attack would result in new legal problems about which we could hardly guess. We thought, then, that those new legal problems would, as in the country's past history, be resolved in the U.S. Supreme Court.

The executive branch decided in secret that if the commander in chief said so—which he did—the custodians of the detainees could disregard what some people in high positions described as the "quaint" provisions of the Geneva Conventions dealing with the treatment of combatant and noncombatant detainees. Indeed, the executive branch decided that in the lawfree zones where detainees would be held, the interrogation methods described in a Cold War–era military training program called "Survival, Evasion, Resistance and Escape" (SERE) could be used. The methods of interrogation had been developed in the former Soviet Union by the NKVD and the KGB and were used in the SERE program to train American military at high risk of capture about Soviet interrogation techniques, such as sleep deprivation, exposure to extremes of temperature, hours in uncomfortable stress positions, and waterboarding. But unlike the SERE program, which was used to train resistance to such torture, the methods were to be used after September 11 for the same purposes they had been used for by the Soviet Union: to extract information.

The incommunicado detention and torture policies were thus mutually reinforcing. The executive branch did not want to acknowledge to the world

---

Former U.S. Court of Appeals Judge John Gibbons delivered the winning argument in the Rasul *and* Al Odah *cases in front of the Supreme Court. (The cases had been consolidated for argument and decision.)*

that it had authorized a program of torture, and thus the torture had to be carried out in places where the law and the public were both excluded.

But the Guantánamo detention operation was simply too large to remain hidden. Thus, while the executive branch's torture position was still secret, habeas corpus petitions were filed in federal court in Washington, D.C., to challenge detention of prisoners at Guantánamo. The executive branch was thus required to make public its position that it could detain noncitizens outside the United States on the authority of the president, with no judicial review by habeas corpus. This was so, the executive branch urged, first, because aliens outside the United States had no rights that a habeas corpus writ could enforce and, second, because the Guantánamo Bay Naval Base, occupied under a perpetual lease, was in a foreign country to which the writ of the U.S. courts did not run. The lower courts accepted both propositions. When *certiorari* was granted by the Supreme Court, I argued that both positions were wrong, and in June 2004, the Court agreed, remanding the cases for hearings in the district court.

Gary A. Isaac: Anatomy of an Amicus

The detainees' lawyers had already struck out in the district court and the court of appeals, and the climate for asking the Supreme Court to hear the *Rasul/Al Odah* case—and invite confrontation with the president in a time of war—could hardly have been worse. So the lawyers for the detainees decided that they had to change the Supreme Court's perception of the case: instead of seeing it as "*United States v. a bunch of terrorists*," the Justices had to see the detainees' certiorari petition as presenting fundamental issues about separation of powers and the rule of law. And the detainees' lawyers decided that the best way to help the Court recognize the importance of the case was through the filing of *amicus curiae*, or "friend of the court" briefs. But not just *any* amicus briefs—and not briefs by the civil liberties and other human rights organizations that the Supreme Court would expect to weigh in. To the contrary, the detainees' lawyers were looking for amicus briefs to be submitted by individuals who were not "the usual suspects"—retired military officers, former U.S. prisoners of war, retired federal judges, retired U.S. diplomats, and the like.

The person charged with implementing this extraordinary amicus strategy was Doug Cassel, then the director of the Center for International Human Rights at Northwestern Law School. Looking for lawyers to write the amicus briefs, Doug contacted me on September 12, 2003, exactly three weeks before amicus briefs were due in the Supreme Court. Doug asked us to submit a brief on behalf of a group of retired military officers and offered a general suggestion that the brief address the applicability of the Geneva Conventions to the detainees at Guantánamo. Three weeks wasn't much time to write an important brief in a landmark Supreme Court case, so my colleague Jim Schroeder and I quickly put together a team to work on it at our firm, Mayer Brown. But writing the brief turned out to be the easy part. Doug had asked us to draft an amicus on behalf of a group of retired military officers, but we had only a single person who had actually signed on to the concept: Retired Admiral John Hutson, former Judge Advocate General of the U.S. Navy. An amicus brief on behalf of one individual wouldn't be terribly convincing, so we not only had to write the brief; we had to get it done in time to show the draft to other retired military officers to try to persuade them to sign on.

One problem, of course, was that Jim and I didn't know anyone in the military, much less any retired military officers. We had both grown up during the Vietnam War era, when many Americans viewed the military with suspicion, if not downright hostility. I hated the very idea of blind obedience to authority, and to me that was what the military represented. I soon learned otherwise.

As the deadline for filing approached, Jim and I began making cold calls to various retired military officers whose names we had been given, to see if we could persuade anyone else to sign on to the brief. It was tough going. Some of the retired officers we spoke with said they disagreed with our arguments. Some told us that they concurred with what we planned to say, but for one reason or another, they were just not willing to put their names on the brief. It was now October 1, and with only two days left before the due date, only Admiral Hutson had signed on to the brief, a distressing fact that made us wonder whether filing the brief might do more harm than good, because a logical implication of our having only one signer might be that all the other retired military officers out there simply disagreed with our contentions.

Finally, on the afternoon of October 1, we heard back from Retired Admiral Donald Guter that he was willing to sign on to the brief. Admiral Guter had succeeded Admiral Hutson as Navy Judge Advocate General and had actually been in the Pentagon on 9/11 when it was attacked. Still, that only gave us two signers, and both were from the navy. We were hoping to add at least one from another branch of the service.

That same afternoon I made a cold call to Brigadier General David Brahms, who had been the top lawyer for the Marine Corps and had been in charge of repatriating U.S. prisoners of war returning home from Vietnam. I talked to General Brahms for some time about the brief and had to underscore that it was due in two days—so he didn't have a lot of time to mull this over. General Brahms heard me out and then asked me to fax him the draft brief so he could look at it. He said he would get back to me but gave me no sense of whether he would sign on or not. In fact, I wasn't sure I would ever hear from him again.

I got my answer soon enough.

When I got home that evening, I went straight to our home computer—this was in the pre-Blackberry era, at least for me—to check my e-mails to see if I'd heard anything from anyone. This message, from General Brahms, was waiting for me:

> GOT IT, READ IT, AGREE WITH IT. I WILL BE HONORED TO BE A
> SIGNATORY.
> THE MEASURE OF A COUNTRY IS HOW IT ACTS IN TIME OF
> PERIL. WE HAVE NOT ALWAYS MEASURED UP. LINCOLN SUSPENDING
> HABEAS CORPUS, ROOSEVELT, THE SUPREME COURT COUNTENANCING
> DISPLACEMENT OF THE JAPANESE AND THE MCCARTHY DEBACLE IM-
> MEDIATELY COME TO MIND. WE CANNOT AFFORD TO FALL SHORT IN
> TODAY'S WORLD; WE CANNOT FORFEIT OUR CLAIM TO MORAL LEAD-
> ERSHIP ON THE WORLD STAGE.
>
> VR,
> DAVID M. BRAHMS
> "JAFL"

Over the course of my career, I've received countless e-mails, but none ever meant more to me than that one. It inspires me still.

The brief we submitted urging the Supreme Court to take the detainees' case made two basic arguments: first, that the military must be subordinate to civilian authority and the rule of law even in time of war; and, second, that the Bush administration's failure to provide the detainees with any process to challenge their detention, as the Geneva Conventions require, would put our troops abroad at greater risk because foreign countries or groups taking U.S. service men and women prisoner would use the Bush administration's example as an excuse to ignore the Geneva Conventions as well. Jim and I originally placed the Geneva Conventions argument first, because we assumed that this would be more important to whichever retired military officers ended up signing the brief. But when we sent the draft to Admiral Hutson, the message came back loud and clear: the rule-of-law argument should go first.

When writing an amicus brief, especially in high-profile litigation like *Rasul*, you hope to influence consideration of the case by drawing attention to a point of view that is different somehow from that presented by the parties themselves. It is impossible to tell what caused particular Justices to vote to hear the detainees' case. But if the extensive media coverage was any indication, it was clear that our brief had struck a chord, precisely because it reflected the first criticism of the Bush administration's "war on terror"—and in particular its Guantánamo policies—from the military itself. On November 5, 2003, the lead editorial in the *New York Times* urged the Supreme Court to "take the case" and noted that the "detainees are being backed not only by human rights groups, but also by some retired military officers who argue that the administration's policies could hurt American troops captured in future conflicts."

Just five days later, the Supreme Court announced that it would hear the detainees' case, and the media continued to cite our amicus in editorials and op-eds applauding the Court's decision. It was gratifying to see the brief receive so much media attention, but out of all the press references, the one that made the biggest impression on me came out of Anniston, Alabama. I remember looking up Anniston in my Rand-McNally atlas; it's a relatively small town, about eighty miles east of Birmingham. In the cataloging of "red states," this was about as "red" as you could get. It's one thing for the liberal *New York Times* to endorse habeas rights for the so-called worst of the worst at Guantánamo, but this editorial from the *Anniston Star* was not what might have been expected:

> The fact that the High Court has agreed to hear the cases is a breath of fresh air for anyone who cares about rights, civil liberty or common decency, or who cares anything at all about the time-honored sanctity of habeas corpus.
>
> Yes, we live in a dangerous world, a world where a terrorist with a bomb or missile may have taken up residence in the next block. But we must not forget what this country was founded on; we cannot turn our backs on matters of justice simply because we happen to feel threatened.
>
> The Bush administration is wrong to assume that just because the detainees were taken during wartime—the early days of the U.S.-led invasion of Afghanistan, which followed the Sept. 11, 2001 terrorist bombings—that they have no rights, that they can be held, some now

for more than 18 months, without benefit of hearing of any sort. In effect, the court's decision to hear the cases of the 16 is in itself a stiff rebuttal to the administration's ham-fisted assertion that the detainees' status was the business only of the executive branch.

Don't take this page's word for it, take it from one of the extraordinary "friends of the court" briefs filed on behalf of the Guantánamo Bay detainees, by three retired U.S. military officers, no less, all men of respected legal standing: "These cases raise issues of extraordinary significance. The judicial branch has a duty to act as a check on the executive branch, even in wartime."

Many of the hundreds of prisoners being held at Guantánamo may turn out to be war criminals, terrorists, or sworn enemies of the United States. But continuing to hold them there, against their will, without giving them due process, goes against the spirit of international law and the very foundation upon which this great country was built.

The *Anniston Star* editorial drove home for me that habeas corpus for the Guantánamo detainees wasn't a "left" issue or a "right" issue. It was fundamentally an "American" issue.

The principal question presented in *Rasul*, however, was whether U.S. courts had jurisdiction over the detainees' habeas corpus petitions. The Bush administration argued that courts here lacked jurisdiction because the detainees were not U.S. citizens and were being held outside U.S. "sovereign" territory. The detainees, on the other hand, argued that technical "sovereignty" was beside the point and that U.S. courts did have jurisdiction because our lease agreements with Cuba stipulated that the U.S. exercised complete "control" over the area of the naval station in perpetuity, so that other U.S. laws, such as the Endangered Species Act, applied at Guantánamo. *Both* sides pointed to language in the same provision of the original U.S.-Cuba lease agreement negotiated in 1903, during the presidency of Theodore Roosevelt:

> While on the one hand the United States recognizes the continuance of the ultimate sovereignty of the Republic of Cuba over the above described areas of land and water [the boundaries of the naval station], on the other hand the Republic of Cuba consents that during the period of occupation by the United States of said areas under the terms of this agreement the United States shall exercise complete jurisdiction and control over and within said areas.

Now that the Supreme Court had agreed to hear the case, we were planning to file another amicus brief in support of the detainees on the merits, arguing that the Court should hold that the detainees were entitled to a day in court in the United States. With so much potentially riding on the meaning of the lease provision that both sides cited, Jim Schroeder and I decided to put our firm's considerable resources to use to try to solve the mystery: just what exactly did the negotiators of the lease mean by their reference to Cuba's "ultimate" sovereignty over Guantánamo?

We started out by borrowing every single book we could find, the older and dustier the better, on the history of the U.S. presence at Guantánamo. We were hunting for primary source materials—drafts of the original lease, letters written to or from the original negotiators, private papers—that might explain what "ultimate" sovereignty meant. The research took us back to the period just after the Spanish-American War, when the United States was also negotiating the Panama Canal Treaty and just starting to project its power in Latin America and around the world. Jim and I figured that we should definitely look at the various collections of Theodore Roosevelt papers—Roosevelt was a prodigious letter writer who reportedly penned over 150,000 letters in his lifetime—and also set out trying to locate the papers of Elihu Root, who was secretary of war under Roosevelt and, we assumed, the person who had overseen the negotiations with Cuba of the Guantánamo lease. We then learned that the negotiations might have been carried out through the State Department, so we expanded our research to include the papers of Roosevelt's secretary of state, John Hay.

We never did find exactly what we were looking for: a draft lease agreement, diplomatic communication, or other documents explaining where the lease's reference to Cuba's "ultimate sovereignty" came from or what it was intended to mean. Nevertheless, our plunge into historical research ultimately yielded a number of pertinent facts that we were able to use in our brief. We found a 1912 State Department memorandum in the National Archives that characterized U.S. authority at Guantánamo as "*quasi*-sovereign" (emphasis mine), and an unpublished 1903 letter from Theodore Roosevelt to John Hay saying that the United States regarded Guantánamo as "ours." We also discovered a draft of Cuban lease terms that provided for Cuban citizens who may have committed crimes on the base to be tried by Cuban courts and governed by Cuban law. But the United States rejected the provision, insisting that U.S. law—and U.S. law alone—would govern at Guantánamo.

When the Court scheduled oral argument, Jim Schroeder and I wanted to be there. We were anxious to be sure we would get in, so we headed for the Court at 5:30 the morning of the argument. Because of the historic nature of the case, the lines of lawyers and members of the public hoping for admittance grew steadily, and a large press contingent was camped out in front of the Supreme Court.

The atmosphere grew more tense once we were allowed inside and seated in the grand courtroom. Finally, John Gibbons stepped up to the podium to argue the case for the detainees. Gibbons was no left-wing partisan—he had served years before as the Chief Judge of the U.S. Court of Appeals for the Third Circuit, and he had actually been appointed by Richard Nixon. To no one's surprise, Judge Gibbons was pressed particularly hard by Justice Scalia.

The Bush administration was represented by Theodore Olson, the Solicitor General, in the Solicitor General's traditional morning coat. The drama was heightened by the fact that everyone in the courtroom knew that Olson's wife had died on one of the planes hijacked on 9/11. For me, the key moment in the entire oral argument came less than one minute into Olson's presentation. Olson began just as the government lawyers had begun every one of their briefs in the Guantánamo cases, by invoking the terrible tragedy of 9/11 and the fact that "the United States is at war." But Justice Stevens immediately cut in, asking if Olson would assert that the courts lacked jurisdiction over the detainees at Guantánamo even if "the war has ended." When Olson responded that the courts would have no jurisdiction even in peacetime, Stevens coolly replied, "The existence of the war is really irrelevant to the legal issue." That to me was the key moment in the whole oral argument: the Bush administration was trying to wrap itself in the flag, and the Court—or at least a number of its members—was having none of it.

After the oral argument, all the lawyers who had worked on our side were invited back to someone's home for a social gathering. We were in a celebratory mood—convinced that we had at least five, and probably six, Justices on our side. Justice Breyer had neatly summed up the "problem" with the Bush administration's argument: it "seems rather contrary to an idea of a Constitution with three branches, that the Executive would be free to do whatever they want, whatever they want without a check."

Although we were confident after the oral argument that we would prevail, it was still tremendously satisfying when the Court handed down its decision on June 28, 2004, and we *knew* that we had won. I had recognized all along that the case was of national, or even international, significance. But I remember being struck by the fact that within minutes of its release, the Court's decision seemed to be the top story on every major news website that I could find. For me at least, that drove home the magnitude of the case as much as anything else.

As a result of the decision in the Rasul *and* Al Odah *cases, attorneys were finally able to travel to Guantánamo and meet with their clients. Guantánamo's days as a prison entirely beyond the law were over. Yet, in many ways, the struggle for justice had only begun.*

David J. Cynamon: Contradiction

What strikes me about the prison at Guantánamo Bay is its incongruity. It sits at the base of rolling green hills on a bluff overlooking the beautiful, sparkling Caribbean. But, inside the razor-wired, green-canvas-covered fences sits a grim, sterile, maximum-security prison, surrounded by concrete, pea gravel, and dirt. It's the kind of place in which, in the United States, we house our most violent and incorrigible convicted criminals, yet most of the detainees have not even been charged with a crime. I have a feeling that someday, long after the prison is finally closed and we restore normal relations with Cuba, this spot will become a tourist attraction like Alcatraz. People who have come to enjoy the warm Caribbean sun and sea will wander in and out of the cells and look with interest at the photos and exhibits but will have no real clue about the torment that occurred here at the epicenter of one of the most shameful episodes in U.S. history.

Thomas P. Sullivan: Imagine

Most of the prisoners at Guantánamo are represented by American lawyers who have volunteered their services *pro bono publico*. Several years ago, a few of my partners and I volunteered to assist, and we have come to represent eighteen men, from Iraq, Libya, Saudi Arabia, and Yemen.

When reading this, imagine that you too had volunteered your services.

Having received the names and prisoner identification numbers of your new "clients"—you haven't yet met or spoken with them or anyone on their behalf—you contact the point person at the Department of Justice and identify your clients. You thereupon enter a bureaucratic maze. Before being permitted to write or visit your clients, you must first obtain a "secret" security clearance, a process which involves the FBI and usually consumes months. When this is accomplished, you receive a telephonic briefing by a DOJ representative, during which you are cautioned not to discuss the case in a room unless the blinds are drawn (my office is on the forty-first floor with an unimpeded view of Lake Michigan) and similar admonitions reminiscent of a John le Carré spy novel. You must sign a lengthy protective order acknowledging, among other things, that it is a serious criminal violation to reveal anything you are told by your client without having the information written and cleared through a screening procedure.

With that, you are qualified to visit the "secure facility" near Washington, D.C., to view classified material relating to your client. You nervously read the contents, then alternate between amazement and amusement as you realize that not only is there little or nothing very secret in the files but that the file often consists only of the statements the prisoner himself made when questioned by U.S. personnel, with innocent explanations as to why, for example, he was present in Afghanistan or Pakistan and what he was doing before being taken into custody.

To get to Guantánamo, you fly to Fort Lauderdale and then continue on to the base on one of two small prop-plane carriers, Air Sunshine or Lynx Air. The planes have a dozen or so seats but no toilet on board. When you check in for the three-and-a-half-hour flight, you're weighed along with your luggage to determine if the plane will be too heavy to fly all the way to the base without a stop to refuel at Exuma in the Bahamas. The plane may not enter Cuban air space, so you fly to the easternmost end of the island, make a right turn, and descend to the airport on the leeward side of the base. There is no prison on that side of the bay, and unsupervised movements are permitted, but amenities such as restaurants or grocery stores are scarce. You stay at the former "CBQ"—Combined Bachelors' Quarters—at an attractive government room rate of approximately $20 per night. A kitchenette and four twin beds furnish each two-room "suite." There are so few visitors that each lawyer is usually housed alone, although recent construction on the CBQ has required some doubling up.

The following morning, a bus takes you and your interpreter (the usual fee is $1,000 per day plus expenses) to the landing at the bay, where a ferry loaded with cars and trucks waits to make the twenty-minute crossing to the windward side. Your fellow travelers are chiefly workers from the Philippines and Jamaica and military personnel. In most places on this side you may move about only by bus or van, accompanied by members of the military Joint Task Force, which includes personnel from the army, navy, and Marine Corps. No electronic devices are allowed, including Blackberries, cell phones, and cameras.

On the first day of your visit, you are taken to an office to be photographed and given a clip-on badge, which you wear in the bus and at the prison but not in public places, and which you must return before you leave the windward side. You are driven to McDonald's, where you may to purchase food and drink for yourself, your interpreter, and your clients. Your driver then takes you to the camp where your client awaits.

The prison is divided into a number of "camps," each of which is enclosed by wire fencing topped with razor-sharp coils, and everything is double gated and securely locked. Soldiers proliferate, mainly young American men and women, looking serious and dressed in camouflage-patterned uniforms and combat boots, most carrying side arms or rifles.

You wait patiently outside the gate. The soldiers who police the entrance are polite and businesslike. One of them opens the gate and motions you and your interpreter in. Inside the compound, you observe that the soldiers' name tags are covered. A soldier runs a scanner over you, front and back with arms extended, looks through your wallet, reviews your papers, and confiscates items deemed inappropriate for lawyer visits such as news articles, books, and magazines. He or she also takes anything that is considered usable as a weapon, for example, paper clips, staples, straws, and combs. You are then escorted by armed personnel to a small, rectangular building that resembles the van of a semitrailer. The soldier opens the door, you and your interpreter enter, and the door is shut and locked.

Most of the detainees are kept in isolation, twenty-four hours a day, seven days a week, without proper medical attention, decent food, or diversions such as radio, television, books, newspapers, magazines, or reading material other than the Quran. By design, most have no contact with fellow prisoners, and opportunities for exercise are limited. Most prisoners are housed in rectangular cubicles, actually small cages, measuring from six-by-eight to seven-by-ten feet, with a raised concrete slab and mattress for a bed, a wash basin, and a toilet. The walls are made of fine wire mesh, which I am told impairs vision if looked through for extended periods. In most of the camps, physical contact among prisoners is prohibited, and oral communication is restricted to shouting to those celled nearby. In one of the highest security camps, known as Camp Six, the walls are not porous, resulting in total isolation. All movements of prisoners require two armed guards, with the prisoners chained hand and foot. Mail from home is sporadic, often delayed for many months while being translated and censored for unauthorized content and heavily redacted.

Jan K. Kitchel: The Kingdom of Guantánamo

We stopped in Exuma, Bahamas, to refuel, and we were allowed off the plane into a tiny airport "lounge," really a cinder-block building where we could buy a T-shirt or a soda and wait for the aircraft to refuel. Across the street, where we weren't allowed, being aliens to the Bahamas, was an inviting bar, with the promise of cold beer.

It was already dark when our plane arrived at Guantánamo, given the tropical latitude. The mess was closed, so our dinner was limited to The Clipper bar, the only bar on the leeward side of the bay, where habeas lawyers "live." Most of the town, and most of the bars, are on the windward side, but letting us wander aimlessly on that side of the base might compromise security, so we were exiled to the leeward side with few people. The other people were mainly Haitian or Filipino contract workers, known as third-party nationals, or TPNs, and the occasional Marine, guarding "the wire" separating us from the frightening Cuban army.

I got up early the next day, and I was the first one into the large mess hall, or galley, which is next door to The Clipper. The Haitian cooks will make you an omelet to order, and whatever breakfast you want, for about $1.83, which is about what they make per hour—the U.S. minimum wage not being applicable in the "Kingdom of GTMO." The food was great, and almost no one came into the mess hall, which easily could have seated 150 people.

I caught the bus to the ferry landing, with my daughter and my compatriots, and we rode a battleship-gray U.S. Navy ferry across the bay to the windward side. That naval vessel was piloted and crewed by TPN contractors, probably Filipinos. TPNs do virtually all the nonprison work on the base, and I was quite surprised that the navy would turn one of its vessels over to guys in Rasta T-shirts.

Howard J. Manchel: Camp Echo

Just before our flight to GTMO left Fort Lauderdale, our pilot appeared in the boarding area to apologize for what would only be a ten-minute delay. "I'm sorry we need to fuel up here." The nine passengers, me included, all nodded our heads, hoping to convince the pilot that we were all in favor of fuel. The first passenger in line, a heavily tattooed contract employee on the island, called back, "Take as long as you need—even an hour if you have to."

Within ten minutes, we were boarding the plane. This was a trip that for me was some ten months in the planning and involved obtaining a top security clearance, so I anticipated a fairly heavy-duty show of security to board the plane. Yet I wasn't even asked to go through a metal detector, nor was my luggage checked—at least not in front of me.

The countryside at Guantánamo is tropical, with occasional views of the bay. Although the natural scenery is beautiful, the base is ugly. There is no doubt in my mind that if Cuba ever got this territory back, it would tear down the base and develop the surrounding area for a resort.

We knew we were approaching the infamous prison camp when we encountered the worst speed bumps imaginable. The jar to the back of the van was so pronounced, we did everything in our power to avoid the next one. At some point an armed soldier, who looked exceptionally young, stopped the van, entered, and checked our IDs.

We continued driving and came upon a construction site where the United States was building another camp, as the buildings that hold the prisoners are called. On the opposite side is a large camp, reminiscent of World War II prison-camp movies, complete with wooden watchtowers surrounded by a tall fence covered with a green tarp and topped with the standard razor wire.

Eventually, we pulled into the parking lot of Camp Echo, where detainees are brought to meet with their attorneys. Here there are no trees, nothing living. The ground is covered with white pea gravel, which serves to reflect the sun and make the area seem brighter than one would think possible. An official escorted us to the entrance, which is about as nondescript as the military could make it. Again green tarp prevented us from seeing inside the gate. When the door popped open, we entered a sally port. When we were all within the first door, the second opened, and we found ourselves facing another soldier dressed in tan fatigues, who told us what we could and could not bring in and who also advised us to use the latrines because the army could not guarantee a restroom escort once we got to the cells.

Camp Echo contains a series of either newly constructed or renovated cells for the purpose of interviews and interrogations, although they are also apparently capable of housing inmates. Each building houses two cells, with each cell divided in half with its own door. One half of the individual cell is a living unit, with a shower, sink-toilet, and a foam mattress that rests on a concrete slab. The other side of the cell is where the interview takes place. The detainee is shackled to the floor by his feet, and the interpreter and I sit across from him. A government-issued card table stands between us.

George Daly: Sending a Message

Inside the gate of Camp Echo a highly serious enlisted woman searched us and had us sign in. Then we were escorted into an interior rectangular courtyard. If I had been dropped there from Mars, I would have known instantly I was in a military prison and not a civilian one. The entire courtyard except for the sidewalks was covered with blindingly white, neatly raked pea gravel. A civilian prison would have a courtyard with packed dirt and occasional grass, for the prisoners to exercise, smoke, and stand around. Here the courtyard was being used to project order and power. Sidewalks bisected the courtyard, forming four rectangles. Along the perimeter of each rectangle the gravel had been meticulously raked into low dikes or levees with sloping sides, about six inches high and six inches wide. Before we came into the courtyard we had been told not to step off the sidewalks. I've since heard that other lawyers were told there were minefields inside the picture frames. Blinded by the whiteness of the courtyard, I unwittingly stepped on one of the dikes. Nothing exploded. Everyone stopped for a moment, but nobody said a word.

Heading back to the ferry in our military jitney after the interview, I thought about Ryoanji, a Zen monastery in Kyoto. Its courtyard contains several large stones surrounded by neatly raked white-sand whorls. Like the courtyard at Camp Echo, it is there to be looked at, not walked on. But it was the difference in their messages that so lanced me, the Zen message of quiet contemplation and the Echo message of power and order. Both courtyards are sacred spreads, but one is sacred to the Zen god of contemplation and interior knowledge, the other to the Devil's Island god of torture. One is for liberation. The other is for domination.

David Marshall: Escort Required

Imprisoning alleged terrorists is the most famous function of the Guantánamo naval base, but it goes on only in a small area. The various military services have a role in it, so it is known as the Joint Task Force, or JTF, area, distinct from the other areas from which coast guard and navy craft carry on that older war, the War on Drugs, and fish refugees from the sea. (Haiti is not far away.)

Our escort picked us up in a van at the ferry terminal. He drove us first to an office building, where I had my photo taken and my permanent JTF-GTMO badge issued. The big type on it read, "Escort required."

Under normal conditions, the escort would then have driven us to McDonald's or Subway to pick up breakfast to go, for ourselves and our client. At every jail and prison at which I had previously visited a client, a lawyer was forbidden to bring the prisoner anything but legal papers. The rules at Guantánamo, though, permit lawyers to bring all manner of food and drink to client meetings. The only limitation seems to be that the prisoner may consume it only during the meeting. For some prisoners—the ones most like me—meetings with habeas counsel become pig-outs. Counsel, always looking for ways to strengthen relationships with suspicious clients, try to bring foods popular in the client's homeland, such as dates, figs, pistachios, and tea. (No, the McDonald's and Subway at Guantánamo don't have extensive menus along those lines, but many prisoners enjoy Western food too.) A common subject to cover in an interview is whether the client would like his lawyer to bring any special treat at a future visit.

I had been alerted that my client would feel free to eat only if we lawyers ate. Always ready to go the extra mile for a client, I had prepared by eating nothing before boarding the ferry.

Prisoners at Guantánamo suffer extraordinary isolation. The popular image of inmates in a prison working together in the laundry, lounging together in the yard, and forming a football team to play the guards does not fit Guantánamo. The isolation is most severe at Camp Six. There, prisoners are permitted to leave their windowless, individual cells at most only once a day for a brief exercise period. The exercise area has walls two stories high, so even there a prisoner can see nothing of the natural world except the sky. Direct sunlight rarely reaches prisoners in the exercise area. Only when in the exercise area can a prisoner communicate with another prisoner, and only then by speaking to one of the few prisoners who has simultaneous exercise in a neighboring, but not connected, exercise area. A prisoner in Camp Six never has contact with another living thing—not even a blade of grass—unless an insect lands on him in the exercise area. I am not counting the gloved hand of a guard who moves the prisoner.

When any prisoner is moved from a camp, he travels by van. The prisoner has his feet shackled together and his hands shackled to his waist. A hood is placed over his head. He is placed in the windowless back of the van and driven to his destination.

Wherever a prisoner meets his lawyer, he does so with one ankle chained to a ring in the floor. If the meeting lasts the entire day—and it usually does—the ankle will be so chained all day, except for meal and toilet breaks. I have visited many people in custody, but I have never seen anything like these conditions before.

Andrea J. Prasow: The Other Side of the Island

"Do not wave, point or gesture toward the Cubans." This warning appeared on the brief I received from the marines for the five-mile run I signed up for at Guantánamo. The race started at the Northeast Gate to Castro's Cuba—the gate through which two old Cubans still cross every morning to work on the base and return every evening to their homes—and ran along the barbed-wire-fence-line perimeter. It ended at Kittery Beach. Life as a lawyer in the military commissions system is certainly different than it was when I was habeas counsel.

The life of a habeas lawyer at Guantánamo is circumscribed and varies significantly from that of lawyers who represent the handful of detainees who have been charged with war crimes before a military commission. Everyone else is simply detained without any charge at all (and they do not have military attorneys, only civilian counsel, for their habeas corpus cases). As civilian habeas counsel, you must sleep on the leeward side of the island, in the CBQ that is a cross between a roadside motel and a dorm. You cannot travel alone to the other side of the island. You cannot rent a car, go out for a late dinner, jog along the road to Camp X-Ray, or go snorkeling. In many ways, the limits are helpful—they used to remind me constantly of how unpleasant life on the island can be. No matter how tired, sweaty, and dirty I felt, I knew that my clients were suffering so much more. Now, as a Department of Defense employee "on orders," I am free to roam the base as I please, unescorted for the most part. Now, when I go to the beach or have a barbeque with my colleagues, I feel guilty. Recently, I set out for a run after work at the base. It had just started raining, and I thought about turning back. But I reminded myself that there were hundreds of men on the island who would give anything to be able to run free in the rain. So I ran and thought about them every step of the way.

Patricia A. Bronte: GTMO Arrest

Despite some prodding, the Department of Justice waited until the last business day before the trip to send me the country and theater clearances that would allow me to be on the base. In a rush to finish some other matters on the Friday before my departure, I printed the two clearances attached to the e-mail and put them in an envelope with my other travel documents. That turned out to be a big mistake. I arrived at the base at about 5 p.m. on a Sunday. When asked to present my clearances, I pulled out the two documents I had printed the Friday before. Unfortunately, the DOJ had sent me two copies of the theater clearance and zero copies of the country clearance. I could not reach the DOJ because it was Sunday night. Although everyone at the base knew that I was authorized to be there, no one seemed to have the authority to allow me to stay there without the magic country clearance.

Initially I was escorted to a guard office adjacent to the airport, where I waited two hours while a guard attempted to reach someone at the base who could resolve the issue. The authorities finally determined that I needed to go to the windward side of the base. Armed Military Police (MP) helped me haul my baklava-laden luggage onto a speedboat, all the while thanking me for being so "compliant" and apologizing that the trip might be uncomfortable. Foolishly, I thought they were worried I might be seasick. One MP handed me a rope that was tied to the prow of the boat and told me to hang onto it. I soon discovered the wisdom of this advice, as the boat sped across the bay. The trip that ordinarily takes twenty-two minutes by ferry lasted only three minutes. I am certain I would have flown overboard if I had not clung to the rope.

Once on the windward side, we climbed about fifty stairs from the boat landing up to the Badging Office, hauling my luggage with us. We waited in the Badging Office for about half an hour for someone from the office of the Staff Judge Advocate (SJA) to arrive. The SJA provides legal advice to the military at GTMO. After several minutes of consternation about my plight, the SJA announced that he might be able to locate the missing country clearance—because, of course, it had originated with his office. We soon returned to the leeward side of the base, and I arrived at the CBQ exactly three hours after my plane had landed.

Jerry Cohen: Honor Bound to Defend Freedom

I came to the Guantánamo Bay Naval Station as a volunteer lawyer for a detainee and remembered my own military service fifty years ago. Yes, fifty. My first impression of the military people—officers and enlisted personnel of Joint Task Force–GTMO—and of the naval base itself was how similar it was to the people and facilities of my awakened memories of long-ago service.

Joint Task Force–GTMO is peopled by officers and enlisted personnel of the army, navy, marines, and coast guard, supporting civilian employees of the DOD and contractors and "observers" of the CIA. My own observations of the detainees were preceded by observations of, and interactions with, the enlisted men and women who guided, searched, and chaperoned me, who chatted with me in the galley or Naval Exchange and, as I watched, escorted detainees to and from interview rooms and handled counsel requests for special relief.

They were mostly young men and women, ranging in age from nineteen to twenty-five, at a turning point in their lives, and a few were noncommissioned officers and officers in their late twenties to thirties who were going the distance of a military career. All are subjected to a discipline and motivation system that includes slogans such as "Honor Bound to Defend Freedom." This slogan is emblazoned on walls and gates and reinforced by a ceremonial saluting exchange: the lower-ranking person salutes and says, "Honor Bound," and the senior replies, "To Defend Freedom." It struck them and the intruding civilians as hokey, so they reduced it to a junior's "Honor Bound" greeting, met with the senior's reply, "Honor Bound." Later, there was a general trend toward a mere silent exchange of salutes, often with a smile.

Why bother? It matters because patriotism is an element of a soldier's or sailor's motivation to enlist, reenlist, and serve honorably. Set aside blandishments of training, structure, bonuses, college help, and travel. None would suffice absent the element of patriotism—that and a sense of mission and a willingness to believe in the organization and its duty assignments. Embarrassment at the sentiment of patriotism is covered by pretended cynicism.

Other motivating slogans include periodically posted values, such as "Leadership," "Courage," "Obedience," and "Compassion." My reaction to the last value made me rethink my own cynicism and reflect on the relation of the guards to detainees—I saw once harsh captors become gentler over time. They wouldn't wholly reveal feelings and judgments to me, given our separate roles, but there were hints of mutual understanding.

In some ways the young soldiers and sailors are captives. They don't sign up for JTF-GTMO. They are deployed for duty tours that can last years. They are now trained to serve as humane jailers in a jail where they cover their own name tags, follow scripts of addressing detainees and visiting lawyers, cope with challenges of an unusual prison population and glib lawyers, and carry out orders, fair or otherwise. Past trainings, exercises of aiding torture and misguided interrogation techniques, have moved into a shadowed past. Most practitioners of those sinister excesses have been redeployed, including generals and Cabinet-level officers. At intermediate rank levels we find brave JAG prosecutors who spoke out and acted, at high risk, against perversions of military honor and legal standards, offset by higher-level opportunists in the chain of command seeking advancement by adopting those perversions.

Some of the current guards have empathized with detainees, advocated for them, filtered general declamations of the "worst of the worst" against their own observations of their charges—good and bad, compliant and challenging, healthy and sick, harmless and dangerous. This has been one part of their coming-of-age experience, mixed with the usual stilted exchanges and ennui of military life.

The soldiers and sailors have also gone through a prolonged observation of the visiting lawyers and translators. I was greeted in early visits with a stiff, even hostile formality. It changed. We are no longer the devious practitioners of "lawfare" (the idea of war waged through the courts and legal procedures) in the eyes of most of them. They now realize we have a role that adds legitimacy to their roles, that we join with them as a team working for the justice that makes freedom meaningful.

The soldiers and sailors, when sworn into service, took an oath to defend the Constitution. So did the lawyers. Together, we're honor bound to fulfill it. If only their former commander in chief, President Bush, had been similarly bound.

Jessica Baen: Season's Greetings*

To those of you fortunate enough to miss the holiday festivities, I thought I'd send season's greetings on behalf of the Joint Task Force–Guantánamo. Pour yourself a mug of some heavily doctored seasonal beverage and close your eyes for a moment to picture the Christmas-tree display in front of the Navy Exchange, in between the Subway sandwich shop and the gift shop—the one with the "Kisses from Guantánamo Bay" shot glasses and the "Sinking our teeth into the Middle East" T-shirts.

Swathed in fake cotton-ball snow stand no less than fifteen synthetic Christmas trees. Each tree has its own theme, collectively representing every facet of Guantánamo life, except, of course, for one. McDonald's

---

* *This selection is based on an e-mail sent by Jessica Baen to a colleague in December 2007.*

and Subway each have their own tree, which sport take-away boxes and paper cups as ornaments. The Guantánamo Youth Center has a tree, as do the Guantánamo Police and Fire Departments, with yellow police-tape garlands. The contractors have a tree festooned with electrical wire and toy trucks, with a hard hat perched on top. There's a "third-party national" tree decorated with foreign flags, representing the migrant laborers and refugees who provide Guantánamo with most of its civilian labor, and a "GTMO Latino Families—new generation" tree, with smiling photos of the new generation.

A lot of the decorations are cute and clever, in a banality-of-evil sort of way. My favorite might be the sick tree. It's draped in hospital-bracelet chains, with pill bottles, urine-sample vials, and syringes hanging from its branches. With all these resources so readily available, I wonder, why hasn't our client received proper eyeglasses, despite having asked for them for over a year? His vision has been deteriorating severely due to so many years of confinement in his small cell, where he is unable to focus his eyes beyond the walls a few feet away. On top of the tree is a star wrapped in an ace bandage, and if you read the dangling prescription bottles carefully, you'll see they're for "Holiday Cheer: 100 mg. Take once a day as needed. Signed: Dr. S. Claus." Faced with the prospect of reintegrating into the real world of American denial just four days before Christmas, I consider the bottle with mild interest before I snap out of it.

But wait, something's missing. No barbed-wire garlands, no orange? Given the rather literal interpretations favored by the tree designers, it's all too easy to envision the one tree they thought it best to omit.

Happy Holidays.

3

Uncovering Guantánamo's Human Face

First Impressions

By the time lawyers were first permitted access to Guantánamo detainees in 2004, their clients had been imprisoned for more than two and a half years without access to a court or the outside world. Many had been subjected to torture and other abuse. All had endured unremitting isolation and the effects of a detention system designed to instill hopelessness, fear, and despair. Guantánamo, the detainees knew, was a lawless zone, and for many of them, lawyers were part of that lawless system.

For many lawyers, these first meetings involved an effort to win their clients' confidence and trust. Lawyers listened as detainees began to tell them their stories and to explain the hardships and mistreatment that they had endured and continued to confront.

The lawyers had been told by the highest level of the U.S. government that their clients were "the worst of the worst." But that unfounded assertion became more and more absurd over time, as lawyers learned more about their clients and fought for their right to a day in court.

Thomas P. Sullivan: You Have the Bodies

You see your client seated behind a table, one leg shackled to the floor. He is young, bearded, swarthy, and does not speak or understand more than a few words of English. If you haven't met before—and often even if you have—he suspects that you and your interpreter are secret agents for the U.S. government who have come to pry information from him. After repeated assurances that you are there to help him, you discuss the state of the legal and political efforts under way to have him and the other prisoners returned home. There is a problem here: there is no real news to report, at least no good news. The conversation consists chiefly of you trying to explain why no progress has been made to get a hearing before a tribunal that will require the government to explain why he and his fellow prisoners have been held in jail for so many years.

You try to curry favor by offering McDonald's and baklava; both often go untouched. Your self-serving protestations of loyalty to him ring hollow. You find it difficult if not impossible to respond to questions about why, when your government preaches liberty and fair dealing for all, it confines citizens of other countries, mostly Islamic, for years without hearings, and why your Congress and courts not only fail to afford relief but affirmatively take steps to bar it.

At the end of the visit, your client expresses his sincere appreciation for your having come and assures you he knows that not all Americans support their government's repressive treatment of the men imprisoned at Guantánamo Bay. You are taken aback and embarrassed at being met with kindness and solicitude from a man whom your government has caged for years for no discernable reason. You promise to write and keep your client informed and to continue working on his behalf to correct the injustices visited on him and his fellows. He responds with polite but understandable skepticism. The interview closes on this ambiguous note.

You return to Fort Lauderdale, with time to reflect on the contradiction between the prisoners' plight and the Joint Task Force motto, prominently displayed throughout the base, "Honor Bound to Defend Freedom." You are a few days older, but without any greater understanding than when you came as to why our government is spending our money and using our armed forces to imprison your clients.

Baher Azmy: Shipwrecked

I first saw him on a TV screen. Before my initial meeting with Murat Kurnaz in October 2004, the U.S. military police escorted me—the third civilian lawyer to enter the inner sanctum of Guantánamo's Camp Echo—through several fifteen-foot-high locked gates and into the guard booth of the world's most notorious military prison. On my way to the booth, walking across gravel made bright white by the blazing Caribbean sun, my status as a civilian—clean shaven, dressed in a tie and formal shoes—was punctuated by the loud sounds of practice machine-gun fire in the distance.

The military showed me the surveillance they would employ during my otherwise private meeting with my client: he was on a video screen, waiting for me. The image was blurry, like the grainy picture on a store security camera or a late-night news broadcast's depiction of a wanted menace, and it was unsettling: here was a man with a beard and hair seemingly befitting a prehistoric warrior. Prior to the Supreme Court's 2004 decision in *Rasul v. Bush*, which first opened up the camp to law, lawyers, and therefore a minimal amount of scrutiny, Bush administration officials had claimed that all the detainees in Guantánamo were a sort of maniacally diabolical lot—not only were they "trained killers," but they had nearly superhuman ability to, for example, "gnaw the hydraulic wires of a C-17 transport plane." I was naturally distrustful of these claims, but this first image obviously did not advance my skepticism. Another military guard carried out what appeared to be his somber duty, instructing me to push away from the table in case the man lunged for my throat.

Leaving the guard booth, we walked toward the hutlike structure in Camp Echo that housed the detainees' cells, mindful to stay within the gravel walking lanes manicured by the lowest level military personnel. An impossibly young soldier who had been "preparing" my client for the visit told me, "He says he doesn't want a translator." I exchanged concerned looks with Belinda, the German translator I brought all this way to translate our interviews. "You sure you're talking about Murat Kurnaz?" I asked. "He doesn't speak English." The guard replied, "No he speaks it good enough. And he's pretty adamant—he doesn't want a translator." "Since when does he speak English?" I persisted. The guard didn't know, and obviously neither did Murat's family, who hadn't communicated with him in the three years since his U.S. detention began.

I regretfully sent the translator back to the civilian side of Guantánamo and prepared to meet Murat alone. When the door to our meeting room opened, he was seated, squinting at the incoming sunlight. He was dressed in a short, tan shirt and cotton pants—the color designating him neither cooperative nor uncooperative. With a flowing beard and red-brown mane of hair, he looked like someone who had been shipwrecked on a desert island, which, in a sense, he was. He shook my hand and motioned for me to sit across from him on the flimsy plastic chair, as if he were welcoming me to tea in his home. I tried to sound confident. "Murat, my name is Baher Azmy. I am a lawyer. I do not work for the U.S. government. Your family in Germany asked me to help you." I handed him a handwritten note from his worried mother to help convince him that I was on his side. The simple honesty and loving reassurance of her message still moves me: "My dear son Murat, You will be visited by an American lawyer whom you can trust. Murat, your brothers go to school and we have been for vacation in Turkey. We were shopping with [your wife] and she is loving you." As I watched his pained expression while reading his first message from home—his first taste of humanity in three years—I felt as though I was delivering a crumb of bread to Robinson Crusoe.

I explained that his mother and German lawyer had been fighting for years for him, that Guantánamo had become an international embarrassment, and that millions of people in the United States were opposed to it. Because he had been held incommunicado for almost three years, he had no idea anyone even knew of Guantánamo's existence, or his existence. I also told him that I was born in Egypt, a Muslim, and was a law professor with great faith in the American legal system. "You have sued President Bush?" he asked. "Yes, you and I have sued him. And I will do everything I can to help you," I answered. To my relief, he said with a heavy German accent, "This is goot."

The second day of my visit, I brought him McDonald's coffee and a half-dozen packets of sugar to satisfy what I knew about the Turkish coffee culture, as well as an apple pie; he ate with wondrous nostalgia for his mother's version. On subsequent visits, I became more adventurous in what I would bring to our meetings: dolmas, baklava, cheese, pita bread, Turkish figs, fresh garlic (his request), subs, pizza, Filet-O-Fish sandwiches, fries, hot peppers (also his request), Jolly Ranchers, cookies, fresh fruit, canned fruit, dried fruit, melting McFlurries, and even a packaged shrimp cocktail. I was shopping for a starving man. I also brought him Starbucks, but, to my surprise, he preferred McDonald's coffee.

We spent eight hours a day for the next four days talking—about everything—and I spent a total of over sixty hours with him on four subsequent visits. Murat is the furthest thing from a hardened terrorist. I lived in downtown New York during September 11 and remember the haunting smell of the smoldering rubble twenty blocks south, so in the course of conversations, I was curious to hear what Murat thought of this monstrous act. Murat repeatedly rejected the logic of terrorism. "My mother and father go to malls and airports in Germany. Why would I want terrorists to kill them?" he stressed. Also, the Quran commands never to kill women, children, or men not in battle and also condemns suicide killings—only God chooses when we die. But Osama bin Laden and Hamas believe that such suicide killings are a necessary response to oppression, I pushed, playing devil's advocate. Murat had never heard of Hamas.

And Osama bin Laden? In Murat's military hearing in which he was given an opportunity to speak, he said,

> I hate terrorists. I am here having lost a few years of my life because of Osama bin Laden. His beliefs show Islam in the wrong way. I am not angry with Americans. Many Americans died in the September 11

terrorist attacks. I realize the Americans are right to stop terrorism. All countries should do the same thing. . . . If any Muslim talked to me about terrorism, I would tell them to their face it was wrong. I would do everything I could to stop them. I don't have any proof to show you, but I didn't harm or kill anyone.

The United States knows that Murat Kurnaz has no connection to terrorism and logged this fact no less than five times in his classified "file." According to his file, the U.S. military itself concluded that "Kurnaz has no connection to al Qaeda, the Taliban or any terrorist threat," and "the Germans have confirmed he has no connection to al Qaeda." The government resisted for years permitting disclosure of this information, but as a result of a Freedom of Information Act litigation we brought on his behalf, it is now public and indisputable that as early as 2002, the United States recognized that Murat had nothing to do with terrorism. Yet it suppressed this information and continued to imprison him.

Joshua Colangelo-Bryan: Habeas on the Gate, Part I

"We'll be watching," the sergeant said, pointing at a video monitor inside Camp Echo's guard booth, "for your protection." The monitor showed a grainy image of a table and chairs in a small room. To one side was a tiny cell, partially hidden behind a steel mesh wall. I was about to have my first meeting with a Guantánamo Bay detainee in a room just like that.

"You have any questions before you go in?" the sergeant asked. I certainly did. Donald Rumsfeld had said that the detainees were "among the most dangerous, best-trained vicious killers on the face of the Earth." President Bush had said that they had been "trying to kill Americans." The chairman of the Joint Chiefs of Staff had said they would chew through hydraulic cables to bring down airplanes. I didn't buy that kind of rhetoric wholesale, but it wasn't hard to imagine that there were at least some nasty characters among the Guantánamo prisoners. It was impossible not to wonder if I was going to meet one.

These questions had been on my mind ever since my corporate law firm had agreed to represent six Bahraini detainees several months earlier. According to a document the government provided to us under court order, the client I was about to see had received military training in Afghanistan, had gone to Bosnia to fight, and had been arrested in connection with a bombing in Saudi Arabia. A day earlier, on the small prop plane that ferried us to Guantánamo from Fort Lauderdale, I read news stories on the Internet that described this man as an al Qaeda recruiter. For a moment, I pictured myself sitting alone with a big, bearded, menacing Arab who would reach across the table for my throat.

Figuring that the sergeant was just asking if I had questions about logistics, I said I was ready. A military guard escorted my interpreter, Karim, and me away from the centrally located guard booth and toward one of a series of small wooden buildings that were spread out around Camp Echo's gravel compound. The buildings were on short stilts, and despite resembling low-rent beach cabanas, they housed interview rooms and cells like the one on the monitor. Beyond the buildings, and surrounding the camp, were several fifteen-foot-tall chain-link fences, each topped by razor wire and covered with green tarps, evidently to keep people from looking in or out. We walked up to one of the buildings, where a guard held the door slightly ajar. I nodded to him and, more tentatively than I might have liked, went inside.

Jumah Al Dossari sat at a table, flanked by guards. He saw me, and his face broke into a warm smile. As I walked toward him I sized him up, a habit I had developed as a kid on public school playgrounds in New York City. I guessed he was about five foot six and 140 pounds—not exactly a gladiator's build. I started to feel a little stupid for having worried about meeting a vicious killer. Besides having a short beard, Jumah didn't match my overwrought mental image at all.

One of Jumah's ankles was shackled to a bolt that was attached to the floor. He struggled to get halfway to his feet. We shook hands. "Assalamu alaikum," I said. Having exhausted my Arabic, I looked to Karim for help. "I'm Josh Colangelo. I'm your lawyer. It's very good to meet you."

"Hello, I am Jumah," he said in heavily accented English, before shaking hands with Karim and switching to Arabic. "Thank you for coming. I have been waiting for your visit. Please sit," he said, gesturing to the table. Jumah was doing his best to be a gracious host despite his shackles and our surroundings.

Once we sat down, the guards left.

"Do I understand correctly, then, that you received my letter?" I asked, referring to correspondence I had sent two months earlier. Jumah nodded. "As I said in my letter," I continued, "I'm a lawyer with a firm called Dorsey & Whitney. I work in New York. Your brother, Khaled, asked my law firm to represent you. When did you find out that you would be seeing me today?"

"This morning they told me I was moving, but they did not say why."

"I'm sorry about that. Do you normally stay somewhere else?"

"Yes, I am in Camp Five." Jumah gestured to the cell that sat two feet away from us, sealed off from the rest of the room by a steel mesh wall. "This is worse than Camp Five."

The cell next to us couldn't have been much smaller. The main section of it was as long as the concrete slab that served as a bed and no wider than five feet. The cell had another small area for a shower, but it was locked off by a heavy steel door. As there was nothing in the room except the cell and our meeting area, anyone spending a night there would be completely alone—except for the remarkably loud drone of an air conditioner that must have been on its last legs.

One thing I had been worrying about was whether Jumah would be able to trust a thirty-something, white, short-haired American who showed up at Guantánamo claiming to be his lawyer. It seemed likely that the only people fitting my description he had seen over the prior thirty-two months were guards, interrogators, and the like. Maybe he would think that this was just some CIA agent's ruse.

I attacked that issue first. "I thought it might be hard for you to believe it was really Khaled who sent me here. So I asked him to tell me a few personal details about you that only people close to you would know. Do you mind if I share those details with you?"

"No, please tell me."

"Khaled said that when you were a child, your favorite beach was Half Moon Beach."

Jumah smiled as if savoring a memory. "Yes, Half Moon Beach," he said in English.

"Khaled also told me that you loved the movie *Jumanji*." Jumah smiled again. "I am a little embarrassed to say that I asked if it was from somewhere in the Middle East, and Khaled had to tell me that it's an American movie."

Jumah laughed. "You don't know this movie?"

"No, I've never seen it." I later Googled the film and learned that it starred Robin Williams and was about kids playing a board game. It wasn't my kind of cinema, and it had struck me as an odd favorite for a supposed jihadist.

"You should see it," Jumah said. "It's very good."

"Jumah, unless you have questions about what Khaled told me, I would like to explain why we agreed to represent you."

"Yes, that would be good," he said.

"I don't need to tell you that the government has classified you as an 'enemy combatant.' The government claims it can hold anyone it calls an enemy combatant in jail forever without a trial. The government claims that enemy combatants do not have any rights at all—but I guess you know that already. Now, you might disagree, Jumah, but personally, I don't think that's right." Jumah chuckled and nodded. "If someone might be in jail for life," I continued, "I believe the person deserves at least a fair hearing to determine if he has done something wrong. My law firm feels the same way, and that's why we agreed to represent you. It's really as simple as that."

"I am very grateful to you and your law firm," he said.

"You're welcome, but we believe that we're obliged to provide legal help to people who would not otherwise have it. We call it *pro bono* work, which means that we aren't paid for what we do." For a minute, I felt like I was trying to sell an idealistic law student on the idea of working for my firm because it had a social conscience. I felt a flush of pride, reflecting on the fact that I was actually telling the truth.

"I am still grateful," Jumah said. "In your letter you said that there was a court case for the detainees. Can you explain this?" he asked.

"Sure. In June of this year, the Supreme Court—the highest court in America—ruled that detainees at Guantánamo can bring court cases. Specifically, the Supreme Court said detainees are entitled to bring habeas corpus petitions. A habeas petition is made by someone who is in jail. The petition requires the government to produce evidence in court, showing that there is a legitimate reason for holding the person. The person can respond to the government's evidence and submit his own. Then, a court decides if the person should be held in jail."

"But isn't the Supreme Court part of the government? If the government says we have no rights, how can the Supreme Court say something else?"

"Wait," I said with mock exasperation. "Are you asking me hard questions already? Nobody told me I'd have to answer hard questions."

Jumah laughed. "Yes, I have many hard questions."

"OK, let me try to answer. You're right that the Supreme Court is part of the government. But if I say the government claims you have no rights, I'm actually talking about the President. The Supreme Court and the President are both part of the government, but they're separate. Under some circumstances, the Supreme Court can tell the President what to do." Not knowing how much sense this would make to someone who grew up in a Middle Eastern monarchy, I drew a diagram, trying to illustrate the separation-of-powers doctrine.

"I can make one of these . . . petitions?"

"Actually, we've already brought habeas petitions for you and the other Bahrainis."

"Thank you. What evidence has the government shown to the court about me?"

"Well, nothing yet. We still have some preliminary issues to resolve, but we hope to have hearings relatively soon."

In fact, the government had just made a motion to ask that our petitions be dismissed, arguing that the Supreme Court decision was simply a formality that did not give the detainees any rights beyond filing a piece of paper in court. I decided against trying to explain the intricacies of motion practice just yet because we had already covered some nuanced ground and I didn't want Jumah to think we were stopped in our tracks before even starting.

"I'd like to explain some other things about our work. In America, anything that a lawyer and client talk about is confidential. The court has ruled that the right to confidentiality applies here. I will do everything I can to preserve that confidentiality, but unfortunately I can't guarantee it."

"That's because everything you say is classified or secret. If I write down your words, my notes become secret. At the end of our meeting, I will be required to hand over my notes to the military. The military is not supposed to read them. They are supposed to send them to what is called a 'secure facility' in America, where I will be able to review them. But, again, I cannot guarantee that my notes won't be read. So if you want to say something that you don't want me to write down, please tell me."

He wasn't fazed. "I have nothing to hide."

I looked down and noticed a plastic bag near my feet that I had forgotten about entirely. It was filled with items from Sahadi's, a Middle Eastern specialty shop in Brooklyn.

"Jumah, I realize it might threaten national security, but they actually let us bring in food. Would you like to eat something?"

"If you eat with me."

I took out pastries, dried fruit, cookies, and other things that had seemed likely to survive the day-long trip to Cuba. I motioned to Jumah to eat. He motioned to Karim and me to eat. The standoff lasted for a moment. Then, we all grabbed stuff and started passing it around.

It seemed like a good time to find out if Jumah would be willing to tell me about himself. "Jumah, if you don't know it already, you are going to find out that lawyers can be really boring. I'm sorry to say that your lawyer is no exception. Sometimes, I ask very annoying questions until I get all the information I need. I don't do it to make people miserable. It's just that lawyers need to be very precise sometimes in what they say about their clients. How would you feel if I asked you some of those boring, annoying questions now?"

"Tell me what you want to know."

"Would you tell me about your family?" I hoped letting him know that he had control over our conversation might distinguish me from an interrogator. I also hoped that talking about family would be a safe place to start. It was.

"My grandfather was a tribal chief in Bahrain," Jumah said. "My father had a construction company in Saudi Arabia, where I grew up." Jumah had joint Saudi Arabian and Bahraini citizenship. Bahrain sits off the coast of Saudi Arabia, and the two countries are linked by a causeway. "I have several brothers and sisters. One of my sisters married a Bahraini prince. I was married when I was twenty-one, but we were divorced in 2000."

"I apologize for my ignorance, but is divorce common in Saudi?" I asked.

"Before it was not, but it is more common now. My marriage was not good. I was very young, and there wasn't enough feeling in it."

"Divorce is hard."

"Were you divorced?" he asked.

"No, I've never been married, but my parents made everyone pretty miserable when they got divorced. I was a young kid."

Jumah nodded and said that he had a nine-year-old daughter named Noora. He looked at the table for a moment or two, evidently thinking about her. Looking back up and with plaintive irony he said, in English, "Don't worry, be happy," before going quiet again.

The absurd image of Bobby McFerrin handing out buttons with smiley faces to detainees flashed in my mind.

After a moment, Jumah asked, "Joshua is a Jewish name. Are you Jewish?"

The question caught me by surprise, and I had a sinking feeling that things were going to get anti-Semitic. It's not that I would have abandoned the case or anything—I have heard well-heeled, paying clients say racist or sexist things—but I always lose a little enthusiasm when a client shows that side of himself.

"No, I'm not. Joshua was just a popular name in the neighborhood where I grew up."

"Oh," he said, sounding slightly disappointed, "I heard the best lawyers were Jewish."

Quickly, and obviously for my benefit, he added, "But I'm sure you're good too."

It was approaching noon when our meeting was to end. I was slated to see Jumah the next day, but I resisted telling him we were almost finished for the morning. We had been talking for several hours, and Jumah seemed to be soaking up all the human interaction he could get. At around 11:50, I said I would have to go, but I would be back the following day. A minute later, a guard knocked on the door and yelled that our time was up. Jumah, Karim, and I kept talking until the guard opened the door and came in.

As I was stepping outside, I looked back to reassure Jumah that we would see him the next morning. He flashed a crooked smile and, in English, said, "See you later, alligator." It was as if I'd been struck dumb. I know that phrase, I said to myself, and I know that there's something I should say in response. But hearing a "vicious killer" at Guantánamo Bay say "See you later, alligator," proved too much for me.

After waiting through two beats of my stammering, Jumah almost nailed the punch line, "After a while, crocodile."

Mark P. Denbeaux and Joshua W. Denbeaux: Questions

When lawyers first meet with clients, they are often bombarded by questions, especially when the detainee is not familiar with the common law adversary system or the civil law tradition of Western Europe. The following questions are from the notes of our meetings with our two clients, both Tunisians who speak no English. Tunisian lawyers have been arrested for criticizing the government during court arguments, and when we first met our clients, we were unaware of the different understandings of the role of lawyers in other parts of the world.

1. Who is paying you?
2. Why are you doing this?
3. Do you work for the government?
4. Do you think that I know something?
5. The interrogators know everything. I have told them everything, over and over again. Why do you keep asking?
6. Are you my new interrogator?
7. Why do you want to know the name and address of my family?
8. I do not know how many days that I have been at Guantánamo. How could I tell?
9. Do you think that the courts will make Bush let me go free?
10. You say that the court helped me last year, but why am I still here?
11. Does the court have guns or bombs? How can they stop the American army?
12. What difference does it make if the Congress and the courts share power with the president?
13. Do you care about me?
14. Why do you care about me? You do not know me.
15. Do you know that everyone here is a Muslim? Why is that?
16. If I were not a Muslim, I would not be here. Does America hate all Muslims?
17. Isn't the name Joshua a Jewish name?
18. Are you Jewish?
19. Could you send me something to read?
20. Do you know that I have nothing to read but the Quran?
21. How can you help free me from the American army if you cannot send me newspapers? What about soccer magazines?
22. How is the Milan soccer team doing?
23. So what if there are elections—will that stop the army and make them let me go home?
24. Can I have an English-Arabic dictionary?
25. What is the reason that I am here?
26. How can you help me if you do not even know why I am here?
27. You know the reasons, but the reasons are secret so you cannot tell me what they are?

28. How can telling me the reasons that I am here hurt America?
29. Did you know that Pakistanis do not speak Arabic?
30. Do you know that Pakistanis want all Arabs to leave?
31. I see a dentist, but I never have my teeth cleaned. Because of my heart problems, I have to be very careful about infection. Can you get my teeth cleaned?
32. Can you bring me toothpaste?
33. If I am an enemy combatant, who would be afraid of me?
34. What could I do to anyone? Is the American army afraid that I will hurt their planes or hurt their soldiers?
35. How are you different from the interrogators? They want me to talk, and they tell me nothing. You want me to talk, but you will not tell me anything!
36. Why can you not call me by telephone?
37. Why does it take so long for you to arrange a visit?
38. You are my lawyer; you say that you can help me, but you can only see me when the government says you can?
39. You say the Supreme Court has said twice that I have a right to go to court?
40. Why have you not gotten me to court?
41. Thank you for the food, but this is Ramadan. I will eat it later tonight. Do you mean that you cannot leave food for me to eat after sundown?
42. Do you know that I never get any mail from you or anyone else?
43. Why don't you send me mail?
44. When will the army let you come again?

Julia Tarver Mason: Melting the Ice

Photographs and recording devices are not permitted at Guantánamo. It is difficult to bring the humanity of these individuals back to the American people and the world. But let me tell you about a human being I have come to know at Guantánamo.

Yusef Al Shehri is a client who has been dear to me from the very first time I met him in May 2005. I think this is in part because Yusef was a young boy when he left home. Yusef was only fifteen years old when he left his family in Saudi Arabia. By his sixteenth birthday, he had been captured by Pakistanis and then traded to the U.S. military. He was blindfolded and bound and shipped all the way to Cuba in a military airplane under harrowing conditions.

I did not meet Yusef until three years later, in May 2005. And when I did, I was not sure exactly what to expect, especially since the government had done such a great job in the public relations department by constantly telling all of us that the men at Guantánamo were "dangerous" and were "the worst of the worst." But what I found when I first met Yusef was not a dangerous man but instead a timid young boy who was far away from home and scared.

Yusef was eighteen years old and visibly nervous when we first walked into the room to meet with him. His hands and feet were shackled. It was clear that he was not sure if he could trust us. We knew that in the past interrogators had impersonated attorneys in order to try to coerce prisoners to talk. So we expected that it would be difficult to gain our client's trust. But we were able to break the ice with Yusef because we were able to show him photographs of us standing with his family, with whom we had previously met. Even more important, we brought letters and correspondence from them. That almost immediately melted the ice in the room, and Yusef began to warm to us. He began to smile. Over time, he came to trust us. And even later, as we taught Yusef about the United States and the rule of law, he began to develop something very powerful: hope.

Sarah H. Lorr: Comfort Foods

As a second-year law student, I did not anticipate that I would be visiting the U.S. naval base at Guantánamo Bay, Cuba. When I was offered a spot in the International Justice Clinic at Fordham Law School, I eagerly accepted, but I did so knowing that there would be no opportunity for client contact. I looked at the clinic as an opportunity to combine my nascent legal skills with my longstanding belief in the need for a just and fair judicial system.

In September 2008, my professor, the director of the clinic, Martha Rayner, told me there was a possibility that I could accompany her on her October visit. Just two weeks before the trip, we received word from the Department of Defense that my theater clearance had come through.

The week prior to my trip to Guantánamo was characterized by an obsession with detail. I prepared for my visit as though I was preparing for my Contracts final or an on-call day in Torts. It seemed imperative that I know each fact, each piece of information associated with the case. I was very aware of how short our visit would be, how two full days would turn into four short meetings, with much time lost to translation, both cultural and linguistic.

Arriving at the camp, after going through several sets of identification checks, we were met by several guards. They went through our belongings and kept catalogued lists of the food attorneys brought their clients. We came with a load of Yemeni groceries purchased by a clinic teammate for the trip: fresh dates, a pomegranate, nuts, dried figs and raisins, flatbread with spices, a box of baklava, and other pastries. We also had two extralarge McDonald's coffees and a steak-and-egg breakfast sandwich. I still haven't been able to understand the military interest in monitoring the food we brought. Our client was awaiting our visit on the other side of the barbed-wire fence. It was the knowledge of my client's humanity that propelled my interest in the case in the first place, but until meeting him, his individuality had become almost theoretical.

Predictably, our client seemed to meet our legal advice, indeed our very presence, with a mix of cautious optimism and deep distrust based on five years of captivity without judicial review. As we wound our way through a lengthy agenda prepared by the clinic, I got a glimpse of the individual we were representing. For stretches, he would talk a mile a minute, his voice racing so quickly that I was confident I would have trouble following even in English. At other moments, he would meet an earnest question with a sarcastic quip and break into a large grin, revealing a taste of his cynical and straightforward sense of humor.

As we discussed the intricacies of his case, trying to fill gaps in our own understanding of the facts and to explain some of the complexities of his legal situation, our client participated and ate. Over the course of the first day, he ate almost ceaselessly throughout both meetings. He not only drank four extralarge coffees, but he also ate a McDonald's breakfast sandwich, an entire box of baklava, two candy bars, and snacks of pumpkin seeds, nuts, and fresh figs. After he had polished off the entire box of baklava and two candy bars, Martha offered him a cookie. He protested, explaining that he was on a diet and watching his calories. He laughed, not cynically but in good humor. And then, after a break, he continued eating.

Back at the CBQ, other attorneys reflected on their day. Attorneys shared stories of frustrating encounters, difficulties gaining trust, or minor breakthroughs that had occurred. The subject of food came up again and again. One attorney told a story about a detainee from Yemen who consumed an entire bottle of honey during a three-hour afternoon session. He began by pouring the honey into his tea, graduated to spreading it onto pita bread, and ended by pouring the remainder of the honey directly, and unceremoniously, into his mouth.

This story, like my own client's capacity to consume, is telling because of its simplicity. Beyond hunger, the desire for comfort foods is such a basic human desire. The fulfillment of such a simple craving in the face of so many human needs and rights denied reveals both the depth of the problem at Guantánamo and the value of maintaining the legal battle to free these men. Witnessing the fulfillment of such a simple need revealed to me that notwithstanding all those true challenges to humanity, and the need for legal principles to guide my work, something important and human has survived within my client and all the men at Guantánamo.

Joshua W. Denbeaux: Lieutenant Commander Feces Cocktail

One of the more memorable experiences of my first trip to Guantánamo was when I was finally brought over for the first meeting with our clients in the secure facility in Camp Delta. Before the military officials would allow us to see our clients, they made us look at a sample cell where the interrogation would take place, pointing out that we would be videotaped for our own protection and stating that there was a system for extracting detainees who chose not to talk to their lawyers. The "system" looked like an updated Darth Vader costume, with black hoods, black helmets, black plastic gloves, black vests, black arms and legs, the whole bit, including five-foot-long shields. We asked if any lawyer had ever requested this means of establishing or continuing the attorney-client relationship. None had.

The officials also told us that the reason they were filming everything was to protect us because detainees, when their lawyers came in, would give them feces cocktails. The lieutenant commander who advised us of this explained that the feces cocktail was urine with feces in it, thrown in the face of the lawyer.

Shortly thereafter, we finally met our client. Rafiq was seated at a table chained to the floor: long face, balding, with a shy smile and a long beard. We noted immediately that there was no possibility that feces cocktails could be thrown at us because he was seated at the table chained to the floor with no container, no feces, and no urine. It was embarrassing to imagine that your client would ever have reacted that way.

When we returned home, we sent an e-mail to the other habeas lawyers asking if any had ever had a feces cocktail thrown at them or had ever heard of anyone else having such an experience. None of the lawyers had. Rather, this was a standard presentation by some people in Guantánamo to interfere with the attorney-client relationship.

At the end of the first meeting, Rafiq told us he'd concluded that there was absolutely nothing we could do for him. He said he appreciated our coming, but we could not help him, so it was a waste of our time. He said that he hoped he would not, and that he would rather not, see us anymore.

I said, "Rafiq, if you were with Osama bin Laden and you were a part of 9/11, there is nothing I could do for you."

He said, "What's 9/11?"

I said, "The World Trade Center."

He said, "What's the World Trade Center?"

And I said, "The Twin Towers."

He then said, "The Twin Towers? I had nothing to do with that." It was remarkable: 9/11 meant nothing to him, the World Trade Center meant nothing, and he was fully familiar with the Twin Towers but was shocked that someone would think he was involved in that. And it turns out he was never accused of being involved in it.

I added, "But if all you were was a soldier shooting at Americans, then you will be locked up for a few years, then you'll be released."

He said, "I never shot at anybody," as he waved his badly damaged left hand, which was missing parts of three fingers.

"Well if you were not shooting at people, and you were not part of the 9/11 World Trade Center Twin Towers, a lawyer should be able to help you."

"They haven't helped anyone else." Finally, he said, "All right, I will let you try to help me. I will agree to have you be my lawyer, but I will never sign any piece of paper because the last time they tortured me they used things I said in an untruthful way. If you will take my word for it, then you can be my lawyer. If you won't, that's it." I tried to explain to him that the protective order setting forth procedures in the habeas corpus cases required that he sign something, showing he approved my representation of him. He said, "You are never going to get me out of here if you can't be my lawyer without making me sign a piece of paper." It was a compelling statement.

Shawn Nolan: The Riddler

The teenage-looking guard opened the door to the cement shoe box that was our meeting place. Our client exploded with, "Welcome to my American lawyers!" Addressing the young army personnel, he boomed, "Get some coffee for my very important American guests!" The guard looked shocked and had no idea what to do or what our client was talking about. Then our client laughed. He always laughed. He called himself "The Riddler." He loves riddles.

We started our visit introducing ourselves, trying to explain how we got involved, trying to convince him that although we were federal defenders, paid by the government—the same government holding him— that we were there to help. A two-hour civics lesson ensued, but all he wanted was cigarettes.

You see, the interrogators give him cigarettes whenever he talks with them. He talked to them all the time so he could get cigarettes. You could see the addiction in his eyes, his quivering mouth and shaking fingers as he asked us over and over for cigarettes. But lawyers are not permitted to bring cigarettes. We spent the entire morning trying to talk to him about his life, his capture, his jailing by the Taliban, his awful existence in Guantánamo, but all he wanted was tobacco. He made us promise that we would ask over lunch to bring him cigarettes. We did. The guards refused. They know.

We returned after the lunch break. He was shaking in anticipation of the tobacco that we were not permitted to bring. We brought some pizza from the local Subway. He covered it in hot sauce. Then he ate the extra hot sauce right out of the packets. He couldn't get enough.

The psychosis from isolation was all over his face and everywhere in his behavior. By the end of the day, we convinced him that we really were there to help. He cried when we left. He didn't want to be left alone again, but there was nothing we could do to ease his pain.

David McColgin: Skepticism

I visited Muhammed in Camp Echo, which at the time was used both for punishing detainees and for attorney interviews. Detainees are kept in isolation there in a small cell with an adjoining space for interviews containing a table, chairs, and a bolt in the floor for ankle shackles. When I went into the room with my investigator and our interpreter, my client Muhammed was already seated and shackled to the floor. He made no move to greet us, and he viewed us suspiciously. He had been brought to Camp Echo the night before and had assumed it was for punishment. But he couldn't figure out what he had done wrong. He had spent the entire night wondering about it.

When we explained that we were part of the legal team that would be representing him, he was perplexed. The letter that a fellow detainee had sent on Muhammed's behalf asking for legal help had been mailed nearly a year and a half earlier. The government had prevented any attorney from seeing him since the letter was sent. Muhammed had forgotten about it and had given up hope that an attorney would ever come to see him.

"Who are you?" Muhammed kept asking, as he eyed us warily. We explained that we had been appointed by a court in Washington, D.C., to represent him. The notion that the same government that had imprisoned and abused him without recourse for over three years would now appoint a lawyer to help him seemed bizarre at best. His country, Afghanistan, had no such system of public defenders or appointed counsel. He was convinced it was all a trick to interrogate him.

We spent some time explaining that in the United States the courts can and do appoint lawyers to represent people to protect their legal rights. It took several hours to convince him that we were not interrogators and that we really were there to be his legal advocates. By the end of the day, he did ultimately believe us and signed an authorization for us to represent him—a document required by the government in order for us to continue to see him each time we went to Guantánamo.

Ramzi Kassem: Imposture

Urban Virginia. A long day spent reviewing classified documents the U.S. government wishes to use as evidence against my clients, prisoners at Guantánamo Bay, Cuba. I step out into the cool fall night and immediately spot a band of men in bright orange jumpsuits merrily crossing the street. A moment of initial shock, then a sobering thought sets in—it is Halloween night, and *Harold and Kumar Escape from Guantanamo Bay* had scored a box-office smash earlier in the year.

•   •   •

Leeward Side, U.S. Naval Station at Guantánamo Bay. I go for a walk at dusk wearing short sleeves, forgetting that at GTMO, the night belongs to ravenous mosquitoes. On a dimly lit, dusty pathway leading to a small, secluded, and picturesque Caribbean beach, I am approached by two haggard-looking men. In rapid-fire Spanish, they ask if I am Cuban, tell me they are refugees from the other side of the island, that they want people in the United States to know they are stuck here at the base. They abruptly walk away when they see the oncoming headlights of what might be a military police vehicle.

•   •   •

Aboard the morning ferry crossing the bay. The prison camps are on the other side. One of the lawyers asks why I am wearing a suit in the dense tropical humidity. Another lawyer volunteers that he might start wearing a suit as well. After all, he wears one for his clients States-side; why not follow the same protocol in Cuba? A third lawyer jokes that as an Arab I have to wear a suit, lest the military guards mistake me for a detainee and refuse to let me out of the prison camp at the end of my client meeting.

•   •   •

McDonald's, Windward Side. The lawyers are purchasing the usual heart-hostile, Muslim-friendly fare for their clients who are not on hunger strike. This typically consists of egg-'n'-cheese biscuits, hash browns, apple pies, coffee, and juice. Our military escort is going around informing attorneys which of their clients agreed to meet with them and which ones declined. Todd is the escort's first name, though he is under orders not to share it with detainees' lawyers, and his Velcro name tags have been removed from his uniform.

Todd approaches me and asks in a hushed tone how my client ISN 87471 is doing. He asks me to let ISN 87471 know that Tarek sends his regards. Todd explains that back when he was on cellblock guard duty, he tried to treat the prisoners decently. My client and the other detainees had fondly renamed him Tarek. Now that he has been reassigned to escort duty, Tarek often worries about how the detainees are faring with the other guards.

•   •   •

Sally port, Camp Five. The sun is blazing bright. This is where inbound attorneys and interpreters are frisked and wanded down by military guards before entering the prison camp's perimeter. We are informed that contraband comes in numerous and unpredictable guises. Its avatars have included such disparate items as straws, socks, human rights reports, thermal underwear, and spoons (but sporks are okay). Accordingly, bags of food are searched and their caloric content inventoried; legal papers are scanned one by one.

A high-ranking officer passes by on his way out of the camp. As he is saluted by the guards who were searching me he says, "Honor bound," and they respond, "To defend freedom, sir!"—thereby completing the Guantánamo detention operations group's motto. On this island, freedom has become the jailer's salutation.

Though the rest of the lawyers have been dropped off at other camps for their meetings and I am alone, a sally port sentinel asks if I am an interpreter for one of the attorneys.

•   •   •

Camp Five entrance, inside the wire. A guard with his name tag covered with black masking tape meets me at the entrance point to the imposing gray concrete structure. The guards cover their names and use call signs among themselves to prevent prisoners from learning their true identities. The authorities say this is necessary to forestall future retaliation by the prisoners after they are released; some of the more cynical lawyers say the guards are ordered to cover their names to avoid liability for abuses perpetrated.

The guard asks me for my call sign. I look befuddled. He asks which agency I represent. The head guard intervenes and clarifies that I am habeas counsel, not U.S. government. I am ushered on to another guard, who is stationed inside the entry point. The prison is kept uncomfortably cold. That guard leads the way to a thick steel door, then turns around and asks at what restraint level I would like the detainee to be placed. For a split second, I am tempted to request the usual, just to see what that might be. The head guard's voice crackles into my escort's earpiece. The guard nods: habeas counsel.

•   •   •

The man they call ISN 87471 is seated on a steel chair in the middle of a small, brightly lit room surrounded by barren walls and under the constant gaze of a surveillance camera. He is shackled to a steel loop jutting out of the floor and is wearing an orange jumpsuit which, at Guantánamo, denotes punishment status. Such privileges as a mattress or thermal underwear have been taken away from him because he has persisted in his hunger strike in protest of his indefinite imprisonment. He has explained that he will remain on strike until the U.S. government ceases to refer to him as an enemy combatant and returns him to his homeland.

The years on hunger strike have taken their toll on my client—he is emaciated in the extreme and bruises are still visible on his face from a recent run-in with the riot squads routinely deployed at Guantánamo to intimidate prisoners.

ISN 87471 prefers to go by his given name or by Abu Aisha—father of Aisha. His mother's name was Aisha and, when the thought of freedom finds its way into his cell, he fantasizes about marrying, begetting a daughter, and naming her Aisha in honor of his mother.

•　　•　　•

In our initial encounter over two years ago, Abu Aisha was wary. Prior to meeting me, the last Arab American he had seen was in the Bagram prison in Afghanistan. My client had been taken there following his abduction in Pakistan and rendition to the U.S. military, in exchange for the usual hefty ransom. That Arab American man spent his first two meetings with Abu Aisha pretending to be a humanitarian aid worker interested in my client's well-being. He subsequently revealed himself to be an intelligence agent and oversaw interrogation sessions too numerous to count in which Abu Aisha was beaten and otherwise tortured. The agent relished threatening to send my client to Egypt or Israel, "where they like to use men like women."

•　　•　　•

Today, Abu Aisha recalls how not so long ago Guantánamo interrogators would tell him and the other prisoners that their attorneys were "Jews and homosexuals." The idea was that devout Muslims would not wish to deal with such people. Abu Aisha paused, then scoffed: "So what if they're Jews?"

•　　•　　•

Abu Aisha and I conclude our meeting shortly before prayer time. Before we part, he tells me that most Guantánamo prisoners only kneel twice during prayer in Cuba because they consider themselves travelers in this land, individuals here transiently who will soon return home. Abu Aisha confides that he recently reverted to the default practice of kneeling four times.

George Brent Mickum: Little Victories

The harsh sun and the glare off the white gravel at Guantánamo Bay's Camp Echo make it difficult to see into the small enclosure where Bisher al-Rawi is seated at a tiny folding table. Two marines have escorted me to his prison hut.

Bisher and his friend, my other client, Palestinian Jamil al-Banna, are among half a dozen U.K. residents at Guantánamo. Bisher, who is thirty-eight, was born in Iraq, where his father was arrested and tortured by Saddam Hussein's regime. His family fled to Britain and was granted permanent residence. He has lived in London for twenty-two years. But if he is released, the United States intends to repatriate him to Iraq. The British government, which is responsible for his arrest, has been unwilling to intervene on his behalf.

A small, slightly built man, Bisher is wearing an oversized, orange jumpsuit that swallows his diminutive frame. A flourishing black beard extends several inches in all directions. Bisher rises with difficulty. His feet are shackled at the ankle by an eighteen-inch chain that runs through an O-ring that is set into the concrete. His hands are manacled closely together in front of him and attached to a chain around his waist. He grasps my hand in both of his and gives it a single short thrust up and down. He does not let go of my hand. His smile is genuine. "How pleased I am to meet you," he says. I ask the military policeman to remove the restraints. After some discussion, his hands are released, but his feet must remain secured. Victories here are measured in very small increments.

I am the first nonofficial civilian Bisher has been allowed to see after more than two years of imprisonment in three countries. Although Bisher has never met me, he must retain me at the conclusion of our first meeting by signing a form prepared by the military. If he fails to do so, the military will refuse to recognize me as his counsel. Such are the rules of engagement.

Bisher looks at me and raises his eyebrows slightly. "Where shall I start?" he asks. "I guess you have a great deal to tell me," I respond. Bisher throws his head back and laughs: "Very much. So very much!"

Next to us is the cell where Bisher is being held in isolation, twenty-four hours a day, when he is not being interrogated or talking with me. It is six feet by eight feet. A surveillance camera in the ceiling monitors his every move. Thick metal mesh, approximately one inch square, encloses him. There is no window. Bisher has been transferred to this cell from another camp where he was caged in a wire mesh enclosure that was roofed but otherwise completely exposed to the elements.

If he is not being punished for some minor transgression—and punishment occurs frequently—Bisher is allowed outside his cell three times a week for thirty minutes at a time. Then he is escorted by two guards to a roofed, fenced enclosure on a concrete slab that is, perhaps, fifteen feet by fifteen feet. He is alone in the enclosure.

Over two days, Bisher and I discuss his brief arrest and release by British officials in London. We then discuss Bisher's subsequent and fateful business trip to Africa to start a peanut-oil factory with his brother and three other colleagues, including Jamil al-Banna. We discuss their detention by Gambian authorities and Bisher's interrogation there by U.S. agents, before he was illegally rendered to Bagram Air Base in Afghanistan, where Bisher was imprisoned underground in total darkness for weeks.

We discuss the horrendous conditions and the brutal treatment Bisher received there. Men were hung from the ceiling in chains, and the screams of brutalized men prevented him from sleeping. We discuss his lengthy incarceration. I remind him of the world beyond the gulag, about his family and world events, like the United States' recent invasion of Iraq.

Only once during my two days with Bisher does he betray any sense of bitterness, and even then it is fleeting.

> Do you know what disappoints me most? I am disappointed in American justice. I expected so much more. When we arrived at Guantánamo and realized we were in U.S. custody, I was confident my situation would be resolved. I assured my fellow prisoners that it was good to be out of Afghanistan and in American hands and that we would be fairly treated. After two years, I am no longer so foolish.

A government that engages in such abhorrent behavior has lost its capacity to be moved by the pleas of a lawyer to treat his client fairly and return his toilet paper.

John Connolly: The Surgeon

About three hours into my first meeting with a detainee at the Guantánamo Bay military prison, the detainee asked me about a faint scar on my face. The scar runs around my left ear and partway down my neck, in a rough outline of a question mark. It was the second time in twenty years that someone had asked me about that scar. The two instances could not have been more different, but the people who asked had a memorable similarity: both were surgeons.

My law partner Bill Murphy and I first traveled to the Guantánamo prison in May 2005. We knew very little about our client, Ayman Batarfi, and had no idea what he had done to end up in Guantánamo.

Once we got to the prison, we were led to a prefabricated shack about the size and shape of a campground cabin. The marine guards opened a steel door, and there, sitting behind a flimsy card table with one ankle chained to the floor, was a man who—who could not possibly have been a terrorist. For one thing, I towered over him. He was a portrait of shyness: head slightly bowed, eyes peering upward, uncomfortable grin. He shook our hands like anyone else and greeted us in very good English—quite a relief since we had not brought a translator. After a few minutes of preliminaries, he proceeded to tell the most extraordinary story I had ever heard, culminating in early December 2001, on a mountaintop in the Tora Bora region of Afghanistan, where Ayman unexpectedly met alone with Osama bin Laden—and basically asked him what on earth was happening and how could it be stopped.

After several hours, Ayman came to a pause in his story and leaned back. My hand ached from continuous note taking. Bill and I took a breath as we tried to absorb the assault of facts. In that quiet moment, Ayman pointed to my face and traced a question mark in the air. "What type of operation?" he asked. Well, I thought to myself, he *is* a surgeon.

Not that I had any reason to doubt it. We had just learned that Ayman was born in Egypt, lived as a child in Yemen, grew up mostly in Saudi Arabia, and went to medical school in Pakistan. He trained under one of the most prominent orthopedic surgeons in Pakistan. Many detainees ask their lawyers to send sports magazines, comic books, and novels. Ayman asked for a dense medical treatise on orthopedic surgery. Ayman's specialty in Pakistan was repairing pediatric wrist fractures with external fixators. His eyes brightened as he tried to explain this procedure to two American lawyers who weren't sure whether the arm bones were the ulna and radius or the tibia and fibula.

It dawned on me that severe bone injuries were rampant in a part of the world flooded with rifles, land mines, and bombs. Young Dr. Batarfi had treated many Afghan refugees with horrific injuries that had been untreated or mistreated in Afghanistan. Taliban-controlled Afghanistan needed help from everyone who could offer it, so in the summer of 2001, during a break in his postgraduate studies, Dr. Batarfi traveled to

Afghanistan both to continue his studies and to offer his services as charity to a desperate people. That fateful decision eventually led to Ayman's
seizure by Northern Alliance forces (who despised all Arabs in Afghanistan) and to his subsequent "sale" to U.S. forces. Ayman's full story is too
long and too complex to recount here, but through six years of incarceration Ayman has unequivocally (and convincingly in our view) maintained
that he was never a member or supporter of al Qaeda or any terrorist organization, that he has never been an enemy of the United States or its allies,
and that he wants nothing more than to return home, where he could do
so much good, before he loses his mind and his surgical skills.

Ayman's professional interest in my scar triggered a memory. Sixteen
years earlier, a visitor from the medical campus was researching a legal
issue in the law library, and I helped him find some unremembered treatise. He was standing immediately to my left while I was bent over the
book. "Parotid gland?" he asked, out of the blue. "Surgeon?" I replied.
(We were both right.) At that time, as a beginning law student, I had
only a rudimentary knowledge of due process as a legal construct. But
I had a visceral understanding of what it meant as an American value.
The enemy at the time was the Soviet Union and China—totalitarian
regimes that treated individual justice as a state weakness. Some of our
nominal allies were no better (Iraq and Afghanistan come to mind).
In 1989, you could not have convinced me that American authorities
would claim a right to incarcerate an individual, any individual, for six
years or longer without a charge, without a lawyer, and without a trial.
I would not have believed that my country would establish a prison in
a remote part of the world chiefly to avoid the reach of the American
judiciary. I certainly would not have imagined that American law would
permit unconvicted detainees to be waterboarded, chained in stress
positions, slapped, sound blasted, chilled, isolated, and psychologically
tormented.

Sarah Havens: Match Maker

My first trip to Guantánamo was in January 2005. That's when I met
my fiancé, Doug, who was then another attorney with a different office of
the same firm. That's also when I met Ali, a young Yemeni detainee and
one of our firm's dozen clients. Ali was seventeen when he was arrested
in Pakistan, a hapless kid who had been involuntarily towed along in his
older brother's misadventures. Recognizing that Ali doesn't belong in
Guantánamo, in 2005 the U.S. government put Ali on a list of people who

were "cleared for transfer" to their home countries. More than three years later, Ali still sits in Guantánamo.

In his seventh year of detention, Ali is now nearly twenty-five—an age at which most Yemeni men are already married with children. While he has been in Guantánamo, Ali's two younger brothers were married in a joint wedding, leaving Ali as the only single brother. From his cell, Ali wishes for a bride only slightly less than for his freedom—and were his release not a prerequisite to his marriage, the order might be reversed. Ali's mother has a bride picked out for him, the sister of his brother's wife. I met his brother's wife and assured Ali that if his bride looks anything like her sister, he will be quite pleased with his mother's choice. At this news, Ali blushed.

Although Doug and I never told our clients of our personal relationship, Ali did not need to be told. In meetings at which I was not present, Ali lectured Doug for the better part of an hour about the importance of marriage and hinted, not too subtly, that he thought I would make a good wife. Doug managed to dodge the subject for a few months, but Ali eventually won Doug's promise that we would be engaged before our next visit to Cuba. When we returned to New York, Doug kept his promise and proposed.

On our next trip, Doug and I visited Ali together and informed him of our engagement. He smiled at first but then shrugged his shoulders and said, "If your marriage is happy, you will go off and forget me, and if it doesn't work out, then you will say it is all my fault. Either way, it's no good for me."

No matter what happens, I will never forget Ali. I only hope that one day soon our courtroom battles will mean that he can start counting the days until he meets his bride.

Carolyn M. Welshhans: A Scream in the Darkness

I walked into our first meeting with our client with another lawyer from my firm and our interpreter. Our client, Abdul Haq, was facing the door. Abdul was thirty-five years old. He is known by the government as ISN 004, meaning he was the fourth person sent to Guantánamo. He was on the first plane of prisoners brought there. Abdul Haq is small and slight and quiet. He was seated at a white, plastic lawn table. One of his feet was shackled to the floor, and he was shackled around the waist. Abdul did not look at me with hatred or disgust. He actually was not looking at me at all. He was slightly cowering in his white, plastic lawn chair, and when he finally did look at us, it was clear that he was afraid that we had been sent in to beat him. I will never forget that image. I also will not forget that while I had sat on an airplane listening to my iPod and wondering if Abdul Haq was going to glare at me, he had been moved to a cell, given no information, and left to believe that someone eventually was going to come through the door and abuse him.

Like most of my clients, Abdul Haq does not like to discuss how he has been treated over the past five years. Part of it is fear of reprisal because he believes that the guards listen to our conversations. Part of it is because of the shame he feels over what he has been subjected to. And part of it is because it is just too much for him even to begin talking about it. Abdul Haq did tell me once that he had been so abused that he thought that he was going to die and that if he had any information of any value, he would have told the Americans at that instant just to get the abuse to stop. It is no wonder that getting Abdul Haq to trust us is a constant struggle. Sometimes he refuses my letters; sometimes he reads them. Sometimes he refuses my visits; sometimes he meets with me. At all times, Abdul Haq remains quietly polite and thanks me for wanting to help him.

Our next visit of the day was with Abdullah Wazir Zadran. Abdullah did not cower. He leaned back in his chair, slouched, and crossed his arms. Abdullah was twenty-six, the same age as one of my brothers, and both of them have medium-shade brown eyes. It hit me very hard that it could have been my brother in a cell thousands of miles from home. With the crossed arms and the instant volley of questions (Do we have a letter from his mother? Who is paying us to represent him? Why should he believe us?), I expected to encounter more hostility from Abdullah, but it never came. He did remain cautious. Abdullah's stance finally relaxed with about thirty minutes left in our meeting. He uncrossed his arms, and he agreed that he would like to see us again.

At subsequent meetings, Abdullah continued to ask many questions. He wanted results. He wanted to know what good a lawyer can do for anyone at Guantánamo. He does not accept "I don't know" as an answer to anything. At one meeting, Abdullah said that he was tired of discussing his case. So I offered not to ask him any more questions about it. Instead, we would just discuss his life in Afghanistan and my life in the United States. Abdullah said that he liked that idea, and then five minutes later, he started asking me questions about his case.

Like all my clients, Abdullah was arrested far away from any battlefield. He was arrested in Pakistan by Pakistani border guards who turned him over to the United States at a time when our country was paying thousands of dollars—more than people in that part of the world make over many years—for anyone accused of being a member of al Qaeda or the Taliban. Abdullah has been accused of making a suspicious trip to Pakistan in the company of an acquaintance alleged to be a member of al Qaeda. He is not accused of attacking U.S. or coalition forces. In fact, Abdullah was making a routine trip to Pakistan to buy supplies for the tire store owned by his family. One of our incredible interpreters traveled to Afghanistan and met with the families of some of our clients. She returned with many pictures of the large and impressive tire store. This evidence was not difficult to obtain, and it bewilders us that our government has not made the same effort to determine whether the people it is holding are innocent civilians, sold to the United States by unscrupulous border guards.

We were very eager to show these pictures to Abdullah, and he was eager to see them. The officials at Guantánamo cleared the pictures rather easily and gave us permission to show them to Abdullah. But it has been a constant struggle to leave Abdullah with color copies of these pictures that he can study in private. The officials at Guantánamo keep giving him Xeroxed, black-and-white copies that are smeared and blurred to the point where it is impossible to see anything. Abdullah's excitement over the pictures stems in large part from the fact that some of them feature his friends and family, including his two little boys, whom he has not seen in more than four years. Abdullah also understands that the pictures demonstrate the existence of the tire store and provide evidence that his trip to Pakistan had a legitimate business purpose. He asked how anyone could continue to believe that he had a nefarious reason for going to Pakistan, and he wanted to know when someone from our government finally is going to investigate the lies behind the accusations. I was worried before that first visit that Abdullah would be young and radical and want nothing to do with me. What Abdullah wants are answers to his piercing questions about why he is at Guantánamo.

Our last visit on that first trip was with Dr. Hafizullah, a sixty-year-old pharmacist. Whereas most clients take at least several visits to accept that we are not interrogators in disguise, Dr. Hafizullah believed that we were lawyers from the beginning. He wanted to talk about proof and evidence and how to present his case. Dr. Hafizullah had served under the pro-American Karzai government in Afghanistan. He served as a district administrator in his hometown, and then he was appointed to a commission of elders that worked with local authorities as a liaison with the citizens. Yet Dr. Hafizullah found himself at Guantánamo. Like many prisoners, his initial arrest may have been the result of lies told by political enemies. Why he remains at Guantánamo after all this time is a mystery because plenty of evidence exists that he is the sort of person that the new and struggling Afghan government desperately needs. At his first hearing at Guantánamo, held nearly two years after he was first sent there, Dr. Hafizullah requested witnesses who could attest that he was a supporter of democracy, had actually been imprisoned by the Taliban, and was innocent of any allegations to the contrary. Two of these witnesses were former governors of provinces in Afghanistan. The U.S. government declared these witnesses "not reasonably available" on the grounds that the Afghan government never got back to the State Department on a request to find them. Rather than our government's taking it upon itself to locate two former high-ranking officials, it proceeded to hold Dr. Hafizullah's hearing without any witnesses on his behalf and then cited that hearing as grounds to continue to imprison him.

Dr. Hafizullah desperately wanted some books in Pashto so that he could have something to do to pass the time. He was in Camp Five, and he remains there more than a year after our first visit. Camp Five is the equivalent of solitary confinement. The doors are solid metal, so Dr. Hafizullah can neither see nor talk to any other prisoners. He has nothing to do all day long, and the lack of any human contact is an overwhelming blow to a man who is educated and accustomed to being surrounded by stimulating conversation. At the end of our first visit, Dr. Hafizullah said, "If you can help one prisoner get released, it will be like you are bringing someone back from the dead," and then he shook our hands. He said it with tears in his eyes and with a very quiet dignity. Every day that I have worked on Guantánamo cases since then, I have thought about Dr. Hafizullah's plea. For a man who was used to being the most impressive person in any given room, it could not have been an easy thing to say to three strangers. It felt like I was witnessing a scream in the darkness, but I am determined to show him that he was right to trust us.

Rendered: How the Detainees Got to Guantánamo

Among the most chilling and heart-wrenching stories are how the detainees wound up at Guantánamo—an ordeal that might involve being swept up, taken from their homes and families, and forced to endure a journey of hardship and abuse.

Melissa Hoffer: Abducted

Before arriving at GTMO, Mohamed Nechla, Lakhdar Boumediene, Hadj Boudella, Belkacern Bensayah, Saber Lahmar, and Mustafa Ait Idir were all living ordinary lives in Bosnia-Herzegovina. Mohamed and Lakhdar worked with children orphaned in the civil war. Mustafa repaired computers and provided technical support services. Saber and his wife were expecting a child.

In October 2001, their lives were shattered when the United States insisted that Bosnia arrest the six men—all Muslims of Algerian descent—based on unfounded U.S. allegations that they were involved in a plot to bomb the U.S. embassy in Bosnia. One by one, each man was taken into custody.

The men spent three months in jail while the federal prosecutor investigated the charges. No stone was left unturned—investigators searched computer files and phone records, and they questioned witnesses and the men.

Finally, the federal prosecutor recommended to the Bosnian high court that the six be released. He had identified no evidence to justify their detention. The high court agreed and ordered their release.

Despite this order, the United States placed tremendous pressure on Bosnia to turn over the six men to U.S. custody, threatening to withdraw support if Bosnia failed to comply. As the six were released from jail in Sarajevo on January 18, 2002, they were handed over to nine soldiers and then hooded, handcuffed, and jammed into waiting vehicles. The huge crowd of community members that had gathered to protest the seizure tried to prevent the cars from passing; wives strained to catch glimpses of their husbands. Abducted in plain daylight, the men were taken to Guantánamo.

Rebecca Dick: Meeting Wazir

I understood why the government had wanted to question him. Wazir was arrested while traveling on an intercity bus in Pakistan, carrying a large sum of cash and a secondhand satellite telephone. At the time, members of al Qaeda were fleeing from Afghanistan into Pakistan. Arrested along with Wazir was an acquaintance, riding the same bus, who was accused of being a "known al Qaeda bomb maker."

This was the government's story, and Wazir admitted all of it. But there was more, he said. His brother owned a tire shop in the central bazaar in Khost, a city in eastern Afghanistan. The shop had been founded by their father and was well established. They purchased their inventory from Pakistan. Periodically, either Wazir or his brother would travel to make the purchase arrangements in person with their Pakistani suppliers. Having no access to banks, they carried cash for their purchases. Since there was neither a wire line nor a cellular telephone network, they communicated with home using the satellite phone. As for the acquaintance, whom Wazir had encountered by chance, Wazir didn't think he was either al Qaeda or a bomb maker but didn't know him very well.

I asked Wazir's brother for a picture of the tire shop and promptly received twenty-five pictures of the largest tire store I have ever seen, with tires of all sizes, from tractor and truck tires on down. Who was Wazir? A young businessman with close family ties or a dangerous terrorist intent on murder? I asked Wazir to describe the life in Afghanistan to which he expected to return if released. He answered softly and slowly, fondly describing the life that was passing him by. If his story was faked, he is a remarkable actor.

Each weekday morning, Wazir, his wife, and their two young sons awoke in the large compound outside Khost that they shared with his brother, his brother's family, and their parents. His mother cooked breakfast for everyone. Then Wazir, his brother, and his brother's sons (not his daughters) piled into the family car and drove into Khost. The boys were dropped off at school. Wazir's sons would attend when they were older. Wazir and his brother then drove to the shop, which was nearby. They swept the floor, rolled the biggest tires out in front as a form of advertising, and pulled their stools alongside them. There they sat, chatting with each other and neighboring shopkeepers when not waiting on customers. They discussed the weather, current events as heard over BBC Radio, gossiped, drank tea, and ate snacks they had ordered from a shop across the street. Cricket was another topic. Wazir had become a fan while living as a refugee in Pakistan during the worst of the fighting against the Soviet invasion. At noon, Wazir's brother went into the bazaar to buy food for lunch, then cooked it on a stove in a small kitchen on the second floor of the shop. Early in the afternoon, the boys walked to the shop from school. They spent the afternoon studying and playing on the second floor. At some point Wazir's brother would go into the bazaar again to purchase food for dinner and other household necessities. They would have a final round of tea from the establishment across the street and then, at dusk, sweep and close up the shop and drive home. In the evenings, Wazir would sit with his family. "That was my life," Wazir said quietly. "That is what I will do if I am released."

David Frakt: Mortal Fear

Mohammed Jawad was a functionally illiterate boy from the Pashtun tribal region of Afghanistan. He had been arrested on December 17, 2002, in Kabul by Afghan authorities in connection with a hand-grenade attack on a jeep containing two U.S. Special Forces soldiers and their local Afghan interpreter. The attack took place in broad daylight in the early afternoon in a crowded public bazaar in central Kabul. It was the first attack on U.S. forces in Kabul since the United States had invaded Afghanistan in the fall of 2001. Fortunately, none of the victims had died in the attack, but each had sustained injuries. Mohammed was about sixteen at the time of his arrest. Like many Afghans, he did not know his exact age or birth date. Mohammed was arrested and was taken first to an Afghan police station and then to the Interior Ministry. Representatives from the U.S. embassy and from the U.S. military immediately demanded that those responsible for the attack be turned over to the United States for questioning. For reasons that remain unclear, the Afghan government decided to let Mohammed take the fall. When Mohammed denied responsibility for the attack, the police threatened that he or his family would be killed if he didn't confess. Because he couldn't write, a confession was prepared for him. The confession was in Farsi, a language Mohammed could not even speak, much less read. In lieu of a signature, the police placed Mohammed's thumbprint at the bottom of the confession, explaining to him that it was "release paperwork."

Late that evening, the interior minister turned over Mohammed to the U.S. military, telling the Americans that he had confessed and was solely responsible for the attack. Mohammed was handcuffed, and a blindfold and hood were placed over his head before he was whisked away and taken to an American military base on the outskirts of the city. Upon arrival, he was given a medical exam, strip-searched, and then forced to pose for a series of deeply humiliating nude photographs. After he was allowed to put his clothes back on, he was again handcuffed and hooded and then taken to another building on the compound for further interrogation. It was nearly midnight when the interrogation began.

The interrogation techniques were designed to reinforce the shock and fear of captivity. Again, Mohammed denied complicity. But the U.S. interrogators refused to accept his denials and continued the interrogation for several hours that night, well into the early morning hours, until they were able to extract another confession. Unfortunately, the precise details of the interrogation session and the confession will probably never be known. Although the entire interrogation session was videotaped, the videotape was later determined to be "lost" when I requested that the prosecution provide me a copy.

Later that morning, Mohammed was transferred to Bagram prison. At that time, Bagram prison was being run by the infamous 377th Military Police Company from Indiana, responsible for some of the worst prisoner abuse of the entire "war on terror." Just the week prior to Mohammed's arrival, prison guards at Bagram had beaten to death an Afghan taxi driver, Dilawar. The cruel and abusive treatment of prisoners at Bagram continued throughout the winter of 2003. Mohammed was subjected to a variety of abusive tactics there, including beatings, hooding, being pushed down the stairs, and being chained to the wall. He heard the rumors from other prisoners about the deaths of other prisoners and heard the screams of other prisoners being tortured. He spent forty-nine days at Bagram in mortal fear. Eventually, he was transferred to Guantánamo.

George M. Clarke III: Letter from Tawfiq

The following is a letter I received from my client Tawfiq. It appears in its original form.

> To Mr. George M. Clarke,
>
> I am sending you this letter and hope from Almighty God that you are in good health and in high spirits. I am writing this letter as you asked me to write the story of my detention and kidnapping from Iran and my sale to the Afghan government and then selling me again to the American government. Following is my story as I remember; a long time has passed since this happened.
>
> As I was sick, I was living at a home of an Iranian. This home was raided by the Iranian intelligence serivices; they started firing using AK47 rifles. Then they detained and moved me, using a small truck, to a detention center that belonged to the Iranian intelligence services. Then they started abusing me by hitting me. They took away all the money that was in my possession. I had

2400 dollars, 800 Saudi Riyals, 6000 Pakistani rupees. They also took away my Yemeni passport, my personal identity card and my clothing which were with me at the time of detention. I remained in this dreadful prison for approximately one month and two weeks. The treatment that I received there was very bad.

Then I was moved to another prison that also belonged to the intelligences services which was much worse. There were other detainees besides me. I remained there approximately for one full month. They told me that I will be moved to Tehran and then to my home country Yemen and therefore I was very delighted. Then they shackled me and wrapped a shawl over my eyes so I could not see anything and moved me by air.

When we reached Tehran, they took me to a prison that was underground. The treatment that I received there was very bad. I have no idea how long I stayed there. Eventually they transported me to an Iranian city called Mash-had, an Iranian border city to Afghanistan. I stayed in a dreadful and a horrible prison; it seemed as if there was no possibility of life. It was a very strange place as if it is a city of ghosts. I stayed there for two weeks and I felt as if I have spent two years there. There they intentionally provoked me sometimes by ill treating me. Then they took me to a room that had a few computer systems. Pointing to a computer screen, they said, "This is your photograph. If you say anything about what happened to you in Iran, we will kill you," and they threatened to kill me. Then they took me along with nine others to the airport while shackled and wearing dark glasses that prevented any vision.

There was a plane waiting for us. I am not sure if it was an American or an Afghani plane but its military crew belonged to a certain military force that was heavily armed.

We were moved to Afghanistan under a deal between the Iranian and the Afghan governments. The Iranian government was able to fool the Afghan government that we belonged to al Qaeda organization. During the war, the Afghan government had detained ten Iranian individuals who belonged to the Iranian intelligence services. This was a commercial deal between the two governments to exchange us, the prisoners of war, in return of the Iranian spies, although Iran actually had its agents as members of al Qaeda; however, regretfully this was my fate. With the grace of

God this is my story in Iran, in a much shorter form than what actually happened, as this is what I remember very well.

This was nothing but a game that was played by the Iranian government on the Afghan government so that it can get back its intelligence agents who had collected large amount of information concering the presence of Americans in part of Afghanistan; thse agents had obtained maximum amount of intelligence. If the Afghan government had handed these ten to the American government, then the American government could have obtained much more important and useful information compared to what they got from us through torture.

Allison M. Lefrak: Trapped

Ghanim was born in the eastern part of Saudi Arabia near Kuwait in 1978, the oldest child in a large family. His father was an executive with the Arabian-American oil company ARAMCO. The al-Harbi family had many American friends—colleagues of Ghanim's father. Ghanim was still a young boy when Iraqi forces under the command of Saddam Hussein occupied Kuwait and threatened to invade eastern Saudi Arabia. Several of Ghanim's cousins who were living in Kuwait at the time were either killed or taken as prisoners of war by Iraqi forces. Ghanim's family supported the American mission during the Gulf War that followed the Iraqi invasion of Kuwait.

After graduating from college, Ghanim went to work for the International Islamic Relief Organization. In 2000, Kuwait and eastern Saudi Arabia once again fell under the imminent threat of occupation by Saddam Hussein and his forces. With memories of the 1991 occupation still fresh in his mind, Ghanim began to consider obtaining some military training. As he explained, the Quran teaches that the eldest son in the family should be prepared to protect and defend his family. Accordingly, Ghanim began his search to fulfill what he viewed as a holy requirement. Saudi Arabia has no draft, reserves, or military recruitment. Ghanim applied to the Saudi Arabian Navy but did not receive a response. He then sought a civilian facility where he could obtain defense training. Unable to locate anything of the sort in Saudi Arabia, and upon a recommendation from a friend, Ghanim decided to take a three-month leave of absence from work to attend a self-defense program offered by the al Farouq training camp in Afghanistan. His understanding of the camp was that it was not affiliated with any political or religious group and that it was funded by Muslim charitable organizations. This understanding was reinforced when he arrived and learned that attendees were not permitted to discuss politics or religion.

While Ghanim was at the camp, a high-profile leader of the Northern Alliance was killed, and the borders to Afghanistan were closed. Ghanim remained hopeful that he would be able to return home as soon as the borders were reopened, but a few days later the attacks of September 11 occurred. Shortly thereafter, the Americans began bombing Afghanistan. Ghanim was trapped. Eventually, he met up with some other men who were trying to flee Afghanistan through the mountains. While they were trying to escape, Ghanim was hit by shrapnel from an American bomb and seriously injured. He made his way to a hospital in Jalalabad, which had been taken over by the Northern Alliance when it prevailed over Taliban forces in Afghanistan. Ghanim remained at the hospital for six weeks. During that time, he repeatedly asked if he could be taken to Pakistan, with the hope that he could get home to Saudi Arabia from there, but he was told that was not possible. Frustrated, and hopeful that the Americans might help him, Ghanim asked to be turned over to American forces. Northern Alliance troops sold Ghanim to American troops for a "bounty" of $5,000. To this day, Ghanim does not know what false information Northern Alliance troops gave the Americans in order to secure the bounty.

Female Attorneys

One of the most challenging aspects for female lawyers representing Guantánamo detainees has been addressing cultural sensitivity around gender issues.

Patricia A. Bronte: Offending the Fashion Gods

The morning I first visited a client at Guantánamo, I knew my client might not exactly embrace the idea of having a female American lawyer. He had been sitting at Guantánamo for several years without seeing anyone but guards or interrogators. He had seen little that would inspire confidence in the American justice system. And the fact that I was female was not going to help. In Saudi Arabia, my client's homeland, women are not permitted to drive or even to travel without being escorted by a close male relative. They must cover their bodies from the eyes of the world, and eye contact with any man except a spouse or close family member is strictly forbidden.

I had done my homework. I needed to wear loose-fitting clothing that covered my arms and legs—not a problem. But I also needed a head covering. I am not graceful with scarves, so I chose something called the "Amirah" (or princess) hijab, a two-piece contraption. The first piece is like an oversized headband that covers the top of the head and the ears. The second piece looks like a large-mouthed funnel. The mouth frames your face, and the rest drapes your head and shoulders.

You may have seen lovely dark-skinned women wearing hijabs. That is not what I looked like. I have pale skin, freckles, and blue-gray eyes. Picture Alfalfa (of Spanky's Gang) dressed like a nun. Perhaps that is why the young U.S. soldiers threw me hostile glances—I had offended the fashion gods. I fancied at the time that they resented my donning what they perceived as the uniform of our Muslim "enemies." But the worst part of the hijab is that it puts two layers of fabric over each ear. That, combined with the loud air-conditioner units in the interview room, made it very difficult for me to hear.

More troubling than the unfamiliar attire, though, was the fact that I would not be able to make eye contact with my client. In our culture, looking someone in the eye is a sign of respect. It is also a way of gauging another's understanding, reactions, and truthfulness. I had never tried to meet with a client without looking him or her in the eye. I wasn't sure I could do a very good job of communicating without eye contact. Fortunately, I was working with a very good Arabic-English interpreter. The client seemed to engage with the interpreter, and over the lunch break I pumped the interpreter for a detailed account of the client's nonverbal reactions to my words. At one point during the meeting, the interpreter told me not to sit so close to him, because that was causing the client to look away from the interpreter so as not to catch a glimpse of me. All in all, that first visit went relatively well. The client and I got used to the rhythm of speaking in short bursts and waiting for the interpreter's translation. And despite the client's conservative religious views about interacting with women, he seemed to accept having a female lawyer.

Not all my clients have cared whether I wore a hijab. Once I was meeting with a Saudi client, and he asked me if I wore the hijab all the time. (I am quite sure he knew that it was not part of my regular wardrobe.) I said no, that I only wore it during our meetings as a sign of respect for him. The client said, "Why don't you take it off, then?"

Some of my Guantánamo clients have also been comfortable making eye contact with me. During my first meeting with a Yemeni client, one of the first things I asked him, through the interpreter, was whether he minded if I looked him in the eye. After a bit of back-and-forth between the interpreter and the client, the answer came back as a sharp "No!" Thinking that the client did not want me to look him in the eye, I spent the entire morning looking down at the floor. During the lunch break, the interpreter said, "Pat, you really should look at your client when you're talking to him." I had completely misread the answer to my initial question; the client was perfectly fine with the idea that we would have eye contact. He probably thought my excessive interest in the floor was a sign of mental disturbance.

I have now visited clients at Guantánamo about fifteen times, and I have yet to meet a client who was unwilling to have a female lawyer. Most of my clients seem to look upon me as a kindly aunt. It has been a while since I wore a hijab because the clients I have been meeting most recently do not care whether I cover my hair. But I did have a hijab panic recently, when unexpectedly I was required to meet with a male colleague's client. I had not brought a hijab with me, and I knew I would not find a suitable substitute at the Navy Exchange. The night before the meeting, I scoured my suitcase for something that would cover my hair. I found a dark-blue tank top. If I slipped the armhole around my face just so and bunched the fabric under my chin with the aid of two binder clips, I thought the tank top could just about pass as a hijab. Well, okay, it actually looked quite ridiculous, but it did cover my hair. Fortunately, a fellow habeas lawyer saved the day by loaning me a two-tone scarf (green and purple), which I just managed to keep on my head during the meeting.

Kristine A. Huskey: Connecting

I braced myself for the Middle East, where I had traveled to meet the family of our client, who was being held at Guantánamo. Though the temperature was in the eighties and nineties, I had brought long sleeves, long skirts, a suit two sizes too big, and head scarves. I wondered how much I would be allowed to contribute to the discussion, whether I would even be allowed to talk. For the first time in a long while, I felt completely unsure of myself, how I would approach the situation, how I would react. Would my feminist proclivities prevail, come hell or high water?

We walked into the conference room at the Kuwaiti City Sheraton, one female lawyer in a very baggy business suit and four men years my senior. The families were there, seated around a large conference table. By "families," I mean fathers and brothers, ranging in age from twenty-five to seventy-five. There was not a female among the eighteen or so individuals who were wearing the traditional floor-length white thobe and Saudi headdress—a ghutra and tahiyah. Think Omar Sharif and *Lawrence of Arabia*. I felt very American and very female.

At the beginning of the intake, the father or brother, as it was in most cases, was very shy with me and looked at the translator when speaking. They would not look at me even when I was speaking. I was not surprised. Living in Saudi twenty years ago had given me insight into a very conservative approach to Islam. I did not think that Kuwait was as strict as Saudi Arabia, but I was intent on erring on the conservative side. So I tried to be shy and "nonchallenging." I didn't look them in the eye; I didn't try to force them to look at me. Instead, I spoke quietly, in singsong, asking gentle questions and looking at the far wall or at my notepad. But soon the emotion of speaking about the missing son or brother overwhelmed them, and by the end, the intake became a conversation between two people, both concerned with the same thing—a human being. In the end, those Muslim men looked me in the eye as they spoke, with tremors in their voices. I do not pretend to have been affected in any way similar to the family member whose son or brother was missing. But it was that missing life that bound us at least in that moment, and it did not matter that we were separated by a panoply of factors: gender, history, culture, geography—to name a few. It was simply about a person.

Allison M. Lefrak: Guilty Feelings

In deference to our clients' religion, I decide to cover my hair with a head scarf for the initial meetings. As the guards slowly inspect the documents and other items that we plan to bring into the meeting with our Saudi client, Ghanim al-Harbi, I reach up and adjust the scarf on my head. It feels strange to wear such a thing—especially in the hot Cuban sun, where a ponytail would probably be the most practical hair style. Perhaps I shouldn't wear the scarf if I don't feel comfortable in it. In the end, I decide to wear the scarf to the initial meetings. As my mother told me growing up, it's always better to be overdressed than underdressed. On this theory, I have continued to wear a head scarf to all subsequent client meetings in Guantánamo.

The first time I meet Ghanim al-Harbi, I extend my hand to him. My colleague, who met with Ghanim once before this meeting, introduces me. Our interpreter, Mahmoud Khatib, simultaneously translates the introduction. Ghanim lifts his arms across his chest and bows his head slightly. I retract my hand, confused as to why he has declined to shake my hand. Ghanim asks Mahmoud to please explain to me that he is not permitted to touch a woman who is not a family member as it will render him unclean for prayer. He intends to pray during the lunch break today, and he cannot be certain that the guards will allow him to wash his hands before doing so. For this reason, he does not shake my hand, and he begs me not to take offense. The sincerity of his apology is obvious even when delivered through Mahmoud. I make a mental note not to extend my hand to any of our clients in future meetings.

In July 2007, I return for my second trip to Guantánamo. I am nearly five months pregnant, just beginning to show, and I have not yet decided whether to share the news with our clients. After meeting the men three months earlier, I wrote letters to them and received correspondence in return. I feel the beginning of a professional friendship forming with each of them. For that reason, I would like to share the news of my pregnancy with them in the second meetings. But at the same time, I feel guilty sharing my happy news with men who have lost years of their lives trapped in this prison far away from their family and friends. Two of my clients desperately hope to marry and have children upon their release. My third client, Ravil Mingazov, has a young son named Yosef. The boy was only one year old when Ravil fled religious persecution in Russia in search of a more hospitable place to bring his family. Yosef is now six years old, and his grandmother, Ravil's mother, tells us that he asks about his father frequently. How can I possibly share the news of my pregnancy with a man who has been deprived of the joy of seeing his own son grow up? I decide not to say anything about the pregnancy—at least not this time.

Andrea J. Prasow: Behind the Veil

We take extra steps to try to gain the client's trust. I wear long, loose clothing and cover my head. At first I found it a bit awkward. I was constantly adjusting my hair, worried that if even a stray strand emerged, I would lose any trust I had gained. But I have learned that most of the detainees recognize that I do not ordinarily dress that way and simply appreciate the gesture of respect it signals. After a while, the scarf becomes just another item to pack along with sunscreen.

But not to the guards. During the early visits, guards would ask why I was wearing a scarf. They seemed surprised when I explained that it was customary for women to cover their heads in many Arab countries and that I did so as a sign of respect for their culture. And I was left to wonder what sort of cultural training, if any, the guards had received before being assigned to this curious place.

In Yemen, visiting with my client's family, I was grateful for the scarf (I hesitate to call it *hijab,* which often is taken to mean "modest," for am I not otherwise dressed modestly?). When I arrived at the airport in Sana'a, Yemen's capital, I felt strangers' eyes on me and quickly covered my head. I wore local clothing on the street, unlike some of the female tourists I saw. Although I did not wear a veil over my face, I looked like I belonged, in contrast to my male colleagues who drew their own stares for being tall, pale-skinned, and dressed in Western clothing. I felt safe.

And suddenly, in Sana'a, being a woman was a blessing. I was allowed to enter the private world of women's parties and women's living rooms. I saw women's faces; I shook women's hands. And I felt lucky.

Family Members

With Guantánamo detainees imprisoned in virtual isolation year after year, lawyers often became the sole link between the detainees and their families.

Ellen Lubell: A Son like Him

A tentative, distant ring began, then repeated. A woman's soft soprano voice answered on the other end in Arabic. "Allo?"

We had just called Aziz's family in Algeria for the first time. Our interpreter on the call, Ali, was a gracious, well-educated man, originally from Algeria, now living in upstate New York.

"Salaam alaykum," Ali replied. He explained who we were. Muffled voices surfaced in the background, and then the woman again, sounding timid.

"I'm not sure who she is," whispered Ali to us in English, "maybe a sister. She's going to get Aziz's brother, Hamid." The static on the line seemed charged as we waited and listened to one another breathing.

"Allo. Salaam alaykum," a man's more assertive voice this time. Hamid knew who we were.

"Thanks so much for calling," he began. "Our family is grateful to you for helping Aziz. Is he in good health? Do they treat him well?" Hamid's questions tumbled out. He was clearly the protective older brother, trying to sound in charge. "We've been worried. Tell us everything. Aziz's letters stopped coming. Do you know why?" he asked.

It hit me then: we were the first people this family had spoken with in four years who had seen their brother, their son, alive, who had heard his voice. They had last seen him in 2001, a young man of twenty-five. They had exchanged good-byes with him at the airport as he boarded a plane to Mecca. His call a few months later told them he planned to travel longer than anticipated. They heard nothing after that until his letter from Guantánamo. No visits, no calls permitted. No explanation. In 2003, a phone call came from an accountant in Sudan, who had been with Aziz in Guantánamo. He offered greetings. That was all. Aziz was now thirty-one. His sporadic letters from prison, black lines of the censor scoring each page, told them little.

"Aziz is well, but he misses all of you," I answered Hamid. "He's received your letters but can't read much of what you've written because they're censored by our military. I don't know why you're no longer receiving letters from him." I wondered if the censors were to blame or if Aziz, in despair, had given up writing. I went on. "Aziz would like news of the family. Did Shada have her baby?"

"Yes," said Hamid. "Hassan is now five years old."

"Hassan! That's the name Aziz picked out for Shada when she was pregnant."

"That's right," said Hamid. "It was Aziz's choice."

"And Gabir—is he well? And Farid and the others? Your parents?" I asked.

"Gabir is now married. My sister Basma has moved to the city of Annaba with her husband. We're all well," answered Hamid.

Our conversation seemed almost ordinary for a moment—inquiries into health, a child's birth, the daily routine of normal life. Then Hamid's voice again. "My mother would like to speak with you."

After a pause, an older woman spoke. She sounded slightly formal. "Thank you for everything you have done for Aziz and our family. We're so grateful." Her words were simple enough, but there was a catch in her tone, the way she spoke her son's name.

My breath faltered. "We wish we could do more," I said with difficulty. I was conscious of each word I spoke. "Aziz is wonderful. We liked him so much. He's in a very hard situation, but he's strong. I would be proud to have him as a son."

I waited.

"Thank you," she said, almost imperceptibly. A long moment passed. "When is he coming home?" Her voice was breaking.

"We don't know." My words seemed small. I knew they were inadequate. It was then she began to sob.

"We're trying everything possible to get him out of prison. We know Aziz has done nothing wrong. We are so sorry for what our country has done." I thought of my father, a Belgian Jew who had fled for his life to the United States—for him a sanctuary of human rights. I was grateful he was not alive to witness what the United States had become.

Jana Ramsey: A Weeping Father

Two members of our legal team first met Fahd in June 2006. Fahd was delighted to meet us and discuss his legal case. But having spent more than five years in Guantánamo, mostly incommunicado, Fahd's primary concern was for his family. So before discussing anything else, Fahd asked the team to call his father and let him know that he was well, but desperate for family letters. So one afternoon back in New York, we sat down in an office and simply dialed the number that Fahd had given us for his father in Saudi Arabia.

We weren't overly optimistic at being able to reach Fahd's father. Even if Fahd had remembered the number correctly after being imprisoned for years, there was no way to know if the number had been changed, and we couldn't simply check the Saudi yellow pages. But luck was with us, and we reached a family member on the first try. Through our translator, we asked to speak to Fahd's father, Omar. My colleague, who had met with Fahd, explained that we were lawyers in New York. Fahd, who was in Guantánamo, had written us a letter asking us to represent him. We were just back from visiting the base, and we wanted to call to let him know that Fahd was in good health and anxious to hear how his family was.

Clearly stunned, if unfailingly polite, Omar obliged by updating us about the health and status of various family members that Fahd had asked about. Two of Fahd's brothers had gotten married and had children. Another brother who had been married for some time had three children now, two boys and a girl. Two sisters had children, one sister was going to be married in the coming month, and two other sisters had entered college. Fahd's youngest brother was in his last year of elementary school. Omar's voice was neutral and calm as he went through each significant family development of the past five years, as if he were simply reading from a list of his family's achievements.

Omar had finally arrived at the youngest family members when he stopped suddenly. As if the reality of who we were and why we were calling had just sunk in, Omar asked again if Fahd was well, this time with some urgency in his voice. How did Fahd look? Were we sure he was in good health? He had heard there was torture at the base—what did we know about that? We repeated what we said at the beginning of the call: that his son was fine and that we were there to make sure that he came home as soon as possible.

There was silence on the line. Then we began to hear muffled sobs. The translator said quietly, "He is weeping."

We waited for Omar to continue, some of us discreetly wiping our own eyes. When Omar was able to speak again, the words began rushing out. He began telling us again about his family, this time not as if we were simply strange foreigners with an unusual interest in his family but with the realization that we were a link to the son that he had not seen in five years. If he could not travel to Guantánamo and see Fahd in person, he had to impress on us that there was an entire family who missed Fahd desperately and prayed every day for his safe return. Omar took particular care to assure us that Fahd's eight-year-old daughter, whom Fahd had not seen since she was an infant, was healthy and was doing well in the third grade. The conversation gradually wound down, and we hung up after assuring Omar that we would call again soon and urging him to give our best wishes to the whole family.

Even if we could not promise our clients that they would ever get their day in court or the opportunity to clear their name, we could guarantee that they would not be forgotten, trapped in a secret prison far from their families and invisible to the world.

Mark Wilson: Like Gold

Five of us gathered on the third-floor porch of our guesthouse in Kabul, Afghanistan. I had not expected the dry, sixty-degree weather in March. Only the dust that rises from the day's vehicle traffic marred a cloudless sky. The rooftops of Kabul and "Radio Tower" Hill and the snow-covered peaks of the Hindu Kush formed an incomparable backdrop to the photos we took of one another. Muhammed's two brothers and his elder cousin were captured digitally—their images to be carried back with us to Philadelphia, later to be shown to the brother who had been physically taken from his home in Paktia more than five years earlier. The images were gold to us—perhaps as valuable as the meetings we had with influential Afghan officials during our week in Kabul and the signed declarations of Muhammed's innocence that his brothers had just

Central Islip Public Library
33 Hawthorne Avenue
Central Islip, NY 11722-2498

delivered to us from his village elders. Those images of my colleague (David McColgin), me, and the Qasim brothers, with the physical beauty of Kabul, would help to earn the trust of Muhammed. Those images would be the first concrete evidence to him in his lonely cell thousands of miles away that his American lawyers really were trying to help him.

One year later, in March 2008, I held my copy of one of those images as David and I spoke with Muhammed on a conference call with our interpreter. Muhammed was describing the celebration that his village had made for him on his return the day before. I marveled at the value of that image in my hand.

Sahr MuhammedAlly: In Their Own Words

I was in Kabul in early 2008 to learn about trials of former Guantánamo and Bagram detainees, which began in October 2007 and were taking place in Pul-e-Charkhi prison in the outskirts of Kabul. The Afghan National Defense Facility (ANDF)—more commonly known as Block D of Pul-e-Charkhi prison—was built by the United States to house detainees transferred from Guantánamo and Bagram.

While in Kabul, I met with family members of Guantánamo detainees. The family members I met all described to me the anguish at not knowing where their loved ones were after they had been taken by the Americans. Families described how in some cases American soldiers knocked on the door and requested a meeting with their relative. Abdullah Muhajid's brother Fareed Ahmed told me,

> My brother was arrested by the Americans. The Americans said that they had an hour's business with him. My brother invited them for tea. The Americans said they will have tea on the base. He went with them. One hour became two and then four hours. I collected the village elders and went to the base. An Afghan National Army commander said Abdullah will be released at the end of the day. He never came back.

Mohamed Qasim Fareed's brother Jameel was in Karachi, Pakistan, for work when he heard that his brother had been taken by the Americans. Jameel left Karachi immediately and returned home. He told me,

> My mother was home when the Americans came. She told me that the Americans were calling out for Mohammed Qasim. When my brother answered, they said, "We have five minutes' business with you. Come

Central Islip Public Library
33 Hawthorne Avenue
Central Islip, NY 11722-2496

with us, and then you can return." Those five minutes became six years.

Hayatullah, brother of Ghulam Rohani, who was detained in 2002 and transferred to Block D in 2007, recalled his family's efforts to search for his brother:

> We did not know who took him—the Americans or the Afghans. We thought maybe someone took my brother's money and killed him. My family went looking for him village to village. We thought he had been kidnapped. Then we heard on the radio that people captured by the Americans were taken to Guantánamo. We did not know what Guantánamo was. Many months later we received a letter from my brother through the Red Cross. He said that he was in Guantánamo.

All the family members I met told me how after several months of having no idea where their relative was, they suddenly would receive a letter through the International Committee of the Red Cross (ICRC). ICRC letters have been the only form of communication from detainees being held in Guantánamo and Bagram. Family members said that these ICRC letters were infrequent and heavily redacted. "Sometimes it was hard to understand what my brother was writing because there were so many black marks. Sometimes entire paragraphs were redacted or sometimes we could only read the beginning and end of a sentence," said Abdullah Wazir, brother of Zahir Shah.

In January 2008, the ICRC negotiated an agreement with the United States and set up a call center at its Kabul office for families to see and talk to their loved ones who were being held in Bagram and whom they had not seen in years. Families were allowed to talk for twenty minutes at a time.

Prolonged absence has caused psychological distress for families. A cousin of a Guantánamo detainee expressed how the five-year separation has affected his family:

> My family and elders are upset. We have no involvement with the Taliban. My cousin has not hurt anyone; there is no reason for custody. We are disappointed that my cousin is still in custody. [My cousin's] separation from his family is torture. Taking him away for five years is torture. It is very hard on his wife and on his children. If there are

problems with detainees then charge us. He is innocent. If mistakes were made, they should not be repeated. We are poor people. This is creating inconvenience and defaming our community.

When I asked how Abdul Wahid, brother of Izatullah Nusrat, who had been detained for five years, felt about his brother's absence, he replied, "I cannot express the pain and sadness. You put yourself in my shoes. This is injustice. First my brother was taken and then my old disabled father." Wahid's eighty-year-old father, Nusrat Khan, who is a paraplegic, was also detained in Guantánamo for three years before his release in 2006.

Abdullah Wazir's brother, Zahir Shah, has family who lives in Khost, near the border with Pakistan. Zahir explained that his brother had traveled to Pakistan to buy supplies for the family's spare-auto-parts shop but was arrested by Pakistani authorities and then transferred to U.S. custody. His brother has been detained for more five years and was transferred to Pul-e-Charkhi in 2007. He lamented the lost time with his brother, saying,

> The reason why he was transferred is because they did not find any evidence against him. My brother does not know the charges against him. Perhaps the Pakistanis have accused him. I don't know why my brother is still in jail. If my brother has committed a crime, he should be punished. But he spent five and a half years in jail for what? . . . Tell us what he has done. What are the charges? Let us know the sentence so we know how much longer to wait. If convicted—fine. We need to know.

Fareed Ahmed, brother of Abdullah Mujahid, explained that some detainees are not told that a family member has died. It's difficult to convey the news of the death of a family member. Fareed recalled,

> Our father died while Abdullah was detained. My brother was killed in a traffic accident. Abdullah does not yet know about them. When I met him in Pul-e-Charkhi, I told him that our father had a cold and could not come. I was so happy to see Abdullah that I could not tell him that Baba had died. Our life in the absence of my brother was tough. We lost our father, our brother, and we did not know if Abdullah was ever coming home.

Children of detainees not only grow up without their father but have a difficult time reestablishing a relationship when their father is released.

Abdullah Wazir's brother, Zahir Shah, recalled when his brother met his children. "I brought my brother's family to Pul-e-Charkhi. He has two sons who are eight and nine and a daughter who is six. The children visited their father, but they did not feel close to him because they have not seen him in over five years. My brother was very sad. But I told him it will take time."

Detention is also financially devastating when it leaves families and children to fend for themselves in the absence of the family's financial provider. In Kabul, the head of an Afghan human rights organization told me how several women approached him to see whether he could facilitate their divorcing their husbands, who had been detained in Bagram and Guantánamo. Divorce, although permitted under Islamic law, is frowned on in conservative cultures. But my colleague explained that a few wives of detainees are desperate, as they do not have any other male family support. They become vulnerable to rumors of ill repute: they have a desperate financial need to sustain their children. Protection by a male family member especially in Pashtun culture is necessary for women to enjoy basic freedom of movement. Although the strict rules in place under the Taliban that women could not work are no longer applicable, wives of detainees who do not have extended family support find it difficult to find work and provide for their children in war-torn Afghanistan.

Interpreters

In every other circumstance, the U.S. government offers a prisoner an interpreter when it seeks to deprive him of his liberty. But not at Guantánamo. A small, courageous group of interpreters has filled the gap created by language barriers between English-speaking lawyers and primarily Arabic-speaking clients.

Carolyn M. Welshhans: Heroes in Any Language

Many things have been written about Guantánamo. People have written about the legal, ethical, medical, psychological, and religious implications of that horrible prison. Writers have discussed the numerous, astounding, and outlandish ways our government turned its back on justice. Little attention, however, has been paid to interpreters. The vast majority of prisoners at Guantánamo do not speak English. They speak Pashto, Dari, Russian, Farsi, Arabic, and other languages. Therefore, in order to communicate with clients, lawyers must bring interpreters with them to Guantánamo.

These interpreters are nothing short of courageous. They have made individual decisions to reach out and get involved in the Guantánamo litigation. These brave men and women realized that they could not stand by silent while fellow human beings suffered, and so they offered an incredible gift: their voices. They submitted themselves to thorough background checks in order to obtain the necessary security clearances to travel to Guantánamo. They asked employers for permission to take off work, days at a time, for trips to Guantánamo. They explained to loved ones, including small children, why they would be away from home. In fact, because there is such a shortage of security-cleared interpreters, they devote even more time to Guantánamo trips than the attorneys do. Many of these individuals volunteered before much was even known about Guantánamo. The interpreters did not know how their neighbors or the country as a whole would react. Many of the interpreters are first- or second-generation immigrants, and they face possible discrimination within their new country if they are accused of being "soft on terrorism."

The interpreters do much more than simply translate words. They also explain legal concepts to clients completely unfamiliar with the American judicial and political systems, and they navigate cultural differences. In addition, the interpreters serve as psychologists, advisers, and perhaps most important, surrogate family members. Clients' faces light up when they see an interpreter whom they have come to regard as a trusted friend. It is a visible relief to them to be able to talk to someone in their own language and to someone who understands something about their customs, their home, and their old way of life. The interpreters get to share in such moments of happiness, but these moments are all too fleeting. Clients miss their families desperately, and seeing the interpreters reminds them that they have been separated for years from children, wives, brothers, and fathers. Sometimes, clients rail at the injustice of their situation. There is little to say other than to agree with them. But the lawyers are one step removed, and it is the interpreters who hear the emotions firsthand. If clients' stories are that hard for me to hear, I cannot imagine the emotional burden that the interpreters carry. Yet I have never heard one of them complain. I hope only that they realize just how much they have helped the prisoners at Guantánamo.

Masud Hasnain: Karma Sutra

I have interpreted for more than thirty different law firms or solo lawyers at GTMO. I have also had numerous outrageous statements to interpret. What happened this week, however, was the crème de la crème.

The client was open and friendly, apparently for the first time, and we talked about many things including how old the client's father was and how old the lawyer was. The lawyer said he was sixty-five. After a bit of legal discussion, the client asked if the lawyer played sports, because he looked so vigorous. Was he strong? I touched the lawyer's bicep and said he was strong.

We resumed our law talk. The lawyer was explaining some action that he was planning to do or submit on behalf of the client, when the client suddenly asked if the lawyer would allow him to ask a very frank and embarrassing question. I had to ask the client to repeat his statement to make sure that I was understanding correctly. The client, who spoke some English, initially repeated in Arabic that he is too shy to ask but wants to ask this question. The lawyer asked the client to "please" go ahead, not knowing what he was getting into.

CLIENT: You said you are married, right?
LAWYER: Yes.
CLIENT: How old is your wife?
LAWYER: Sixty-four.
CLIENT: But she is too old, and you look so energetic and healthy. You need a much younger woman to satisfy your desires.
LAWYER: No, no, no. I am very happy with her. I have been with her for forty-five years. In fact, it is illegal in the U.S. to have a second wife.
CLIENT: You are very vigorous. Should not you have a younger wife?
LAWYER: She is a vigorous sixty-four-year-old.
CLIENT: Do you sleep with her?
INTERPRETER: What do you mean?
LAWYER: Every night.
CLIENT: No, no, not that. Do you have sex with her?

It took me some time to interpret that. The lawyer could tell by the expression on my face, but I eventually translated.

LAWYER: Yes, of course.
CLIENT: When?
LAWYER: What do you mean?
CLIENT: When was the last time?

There was a long pause.

LAWYER: Actually the night before I was flying here, she asked if I
wanted to have sex, but I said that I was worried about going to
GTMO and therefore we will do it after my return. Last Sunday
night was your fault.
CLIENT: Tomorrow night will also be my fault?

In the middle of this conversation, the client had asked if he could use
the restroom. I had stood up and turned on the light, which is a signal to
the guards in their guardroom that we needed some assistance. It takes
the guard five to ten minutes to come to the meeting room. We resumed
our discussion.

I knew we were getting into troubled territory. However, with good
karma, there was a knock on the door, and the guards came in to take the
client to the restroom, and we had to leave the room.

I asked the lawyer later why he talked about such intimate things. He
said that was the first real conversation that he had ever had with the client. He was going to answer any question that the client asked.

I guess the lawyer's wife will understand.

Murray Fogler: The Interpreter Flap

One of my clients, Bashir Ghalaab, is an Algerian who was arrested in
Pakistan. Another prisoner, Sami al-Hajj, had listed Bashir on a form that
he gave to his own lawyer as someone who wanted a lawyer.

This time, I got no guff from the government about needing proof of
authority to represent Bashir, at least as far as arranging a trip to visit him.
Now I needed an interpreter. I had heard that Clive Stafford Smith, another habeas attorney, would be in GTMO around Memorial Day 2008
with Felice Bezri, one of the most experienced Arabic interpreters, so I
made plans to be there at the same time to share Felice.

Clive's plans changed, so I began communicating with Felice directly to arrange his trip. A week before we were scheduled to leave, we
heard that the government had revoked the security clearance of another

longtime Arabic interpreter, Ashraf Michael. I began peppering the DOJ lawyers with questions about Felice's clearance. Two days before the holiday weekend, I was advised that Felice was no longer cleared to go to GTMO. No reason was given. Ashraf and Felice had each been to GTMO over a hundred times.

Scrambling, I received a recommendation to try Amjad Tarsin, a law student at Michigan, who had interpreted for many attorneys in GTMO. Amazingly, he was willing to go with me on short notice. I submitted his information to the DOJ lawyers, but after a couple days no clearances had come. The day before we were to leave for GTMO, the government revoked Amjad's clearance too. Still no reason was given. I thought my trip was sunk.

Not expecting any positive result, I reached out to one more interpreter, Masud Hasnain. He had just returned from GTMO the previous day. Would he be willing to drop everything and leave the next morning for GTMO, subject to getting the required clearances? Yes! But he doubted the DOJ could process the clearance papers in the two or three hours we had before the end of the day.

Incredibly, a couple hours after the close of business on the day before the trip, I received word that clearances for Masud and me would be granted. These clearances were e-mailed to me as I was leaving for the airport, and the trip thereafter went forward without a hitch.

Joshua W. Denbeaux: Secret Weapon

Many clients believe we aren't lawyers but military interrogators who impersonate FBI agents, White House officials, Red Cross officials, and lawyers. Unbeknownst to us, we had a secret weapon: our translator.

Before we arrived we knew virtually nothing about our clients or their cases. We knew Mohammad was from Tunis. That was all. We did not know if he spoke French or Arabic or both. The Department of Justice and the Department of Defense would not tell us what language he spoke. It was expensive to bring a translator. The trip took five days, including two days for travel. We decided that Arabic was the most conservative bet, and we knew a Unitarian minister who had been trained in Arabic: Rev. Dr. Justin Osterman, the minister of the Central Unitarian Church in Paramus, New Jersey. He volunteered to go, even though he was not confident of his Arabic. He was out of practice. He had been trained in Arabic while serving in the U.S. Air Force. Although he had six months to prepare and update his Arabic skills, even by the time we appeared in Mohammad's "questioning chamber" he was not fully up to speed.

And therein lay our secret weapon: how stupid would a prisoner have to be to believe that interrogators would bring an incompetent translator to Guantánamo? Only habeas corpus counsel would do that. So during the first five minutes of conversation, when Justin's Arabic limitations became apparent, we also demonstrated to Mohammad that we were not interrogators. It took less than five minutes of confusing translation for Mohammad to drop his concerns about our legitimacy. Of course, we did not learn that right away. Mohammad did not share that insight with us until the end of the second visit during that trip. The trust obtained from our rusty translation was increased at the cost of efficient translation.

Allison M. Lefrak: Translating Justice

When my colleague Doug tells Ghanim that the Supreme Court will be hearing a case in the fall of 2007—yet another challenge to the Bush administration's claim that prisoners at Guantánamo can be denied the constitutional right of habeas corpus—Ghanim politely interrupts and asks us to please show him where in the U.S. Constitution the right of habeas corpus is provided for. He shuffles through his papers and pulls out a copy of the Constitution. Doug reaches for the document and stares at it blankly. I lean over and see that the U.S. Constitution has been translated into Arabic. Where did Ghanim get such a thing? He tells us that a fellow detainee's attorney had the Constitution translated for him. Doug, realizing his limitations, passes the document to Mahmoud, our translator, and together they locate the appropriate provision for Ghanim to read. I have no doubt that Ghanim will later be pointing this out to his cellmates as he provides them with any useful tidbits of new information we may have shared with him in today's meeting.

4

Red Tape and Kangaroo Courts

The list of things that are prohibited in the camps is, itself, prohibited in the camps.

—George Clarke

Barriers to Representation

After the Supreme Court's June 2004 decision in Rasul v. Bush *granted attorneys the right to see their clients, the U.S. government immediately sought to restrict attorneys' access to Guantánamo and to the detainees. It claimed, for example, the right to monitor lawyers' conversations with their clients and demanded that attorneys obtain authorization from a detainee even before meeting with the detainee for the first time. Ultimately, under a federal district court's supervision, a compromise was reached, resulting in a "protective order" that would govern lawyers' visits to Guantánamo, communications with detainees, and handling of classified information in the years that followed. Although the government did not achieve all it wanted, the protective order made legal representation and access to the courts far more difficult than it should have been.*

David H. Remes: Negotiating the Protective Order

One early challenge in the habeas litigation was negotiating a protective order with the U.S. government. The order governs our handling of classified information and "protected" information (certain unclassified information too sensitive to be made public) and establishes procedures for visiting and communicating with clients. Early on, the two sides submitted to District Judge Joyce Hens Green, who was then coordinating the cases, a proposed protective order that reflected points of agreement, accompanied by a report setting out three significant points of disagreement: the number of "secure facilities" where classified information would be kept, information sharing among habeas counsel, and public comment by habeas counsel. Judge Green ruled for us on two of these points. First, she ruled that counsel in different habeas cases could share classified documents and information. Second, she ruled that we could comment publicly on information in the public domain that was classified, as long as we didn't indicate that we knew the information was classified. Unfortunately, Judge Green ruled against us on the third point, which proved to have great practical consequence. With habeas counsel located throughout the country, we requested that the government provide "secure facilities" in several major cities. U.S. courthouses throughout the country had such facilities. Judge Green, however, provided for only one secure facility, to be located in Crystal City, Virginia.

With only that one secure facility available, all habeas counsel, wherever located, had to come to Washington, D.C., to review their client meeting notes and their clients' legal mail and to prepare briefs and other court filings containing classified information. The resulting time and expense that every trip entailed, on top of the time and expense of visiting Guantánamo, was a heavy burden for all non-Washington-based habeas counsel, but most of all for the solo and small-firm practitioners and public-interest lawyers.

Also, under the protective order, all communications by a client to his lawyer were presumed to be classified unless and until reviewed and cleared by a "privilege review team." (The PRT, as we called it, was bound to keep the communications confidential.) Accordingly, we could not leave Guantánamo with our client meeting notes. Instead, the military was responsible for transmitting our notes to the secure facility in a secure manner. Initially, the military's idea of secure transmission was dropping the material in a mailbox in Florida. Early on, the military managed to use an incorrect zip code. A batch of our mail sat for weeks in a basement of the Department of Homeland Security before the mistake was discovered.

The PRT often refused to clear client meeting notes and clients' letters, which could not reasonably be classified "secret." One of my favorite examples is the PRT's refusal to clear a map of the camps drawn for me by one of my clients. The military went to great lengths to prevent prisoners in one camp from having a sense of the layout of other camps or the location of the camps in relation to one another. Thus, when the military brought a prisoner to meet with his lawyers at Camp Echo, where lawyer-client meetings were held, the military loaded the prisoner—manacled, blindfolded, and facing toward the rear—into the back of a small pickup and drove the prisoner around the winding, hilly roads of the camp complex before arriving at Echo. We viewed this procedure as one of several means the military used to discourage prisoners from meeting with their lawyers.

During one of my early visits to the base, the prisoners were engaged in a hunger strike to protest their conditions and open-ended detention. My client began to describe the hunger strike to me, but I soon became confused about where particular events were happening. To clarify his account, my client drew me a detailed map of the prison complex showing the locations of the camps and identifying by name the cellblocks in each camp. This information was common knowledge among the prisoners. But when the map arrived with my notes at the secure facility, the PRT refused to clear it. I requested a meeting with the head of the PRT—a veteran spook who called himself "Kent Bond"—to complain about the PRT's refusal to clear that and other information in our notes. In our meeting, I asked "Kent" if the prisoners already knew the information in the map. "Kent" speculated that the map might help confederates of the prisoners on the outside attempt a rescue. I pointed out that anyone attempting to land on the base without authorization would be blown out of the sky if approaching by air or blown out of the water if approaching by sea.

"Rules are rules" was his reply.

Patricia A. Bronte: Classified Art

In June 2007, I received a call from the PRT, which had reviewed correspondence sent to me by my client. The PRT explained that there was nothing classified in the letter itself but that the client had drawn a beautiful border of vines and flowers around the letter. The PRT said that it couldn't review the colorful artwork for classified information because it didn't understand art. So the PRT person redacted the artwork and sent me the letter. The fax cover sheet had a note saying, "This is the letter without the drawing as we discussed from ISN 200. The original has been marked classified as it has the drawing and will be maintained in your safe [at the secure facility]."

The PRT also wrote this note at the top of the letter: "This letter is unclassified without the colorful drawing along the edge. The contents have no classification concern."

David J. Cynamon: The Wrapper

Many of our meetings with prisoners at Guantánamo take place in Camp Iguana, a collection of two-room wooden huts about a mile from the main prison. Although these meetings are purportedly privileged, each room is subject to surveillance by closed-circuit TV.

One of my clients enjoys dark-chocolate candy, so I make sure to bring some to each of our meetings. He speaks fluent English, having attended graduate school in the United States. On one trip, I brought him a bag of Dove dark-chocolate candies, which come in red foil wrappers and contain little sayings, something like fortune cookies. We were eating the candy and exchanging our wrappers. He opened one and started laughing. He handed it to me, and I laughed as well because the short sentence encapsulated his life at Guantánamo and my frustrated inability to accomplish anything useful for him in my capacity as a lawyer: "You are allowed to do nothing." I told him I was going to keep the wrapper as a memento and send it to him when he returned to Kuwait. So I noted the date of our meeting on the wrapper and put the wrapper into my wallet.

As I left the interview and was headed back to the bus, the escort said, "The SOG [Sergeant of the Guard] wants to see you." This is never good news. I followed the SOG into a room. He looked at me and said, "Did you bring anything out of the interview that you weren't supposed to?" I had no idea what he was talking about and said so. He replied, "Are you sure you want to stick with that story?" I got annoyed and said I had done nothing improper. He then asked, "Did you put something in your wallet during the interview?" I stared at him incredulously and then removed the wrapper from my wallet, handed it to him, and said, "You mean this candy wrapper? I kept it because it says everything there is to say about this place." He read it, looked somewhat sheepish, but said, "You understand, when we see you put something in your wallet like that, we assume you have something to hide. Everything that goes into and out of those interview rooms has to be inspected by the guards."

I guess he concluded that I was not trying to pass any secret messages on to al Qaeda because he graciously allowed me to keep the wrapper.

Baher Azmy: My Contribution

In the early days of habeas visits to Guantánamo, the DOD assigned a civilian lawyer to accompany habeas counsel, presumably in case disputes arose about protocol or "law." I managed to get along perfectly well with the thirty-year-old woman, Katherine, who was on the island during our visit. One evening, taking the ferry ride home across the bay to the CBQ, I fell into a glorious nap, fueled by soft, steely beats of some reggae music from my iPod. As we approached the ferry station, I woke up to find Katherine standing over me, holding a document and smiling awkwardly. She pointed to my iPod and asked, "Did you have that in the meeting with your client today?" I was still a bit groggy from the nap but apologetically answered, "Well, I guess so. It was in my backpack that I took into the meeting, and the guards didn't tell me to take it out." She then showed me the document in her hand—it was the court-imposed "protective order" that set the guidelines for our client visits. She pointed to the list of items prohibited in client meetings, which included "Recording Devices," such as tape recorders, digital recorders, video cameras, and digital cameras.

As we walked off the boat onto the dock, I explained that iPods really only record from a computer and do not record what I think I ridiculously referred to as "ambient sound." So clearly, I reasoned with her, this wasn't prohibited. She resisted; our words got heated, not least because I wasn't sure what the end game would be. Was I going to lose my security clearance? Spend the night in the brig? Be designated an enemy combatant? She said she'd have to call Colonel Keys.

The colonel insisted that the "recording device" would have to be confiscated to be "scanned by intel." Relieved that I wasn't going to be taken into custody, and confident that nothing on my iPod could be construed, even under the most liberal interpretation, as a message of jihad, I mentioned that "the only offensive thing on it is some disco." Katherine wasn't amused.

During my next visit to Guantánamo, I was pleased to observe a large sign posted on the outside gates of Camp Echo listing prohibited items in large type; it *expressly* listed iPods. I joked to Tom Wilner, one of the first civilian counsel to visit the base, that we were each equally responsible for making fundamental law in Guantánamo—he helped bring the Great Writ of Habeas Corpus, and I forced the military to put lawyers on notice about iPods.

H. Candace Gorman: Is Yossarian Back?

When I visited my client Abdul Hamid Al-Ghizzawi in Guantánamo in September 2007, he brought with him two letters that he had been working on since the summer. The letters were written in Arabic, one six pages in length, the other only one. The six-page letter described the torture that he had been subjected to since being picked up by bounty hunters. The one-page letter contained instructions upon his death. Al-Ghizzawi wanted to spend our meeting going over the letters so that if they got "lost" in the mail, the information would be recorded in my notes.

For most of the first of our two meeting days, Mr. Al-Ghizzawi read his letters to me, elaborating or explaining as necessary while I took notes. At the end of our two-day visit, I had nineteen pages of notes. Most of the notes concerned the torture that Al-Ghizzawi was subjected to while in the hands of the United States. As his physical health deteriorated, Al-Ghizzawi began preparing for his own death. He was not concerned with his own demise, but he was concerned about his wife and young daughter. He wondered if it was possible that whatever disease was killing him was in his system before he ended up at Guantánamo and whether his wife and daughter were exposed to those illnesses that were killing him. As he received no answers from the military, he could only fear the worst. In addition to preparing his last will and testament, Al-Ghizzawi also gave me instructions upon his death. His instructions were simple: he wanted to have his body tested to determine what killed him. He further wanted the results provided to his wife so that she and his daughter could be tested to ensure they did not have the same diseases. I did not have the heart to tell him that his simple request would never be honored by my country. I promised him I would do the best that I could.

As required, I submitted my attorney-client notes to the government at the end of my visit, and Mr. Al-Ghizzawi's letters were turned over to the guards. Both would be read by the government censors before being mailed to me. A month later I received the one-page will and three pages of the six-page letter describing his torture. A memo from the government explained that the other three pages of the six-page letter were being withheld because they were "classified."

It was another month before I got my notes back from the government, without two pages that the government declared classified. When I received my meeting notes by fax, there was a memo telling me that pages 2 and 5 were classified. Even before I reviewed them, I knew that some of the information that was deemed classified in Mr. Al-Ghizzawi's letter was not being considered classified in my notes. To figure out what was being classified from my notes, I had to travel to Washington, D.C., to review everything in the secure facility.

Another attorney suggested that I submit my notes sentence by sentence in an effort to determine what information was classified. I took each of the twenty sentences from the two pages of notes that the government said were classified and typed each sentence separately onto sheets of paper on the governments' secure computer at the secure facility. I knew all twenty sentences could not be considered classified, and this was a way to figure out exactly which facts the government was trying to keep out of the public eye. I submitted the twenty pages with sentences that said such things as "They beat him if he made any sound or if he complained about how much it hurt"; "Had several body-cavity searches with crowds around him laughing"; "They took pictures of him naked. Men and women were watching him and laughing"; "They were brought out to the runway naked. . . . While they were standing on the runway, they were made to sit like a dog on all fours—pictures were taken—they were made to pose with their heads all held a certain way with the goggles on."

I submitted the line-by-line notes to the government, and less than a week later I received by fax sixteen of the twenty pages marked unclassified. In a subsequent visit to D.C., I reviewed the four sentences that were still considered classified. I realized information that was determined to be classified in my notes was cleared in the three pages of Mr. Al-Ghizzawi's letter that were unclassified. Although it took months to work through this, in the end everything that Al-Ghizzawi told me was cleared either in his letter to me or in my notes.

Murray Fogler: The Next Friend Catch-22

My first client, Salim Adem, a Sudanese national, was arrested in Pakistan at his home. His name was one of several listed in a letter written by another prisoner, named Bisher Al-Rawi, an English speaker who was represented by another lawyer, Brent Mickum, who had apparently asked his client to find out if other prisoners wanted representation.

Because there was no evidence of Adem's desire for a lawyer other than the Al-Rawi letter, I filed a habeas petition for him, listing Al-Rawi as his next friend. After the typical delay for security clearance, my co-counsel and I began making plans to visit our client. We were astonished to learn that the government would not approve our visit. It said we had no proof that Adem wanted us to be his lawyers.

Of course, the only way we could get the requisite proof was to visit Adem at GTMO. The existing protective order, which restricted attorney-client communications, specifically provided that a lawyer had only two visits with a detainee to secure written authorization of representation. The government took the position, however, that some initial proof of authority was required before we could even visit for the first time.

We filed a motion to compel the visit. It ended up before Magistrate Judge Kay, who had been selected by other federal judges to hear procedural matters such as this one. Judge Kay set a hearing, but then attempted to "mediate" our dispute. The government had no interest in compromise. So we reurged our motion. After a few more weeks, Judge Kay issued a lengthy opinion, granting our motion and ordering the government to let us visit.

With Judge Kay's order in hand, we made plans for our trip. But the government appealed Judge Kay's order to the district court and refused to process our request. We delayed our trip again but requested permission to travel, leaving on a Monday morning. The Friday before our flight, District Court Judge Richard Roberts affirmed Judge Kay's order. Our clearance papers were faxed at 8 p.m. that Friday night.

Thanks to the government's red tape and foot-dragging, it had taken us over eight months to get permission to see our client. When we finally saw him, he had changed his mind. He no longer wanted a lawyer. He was bitter and stubborn and would not give us written authorization to permit us to represent him.

Unbeknownst to us, his Administrative Review Board had months earlier recommended his release. This was news to us: the government evidently found no need to tell us since it believed Adem wasn't entitled to a lawyer in the first place.

David McColgin: Major Malfunction

Nothing, even access to our clients, can be taken for granted in the Guantánamo litigation. Our first major battle was just for the right to talk with our client. When we were assigned to the case, the government was refusing permission for an attorney to visit Guantánamo to conduct an interview. The government attorneys claimed that since this detainee, an Afghan named Muhammed, had filed his request for legal help and for release indirectly through another detainee, I would first have to get written "authorization" from Muhammed directly before going to see him. But the government would not allow me to write him to get this authorization. It was a perfect Catch-22. Without the authorization I could not see him, and without seeing him I could not get the written authorization. I have since learned that such Catch-22s epitomize Guantánamo litigation.

Ultimately, a federal magistrate judge ordered the government to permit an attorney visit, and I added Muhammed's name to the list of detainees I was to interview on an upcoming trip to Guantánamo. I submitted the list through the government to the authorities in Guantánamo, but the government then appealed to the federal district court judge assigned to the case, who stayed the magistrate's order and scheduled a hearing on the issue for the day *after* my return from Guantánamo. When I arrived in Guantánamo, however, I was ecstatic to discover that the authorities still had Muhammed listed for an interview with me— someone there had forgotten to take him off the list. So I finally got to talk with Muhammed only because the government's bureaucratic machinery malfunctioned.

Joshua W. Denbeaux: Contraband

In early June 2006, we returned to visit with our clients, Mohammed and Rafiq. In the week and a half before that, in mid-May, President Bush had announced that he wanted to close Guantánamo. Newspaper stories with bold headlines expressed these statements. We brought those newspapers down in order to give our clients a moral boost and because it was relevant to our attempts to persuade them to let us take additional steps to protect them. The protective order forbids sharing current events with detainees. We could share information only to the extent that it was necessary as part of our representation.

When we entered the facilities in the morning, the guards inspected our packages and saw all the newspapers we planned to show our clients. At the end of our meeting, they inspected all our materials to make sure we were not bringing out any contraband. After we came back from lunch, one of the guards looked through my bag and said, "What's this?" He was referring to the newspapers. I told him what they were. I explained to him that I thought this was important information in developing my attorney-client relationship. He said that it was contraband because I was not allowed to share current events with my clients.

Two months later, I received an e-mail message from Terry Henry, a DOJ lawyer, saying that I had violated the protective order by bringing contraband to the prison, that is, the newspapers saying that President Bush wanted Guantánamo closed. If I was ever to visit my clients again, I had to promise not to bring "contraband." The government also reserved all rights to take whatever steps it deemed appropriate against me at some future time. That ominous statement has been sent to us several times and obviously to many others.

Eldon V.C. Greenberg: Ocean View

My first meeting with one of our Guantánamo clients, way back in November 2005, was one of my most poignant. We spent two days discussing our role as lawyers, our client's case, and the suffering our client had endured at Guantánamo. As we were getting ready to leave, I asked our client if there was anything he would like us to send to him. "Yes," he said, "I would like a book with pictures of the ocean." Imprisoned a scant few hundred yards from the blue Caribbean Sea but locked in a windowless cell and hooded whenever he was moved outside the prison walls, our client longed for just a glimpse of the sea's expanse. I promised I would do what I could. Upon my return to Washington, D.C., I purchased a book of photographs of the ocean, carefully blacked out all the text, and removed the hard cover—to reassure the prison authorities that I was not trying to deliver some coded message or potential weapon to my client—and sent the book off through the Guantánamo mail system to my client. The book was never delivered, and inquiries to prison authorities about its whereabouts elicited no response. More than three years later, our client, shut away in the concrete bleakness of Camp Six, is still waiting to see the ocean.

Gaillard T. Hunt: Bibles Prohibited

I went down to Guantánamo expecting to meet some poor wretch beaten down and wasting away from years of solitary confinement. I even took with me a field questionnaire designed to assess the degree of a prisoner's mental deterioration.

I was surprised, then, when ushered into one of the cells in Camp Echo, to be greeted by a mature, gray-bearded gentleman radiating self-confidence and obviously delighted to see me. This was Saifullah Paracha. He was then fifty-eight years old. He had lived in New York for sixteen years. He has an American green card. Before he was seized, he was a businessman and a TV producer. His first thought when a gang of masked men jumped him and took him prisoner was, "This is an American operation. I'll be all right."

Paracha had been imprisoned by the United States at Bagram Air Force Base in Afghanistan for about a year before he was transferred to GTMO. He had a Bible there, in addition to his Quran. He explained that the unity of the Abrahamic traditions is very important to him—not that he was any less a devout Muslim. He told me how much making the Hajj, the religious pilgrimage to Mecca, had meant to him. He was quick to add,

"But when I lived in New York, I once went to a gay wedding." Here was a Muslim for the twenty-first century.

At GTMO he asked for the Bible, which he believed had come with him in a box from Bagram. The Sergeant of the Guard told him he couldn't have the Bible unless the interrogation team authorized it. But the interrogation team had long ago departed, declaring that Paracha had told them all he knew and would be released soon. So he got no Bible.

When I got back home, I bought a ten-dollar Bible, King James version. I left it in the publisher's shrink wrap. I learned from the Internet that a Unitarian-Universalist chaplain had recently been posted to Guantánamo, a woman named Cynthia Kane. So I wrote her a note explaining that one prisoner at least would appreciate a pastoral visit and asking her to deliver the Bible to Paracha. I threw in paperback copies of *Hamlet* and *Julius Caesar.*

I have no idea what happened. Possibly Chaplain Kane got neither the Bible nor my letter, nor *Hamlet* nor *Julius Caesar*. After all, what kind of security system would let a chaplain receive such dangerous stuff through the mail from just anybody? When I next visited Paracha, he had neither seen nor heard of my intellectual care package.

As I was leaving, a staff judge advocate came onto the bus. He was livid. I had breached the protective order. My communication with a chaplain was a serious breach of security. "We're trying to run a prison here," he explained through gritted teeth. I soon gave up trying to defend myself and let the chewing-out run its course.

Matthew O'Hara: I Love Cowboys

Almost every lawyer, no matter what his or her area of practice, is practically addicted to taking notes. There doesn't really have to be a good reason to take notes in meetings—you just do. We accumulate file folders of notes for matters over the years, and most of the time we never look back at them. But it's our habit, and we're not about to stop.

At Guantánamo, though, our notes actually play a special role because of the farcical rules imposed on us by our government and our courts. The rule is that everything our imprisoned clients tell us is presumed to be classified—a secret that, if revealed, would endanger the national security of the United States, a secret that, if we tell anyone else without a security clearance and without a "need to know," will subject us to draconian penalties, including felony imprisonment. At Guantánamo, you're talking to men whom our government has collectively demonized as the "worst of the worst" without ever proving any such thing. For more than two and a half years, the U.S. government even managed to keep their very identities secret. The government did this because it's hard to feel bad about holding supposedly dangerous men you can't see or hear and whose names you don't even know.

So notes for lawyers at Guantánamo are our first tool for making our clients into real people. If we want their voices to be heard—in the papers we write in court, the things we say to reporters, the articles we write, and the talks we give—we have to write down what they say. That way, government censors can review the notes and decide whether what was said can be uttered without risking the safety of the nation. Otherwise, the horrible, the fascinating, the mundane, the desperate things the men at Guantánamo have to say—which have nothing to do with our national security—remain secrets.

On my third trip to Guantánamo, I was a couple hours into my sixth meeting with our client Walid. For four or five hours I had not written down a single word he'd said. When we first met Walid, he was pretty forthcoming as things go between Muslim men who have been imprisoned for over five years without charge and American lawyers who are accustomed to making things happen in American courts for their clients. He started telling us about many things that happened to him during his unexpected journey from Gaza to Pakistan to Cuba. But in these past two days on this last visit, he wanted nothing to do with his "case."

"I love cowboys." So begin my notes from the second day of our meeting with Walid in October 2007. "I love Indians" too. All of a sudden, the hours of religious rambling and the subtle proselytizing and the refusal to talk about what happened to him in Saudi Arabia and Iran and Afghanistan and Pakistan and GTMO and the lethargic lack of interest gave way, and Walid's face lit up. Now he got a chance to talk about something that really gave him some solace: American action movies. Westerns. Rambo. Van Damme. Bruce Lee. Walid had spent his childhood, before his ill-fated first adventure away from home, watching American shoot-'em-up movies.

The truth was, I feared, that Walid had become delusional, but all of a sudden at least, he was happy with these memories to entertain him. Walid had left school in the fourth grade. He suffered greatly since he left home at twenty to perform a religious pilgrimage to Mecca. Walid was now living in a steel cell by himself for twenty-two hours or more a day, with no human contact and no intellectual stimulation. But he knew enough to know that telling these sincere American lawyers his story wasn't going to get him home. Walid knew, like every Guantánamo prisoner, that the American courts, even if they are functional in every other way, had washed their hands of him and all his fellow prisoners. On another visit, my notes with Walid end, "I don't deal with Bush. I deal with God." But the mere thought of cowboys and Indians made his day.

The notes from our meetings with another client, Bilal, are always sparse. We started representing Bilal at the same time we first met Walid. Bilal is from Syria. That by itself will tell you a lot about how he views the world. I could see that he worried that anything he said or did would get back to Syria and that he, or someone he knows there, will pay. He started out professing complete hopelessness and no need for lawyers. In meeting after meeting, hour after hour, and through our effort to be plainspoken and honest, my gut told me that he really wanted to believe that we, his lawyers, were good people who were on his side. But his Syrian view of the world colored all of that.

Bilal said he appreciated us and our efforts. He wanted us to come back and see him. He loved to talk about anything that could occupy his mind—our travels, our activities, our families, history, geography. He really wanted to see a soccer magazine. We once sent him one that I had bought for him at a newsstand in Chicago. But the censors never let him have it.

For all the hard-won rapport we built with Bilal, he measured out facts about himself for us like medicine for a child from an eyedropper. In any set of meetings over two days, we got those few facts he wanted to convey, and then it was time to talk sports and travel. Bilal reassured us that when it's time, when he knows something is actually going to happen—when something is going to happen that makes it possible for even the Syrians to leave Guantánamo—he will tell us everything there is to know about him. Until then, nothing more needs to be said. Europeans and Saudis and Pakistanis and others from countries with good relations with the United States go home, but not Syrians. Other countries chastise the United States for its lawless prison for Muslim men, but none opens its doors to those men. So, Bilal figures, what's the rush? See you in three months. Where else will I be?

Umar, our third client, is from Tajikistan, though he hasn't lived there since he was twelve, when his family fled the civil war that began there when the Soviet Union collapsed. We met Umar in the same little wedge-shaped room with cinder-block walls, a steel door with a window through which you could see in but not out, a small dirty table, and a steel ring in the floor so that your client could be chained to the floor. It was the same stuffy room where we had almost all our meetings with Walid and Bilal. Umar was really quite a sight. He's a big bear of a man who speaks so softly that you can barely hear him. He has long hair down to his waist and a beard that reaches almost as far.

Umar greeted us politely. After some opening chitchat, I started talking about who we were and why we were there and about the rights of Guantánamo detainees. I felt like I was giving an opening statement to a jury. It was extraordinarily nerve-wracking, since this jury had already decided that American lawyers are superfluous in his life. I went on for well over an hour, working up a thirst and apologizing for being so long-winded. I had not touched the pad of paper or the pen on the table in front of me.

The very first thing he told us after I finally stopped talking was that Tajik agents had come to interrogate him at Guantánamo on many occasions. I asked Umar if I could take notes. "Of course," he said. The Tajik officials asked him to become a Tajik secret agent in Afghanistan because he had lived in that country for years. He told them no. They told him in that case, they couldn't wait to get him back to Tajikistan. They would throw him in jail and torture him, "maybe even get rid of [him]." Umar said the Americans knew about these threats because they were always watching and listening. Umar told us that Tajiks are known as "quiet beasts" because of the terrible things they do. Two other Tajiks who were recently released from Guantánamo said that they received the same threats from the Tajik officials. The Red Cross has told him that those men were sentenced to lengthy prison terms in Tajikistan.

"I don't want to go back to Tajikistan. I want asylum. I will go anywhere else. Do anything you have to do to keep them from sending me back to Tajikistan."

Matter-of-factly, he related how his mother had led him and his younger siblings from Afghanistan to Pakistan in 2001, where they had lived in a refugee camp. One day, Umar was in the market in the camp, and the Pakistani police picked him up and handed him over to the Pakistani intelligence service. Umar found himself in a cell in the basement of a building.

They said, "Do what we tell you, and we will let you go. We will take you back to your mother. Just copy what we give you into these notebooks, and you can go home." Umar told us that he had not seen or heard from his mother or the rest of his family since the Pakistani cops grabbed him out of the market six years before.

"'No,' I told them. So then they tortured me a little. And finally I did what they said. I wrote day and night for a month."

I scribbled furiously, filling almost an entire legal pad. The army guards yelled in through the steel door with the one-way glass. It was time for us to go.

"They took me from my cell and put a blindfold on me," Umar continued. "They said, 'Come on, we are going to take you back to your mother.' And we drove for a while, and then they took me out of the car. Then they took off my blindfold, and I was standing in front of the gates of a prison."

This is where my notes end. After the meeting, we walked outside the wire into the bright tropical sun. I said to my colleague and our interpreter, "That guy needs a lawyer."

That same evening, we were in Fort Lauderdale, but my notes were on their way to Washington, D.C., to be reviewed by government censors to see if anything dangerous to our nation's security was lurking there. Walid still loves cowboys, Bilal will get down to business with us when even the Syrians are going to get out of GTMO, and Umar wants the world to know what the Americans let the Tajik agents say to him when they came to see him at the U.S. Navy base in Cuba.

Patricia A. Bronte: A Mother's Death

It was supposed to be a birthday celebration. My client was turning twenty-nine, and I timed my visit so that we could celebrate together. It was Ali's sixth birthday behind the razor wire at Guantánamo.

Ali's father died about twenty years ago, so his mother raised Ali and his brothers and sisters on her own. But five and a half years after Ali arrived at Guantánamo, his mother was diagnosed with cancer. Ali's siblings did not want me to tell him at first, so I explained the situation to a sympathetic JAG officer at the base and requested a phone call between Ali and his mother. The officer did what he could but was unable to relax the government's requirement that the mother travel to the U.S. embassy in Riyadh so that the call could be placed on a secure phone line—an impossibility, given the mother's weakened condition.

Just before I left Chicago for the birthday meeting, Ali's brother told me the sad news: Ali's mother had died. I told the guards I had sad news to impart, and they allowed me to meet with Ali through the lunch hour. My translator considerately did not attend the meeting so that Ali—who has taught himself English and several other languages during his tenure at Guantánamo—might feel less awkward expressing his grief. Ali and I spent five hours together, sometimes talking, sometimes not.

About three weeks later, I received an angry letter from the Department of Justice accusing me of "rais[ing] security concerns" and violating the court's protective order by telling Ali about his mother's death "without providing advance notice to Guantánamo Bay staff or obtaining their approval." So not only was Ali prevented from saying good-bye to his mother (or from knowing why the United States has held him since January 16, 2002), but according to the government, Ali had no right to know that his mother was dead, unless and until his jailers approved the message. A copy of our correspondence follows.

U.S. Department of Justice
Andrew Warden
Trial Attorney
January 7, 2008

VIA E-MAIL
Patricia Bronte
Jennifer & Block LLP
330 N. Wabash Avenue
Chicago, IL 60611-7603
Re:

Dear Pat:

    The Department of Defense has informed us of a troubling incident that occurred at the Guantánamo Bay detention facility. Apparently the mother of your client —— recently passed away. We understand that you informed your client of the sad news during your visit with him on December 17, 2007, with no prior notice to the authorities at Guantánamo Bay. As was, no doubt, foreseeable, your client became quite distraught after your visit with him. The guards discovered him crying in his cell later that night and they had no information about this situation or the reasons for his behavior. Guantánamo has since made arrangements for a mental health counselor to speak with Mr. —— in the event he wants to speack [sic] with someone about this personal matter.

    Providing such news in the way you did, without providing advance notice to Guantánamo Bay staff or obtaining their approval, was bound to raise security concerns and should have been recognized as not in the best interest of either camp personnel or your client. Moreover, your decision to provide the news to Mr. —— without any advance notice is particularly disappointing in light of the fact that various agencies within the government had been working diligently over the past several months, at your request, to arrange a phone call between Mr. —— and his family in Saudi Arabia to discuss his mother's health situation. As you know, that phone call was abruptly canceled by Mr. ——'s family after all the necessary arrangements had been made. I spoke with your colleague Sapna Lalmalani about this matter on or about October 10, 2007 and requested an explanation for the cancellation, but we did not hear anything further from her or you. In the future, the sharing of sensitive information such as this must be arranged through Guantánamo personnel, in strict accordance with the Protective Order. We appreciate your exercise of care in this regard.

Sincerely,
Andrew I. Warden

CC: Sapna Lalmalani

•

JENNER & BLOCK
January 8, 2008

VIA E-MAIL & U.S. MAIL
Andrew I. Warden, Esq.
Trial Attorney
United States Department of Justice
Civil Division, Federal Programs Branch
20 Massachusetts Ave., N.W., Room 6120
Washington, DC 20530
Re:

Dear Andrew:

I am sorry you believe I violated your clients' rights by informing my client —— that his mother died at the end of his fifth year of imprisonment at Guantánamo. I believe —— has the right to know the truth, even though the news would grieve him. That is why I told the guards that I had to deliver bad news to —— and therefore needed to meet with him, without breaking for lunch, from 11:30 a.m. to 4:30 p.m. on December 17, 2007.

Nothing in Judge Robert's Protective Order gives the Administration the right to prior notice of the death of a prisoner's parent, nor does the Administration have the right to decide whether, when, or how a prisoner is informed of his mother's death. As you know, I informed JTF-GTMO that ———'s mother was dying of cancer on July 30, 2007. I have already expressed my appreciation for your work in arranging a phone call between ——— and his family. Unfortunately, a call with his mother was impossible because she was physically incapable of meeting your requirement that she travel to the U.S. embassy in Riyadh. Three days before my December visit to Guantánamo, I learned that the siblings had been unable to go to Riyadh at the appointed time because their mother's condition had become critical. I learned at the same time that Mrs. ——— had died.

There is no way to prevent the grief that follows a mother's death, but I tried my best to impart the information in a compassionate way, and I stayed with ——— for five hours to make sure that he was handling the blow as well as possible under the dismal circumstances. Please call me if you would like to discuss this matter.

Very truly yours,
Patricia A. Bronte

CC: Sapna Lalmalani

Clive Stafford Smith: Underwear

The following correspondence between habeas attorney Clive Stafford Smith and the government appears in its original form.

August 12, 2007

Re: Discovery of Contraband Clothing in the Cases of Shaker Aamer, Detainee ISN 239, and Muhammed Hamid al-Qareni, Detainee ISN 269

Dear Mr. Stafford Smith:

Your client, Shaker Aamer, detainee ISN 239, was recently discovered to be wearing Under Armor briefs and a Speedo bathing suit. Neither item was issued to the detainee by JTF-Guantánamo personnel, nor did they enter the camp through regular mail. Coincidentally, Muhammed al-Qareni, detainee ISN 269, who is represented by Mr. Katznelson of Reprieve, was also recently discovered to be wearing Under Armor briefs. As with detainee ISN 239, the briefs were not issued by JTF-Guantánamo personnel, nor did they enter the camp through regular mail.

We are investigating this matter to determine the origins of the above contraband and ensure that parties who may have been involved understand the seriousness of this transgression. As I am sure you understand, we cannot tolerate contraband being surreptitiously brought into the camp. Such activities threaten the safety of the JTF-Guantánamo staff, the detainees, and visiting counsel.

In furtherance of our investigation, we would like to know whether the contraband material, or any portion thereof, was provided by you, or anyone else on your legal team, or anyone associated with Reprieve. We are compelled to ask these questions in light of the coincidence that two detainees represented by counsel associated with Reprieve were found wearing the same contraband underwear.

Thank you as always for your cooperation and assistance,

Sincerely,
[name redacted]
Commander, JAGC, US Navy
Staff Judge Advocate

•

29th August, 2007

Re: The Issue of Underwear ("Discovery of 'Contraband Clothing' in the Cases of Shaker Aamer (ISN 239) and Mohammed el-Gharani (ISN 269)")

Dear Cmdr. [redacted]:

Thank you very much for your letter dated August 12, 2007, which I received yesterday. In it, you discuss the fact that Mr. Aamer was apparently wearing "Under Armor briefs" and some Speedo swimming trunks and that, by coincidence, Mr. el-Gharani was also sporting "Under Armor briefs."

I will confess that I have never received such an extraordinary letter in my entire career. Knowing you as I do, I hope you understand that I do not attribute this allegation to you personally.

Obviously, however, I take accusations that I may have committed a criminal act very seriously. In this case, I hope you understand how patently absurd it is, and how easily it could be disproven by the records in your possession. I also hope you understand my frustration at yet another unfounded accusation against lawyers who are simply trying to do their job—a job that involves legal briefs, not the other sort.

Let me briefly respond: First, neither I, nor Mr. Katznelson, nor anyone else associated with us has had anything to do with smuggling "unmentionables" in to these men, nor would we ever do so.

Second, the idea that we *could* smuggle in underwear is far-fetched. As you know, anything we take in is searched and there is a camera in the room when we visit the client. Does someone seriously suggest that Mr. Katznelson or I have been stripping off to deliver underwear to our clients?

Third, your own records prove that nobody associated with my office has seen Mr. Aamer for a full year. Thus, it is physically impossible for us to have delivered anything to him that recently surfaced on his person. Surely you do not suggest that in your maximum security prison, where Mr. Aamer has been held in solitary confinement almost continuously since September 24, 2005, and where he has been more closely monitored than virtually any prisoner on the Base, your staff have missed the fact that he has been wearing *both* Speedos and "Under Armor" for 12 months?

Since your records independently establish that neither I nor Mr. Katznelson could have been the one who delivered such undergarments to Mr. Aamer, this eliminates any "coincidence" in the parallel underwear sported by Mr. el-Gharani. Your letter implies, however, that Mr. Katznelson might have something to do with Mr. el-Gharani's underthings. Mr. Katznelson has not seen Mr. el-Gharani for four months. As you know, Mr. el-Gharani has been forced to strip naked in front of a number of military personnel on more than one occasion, and presumably someone would have noticed his apparel then.

Without bringing this up with me, it was therefore patently clear that my office had nothing to do with this question of lingerie. However, I am unwilling to allow the issue of underwear to drop there: It seems obvious that the same people delivered these items to both men, and it does not take Sherlock Holmes to figure out that members of your staff (either the military or the interrogators) did it. Getting to the bottom of this would help ensure that in the future there is no shadow of suspicion cast on the lawyers who are simply trying to do their job, so I have done a little research to help you in your investigations.

I had never heard of "Under Armor briefs" until you mentioned them, and my internet research has advanced my knowledge in two ways—first, *Under Armour* apparently sports a "u" in its name, which is significant only because it helps with the research.

Second, and rather more important, this line of underpants are very popular among the military. One article referred to the fact that "*A specialty clothing maker is winning over soldiers and cashing in on war.*" The article goes on to say:

> In August [2005], a Baltimore-based clothier popular among military service members got in on the trend. Founded in 1996, *Under Armour* makes a line of tops, pants, shorts, underwear and other "performance apparel" designed for a simple purpose: to keep you warm in the cold and cool in the heat.

This stuff is obviously good for the men and women stationed in the sweaty climate of Guantánamo, as we could all attest.

It would be worth checking whether this lingerie was purchased from the NEX there in GTMO, since the internet again leads one to suspect that the NEX would be purveyors of *Under Armour*.

Tom Byrne, *Under Armour's* director of new business development, told *Army Times* that "The product has done very well in PXes across the country and in the Middle East, and we have seen an increasing demand month after month. There is clearly a need for a better alternative than the standard-issue cotton T-shirt."

There must be other clues as to the provenance of these underpants. Perhaps you might check the label to see whether these are "tactical" underwear, as this is apparently something *Under Armour* has created specially for the military.

Under Armour has a line of apparel called Tactical that's modified for soldiers. It features the same styles as civilian tops and bottoms—LooseGear for all purpose conditions, HeatGear and ColdGear, meant for hot and cold weather, as well as a line for women. But Tactical items are offered in army brown, olive drab, midnight navy and traditional black and white.

I don't know the color of the underpants sported by Messrs. Aamer and el-Gharani, but that might give you a few tips. Indeed, I feel sure your staff would be able to give you better information on this than I could (though I have done my best).

On the issue of the Speedo swimming trunks, my research really does not help very much. I cannot imagine who would want to give my client Speedos, or why. Mr. Aamer is hardly in a position to go swimming, since the only available water is the toilet in his cell.

I should say that your letter brought to mind a sign in the changing room of a local swimming pool, which showed someone diving into a lavatory, with the caption, "We don't swim in your toilet, so please don't pee in our pool." I presume that nobody thinks that Mr. Aamer wears Speedos while paddling in his privy.

Please assure me that you are satisfied that neither I nor my colleagues had anything to do with this. In light of the fact that you felt it necessary to question whether we had violated the rules, I look forward to hearing the conclusion of your investigation.

All the best.
Yours sincerely,
Clive A. Stafford Smith

Government efforts to intimidate lawyers and undercut their representation of clients were not limited to the protective order but involved other, less formal types of bureaucratic barriers and harassment. As always, it was the detainees who suffered.

Joshua L. Dratel: No Laughing Matter

What stays with me most about Guantánamo was how so much of what occurred there simply made me laugh—oftentimes inappropriately so, whether ironically, bitterly, sardonically, or otherwise. Yet I could not avoid that reaction. Whether because of the surrealism, the absurdity, the hypocrisy, the capriciousness, or maybe because some events were just plain funny. Maybe it was a defense mechanism, constituting the only alternative to anger and frustration, to the helplessness we experienced when confronted by a system—more accurately a human laboratory—designed and implemented to break human beings physically, emotionally, psychologically, and culturally. Maybe it was because Guantánamo represented such an alternative universe that what occurred there lacked any foundation in the "real" world, and it could be viewed as amusing without significant consequences.

Of course, there were consequences, for real persons absorbing real pain and punishment. But parsing out the wry parts enabled me to move forward in my mission—representing and defending my client—rather than becoming immobilized by the injustice, intolerance, and insensitivity to ordinary human interaction that GTMO embodied. Whatever the reason, I remember constantly resorting to laughter while at GTMO, certainly more than an objective assessment of the situation would appear to warrant.

What events and situations caused that gallows-humor response? I can assemble a partial list. If they do not make you laugh as well, do not feel bad or confused. For some of these items, you had to be there. And believe me, if you didn't have to be there, you wouldn't want to be. For others, well, people did give me odd looks when I laughed. But that could not deter me. If they did not understand, it would be too difficult to explain. Besides, often I did not mind being viewed as a bit unpredictable and inscrutable. That helps when you're navigating a bureaucracy as entrenched as the military and an environment as impenetrable as GTMO.

So here is my partial list of what made me laugh—and still does—whether cynically, incredulously, caustically, or worse:

- How little the interrogators knew about al Qaeda, Islam, the Middle East, or Islamic terrorist organizations, a fact painfully evident from a review of their uninformed and amateurish interrogations of the detainees.

- That after we (counsel for detainee David Hicks) were admonished not to reveal anything, even the slightest detail, about David's living quarters after our first few visits to Guantánamo in early 2004—because such information was "classified"—on our next visit a few weeks later we were told we would not be visiting with David in his cell but rather would be set up in a cell, which had exactly the same configuration as David's, that had been outfitted for the media to view as an example they could write about and photograph. The only intervening event had been the Supreme Court oral argument in *Rasul v. Bush* regarding the Guantánamo detainees' habeas corpus rights.
- How information we were provided was deemed classified but was published on the Internet a few months later.
- That migrant workers from Jamaica and the Philippines were permitted access to the most sensitive sites at or in the detention camps, whereas lawyers—some military and the rest possessed of appropriate security clearances after the most comprehensive background checks—were processed through multilevel checkpoints and searches before being permitted to enter the camps.
- That the twenty-year-old soldier who conducted those searches one day in 2007 inquired of Hicks's Australian lawyers, after discovering Australian currency in their wallets, whether it represented "a lot" of money, as if David was going to swim home, paying his way with Australian currency at ports of call throughout the Caribbean.
- That during David's initial military commission proceedings in August and October 2004, when he was on trial for war crimes, the military assembled a huge show of force and security during the day while the commissions were in session, but at night the commission building was completely unguarded and accessible to anyone who knew the code for the front door.
- How at the initial commission hearings it was instantly apparent to the private Arabic interpreters in the audience (who were working with the defense lawyers) that the interpreters employed by the commission to translate the proceedings for the detainee defendants did not understand Arabic properly.
- That the only military lawyer among the original JAG officers assigned to the defense team who has received a promotion was the lawyer whose client refused to accept a lawyer and instead proceeded *pro se*.

- That the camp administration refused to allow us to send David certain books, such as *To Kill a Mockingbird*, because it had the word *kill* in the title. *Presumed Innocent* was another banned title. Needless to say, we were not successful in getting *Breaker Morant* approved either.
- How David was not allowed to keep *The Torture Papers*, a book I co-edited and gave to him, which traced the U.S. government's torture policy after 9/11 through official memoranda and reports, because the detention authorities claimed it had nothing to do with his case.
- How the camp library did not have books in English for David (but he was offered books in Russian as an alternative to the Arabic, Pashtun, or Urdu texts the other detainees were offered).
- That David received more news—and a fair amount of gossip and sometimes disinformation—from the guards on a regular basis than from his lawyers during our intermittent visits.
- That while I was suffering from two herniated disks in my lower back, I was informed (by the soldiers who observed our meetings on the video cameras that were positioned on the ceiling of each cell) that I could not lie on David's concrete-slab bed to relieve the pain while we met with him. Later we were informed that we could no longer urinate in David's toilet during our half-day meetings with him.
- That as the population of detainees declined steadily from the time I began visiting Guantánamo in January 2004, the number of structures built by private contractors steadily increased, more often than not for no discernible purpose.
- That the iguanas, which enjoyed protected status on the base and thus could roam blithely across roads, parking lots, and wherever they fancied, were afforded more rights and protections than the detainees.
- That base personnel who played the GTMO golf course had to use little Astroturf mats under the ball for most shots because the course grass had been worn away in many places by the Haitian migrants who had been confined there years before.
- How for an extended period of visits a woodpecker worked rhythmically on one of the wooden detainee shacks at Camp Echo, perhaps, we mused, assisting the detainees in a long-term escape plot about as effective as the habeas corpus petitions they had all filed in the U.S. courts.

H. Candace Gorman: The Escort

What can I say? I guess I am special. As far as I know, of all the attorneys representing prisoners at Guantánamo Bay, I am the only one assigned a personal escort every time I visit the base. Whether this is supposed to be a privilege or a punishment remains unclear. What I do know is that I love what I consider to be a privilege. I am first in line to see my client each time I visit because I am driven directly to the prison.

Why do I receive this kid-glove treatment? The story began in July 2006, when I first visited Guantánamo. I had intended to meet with both my clients: Abdul Hamid Al-Ghizzawi, a Libyan who had been my client since November 2005; and Abdul Razak Ali, an Algerian whom I had recently agreed to represent. Unfortunately, when I arrived at the base I was told there was some confusion. According to the authorities, Abdul Razak Ali's name did not correspond to the prisoner identification number I had listed (even though the name and number came from the military). According to the authorities, I had the wrong information, and they would not allow me to meet with my client. I told my escort that I had just received a court order to see Razak Ali, and I wanted to make sure that his superiors were aware of the order. He told me, "Court orders don't work here; we consider those only advisory." I did not argue with him. I just wrote down what he said. To make a long story short, the military decided to disregard the court's "advice," and I was not allowed to see Razak Ali.

As it turns out, there was absolutely no confusion. In trying to clear up the confusion I provided three different spellings for the name of prisoner No. 685. Shortly before leaving the base, I was provided a list of the names and aliases for the detainee whose name supposedly did not match the name I provided. The first name on the list was the very same name (and spelling) that I had provided.

When I returned from that trip to Guantánamo, I filed a motion with the judge asking him to find the government in contempt of court for disregarding his order. In response, the government filed an affidavit from one Commander McCarthy. McCarthy, a military attorney whom I had never seen nor met, alleged that I had decided that I did not want to meet with Razak Ali when I discovered that he was Algerian and not Libyan (as if I had a policy of only representing Libyans). Bizarrely, McCarthy also claimed that I had decided against meeting Razak Ali when I discovered that he was not the brother of my Libyan client (as if I had ever imagined that the two were related). Lastly, McCarthy claimed that I had never really wanted to see Razak Ali because I had really gone to Guantánamo to go bird watching.

Of course, this was nonsense. The authorities were only trying to cover up their own mistakes. It was clear to me that they had read and purposely misconstrued my attorney-client notes from my meeting with my client Al-Ghizzawi. My notes contained many references to Al-Ghizzawi's brother, but that had nothing to do with Mr. Razak Ali. Al-Ghizzawi's brother lives in Libya.

At the hearing, the judge declared that Commander McCarthy's affidavit should be given "no weight." It was a polite and judicious way of calling the guy a liar. Not surprisingly, the good commander was later promoted to captain!

The military does not like it when you nail them, and McCarthy was no exception. I nailed him, so I had to be punished. My punishment is that I have been given my own personal escort, an attorney, whose job is to stay with me at all times while I am on "their" side of the base (except when I am visiting with my client). From the time I leave the ferry each morning until I am put back on the ferry in the afternoon, I am separated from the other attorneys. This means that I get more time with my clients and that I do not have to wait in the lines with the other attorneys.

Being an attorney for a person who is being held without charge for an indefinite period is pretty miserable. On some days, it is even heartbreaking. Most days I find myself frustrated because trying to do my best is not good enough, and I have the added burden of trying to help keep my clients sane through it all. Still, there are some perks. I have a personal escort.

Jim Nickovich: The Force of Time at Guantánamo

When a detainee agrees to see you, his attorney, he agrees to go through the arduous process of being awoken early in the morning. He is then fully searched and chained on his way to meet you and then chained to the floor awaiting your presence. But your military flight from Washington, D.C., to GTMO is delayed. More of your time has been swallowed. You call ahead and let the military officials know you will not be there, but they move the prisoner—chains and all—in spite of your attempt to cancel the meeting. He waits. Time ticks. You do not show. Trust is ruined. There is no naive expectation that the military guard who chained the prisoner and moved him from his prison cell to the room where he was supposed to meet with you explained that your absence was the result of a delayed flight. You finally arrive at Guantánamo, but it is to no avail. Trust is gone. You have failed. Another weeklong trip made in vain. Time marches on—a week of missed opportunities at the office. It is hard to imagine giving up another week. And then you remind yourself that the detainee has given up seven years of his life. Imprisoned without trial. No judge, no jury. No television. No weddings. No family. No friends. Just the slow passage of time.

GTMO is about time. It takes enormous chunks of it from the lives of the men it imprisons. More than 700 of those men, some now reunited with their families, have given years of their lives to the prison without charge, trial, or any evidence of wrongdoing. It takes time from the attorneys who wish to bring justice to the men imprisoned and from the country that has imprisoned them. GTMO has served the ideological purposes its architects intended. The passage of time is GTMO's strongest ally.

Susan Hu: Trip Diary

April 30, 2007

Our last day of client visits was especially difficult and frustrating. The military told us that one of our clients had refused to see us. Experience has taught the lawyers to question these refusals, but nevertheless, the anxiety and uneasiness lingered all day.

We get only two and a half hours in the morning and then three and a half hours in the afternoon to meet with clients. It is so ridiculous that it is almost funny: two and a half hours every three or four months, sometimes every year or even every five years. As I sat in the room with our other client, I wondered what he went through for this short meeting. A soldier may have woken him up at five or six in the morning, shackled and hooded him, and roughly pushed and dragged him to this room, where he may have been waiting for two hours. Someone may have told him that he was meeting with interrogators, making our presence immediately more suspicious. If he was moved from one camp to another for our meeting, he might have gone through an even longer process, just to sit across the table from us while we talk about what is happening in the courts in Washington, D.C., occurrences so remote and unconnected to his daily life of frustrations and indignities. I wondered whether it was all worth it for these men to have this brief time with us. Were we even helping?

David H. Remes: Calculated Inefficiencies

There are many logistical restrictions on lawyers' access to clients at Guantánamo. The military has built calculated inefficiencies into the system of client visits, including the ban on telephone contact and the restrictions on written communication.

Consider simply the time allowed to lawyers to meet with clients. Over time, the Joint Task Force (JTF) restricted the time available for any given lawyer to meet with his or her clients. Although there was an increase in the number of attorneys visiting clients, JTF responded by severely and disproportionately slashing meeting times.

In much of 2005, at least, a lawyer theoretically could meet with clients as many as seventy hours weekly—ten hours a day if he or she started at eight and ended at six and worked seven days a week. Now, as a rule, a lawyer cannot see clients more than twenty-five hours per week. Although officially a lawyer may meet with clients from nine to eleven thirty and one to four thirty (six hours a day, or thirty hours a week), the actual time works out to about nine thirty to eleven thirty and one thirty to four thirty (five hours a day, or twenty-five hours a week) because of lawyer searches at the sally port and other inefficiencies. By special permission, a lawyer may work through lunch, which may add two hours to a day (seven hours a day, or thirty-five hours a week), but I'm not sure how commonly special permission is granted or for how many lawyers it may be granted on any given day. And lawyers are no longer allowed to meet with clients on holidays.

Nowadays, only three lawyer teams are allowed to visit the base at one time. More teams were allowed earlier. Also, it used to be possible to see three or even four clients in a day; now it is possible to see only two. So not only has the time for client meetings been constricted, but the number of lawyers who may meet with clients in any given day and the number of clients a lawyer may see in a day have also been curtailed.

In our early visits to the camp, the military treated our schedules and more generally our role at Guantánamo with contempt. This contempt took passive-aggressive forms. For example, the military would bring a prisoner to Camp Echo a day or more before a meeting with his lawyer and leave the prisoner in the camp a day or more after the meeting. During this time, the prisoner would be left by himself in a cell, with no contact with other prisoners. The military thus made the prisoner accept solitary confinement to see his lawyer.

The military's mix-ups in arranging our meetings were another example of contempt. Lawyers would sometimes arrive at Camp Echo to meet with their clients, only to discover that their clients had not been brought to Camp Echo to meet them. Often our clients due to meet with attorneys in the afternoon were brought in the morning, or clients due in the morning were brought in the afternoon. On one particular day, I arrived at Camp Echo, only to discover that Client A, with whom I had met at the camp the day before and with whom I was supposed to meet that morning, had been returned to his cell and that Client B, with whom I was also supposed to meet that day, had not been brought to the camp at all and seemed to be missing. I asked the guards to put me on the phone with the military lawyer responsible for habeas counsel visits in Guantánamo. When the lawyer took the phone, I voiced my frustration. Client B was not "missing," he replied. "We know exactly where he is."

These restrictions and conditions also sharply increase translator costs, which are already huge, by making each trip substantially less efficient. Instead of paying a translator for three days, the lawyer must pay the translator for six days; and if a lawyer must make two trips instead of one because of the various restrictions, travel time and costs are doubled. All these inefficiencies increase the cost and difficulty of lawyers' meeting and communicating with their clients, compromise their ability to nurture and sustain the client relationship, and enhance the military's ability to undermine effective representation.

Ellen Lubell: A Shackled Prosthesis

Aziz's right leg ached. When he lifted his tan pant leg to show me, I saw the hard, beige-toned plastic, a white sneaker laced at the bottom. The leg widened upward into a black-banded shank, ending in soft rubber that fit against his skin.

His lower right leg, the real one, had blown off in a land-mine explosion in Kashmir in 2001. He was brought to a hospital in Lahore, Pakistan, to recover. The doctors there gave him a good lightweight prosthesis stamped "Made in Germany." It fit him well, and he had learned to walk with it. At the U.S. military base in Bagram, Afghanistan, a beating by U.S. soldiers left it broken, cracked down the side.

"The interrogators here said they would fix it," explained Aziz, who was meeting with us for the first time. "But after they took it away, they said they would not give it back until I confessed. I would have confessed to anything to get my leg back, but I didn't know what they wanted me to say. For months I went without a leg. Finally, they gave me this one. It's too long and heavy, too hard to walk with, and they don't give me new socks to cover my stump when the old ones wear out."

Aziz pulled the stump out to show us, leaving the prosthetic leg and its shoe still shackled to the floor, alongside the good leg. As I looked at what remained of his right leg, I knew I had come to the heart of a new kind of irony.

"Aziz, we should talk about what we'll need to do to apply for asylum," I said, pulling us back. "The U.S. probably won't consider you for asylum. Our Department of Homeland Security may not even process your application. But if they deny you, we will go with that denial to the United Nations and the European Parliament. We'll show them that the U.S. won't accept responsibility for your resettlement and that some country must be found to take you in."

Aziz nodded.

"We don't know how long this will take or whether we'll succeed, but we should start the application."

He agreed.

For hours we went line by line through U.S. government Form I-589. What elementary school had Aziz attended? Where was his father born? He struggled to remember the dates and details. Items on the form that should have been easy to complete—"Applicant's residence in the U.S."; "List each entry by applicant into the U.S."—were problematic, to say the least, with the question of Guantánamo's status as part of the United States or Cuba still under active debate in the courts. "Staple your photograph here" was impossible. Bring a camera to the prison? Ask the military for a snapshot?

"We'll work on the application," I promised him, pulling papers together. "We'll write to let you know when it's complete and ready to be filed. We'll need statements from experts—affidavits. We'll let you know what we can find."

The allotted time for our meeting was nearly over. The guards would come soon to escort us out and take Aziz back to his cell.

Doris Tennant: Terrorist Bake Sale

On January 29, 2007, a national news article, headlined "Potshot at Guantánamo Lawyers Backfires," publicized the nationwide backlash against a high-ranking government official's remarks about volunteer attorneys representing GTMO detainees. Cully Stimson, the Deputy Assistant Secretary of Defense for Detainee Affairs, urged chief executives of the firms' corporate clients to make their lawyers "choose between representing terrorists or representing reputable firms." The article described the vehement and widespread criticism that Stimson's statements sparked. Major companies issued statements supporting "vigorous advocacy for even the most unpopular causes." My law partner Ellen and I were interviewed for the article because the reporter had heard about our two-person firm raising thousands of dollars in donations—partially through a bake sale—to defray the costs of our representation of a detainee. Friends and colleagues just happened to have received our fundraising letter the week that Stimson's remarks aired, and the many notes included with the donations made it clear that they viewed his criticism as yet another reason to give generously. I was quoted in the article, describing the donors' response as "quite an outpouring."

At about 1 p.m. the day after the article appeared, we received an e-mail from the Department of Justice lawyer who had several weeks before given us approval to travel to Guantánamo for the first time to meet our client. His tone was noticeably matter-of-fact as he suggested that the visit coordinator "may have mentioned" a document required prior to our visit—a signed representation regarding the sources of any counsel fees. He noted the recent article about our fundraising efforts, which he admitted were understandable "given the costs associated with litigating Guantánamo cases." However, he also recognized the "amount of time needed to conduct the due diligence necessary to complete the financial representation form." But not to worry—all we had to do was to let him know if we needed "to reschedule [our] trip to have enough time to complete that due diligence."

We could similarly offer him assurance. We advised him that we would comply that very day, so duly diligent were we in concluding that none of our work was funded by terrorists. All our funding came from people Ellen or I knew personally. We signed a declaration that our work was not funded "directly or indirectly by persons or entities we believe are connected to terrorism or the product of terrorist activities, including 'Specially Designated Global Terrorists,'" identified in President Bush's order of September 23, 2001.

Over the last three years, we have been the grateful recipients of contributions from hundreds of people and entities who not only are not connected to terrorism but who support the criminal prosecution of alleged terrorists by application of the rule of law. Naturally, the representation form we signed, requested by a government that had declared a panoply of laws irrelevant, didn't ask us to go that far.

Chuck Patterson: Bureaucratic Bullshit

When I first began my representation of detainees at Guantánamo, I found that the detention camps were a joint project of the DOJ, the DOD, the CIA, and the armed services, overseen by a micromanaging White House. I suspected that I was entering the perfect storm of bureaucratic bullshit. I was right.

1. I first applied for security clearance in December 2006. I had held both secret and top-secret clearances in the Marine Corps. My application was returned several times for minor clarifications (Is your mother's maiden name spelled correctly?) and was not accepted until April 2007. I applied to visit Guantánamo in September 2007 and was told I had no clearance. I applied in November and December with the same result. I finally got there in February 2008.

2. I asked for a joint visit in March 2008, together with military defense counsel for our detainee. I then found out that the command had denied a joint visit by habeas and commission counsel on the basis that they were responsible for different things. I had to cancel the March trip because we wanted a joint meeting. I wrote a request to the Staff Judge Advocate (SJA) of the JTF who had refused the joint meeting and was directed by him to the DOJ. Ten days later the DOJ said to take it up with the DOD. The DOD said they would get back to me. I received a call from the DOD saying I could not travel to GTMO because I had no security clearance. I pointed out that my clearance form from the last visit said that I did. They said, "That was based on what you told us, and that does not appear to be the truth." The next day they e-mailed back to say that it appeared I did have a clearance, but would I mail them a copy of the letter granting the clearance? Of course, I had never received one, so I asked for a copy. None came. The DOD advised me by e-mail as I was about to board my plane to GTMO that the decision would be made by the SJA of the command, and I would probably hear the decision when I got off the ferry after traveling to the base and trying to see my client. When I did get off the ferry, my escort said, "I understand that you have a joint meeting with your client and commission counsel this morning. Is that correct, Sir?" The perfect storm.

3. Coincidentally, about the time I first asked to go to GTMO I was told when checking in for a domestic flight that I was on the Department of Homeland Security (DHS) watch list. I found a site on the Internet with the forms to contest being placed on the watch list. I complied with the requirements. A month later, I got a letter from the DHS

saying that they had checked records with appropriate other agencies and that if there was a correction warranted, they had made it. I had no further problems until I returned to the United States after I had the disputed joint meeting with my client and commission counsel. The immigration officer looked at my passport, told me to wait a minute, left, and came back with a supervisor. They advised me that I was on the DHS watch list.

4. Before going down to Guantánamo on my last trip, the DOD again said I had no clearance. I referred them to their e-mail in which they said I had clearance. I again asked for a document showing I had a clearance. I heard nothing from them and went ahead for the visit (again a joint visit). When I arrived back in Florida, I found an e-mail dated that day saying that I had been issued a clearance and that my trip (from which I had just returned) was approved and I could go. I asked them to give me the date my clearance was granted. They replied "6 August 2007." See no. 1 above. I spend more time dealing with "them" than I do with my client.

Amal Bouhabib: Loyalty

From the outset, I knew that the process of applying for security clearance to visit my client at Guantánamo would be grueling. As a thirty-one-year-old law student, my past ten years—the required span for investigation—have been anything but perfunctory. Since graduating from college in 1999, I have moved over twenty-two times, twice to a country in the Middle East; I've worked as a journalist, a researcher for a nonprofit, and a freelancer; I've written op-eds condemning the Iraq war and criticizing the Bush administration, attended protests and organized peace vigils, all before enrolling in law school at age thirty. Needless to say, the task of tracking down old addresses, domestic and abroad, as well as the names and contact information of former colleagues, associates, friends, neighbors, landlords, etc., was daunting. It's also profoundly paranoia inducing—and not just for me. The special investigators, after all, have to meet everyone listed in the application in person. Several of my friends expressed concern that that they were now "in the system," worried that their participation in a demonstration or neglect to pay taxes one year could now somehow come back to haunt them. I for one agonized for days about whether discussing an ex-boyfriend's psychological issues with a school therapist counted as "seeing a therapist" within the meaning of the application—a question for which a wrong answer could result in either a monetary penalty or time in jail.

But despite my early anxieties, I greatly underestimated the challenge of the one feature I thought would best serve my client: my heritage as an American Lebanese. My mother is American and my father is Lebanese. They met at Vanderbilt University while he was getting his Ph.D. My twin brother and I were born in Alexandria, Virginia, along with my little sister. I chose to move to Lebanon in 1999 to work as a journalist, have some adventure, and get to know some of my father's family. I don't speak Arabic very well because it's a difficult language and we never spoke it at home. My first job was as a hostess in a Georgetown barbeque restaurant, and to this day, in my spare time, I sing in a folk-country band.

If I sound defensive, it is because it is nearly impossible to "prove" how American you are, as an American. Yet this is exactly what the U.S. government asked me to do. I was one of two students at Fordham Law School granted permission by the government to apply for security clearance. We both sent out our applications within days of each other in mid-July 2008. One day in November the other student received a call saying she'd been cleared. That same day I got a call from a special investigator—not the one who had interviewed me the first time around—saying that there was a problem with my foreign passport. (I have a Lebanese passport as a birthright through my father, who is also an American citizen). The special investigator told me that I would have to bring in a copy of both passports and warned me that he was going to have to bring me a paper asking me to renounce my dual citizenship.

Just to be clear, the "problem" with my Lebanese passport was the mere existence of it. And the request to renounce it was the remedy. I don't know if I can accurately express the outrage I felt at this request. Giving up my passport would be akin to disavowing my father and my father's family—I would legally be a stranger in my father's home country; I would lose my inheritance rights; and travel to see my family would be considerably harder. The idea that my connection to another country somehow made me less American than every other lawyer applying for clearance appalled me—not to mention the sheer inanity of the demand. It is purely symbolic to sign a paper for the United States renouncing citizenship. What could it prove that they hadn't already uncovered in their months of investigation into my finances, school records, tenancies, friendships, work life, and romantic relationships?

By the time I met with the special investigator I had already spoken to him a few times, and he was highly sympathetic. He apologized for putting me in this position more than once and said that, as a Muslim, he had been through his own share of racial profiling at the hands of the government. At one point, because he was so apologetic, I assured him that this was probably routine for all persons of dual nationalities. He replied that no, in fact it was not, and that he had other dual citizens—from Australia and other countries—to whom this request was not made. He actually made me laugh when he told me in all seriousness that he had considered refusing to make me sign the pledge but worried that the "higher-ups" might think there was a conspiracy between us because he is Muslim and I am Arab. And he had worked for the government for over twenty years!

I didn't sign the pledge. We went through my passport together, and I answered more questions that were mostly the same as ones on the application. One new question asked, "Which country do you feel most loyal to?" He handed me the request to renounce my dual citizenship, which gave me two options: give up my former country (which did not apply) or renounce citizenship to the dual country. In the alternative, I could write a statement explaining why I could not do so. In retrospect, I now wonder if I should just have signed the damn thing and been done with it, but I don't think I could have. There is something so degrading about being presented with such a request, and I don't think I could have looked at my father again with pride, even if it meant nothing.

So I wrote a statement. I started by saying that I was American first and foremost, that I was born and raised in the United States, that Lebanon was an ally of the United States, that giving up my Lebanese passport would mean forfeiting my legal rights to inheritance, and that my decision not to do so in no way undermined my loyalty to the United States. My special investigator asked me to read it to him, and I did. Somewhat oddly, I broke down while reading it. Under the most relaxed of situations, in the least coercive setting possible, under no threat of any real injustice or mistreatment, I found it profoundly painful and insulting to have to defend myself to my own country.

That was over a month ago, and the semester is now coming to an end, with still no clearance. Over the past few months, I've written to my client, drafted media pieces and motions for the court on his behalf, and examined his facts, all without meeting him or seeing what the government has against him. But with a new president, it seems equally possible that my client will be sent home before I ever get the chance to meet him.

Yasmin Zainulbhai: Zoom Out for a Broader Look: An Unclassified Tale

Perhaps it is natural that fragments of our representation would appear in my dreams. In January 2008, just a few weeks into my work as a law student intern with the Fordham International Justice Clinic, my sleep was occasionally invaded by a strange jumble of images: overhead views of the U.S. Naval Station at Guantánamo Bay, Cuba, orange jumpsuits, mountains of legal documents. Later in the semester I would find myself unsurprised by this sort of occurrence; in fact, my dreams would become more specific, reflecting the everyday workings of our clinic. So it was perhaps inevitable that around April, I began to find myself particularly haunted by a set of information that carries a great amount of weight in Guantánamo litigation, and to which I have no access: classified information.

We currently represent two clients at Guantánamo Bay. While we have been fortunate to participate in the litigation, we have faced an additional obstacle to those faced by every habeas lawyer: law students are barred from applying for security clearance. Since 2005, the Department of Justice has refused to permit law students to apply for security clearance, effectively denying us access to a large portion of the allegations against our client and ensuring that we are unable to visit our clients at Guantánamo Bay. It sounds unthinkable, and yet, for the many law students working on Guantánamo litigation, this is a fact of our representation.

Given this obstacle, we gleaned information from wherever we could. Instinctively, we turned to our trusted and often-searched source of information: Google. One day early in the semester, as we struggled to grasp the complicated and difficult history behind the Guantánamo detentions, we went to GoogleMaps and typed in "Guantánamo Bay." First, a text bubble appeared, asking us if we would like directions to Guantánamo Bay. Out of curiosity, I tried this. I typed my New York address into the address bar and received this message in response: "We could not calculate driving directions between this address and Guantánamo Bay NAS Station, Cuba."

We then clicked on "satellite image." The image was clear, providing an overhead, satellite image of barren-looking land, curving around a blue bay. Boats, with white wakes behind them, dotted the water. The scene appeared peaceful; it was only upon scrolling to the right that a jumble of buildings and roads appeared. This is what we were looking for—this is the detention center, the camps. A zoom bar on the side invited us to explore more closely. We zoomed in, clicking again and again, as though this would give us a better glimpse of what lay inside, perhaps some insight into what life is like for our clients. Finally, we focused in on a group of buildings and clicked to zoom in further. Suddenly, however, the image went blank, and a message appeared: "We are sorry, but we don't have imagery at this zoom level for this region. Try zooming out for a broader look."

Although we were not surprised by this message, it also felt particularly disappointing. Zooming out was the opposite of what we were trying to do. We were trying to zoom in—to learn specifics, about what life is like for our client, about why the government keeps him at Guantánamo. Sadly, there was information that even Google, our trusted friend, could not provide.

And so, classified information took on near mythical importance in our minds. It was as though, tucked away somewhere in a folder stamped "classified" in huge black letters, were the answers to all our questions. In late March, several months into our time at the clinic, our team began work on a document, compiling information and organizing it into a chart. The purpose of this document was simply to aid our representation, to organize and focus our work. The going was slow and tedious and required that we read through a large set of documents. The night after we had finalized the document and sent it out to other Guantánamo counsel, I had a strange dream. I dreamt that the entire document we had just completed had actually been done before, but that it had been deemed classified. Since we had no access to classified information, we had just re-created work that had already been completed by other counsel. Of course, this wasn't actually the case, but still, the dream made me wonder: Were we overestimating the importance of classified information? Does it really contain the answer to why our client is still detained at Guantánamo Bay? The difficulty is that we can't truly know the answer to this question— without access to classified information, it's impossible to assess its true weight.

We will continue to be haunted by the strict control on information that pervades every aspect of Guantánamo litigation, and by everything that the U.S. government does not permit us to know.

Marjorie M. Smith: The Other Man

In early 2005, Mohammed Hassen informed me that another detainee, Mr. Hazi Ahmed, was requesting legal assistance to challenge his detention at Guantánamo. Hassen told me that Mr. Ahmed was in his forties, quite ill, and suffering from severe pain that required him to take several dozen pills a day. After learning of the case, I filed a habeas petition on Mr. Ahmed's behalf on April 1, 2005.

In early July 2005, Judge Richard Roberts, before whom Mr. Ahmed's case was pending, ordered that both the court and I be given a minimum of thirty days' notice before Mr. Ahmed could be transferred from Guantánamo. The court also ordered the DOD to provide me with the facts on which the government based its decision to hold Mr. Ahmed at Guantánamo. Inexplicably, the DOD responded by providing a factual response for a different detainee, a man named Fawaz Naman Hamoud Abdullah Mahdi. When I questioned the DOD about the obvious difference, the DOD insisted that Mr. Mahdi was Mr. Ahmed and suggested that the information provided by Mr. Ahmed's friend was inaccurate.

On August 22, 2005, I was finally given clearance by the DOD to meet with my client for the first time. Upon my arrival, the military police produced Fawaz Naman Hamoud Abdullah Mahdi, a twenty-five-year-old young man who was not on pain medication and who emphatically denied ever being known as "Hazi Ahmed." Without a doubt, Mahdi and Ahmed were not the same person; the DOD had produced the wrong detainee. In the process, the DOD revealed that they had been holding detainee Mahdi incommunicado for more than three years. Mr. Mahdi took advantage of his first opportunity to communicate with a lawyer and immediately signed an authorization so that I could represent him.

I then again asked the government to produce my original client— Mr. Hazi Ahmed—for his scheduled interview. An hour and a half later, the base command responded that their records indicated that a detainee, "Haji Mohammed Ahmed," had been moved from Guantánamo earlier that year, but they refused to provide any information about where they had transferred him.

George M. Clarke III:
Top-Ten Most Depressing and Frustrating Sights in GTMO

10. Knowing your client cannot stand up because he is shack-led to the ground

9. That alcohol (a bad thing most prisoners don't want) is not prohibited in the camps but tobacco (a bad thing most of them do want) is

8. "Honor Bound to Defend Freedom"

7. Having your client teach you how to open and drink from a juice box without a straw and then teaching it to your four-year-old when you get home

6. Military commissions

5. The phrase "we regret we cannot accommodate your re-quest at this time"—implying, contrary to all objective in-dications, that the request stands a snowball's chance in hell of being granted at a later time

4. Having the military escort tell you, once again, that you will be meeting your client in Camp Six because "that's affirma-tive, sir, he's still in there"

3. Your client's face when you leave

2. Feeling the sun in your face as you leave Windward on the fast boat—knowing your client cannot do either

1. The American flag flying above it all

The No-Hearing Hearings: Combatant Status Review Tribunals

One of the main ways the government continued to try to circumvent habeas corpus and deny Guantánamo detainees their day in court was by creating sham military "status" review hearings. Those hearings helped institutionalize a legally and morally bankrupt system of indefinite detention without charge or due process.

Thomas P. Sullivan: "Due Process" at Guantánamo

The *Rasul* decision by the Supreme Court was announced on June 28, 2004. Nine days later, the Department of Defense put into place a new, unique administrative process, to be held before panels named Combatant Status Review Tribunals (CSRTs). The CSRTs were designed deliberately to prevent the meaningful court review that is secured by habeas corpus. The prisoners were refused access to a lawyer, were not allowed to see most of the evidence against them, and were denied the right to call witnesses in their favor or cross-examine their accusers. The CSRTs also routinely relied on evidence garnered through torture and other coercion. In addition, the CSRTs were pervaded by "command influence," and the tribunal members were pressured from above to reach the preordained outcome, finding that the detainees were "enemy combatants."

The CSRT hearings were held between August 2004 and early 2005. Out of nearly 600 prisoners, almost ninety-five percent were found by the CSRTs to be properly classified as enemy combatants and, as a result, could be held without charge or trial indefinitely, potentially for life.

The CSRTs consisted of three officers, with the senior of the three officers being denominated tribunal president, none of whom was identified by name, rank, serial number, or otherwise. The prisoners did not have their own lawyers. A "personal representative," also not identified except by that title, participated in the hearings. It was this person's function to advise and assist the prisoners in responding to the tribunal's inquiries. The personal representatives were functionaries of the tribunals. They were not lawyers and did not act as the prisoners' advocates; they made no arguments on the prisoners' behalf and sometimes even made statements contrary to prisoners' interests. The CSRT regulations expressly provided that "no confidential relationship exists between the detainee and the Personal Representative."

Also present was a recorder, whose identity was also not disclosed. The regulations provided that the recorder had "a duty to present to the CSRT such evidence in the Government Information as may be sufficient to support the detainee's classification as an enemy combatant, including the circumstances of how the detainee was taken into custody of U.S. or allied forces," and "[i]n the event the Government Information contains evidence to suggest that the detainee should not be designated as an enemy combatant, the Recorder shall also provide such evidence to the Tribunal." However, whatever evidence the recorders accumulated about the prisoners was not revealed during the portions of the CSRT hearings that the prisoners were permitted to attend. Clients' CSRT summaries and classified files typically contained no information about how the prisoners were taken into custody and no evidence to show whether they were or were not enemy combatants. These portions of the recorders' presentations, if they exist, were not made available either to the prisoners or their lawyers.

During the first portion of the CSRT hearings, which the prisoners were allowed to attend, interpreters were present; they were required because most prisoners neither spoke nor understood English, the language in which the proceedings were conducted. A provision in the regulations that states, "The Tribunal is not bound by the rules of evidence such as would apply in a court of law," was superfluous, because no evidence was presented to the tribunal during the portion of the hearing attended by the prisoner, save only for the prisoners' own statements, as described below. The "allegations" (sometimes referred to as "accusations")—a few terse declarative sentences—were read, and the prisoners were asked to respond. No evidence or witnesses were presented in support of the accusations. Hence, the prisoners had no opportunity to confront witnesses or view documentary evidence. The tribunals were also permitted to consider evidence obtained through torture and secret evidence to which the prisoners had no access. With rare exceptions, the prisoners were not afforded an opportunity to call witnesses, and in the few instances in which they were given that opportunity, the witnesses were fellow inmates.

As illustrated by the examples that follow, if the prisoners asked the tribunal for details of the allegations, which were stated in short, conclusory form, the tribunal members responded that they neither prepared nor had information about them. The following examples are taken verbatim from four CSRT transcripts, eventually obtained through the habeas cases or under the Freedom of Information Act:

RECORDER (READING THE ALLEGATION): While living in Bosnia, the Detainee associated with a known Al Qaida operative.
DETAINEE: Give me his name.
TRIBUNAL PRESIDENT: I do not know.
DETAINEE: How can I respond to this?

RECORDER (READING THE ALLEGATION): Detainee is a close association [sic] with, and planned to travel to Pakistan with, an individual who later engaged in a suicide bombing. [Name] possibly is the Elalanutus suicide bomber.
DETAINEE: Where are the explosives? What bombs?
RECORDER (TO TRIBUNAL PRESIDENT): Sir, I don't believe I can answer in this session.

TRIBUNAL PRESIDENT: I certainly cannot answer because this is the first time I have seen this evidence. It is my understanding that anything remaining concerning this individual [name] is in the classified session.

When the tribunal president explained that a government exhibit, an FBI letter, must remain redacted, the detainee asked, "If they are classified, what if they are incorrect?" The detainee was concerned about his fate if the documents presented were not correct. He wanted to see the classified documents.

TRIBUNAL PRESIDENT: The classified information cannot be shown to you due to national security reasons. By you participating today, we want to hear your story as well [sic]. We haven't seen any information prior to this. We will take everything into consideration.

TRIBUNAL PRESIDENT: As to the second request, you asked us to check with the Saudi police in [city]. It could prove you were on a humanitarian mission while on leave.
DETAINEE: Yes.
TRIBUNAL PRESIDENT: I denied that request as well, because an employer has no knowledge of what their employees do when they are on leave.

The prisoners were often asked to answer the allegations, but no information or evidence was adduced by the tribunal to support or explain the allegations. In short, the proceedings involved nothing more than the recorders reading terse, unsupported accusations, followed by requests to the prisoners to respond if they chose and examinations by tribunal members about the prisoners' explanations. When these exchanges ended, the open sessions were closed, the prisoners were removed, and the tribunal members met behind closed doors.

H. Candace Gorman: Do-Overs

Mr. Abdul Hamid Al-Ghizzawi has never been charged with anything, nor has he ever been told what he is accused of doing, nor has he been given the opportunity to prove his innocence. In his first CSRT, Mr. Al-Ghizzawi was found not to be an enemy combatant. This finding was apparently unacceptable to the higher-ups, and the military did a "do-over"

CSRT six weeks later. The government claimed that after almost four years of captivity, it had suddenly found new information during that six-week period. This was, as my mother would say, a bold-faced lie. I have seen the classified transcripts of the CSRT proceedings, and I know that no new information surfaced. The only new factor in the do-over tribunal was a new (and more compliant) panel of military judges. The new panel took the same information as the first panel, classified it as secret, and claimed it was new evidence. The predictable result: Mr. Al-Ghizzawi was found an "enemy combatant." The same pattern was repeated in other cases.

Note this declassified portion of an e-mail chain between officials responsible for ordering the do-over:

> Inconsistencies will not cast a favorable light on the CSRT process or the work done by OARDEC [Office for the Administrative Review of the Detention of Enemy Combatants]. This does not justify making a change in and or [sic] itself but is a filter by which to look. . . . By properly classifying them as an enemy combatant, then there is an opportunity to (1) further exploit them here in [G]TMO and (2) when they are transferred to a third country, it will be controlled transfer in status.

Stephen E. Abraham: Inside the CSRTs

The three-member panels of the CSRTs typically ran concurrently. There were three panels a day, and each processed four detainees a day, six days a week, for a total of seventy-two detainees a week. From September 2004 until March 2005, nearly all the CSRTs for Guantánamo detainees were conducted.

I am a lieutenant colonel with twenty-two years of experience as a military intelligence officer, and I have served both on active duty and as a member of reserve components. During that time, I was assigned to the Office for the Administrative Review of the Detention of Enemy Combatants (OARDEC), which oversaw the CSRT process. Prior to my assignment to OARDEC, I served for one year as a lead counterterrorism analyst for the Joint Intelligence Center, Pacific Command, for which I was decorated. I also came to OARDEC with more than ten years of experience as an attorney.

While at OARDEC, in addition to other duties, I worked as an agency liaison, coordinating with various government agencies to gather or validate information relating to detainees for use in the tribunals. In that capacity, I was asked to confirm that the agency did not possess "exculpatory information" relating to the subject of the hearing. I also served as a member of a tribunal and had the opportunity to observe and participate in all aspects of the CSRT process.

Considerable emphasis was placed on completing the hearings as quickly as possible. The only thing that would slow down the process was a finding that a detainee was not an enemy combatant. These conditions encouraged tribunal members and other participants in the process to find the detainees to be enemy combatants.

On one occasion, I was assigned to a CSRT with two other officers. We reviewed evidence presented to us regarding the status of Abdullah Al-Ghizzawi, a detainee accused in the unclassified summary of being a member of the Libyan Islamic Fighting Group.

There was no credible evidence supporting the conclusion that Al-Ghizzawi met the criteria for designation as an enemy combatant. What were purported to be specific statements of fact lacked even the most fundamental hallmarks of objectively credible evidence. Statements allegedly made by percipient witnesses had no detail. Reports presented generalized, indirect statements in the passive voice without stating the source of the information or providing a basis for establishing the reliability or the credibility of the source. Material presented to the panel provided no evidence that the detainee was an enemy combatant. Questions posed by members of the tribunal yielded no answers but instead yielded frustration, the product of a complete absence of factual support for the government's case.

On the basis of the paucity and weakness of the information provided both during and after the hearing, we determined that there was no basis for concluding that the detainee should be classified as an enemy combatant. The validity of our findings was immediately questioned. We were directed to reopen the hearings, to allow for additional evidence to be presented. Ultimately, in the absence of any substantive response to our questions and no basis for concluding that additional information would be forthcoming, we adhered to our determination that the detainee was not an enemy combatant.

The response to this determination was not acceptance but rather a suggestion from my superior officers that I had done something wrong. I was not assigned to another tribunal panel.

I concluded that the CSRT process was little more than an effort to ratify the prior exercise of power to detain individuals in the "war on terror" while paying lip service to the Supreme Court's mandate that the detainees were entitled to a fair hearing. The tribunal process was designed to validate detentions that the executive branch believed it should not have to justify, could not be bothered to justify, or could not justify.

I subsequently learned that two months later, a second CSRT hearing had been convened for Mr. Al-Ghizzawi without his knowledge or participation. The new CSRT reversed my panel's unanimous determination that he was not an enemy combatant. I also learned that this panel also reconsidered and reversed the findings as to another detainee. It appeared to me that this particular panel was convened precisely for the purpose of overturning prior favorable findings.

George Brent Mickum: A Meaningless Opportunity

I was the second habeas counsel allowed to travel to Guantánamo. At that time, many prisoners, including my clients, Bisher and Jamil, had yet to appear before the CSRTs. I wrote to Bisher and Jamil more than one month before traveling to Guantánamo in September 2004, advising them not to appear before the CSRT or participate in the process. My letters were not delivered until after each had participated in his tribunal, a fact that is unquestioned and memorialized in records released by the military. The military's failure to deliver my letters was no oversight: my letters were delivered the day after each prisoner's CSRT hearing took place. The inescapable conclusion is that the military read letters that were protected by the attorney-client privilege.

I advised my clients against participating in the process because the CSRTs were a sham. They were permitted to rely on information obtained under torture. Equally important, none of my clients had a meaningful opportunity to defend himself, confront evidence, call witnesses on his behalf, or have an attorney present. Although Bisher and Jamil never were anywhere near Afghanistan or Iraq, never were involved in any unlawful activity, and never possessed a weapon of any kind, they were powerless to defend themselves against the charge that they associated with Abu Qatada, "a known al Qaeda operative," who has never been charged with any crime or shown to be involved in al Qaeda.

At Bisher's CSRT, he testified under oath about his relationship with the United Kingdom's domestic intelligence service, MI5, and his role as a liaison between MI5 and Abu Qatada. He also testified that MI5 had expressly approved of his role: "During a meeting with British Intelligence,

I had asked if it was okay for me to continue to have a relationship with Abu Qatada. They assured me it was." Bisher specifically asked that the three MI5 agents who had traveled to Guantánamo appear as witnesses to confirm his work with MI5 and Abu Qatada. Recognizing the obvious importance of such testimony, the CSRT "determined that these three witnesses were relevant" and instructed the military prosecutor to make inquiries to determine whether the British government would make the witnesses available to confirm Bisher's account. The British government not only refused to allow the witnesses to appear but also refused to confirm the accuracy of Bisher's account, effectively consigning Bisher and Jamil to indefinite imprisonment.

Later in the proceeding, the CSRT issued the following clarification: "The British government didn't say they didn't have a relationship with you, they just would not confirm or deny it. That means I only have your word for what happened."

Jamil's CSRT hearing was so procedurally defective that it would make good farce if the result were not so devastating. The only evidence against Jamil that the tribunal considered was that Jamil drove Abu Qatada's wife and son to visit him. The evidence against Jamil was so tenuous that Jamil's CSRT hearing was postponed three times and reconvened four times, to allow the military's prosecuting attorney to obtain and present additional evidence to the tribunal. At the conclusion, Jamil's personal representative, a nonlawyer who could be compelled by the tribunal under its regulations to provide testimony against Jamil, took the extraordinary step of formally dissenting from the tribunal's conclusion: "The Personal Representative states that the record is insufficient to prove that the detainee is an enemy combatant."

Marc D. Falkoff: Without Law or Justice

November 19, 2004. I am sitting in an interview cell—really, a retrofitted storage container—in Camp Echo at Guantánamo Bay. Across the table, Adnan sits with his arms crossed and his head down. The guards have removed his handcuffs, but when he shifts his weight his leg irons clang and echo in the bare room. The irons are chained to an eyebolt on the floor. Guards are stationed outside the door, and a video camera is visible in the corner.

Adnan is a small, thin man with a scraggly beard. He looks pale. He looks weak. He has been dressed in a pullover shirt and cotton pants that are dyed iconic GTMO orange.

"I see they're keeping you shackled," I say, shaking my head, trying to communicate that the precaution is unnecessary. My interpreter translates my words into Arabic.

Adnan looks up and smiles briefly, acknowledging the obvious. But he does not meet my eyes.

Adnan has been in this prison for nearly three years, since January 2002. He is only thirty, but he looks much older. He bows his head and stares at his ankle cuffs again.

He doesn't trust me, I write in my notebook.

· · ·

I have been Adnan's lawyer for several months, although Adnan himself doesn't know this until our first meeting. One of my tasks is to explain to him how I came to be his lawyer—and how he and a group of Yemeni detainees ended up suing the President of the United States.

I tell Adnan of the recent Supreme Court decision, *Rasul v. Bush,* that held that the detainees were entitled to their day in court. I tell him of our difficulties in finding out the names of the prisoners, since the military has kept their identities secret for three years. We had learned the names of our Yemeni clients, I explain, only when their families showed up at a human rights conference in Sana'a, the capital of Yemen, seeking help. I explain to Adnan that initially the Pentagon refused to allow lawyers to visit Guantánamo, insisting that our meetings with our clients be monitored and videotaped. I tell Adnan that we convinced a judge that such monitoring would be a gross violation of the attorney-client privilege, and I tell him that eventually we were given the green light to meet with our clients, unmonitored.

We both look up at the video camera in the corner of the interview cell. "They assured me it's off," I say, and we both chuckle.

Finally, I tell Adnan that the government claimed the right to hold him in Guantánamo, without charge or trial, for the duration of the "war on terrorism." Because this "war" is based on an inchoate idea, it could go on indefinitely. For Adnan that means he could be held in this prison forever.

Neither of us is laughing now.

· · ·

to: Personal Representative
from: Officer in Charge, CSRT

Summary of Evidence for Combatant Status Review Tribunal.

The United States Government has previously determined that the detainee is an enemy combatant. This determination is based on information possessed by the United States that indicated that he was a fighter for al Qaida who engaged in hostilities against the United States or its coalition partners.

   a. The detainee is an al Qaida fighter:
      1. In the year 2000 the detainee reportedly traveled from Yemen to Afghanistan.
      2. The detainee reportedly received training at the al-Farouq training camp.
   b. The detainee engaged in hostilities:
      1. In April 2001 the detainee reportedly returned to Afghanistan.
      2. The detainee reportedly went to the front lines in Kabul.

•   •   •

After I finish speaking, Adnan talks to me. He tells me that during his first three years in Guantánamo, he has been interrogated hundreds of times—no charges, no hearings before a judge, only endless interrogations. Then, a month ago, he was brought before a "status" hearing, at which he was accused of being an al Qaeda fighter and of manning the front lines against the Northern Alliance, the United States' newest ally.

I tell Adnan that I saw the "charges" a few weeks earlier, after we successfully asked the court to order the government to provide its explanation for why he was being held in captivity. I tell him that when I first saw the accusations, I thought they looked serious but that when I looked at the government's evidence, I was amazed. *There was nothing there.* Nothing at all trustworthy. Nothing that could be admitted into evidence in a court of law. Nothing that was remotely persuasive, even leaving legal niceties aside.

"*I* haven't seen any of the evidence," Adnan says. "How can I begin to refute it?" He's right. He's never been allowed to see the evidence against him, paltry as it is.

Like all but a handful of the more than 750 detainees who have been held at Guantánamo, Adnan has never been charged with a crime. The only hearing Adnan has ever received was his CSRT hearing, convened to decide whether he was an "enemy combatant." Adnan saw none of the evidence against him. He wasn't given the names of witnesses whose statements would be used against him. He wasn't allowed to challenge witness statements on grounds that they were hearsay or that their statements had been tortured out of them.

And I am not allowed to show him the evidence either, even though I've seen it. All I can do is learn his story, in his own words.

•   •   •

"My case is very clear," Adnan begins.

He had been in an automobile accident in 1994 while serving in the Yemen military, he explains. The accident caused serious head trauma and left him with inner-ear problems and persistent head pain. For the next half-dozen years, he found himself roaming from hospital to hospital and country to country, seeking inexpensive medical care: Yemen, Jordan, Pakistan. Eventually, an acquaintance told him about the health-care office of a Pakistani aid worker living in Afghanistan. Adnan, a man from the desert, considered himself self-sufficient and strong. But his family was poor, and his medical needs were serious. He accepted the Pakistani's charity and thus found himself in Afghanistan in late 2001.

Then history caught up to him. The 9/11 tragedies. The Americans' bombing runs against the Taliban. Like all Arabs caught in Afghanistan, Adnan fled for the border.

Adnan becomes more animated and more frustrated as he narrates his story. "I've told this story hundreds of times to the interrogators. Why don't they listen?"

•   •   •

Combatant Status Review Tribunal
    Summarized Sworn Detainee Statement

DETAINEE: Why have I been here for three years? Why have I been away from my home and family for three years?
TRIBUNAL PRESIDENT: That is what we are trying to determine today.

DETAINEE: Why did you come after three years? Why wasn't it done much sooner after my arrest?

TRIBUNAL PRESIDENT: I cannot answer to what has happened in the past. I was asked to come here now, and I came.

DETAINEE: Why am I not allowed my freedom here?

TRIBUNAL PRESIDENT: Because you have been classified as an enemy combatant.

DETAINEE: How can they classify me an enemy combatant? You don't have the right documents.

TRIBUNAL PRESIDENT: That is what we are here to determine.

DETAINEE: For three years I haven't been treated very well because of wrong information. Would you let that happen to you? What will be your position if you find out what happened to me was based on wrong information and I am innocent?

TRIBUNAL PRESIDENT: Your current conduct is unacceptable. If you keep interrupting the proceedings, you will be removed and the hearing will continue without you.

·   ·   ·

Adnan breaks into metaphor. He describes himself as a caged bird. He sits silent for a moment. Then suddenly his sentences fly out from him in hasty bursts. His words are like caged birds themselves. They throw themselves at the bars of the cage and tumble back in a flapping frenzy.

"Why doesn't the military check my hospital records? Where is the evidence that I ever held a gun in Afghanistan? Why don't they find the medical documents?"

·   ·   ·

MEMORANDUM

FROM: Legal Advisor

TO: Director, Combatant Status Review Tribunal

SUBJ.: legal sufficiency review of combatant status review tribunal for detainee isn #156.

1. During the hearing, the detainee requested that the Tribunal President obtain medical records from a hospital in Jordan. He alleged the records would support his story that he went to Afghanistan for medical treatment.

The Tribunal President denied the request. He determined that, since the detainee failed to provide specific information about the documents when he previously met with his Personal Representative, the request was untimely and the evidence was not readily available. After reviewing the evidence in the course of the Tribunal, the Tribunal President further determined that even if the medical records did exist and contained the information described by the detainee, the information was not relevant to the issue of whether the detainee is properly classified as an enemy combatant. . . .

2. The proceedings and decision of the Tribunal are legally sufficient and no corrective action is required.

•   •   •

The tribunal was not interested in Adnan's medical documents, but I was. His brother sent them to us, and they provided strong support for his explanation for his presence in Afghanistan.

From the Islamic Hospital in Amman, Jordan: "The patient was admitted under my supervision to the Islamic hospital on 07/09/1994 following a head injury. He was suffering from aches and a headache. A clinical test showed blood concentration and hemorrhage above the left eye, and a hole in the left eardrum. The x-ray test showed a broken skull but no brain injury."

From the Yemen Ministry of Defense's "Military Medical Decision Form," dated July 10, 1995: "Diagnosis: 1. Loss of sight in the left eye as a result of eye nerve damage. 2. Loss of hearing in the ears."

From the Al-Thawra General Hospital's "Medical Report," to the Yemen Ministry of Public Health, dated August 18, 1999: "The above-named is hard of hearing. Upon examination, a wide circular hole was detected in his left eardrum. The attached audiography revealed a hearing loss in the left ear. We recommend that he return to the previous center outside for more tests and therapeutic and surgical procedures at his own expense. This is to whom it may concern."

•   •   •

Adnan and I discuss his Combatant Status Review Tribunal, and we agree that it has been a farce.

Adnan didn't know it at the time, but I was already his lawyer in October 2004, when the hearing took place. But I was not allowed to attend. Instead, Adnan was given the assistance of a "personal representative." By regulation, the personal representative had to be a military officer. By regulation, the personal representative could not be a lawyer. If the personal representative had had any legal training, he would have been disqualified from helping Adnan.

Adnan would have been better off without him.

After meeting with Adnan for just eighty-five minutes in preparation for the status hearing, the personal representative wrote an unsolicited letter to the Status Review Tribunal. Adnan was never told of this letter. He was never given a chance to rebut the unflattering portrait of him painted by his own (quasi) lawyer.

·   ·   ·

DETAINEE ELECTION FORM
PERSONAL REPRESENTATIVE: LTCOL [redacted]
PERSONAL REPRESENTATIVE COMMENTS:
No witnesses. Rambles for long periods and does not answer questions. He has clearly been trained to ramble as a resistance technique and considered the initial [interview] as an interrogation. This detainee is likely to be disruptive during the Tribunal.

·   ·   ·

Perhaps if Adnan had a real lawyer at his hearing—one who had not acted as an unsworn witness against his own client—he would have received a fairer hearing. As it turned out, though, the panel was unwilling even to make sure that Adnan understood the charges against him.

·   ·   ·

Combatant Status Review Tribunal
Summarized Sworn Detainee Statement

TRIBUNAL PRESIDENT: Personal Representative, tell us what the Detainee told you yesterday. . . .
PERSONAL REPRESENTATIVE: . . . He said he did not live in al Qaida. This is a case of mistaken identity.
DETAINEE: That is not correct. . . . I am from Orday City in Yemen, not a city in al Qaida. My city is very far from the city of al Qaida. . . .
TRIBUNAL PRESIDENT: al Qaida is not a city. It is the name of an organization.
DETAINEE: Whether it is a city or an organization, I am not from al Qaida. I am from Orday City.
TRIBUNAL PRESIDENT: Are you from Yemen?
DETAINEE: Yes, I am from Orday.

·   ·   ·

I tell Adnan that back in October, when I had first read the unclassified transcript of his Combatant Status Review Tribunal, I was confused by this discussion of "al Qaida City." I had opened an atlas and looked up cities in Yemen.

Sure enough, there it was: al Qaida City, in the Baladiyat Adan region of Yemen, at thirteen degrees north latitude and forty-four degrees east longitude.

I tell Adnan that I had understood. Al Qaida is pretty darned far from Orday City.

·   ·   ·

I ask Adnan how he was taken captive.

He tells me that he was trying to get to the border of Pakistan so that he could make his way to the Yemen embassy and, from there, back home. With bombs dropping everywhere, Afghanistan was dangerous for everyone. But it was especially dangerous, Adnan was told, for Arabs. The Americans were on the lookout for any Arabs in the country.

Adnan arrived at the border town of Khost and made his way through the rough terrain into Pakistan. Almost immediately, however, Pakistani forces picked him up, along with about thirty other men who looked Arabic. Most turned out to be Yemenis. He eventually learned that each of them had been sold to the U.S. military for a bounty of $5,000.

A British historian, Andy Worthington, later explained to me how the Pakistanis ended up detaining these thirty men. Hundreds of al Qaeda fighters, he tells me, escaped from their position in the Tora Bora mountains after the Americans began a long-distance bombing campaign against them. But American military intelligence was unaware that there were *two* routes out of Tora Bora—one down to Khost and the other across the White Mountains. The Americans were focused on the Khost road, oblivious to the actual escape route of the fighters. When the Pakistanis seized the thirty Arab civilians passing through Khost, therefore, the Americans touted the capture as a successful roundup of al Qaeda soldiers. In fact, the hundreds al Qaeda forces from Tora Bora had escaped clean through the mountains.

·   ·   ·

November 20, 2004. My second meeting with Adnan. The leitmotif of our conversation is the uselessness of lawyers.

Yesterday, I'd left Adnan with a folder clearly marked "Attorney-Detainee materials. Privileged & Confidential." I told him that the guards are not allowed to read any of the documents inside but that he is obligated to keep nothing but legal papers in the envelope. He said he understood and placed his notes from our meeting in the envelope.

Today, Adnan tells me that the guards confiscated his folder. He believes they've read all the documents inside. He wants to know of what use I can be to him if I can't even prevent the military from reading his privileged materials.

This was not the last time that Adnan's legal materials were confiscated during the years I have represented him. After three detainees committed suicide in June 2006, the military responded by confiscating every document from every detainee in the camp—looking for evidence, in part, that lawyers had something to do with facilitating the suicides. All of Adnan's papers were taken and never returned.

I tell Adnan that we will make sure the guards understand the rules and that if necessary we will try to get the court to intervene. But I know—and I tell Adnan—that judges are rarely willing to interfere in the day-to-day management of a prison and that we're going to have to choose our battles.

•   •   •

Sometime during our second day together, I begin to feel that Adnan and I have connected. He's still skeptical of my value to him, and he is refusing—for now—to sign the document letting the Department of Justice know that he wants my firm to represent him.

But we're developing a rapport. We're engaged in a spirited back-and-forth about the rule of law, and he's downing a remarkable number of the Filet-O-Fish sandwiches that I've brought him from the Guantánamo McDonald's. The fast food is a welcome change from his bland diet—overcooked chicken and rice, barely ripe fruit, inedible vegetables—that he has grown used to over the past three years. I tell Adnan that I'm surprised the military has let us bring the food in. He tells me that it's not unheard of. Interrogators give out McDonald's food as a reward to prisoners for cooperating during interrogations.

Our discussion turns to the separation of powers in the U.S. government and to the role of the courts. Adnan pauses and asks to borrow my notepad. We take a break from talking. In flowing Arabic script, he begins composing a lengthy letter.

I watch and wait for him to finish. Something about the way he leans over the paper seems odd but familiar. Then I figure it out. Adnan is right-handed, and in order to keep the ink from smearing his Arabic text—which is written from right to left—he has to contort his body.

"So, what's that?" I ask finally, nodding at the paper. He smiles and tells me to have it translated when I return to the States.

Several weeks later, I'm in the "secure facility" in Virginia, near Washington, D.C. This is where, by court order, our clients' letters and the notes from our meetings are stored. Anything our clients communicate to us, the military had convinced the court, could pose a potential national security threat.

A linguist translates Adnan's letter for me. In it, Adnan thanks me for volunteering to represent him and tells me that God will reward me.

He also suggests that I convert to Islam—as a safeguard against the hellfire. I can't help but chuckle at this last part, but I'm moved by the trust he's placed in me.

•   •   •

April 9, 2005. I'm visiting Adnan again, this time accompanied by another lawyer, Jason Knott. The topic for the day: what will happen if and when Adnan is transferred back to Yemen.

We talk about the likelihood of transfer to a Yemeni prison. We talk about the State Department's annual reports on Yemen and about the country's sketchy human rights record.

Adnan asks us about reports that the United States would move some of the detainees to Saudi Arabia, so that President Bush could get rid of his Guantánamo problem. He's also heard that men might be moved to places such as Jordan or Syria to be interrogated through torture. He feels he can handle anything that the Yemen government's thuggish Political Security Organization is likely to mete out, but he's concerned about the treatment he'd receive in a third country.

We explain that the judge has ordered the government to give us thirty days' advance notice before Adnan or any of our other clients is transferred out of Guantánamo. We explain that we proved to the judge's satisfaction that we had legitimate and well-founded fears that the United States might render our clients to other countries to be tortured. Our notice order would provide Adnan protection and enough time for us to get to the court in case the government tried anything like that.

Everything starts to feel topsy-turvy as I'm talking to Adnan. I have just explained to a man from Yemen that we have credible evidence that *my* government has considered torturing some its prisoners and that a judge has agreed with me that the threat is substantial.

.   .   .

June 18, 2005. I've been coming down to Guantánamo frequently, mostly to keep Adnan and the rest of our clients sane. They have no access to the outside world, no newspapers, no television or radio. They are allowed to send and receive infrequent letters to family via the International Committee of the Red Cross, but the military uses the family letters as leverage to try to get the detainees to talk. Most of the men have stopped writing as a result.

We're not allowed to bring the men news from the outside either, unless it "directly relates" to their cases. The detainees' lawyers have a different understanding from the military about what the phrase "directly relates" means. The military, for instance, believes that news of Supreme Court cases dealing with the rights of Guantánamo detainees does not "directly relate" to any particular detainee's case. Remarkable. We just make our own good-faith determinations and continue to do our jobs.

On this trip, Adnan complains about the water. Many people in the camp, he says, are sick from it. It's hard to know whether his claim is true, of course. All sorts of stories go around in a prison environment. It's good to maintain a healthy skepticism when you're talking with someone who's been incarcerated for a long time.

During this trip, I gather sealed bottles of water from my other clients and bring them back to New York. Both have bugs floating in them.

.   .   .

October 21, 2005. My colleague David Remes visits with Adnan.

Adnan tells David, "This prison is like a hideous ghost. The situation is beyond human comprehension. This place is a vicious jungle, without law or justice."

The CSRTs both failed to provide any credible evidence while preventing detainees from presenting evidence or witnesses on their behalf. In many cases, a simple investigation proved there was no basis for detention.

Jonathan Horowitz: Gumshoeing in Kabul

In early September 2008, a few days after I arrived in Kabul, I sat down in an air-conditioned room at a guesthouse with Abdul Wahab and a high school teacher named Ghuam Sadeeq. Five years earlier, American forces had arrested Wahab's brother, Mohammed Zahir, in a night raid at his home. The United States then shipped him off to Guantánamo, accusing him of being a member of the Taliban and of having control of Taliban weaponry.

I was focusing on Zahir's case because his lawyers, Dan Malone and Peter Ryan from the law firm Dechert, hired my small Brooklyn-based investigation firm, One World Research, to do what the U.S. government should have done far earlier and with greater accuracy: determine which, if any, of the U.S. allegations against Mohammed Zahir and other Guantánamo detainees were actually true.

After landing in Kabul, I called the people whom I needed to speak to, such as relatives, friends, and former colleagues of the detainees who Dan and Peter represented. To my amazement and pleasure, they were easy to reach and agreed at the drop of a hat to travel long distances to see me. I barely had the time to rest my knapsack and computer bag on my bed before I began preparing for my first interviews.

It was my fifth or sixth interview when I spoke to Abdul Wahab and teacher Ghulam Sadeeq. With the video rolling, Abdul Wahab openly told me that his brother was, formally, a member of the Taliban. But he also explained that membership per se reflected little about a man's ideology, hatred of the United States, or links to al Qaeda. He described how the Taliban had forcibly conscripted Mohammed Zahir to be a cook, and he said that his brother wasn't a hardened fighter or ideologue.

When I interviewed Ghulam Sadeeq, a man who taught with Mohammed Zahir at the Mirza Khel High School, he explained that the school was nonreligious, with a curriculum that included math, physics, chemistry, biology, geology, art, and languages. Sadeeq recalled how UNICEF and international military forces supported the school. In short, Mirza Khel High School was just the type of school that the Taliban were, and are, notorious for attacking. The more Sadeeq spoke, the more I saw that his interview cast additional doubt on the U.S. allegations against Zahir. Why would a man who devotes himself to teaching join a group such as the Taliban that destroys schools?

More damning than the accusation that Mohammed Zahir was a Taliban cook was the accusation that he was arrested with Taliban military documents in his house. Records from Guantánamo show that Zahir explained to U.S. officials that the Taliban had passed through his village one rainy night when he was not at home and forcibly gave the documents to his wife for temporary safe keeping. Zahir said that when he returned home and discovered what had happened, he notified the governor, but the governor ignored him. So Zahir hid the package in his yard, where Americans later found it.

To confirm this story, I asked Abdul Wahab if I could interview Zahir's wife. He refused. Asking to speak to a man's wife is a sensitive issue, especially since Zahir is from a very conservative part of Afghanistan. But Abdul Wahab agreed to ask Zahir's wife about the package of documents and then travel back to Kabul to tell me what she had told him. A few days later, sitting again in front of the camera, Abdul Wahib told me, in his sister-in-law's words, a similar chain of events that supported her husband's claim, thus calling into question perhaps the strongest evidence the United States has against Mohammed Zahir.

Another of Dechert's clients, Mohammad Rahim, is accused of, among other things, being a Taliban leader who attended a meeting in a mountainous area in February 2003. Rahim's cousin and neighbor, Haji Zakaria, told me that the accusations were ludicrous, stating that the mountainous area was impossible to reach during the snowy winters from their home in Ghazni Province. Besides, Zakaria said, he was with Rahim during daily prayers and meals during that winter.

When I asked why he thought Rahim was arrested, Zakaria launched into one of the most commonly cited reasons for wrongful detentions in the United States' "war on terror." Zakaria described a land dispute between Rahim's family and another family who had people working with international military forces. It was no coincidence, he said, that Rahim was captured after he undertook legal proceedings to settle the dispute and was about to win the claim.

The evidence files that the United States hands over to Afghan officials when each Afghan detainee is transferred back home added to my doubts that Guantánamo detainees were, as Donald Rumsfeld put it, the "worst of the worst." Sabar Lal, another one of Dan and Peter's clients, had the word "None" marked next to the word "offense(s)" in his file. His file named two witnesses, but the United States had no "potential witnesses," "physical evidence," or "photographs." Fortunately, Sabar Lal is a free man today. But this can't dilute the fact that he lived behind bars for several months in Afghanistan after having been detained for years at Guantánamo on sparse, if not false, information.

It's a reality of war that innocent men and boys find themselves behind bars. Afghans I spoke to understood this and didn't initially blame the United States for mistakenly detaining their relatives or for not knowing the intricacies of Afghanistan's people and culture. They did, however, blame the United States for not fact-checking their information and correcting their mistakes year after year. Afghans didn't take lightly to the fact that poor intelligence led to prolonged detention and, by consequence, the collapse of a family business, physical and mental anguish for the detainee, or food not being put on the family's table.

The reasons why the United States detained the wrong people in its global "war on terror" range from the understandable to the ridiculous. Here's a short list I came up with during three different trips I made to Afghanistan in 2008: the government's reliance on untrained translators who misinterpret what people say to them; the government's use of untrustworthy informants who manipulate the United States into detaining, or killing, rivals; profiteers and bounty hunters who provide the United States with false information and detainees in return for cash rewards; the use of coercive and violent detention conditions that push detainees into providing misinformation just so the abuses can cease; detaining people because they are, or were, low-level members of the Taliban even though the Taliban forcibly conscripted people to fight; and arresting innocent people who have the same, or a similar, name as a person who is a legitimate threat.

In reflection, the work that I and other investigators conducted in Afghanistan and other countries around the world persuaded me to believe that the majority of people who have passed through Guantánamo were held on spurious information. But, admittedly, it's tough to know how many exactly. The United States didn't take seriously its responsibility to gather strong evidence against each person it detained. And while many innocent men were held for years on end, the dirty little secret about Guantánamo is that there's a high probability that the government's haphazard information-gathering practices resulted in at least a few people being set free who truly were serious threats to American security.

With this disturbing reality in mind, and as an investigator, my main concern is that the government's numerous agencies, such as the military, the CIA, and the FBI, need to improve the way they collect and corroborate battlefield intelligence and evidence. That my small investigation firm, in a few weeks, was able to punch gaping holes in the accusations against several detainees with relative ease speaks volumes to the government's lazy and callous attitude toward ensuring it was detaining the right people—and not setting the wrong ones free.

Military Commissions

The military commissions were first established at Guantánamo based on a November 13, 2001, order by President Bush to try suspected terrorists of war crimes. The commissions created a rigged system that denied basic due process protections and allowed for the use of information gained by torture and other abuse in order to obtain convictions. The Supreme Court's 2006 decision in Hamdan v. Rumsfeld *struck down those commissions, finding that they violated both the Geneva Conventions and the Uniform Code of Military Justice. Yet, under pressure from the Bush administration, Congress resurrected the commissions four months later—slightly improved but still fatally flawed. In eight years, military commissions produced only three convictions (none involving persons responsible for the September 11 attacks) and undermined the United States' reputation for justice throughout the world.*

Dwight Sullivan: Commissionland

General Omar Bradley is credited with saying, "Amateurs talk strategy; professionals talk logistics." The experience of attempting to litigate military commission cases revealed that it is logistically impossible to have a fair trial at Guantánamo Bay.

Guantánamo had insufficient courtroom space, housing, transportation, and telecommunications to support complex criminal litigation. It also offered defense counsel inadequate access to their clients. Finally, there was an enormous legal difficulty that prevented trials at Guantánamo from being fair: the inability to subpoena civilian witnesses to appear at commission proceedings held there.

Inadequate courtroom space: From the inception of the commission experiment through 2007, there was only one courtroom for the military commissions at Guantánamo. It is a cramped room in a dilapidated structure that is both rat infested and poked from woodpeckers eating insects from the building's bug-ridden, rotting frame. Conspicuous signs warn against drinking the building's water—which no one would be tempted to do since the water that spews out of the building's faucets is orange. The commission room itself prominently features several load-bearing pillars, resulting in obstructed-view seating reminiscent of Fenway Park. But the most significant problem has been the courtroom's size. When the commission prosecution office wanted to hold a joint trial of three defendants in 2006, it couldn't because the courtroom simply wasn't big enough to accommodate more than one defendant and his lawyers at a time. And with only one operating courtroom, the space limitations produced a choke point that severely limited the number of cases that could be tried.

In 2006, to overcome these limitations, the Office of Military Commissions developed an elaborate plan to build a courthouse complex in Guantánamo at an estimated cost of $126 million. Robert Gates, in one of his first actions after becoming the secretary of defense, wisely killed this proposal. In the fall of 2007, construction got under way to spend $15 million to erect a bare-bones prefabricated courthouse surrounded by a military commission tent city. The new facilities were never fully tested before the military commission system went into yet another hiatus following President Obama's inauguration. But given the military commission system's history, there is little cause for optimism that this would have succeeded in producing a viable venue for trials.

Inadequate housing: Housing space at Guantánamo is severely limited. These limitations affected the counsel who were litigating commission cases, the U.S. military personnel who supported them, and the journalists and handful of nongovernmental organization observers who were permitted to attend. Limitations on housing directly interfered with the ability of military commission defense counsel to perform their duties. The U.S. military will not issue a country clearance to travel to Guantánamo Bay unless the individual has confirmed housing available. On several occasions, the Office of Military Commissions' chief defense counsel was directed to limit the number of defense counsel traveling to Guantánamo, particularly when commission proceedings were scheduled, due to a housing shortage.

Inadequate transportation: Traveling to and from Guantánamo is difficult. Although two commercial carriers fly to Guantánamo, during my time in the Office of Military Commissions, commission personnel were prohibited from using them because of safety concerns. So the only way for a commission counsel to travel to or from Guantánamo was aboard one of the limited number of U.S. military flights. Because of those flights' relative infrequency and points of origin far from Washington, D.C., in practice almost every trip to Guantánamo took at least four days. Because commission defense counsel were not allowed to talk to their clients over the telephone, any time an attorney needed to consult with a client about any matter—even if the conversation would take only thirty minutes—the attorney had to devote at least ninety-six hours to accomplish that task. The resulting negative effects on case preparation are obvious.

For example, during the March 2007 hearing in *United States v. Hicks*, more than ninety individuals flew from the Washington, D.C., area to Guantánamo aboard at least three different military flights to participate in or observe the commission proceedings. The only trial participant who was in Guantánamo before the hearing was the defendant, David Hicks. Moving that one individual to the United States would have been far more economically efficient than flying dozens of individuals back and forth from Maryland to Guantánamo for every military commission hearing.

Inadequate telecommunications: Both telephone and computer services were extremely limited in Guantánamo. The limited number of telephone lines that reached the United States were generally of poor quality and usually featured a delay that made it difficult actually to converse. The computer network's bandwidth was extremely limited. And the overly aggressive JTF-GTMO Internet filters often prevented access to websites that were necessary to prepare for trial. Worse still, it was impossible for civilian defense counsel to use the JTF-GTMO computers at all.

Inadequate access to the client: JTF-GTMO imposed unnecessary limitations on the number of hours that a military attorney could meet with a client and on what could be done during those limited meetings. Contrary to practice at most U.S. military detention facilities, where a military defense counsel can essentially meet with his or her client at any time and on any day when the counsel needs such access, JTF-GTMO strictly limited attorney visits to three hours in the morning and four hours in the afternoon, Mondays through Fridays. Weekend and evening visits were generally not permitted.

JTF-GTMO also interfered with the attorney-client relationship by applying inappropriate restrictions on the information that defense counsel could share with their clients. In the case of *United States v. Khadr*, for example, JTF-GTMO officials refused to allow defense counsel to share with the defendant any of the prosecution's evidence in the case. It is simply impossible to prepare for a complex criminal trial without being able to review such materials with the client. The Military Commissions Act of 2006 expressly requires that the defendant be given an opportunity "to examine and respond to evidence admitted against him on the issue of guilt or innocence and for sentencing." Yet JTF-GTMO's operating procedures made it impossible to do so. This not only prevented the defense team from preparing for trial but also undermined the attorney-client relationship. It is hard enough for a U.S. military lawyer to win the trust of a foreign national who has been detained at Guantánamo Bay for many years without due process. It becomes harder still when the defense counsel tells the detainee that he or she has information about the detainee's case but can't share it with him.

JTF-GTMO has also refused to allow detainees to meet with mental health experts working with the defense counsel. The Military Commissions Act provides that "[t]he accused in a military commission under this chapter has the burden of proving the defense of lack of mental responsibility by clear and convincing evidence." How can the defense ever carry that burden if it is not allowed to have a mental health expert examine the defendant? And JTF-GTMO severely limited the number of people who could be in a cell with a detainee at one time. Given the necessity of having a translator present when talking with many clients, this has often prevented members of the defense team from participating in critical attorney-client meetings.

Legal limitation: In addition to these practical matters, there is a fundamental legal limitation that arises from the commission system's location in Guantánamo: compulsory process is not available to subpoena a civilian witness to attend a commission proceeding. As the discussion to the Rules for Courts-Martial explains, "A subpoena may not be used to compel a civilian to travel outside the United States and its territories." In light of the U.S. government's position that Guantánamo Bay is not U.S. territory, it is apparent that neither the prosecution nor the defense will be able to subpoena witnesses to appear at a military commission. This problem is exacerbated because in the military commission system, the prosecution can present its case entirely through hearsay evidence. It is essential for the defense to have an ability to subpoena prosecution witnesses so that they can be confronted and cross-examined about their allegations. But holding the commission trials in Guantánamo extinguishes that ability.

In testimony to before a House subcommittee on March 29, 2007, Secretary Gates said,

> [B]ecause of things that happened earlier at Guantánamo, there is a taint about it. And it's one of the reasons why I had recommended or pressed the issue of trying to get the trials moved to the United States, because I felt that no matter how transparent, no matter how open the trials, if they took place at Guantánamo in the international community, they would lack credibility.

That assessment is correct. But trials at Guantánamo do not merely *appear* unfair; they *are* unfair.

Yvonne R. Bradley: A Rigged Process

In the spring of 2005, U.S. Air Force headquarters sent out an e-mail announcement seeking JAG volunteers interested in working at the Office of Military Commissions (OMC). Although the e-mail announcement offered little information about the position, the job appeared to be one of great opportunity and interest. After briefly thinking about whether to volunteer, I did so.

Several months later, in November 2005, I received a telephone call from the chief defense counsel of the OMC. He called to inform me that I had been selected for a position in the defense office and that he had the perfect case for me. I was then appointed to represent a detainee named Binyam Mohamed, who had been charged with war crimes and would be tried by the commission courts.

I peppered the chief defense counsel with various questions about the commission process. He answered my questions the best he could but seemed unsure about how the process would operate and how the trials would proceed. At the time I did not realize that the commission process was so new and untested that no one knew how any of it would work. Looking back, this should have been my first clue that something was amiss: I was assigned to defend an individual accused of committing a major war crime in a so-called judicial system that was not yet fully established.

I soon learned that rules, regulations, and procedures were being written and implemented before the ink on the paper had a chance to dry. Imagine trying to litigate a major war crime case with schizophrenic rules and procedures. I also quickly learned that the only goal of the military commission system was to establish a rigged court that would guarantee convictions. The entire process was maddening. I often found myself questioning whether the people in charge cared about the Constitution, due process, and the rule of law.

Prior to my appointment as military defense counsel, Binyam Mohamed was represented by civilian defense counsel, Clive Stafford Smith, who had represented Binyam for several months before my appointment. Clive had a wealth of information about our client and provided me with a copy of the charges and other materials. After I first read the charge sheet, I thought the allegations were a joke; I actually laughed. I reread the charge sheet several times, looking for a substantive war crime. I could not find one but saw that there was only one long, complex conspiracy. No murder offense, no mass killings, no death of civilians, no destroyed buildings. Not a single offense that I thought warranted trying Binyam as a war criminal. If the United States was going to try a person in the first war-crimes tribunal since the Nuremberg trials half a century ago, Binyam's case had no business being on the list. This was a sick joke.

There were several other issues that continued to bother me the more I read.

First, how was the government to prove any of the alleged charges in the conspiracy? I could not imagine anyone from al Qaeda taking the stand and testifying for the government. I did not know at the time that the rules and regulations of the military commission would simply be allowed to nullify and suspend the rules of evidence, due process, and the Constitution in order to avoid the need for real and reliable evidence at trial.

Second, it made no sense that Binyam, a non-Arab-speaking Westerner who had recently converted to Islam, was in the inner circle and upper echelon of the al Qaeda organization. Names on Binyam's charge sheet read like a who's who of the supposed al Qaeda membership list: Osama bin Laden, Khalid Sheikh Mohammed, Jose Padilla ("dirty bomber"), Richard Reed ("shoe bomber"), Abu Zubaydah, etc. If Binyam, a janitor and former heavy drug user from London's West End, could make his way to the top of the al Qaeda organization in nine months and dine with the most wanted terrorists in the world, why had the U.S. intelligence agencies been unable to find bin Laden and company and get inside the organization? It appeared that the government was simply throwing mud at the wall to see what would stick, and anything with Osama bin Laden's name on it was likely to fit the bill in a rigged military court.

Another puzzling fact on the charge sheet was that Binyam was arrested at the Karachi airport with an airline ticket to London. He was not picked up by American or coalition forces on a battlefield. Things were just not adding up, and I quickly had concerns about the legitimacy of any of the facts in the conspiracy allegation. If Binyam was an example of a top bad guy, then the entire "war on terror" was being oversold to the American public and the world.

After reading through a lot of material and rereading the charge sheet to exhaustion, the next logical step was to meet Binyam Mohamed. At Clive's suggestion, we left for our travels to Guantánamo Bay, Cuba, the day after Christmas. The first day that Clive and I were scheduled to see Binyam, we decided that Clive would visit Binyam alone. We were unsure how Binyam would react if I walked into the visit unannounced to tell him that I had been assigned as his military counsel without his knowledge or consent. We were also especially concerned about how he would react toward a military attorney representing him, given that he repeatedly said that he had been tortured and mistreated by U.S. officials including the CIA, the FBI, and military guards.

Binyam described in detail how, after being rendered to Morocco and Afghanistan by American officials (before he was taken to Guantánamo), he was tortured, abused, mistreated, and drugged for years. Binyam's torture included being cut on his penis, being kept in pitch-black rooms for weeks, being held in stress positions with his arms stretched over his head for days on end, and being forced to endure weeks of loud, blaring, non-stop music and sounds of others being beaten and tortured. Sometimes his food was drugged; other times he was deprived of food and water. He was also forced to defecate and urinate on himself. And with a gun pointed at his chest, officials threatened to kill him.

Binyam gave Clive the okay for me to visit. I dressed in civilian clothes rather than in my military uniform to distinguish myself from the guards and to establish some type of trusting relationship. I am not sure who was more apprehensive and nervous during the visit, Binyam or I. Admittedly, Binyam had every reason in the world to be apprehensive and anxious. After all, I was a U.S. soldier, and I represented the American military system that had abused and mistreated him. Moreover, my presence could be another Guantánamo trick. It had been reported that interrogators occasionally pretended to be lawyers to trick detainees into talking, including by promising to send them home if they cooperated and spoke to them. Therefore, Binyam rightfully had reason to be nervous about my visit.

I, on the other hand, should not have been nervous or apprehensive, but I was. Here I was, a seasoned former death-row attorney who had sat face to face with dozens of convicted murderers and serial killers, nervous and afraid of Binyam Mohamed, not because he had been convicted of any wrongdoing but simply because he had been labeled a terrorist. I suddenly realized the ugly power of fear, labeling, and misinformation. I realized how propaganda could be used to keep people fearful and the truth hidden.

I left my visit with Binyam with an entirely different set of emotions. I felt confused, angry, mad, and bewildered. I realized in a span of three or four hours that very little if anything I had been told about Binyam as a terrorist detainee and about Guantánamo was probably true.

During our meeting, I said very little, but I observed everything. Every little detail in Binyam's body language, gesture, action, voice, tone, reflection, demeanor, and behavior negated every single thing I had been thinking and had been led to believe about him and about Guantánamo. Binyam was not a big bad terrorist, not "the worst of the worst," not a mad man, not al Qaeda, and not a jihadist. Binyam was simply a man who wanted to be left alone and returned to London.

On October 20, 2008, all commission charges against Binyam Mohamed were dismissed without prejudice by the Convening Authority. However, within minutes of learning that the charges had been dismissed, the prosecutor called and stated that Binyam would be recharged within thirty days. Apparently, the government had dismissed Binyam's charges as part of a political ploy to "clean up" any taint that emerged when the leading prosecutor on Binyam's case suddenly resigned from the office. This was now the fifth or sixth prosecutor to leave the office in protest and then to critique the system as unfair.

In addition, about two weeks prior to the dismissal of the commission charges, the Department of Justice, in Binyam's habeas corpus case, inexplicably dropped all major charges including the allegations of the "dirty bomb plot" and plans to bomb buildings inside the United States. The DOJ suddenly dismissed charges after a federal judge ordered the government to provide the defense with requested discovery and exculpatory materials.

Finally, on February 23, 2009, after seven years in custody, Binyam Mohamed was released from Guantánamo without trial and without a conviction. Ironically, he was flown to freedom from Guantánamo to the United Kingdom on the same type of Gulfstream aircraft that the CIA commandeered from Jeppesen Dataplan to fly him across the Middle East for torture and rendition. The U.S. government neither apologized to Mr. Mohamed for improperly detaining him for seven years and stealing seven years of his life nor recognized or admitted its role in his torture and rendition.

Muneer I. Ahmad: Commission Law

The military commissions were a crude parody of a justice system. For years, they took place in a former dental clinic at Guantánamo that had been redecorated with plush carpeting, blue velvet curtains, and mahogany furniture so as to mimic a courtroom. Under the original military commission system, there was no judge, and yet the presiding member of the commission wore a black robe and carried a gavel. The rules of the commission were promulgated, on a rolling basis, by at least three different bodies within the Pentagon, and the rules changed constantly. Indeed, the hastily constructed nature of the commission room mimicked the substantive deficiencies of the system. Defendants were promised that the system would be "full and fair," yet evidence obtained through torture was initially admissible. A rule change midcourse ended this practice, but even then, evidence obtained through cruel, inhuman, or degrading treatment remained admissible. Double and triple hearsay was also admissible, and the government could use secret evidence and close proceedings to the public at will. There were no rules of discovery, no rules of decision, and no rules of precedent. The commissions masqueraded as law—indeed, we were told to refer to the ever-changing body of rules as "Commission Law."

In light of the shallowness of the system, one of our litigation goals was to expose the deception, to pull back the mask and reveal that what lay behind was not a system of justice but a political will to produce convictions. We openly decried the commissions as a sham, mocked the lack of rules and regularity, and sought to dramatize the illegitimacy of the system. Our consistent argument was that the trappings of law—gavels and blue velvet curtains—were substituting for a truly fair system.

In the process of exposing the illegitimacy of the military commissions, in our client Omar Khadr's eyes, we tore the mantle of legitimacy from law itself. Although habeas corpus proceedings in Washington, D.C., had gone on for over a year prior to the first military commission hearing in Omar's case, in January 2006, the commission hearing was the first legal proceeding of any kind that Omar had ever witnessed, much less participated in as a party. And although the experienced observer could see easily through the artifice of the commissions, for Omar, brought to Guantánamo when he was age sixteen, this was the only legal system he had ever seen or known. The commissions, then, came to represent for Omar not the perversion of law but its operation. Our advocacy helped Omar understand how the terminologically and ritualistically rich discourse of a courtroom could mask, soften, and plausibly deny the operation of political power, thereby preserving the prevailing power relationship in which the government held not merely all the cards but all the guns.

Indeed, through the commissions, Omar experienced exactly how an elaborate, well-dressed, and well-spoken system could, under the claim of law, disregard, and thereby sanction, his treatment at Guantánamo. Among the first experiences he had in the commissions was watching the presiding officer chastise me for having claimed repeatedly that Omar had been tortured. By doing so, the presiding officer argued, I had impugned the reputation of the government and thereby of the prosecution. Here was a system of law that found a defense allegation of torture distasteful—uncollegial—while leaving unexamined the underlying practices of torture, enacted on the body of the young man sitting before it. To Omar's ear, and indeed to mine, the voice of law sounded unmistakably like that of his captors and torturers.

Joe McMillan: The United States on Trial

The first trial by military commission in the so-called "war on terror" took place at Guantánamo in July–August 2008. The accused was Salim Ahmed Hamdan. Hamdan had been captured in Afghanistan in November 2001 and incarcerated at Guantánamo since late April 2002. He was charged with the alleged war crimes of "conspiracy" and "providing material support for terrorism," primarily on the basis of his admitted conduct in serving as a driver and auto mechanic for Osama bin Laden from 1996 until the fall of 2001.

The initial effort to try Hamdan before a military commission was scuttled in June 2006, when the U.S. Supreme Court struck down the military commission scheme established unilaterally by the executive branch (pursuant to President Bush's military order of November 13, 2001).

The Bush administration quickly mobilized to revive its plan to conduct trials by military commissions, introducing draft legislation into Congress for that purpose in September 2006. By mid-October 2006, without the benefit of any public hearings, and just prior to breaking for the midterm elections, Congress passed the Military Commissions Act of 2006 (MCA). This statute provided the legislative approval that had been missing from the president's initial scheme. Although there were a few additional procedural protections for defendants (for example, the right not to be excluded from his or her own trial), the statute largely endorsed the pretrial and trial procedures that had been put in place under the original plan promulgated by Defense Department regulations.

New criminal charges were sworn out against Mr. Hamdan in April 2007. In addition to "material support for terrorism," the original charge of "conspiracy" was reasserted, despite the fact that a plurality of the Supreme Court had determined that no such offense existed under the laws of war.

I first met Mr. Hamdan at Guantánamo in mid-April 2007, after traveling two days from Seattle to get to the base. After obtaining security badges, I proceeded to Camp Iguana, where I was ushered into a plywood hut with several chairs and a worn-out sofa pulled up to a single table in the middle of the room. Sitting at the table was Mr. Hamdan, in beige prison garb, with a shackle around his ankle secured to a large eyebolt in the floor. I was there with one of my co-counsel, a paralegal from the Office of the Chief Defense Counsel, and our translator. Mr. Hamdan looked exhausted and wary, not at all like the one precapture photograph of him that I had seen previously. The swearing of charges meant that his case was likely to move forward quickly. In addition to introducing me and reporting on procedural status, the purpose of our visit was to discuss generally the manner in which we proposed to defend Mr. Hamdan at trial. Unfortunately, we did not make much progress during that first visit. The isolation in which Mr. Hamdan had been held for months, and the continuing uncertainty and stress of his indefinite detention, made it virtually impossible for him to focus on substantive matters. After an initial period of rather disjointed discussion, which did not succeed in coming to grips with the many pressing issues that needed immediate attention, we were forced to sit silently with Mr. Hamdan as he struggled to contain his emotions arising out of the conditions of his confinement and the apparently hopeless situation in which he found himself. It was immediately clear to me that there were huge obstacles to overcome before any effective defense could be presented—obstacles that did not merely arise from the muddled state of the law embodied in the MCA, or from the paltry discovery provided by the government, but from the psychological condition of our client.

By May 2007, Mr. Hamdan's charges had been referred by the convening authority, and a military judge had been appointed to preside over his trial. The arraignment was set for June 4, 2007. In May, during my second trip to Guantánamo, we filed our initial motion in the criminal case, a motion to dismiss for lack of personal jurisdiction. Pursuant to the MCA, military commissions have jurisdiction only over "unlawful enemy combatants," and the CSRT findings on which the government wholly relied to establish that status made no mention whatever of "unlawful" combatancy. The government argued, in essence, that the language of the MCA itself, as well as presidential findings, established that captured Taliban and al Qaeda fighters were "unlawful enemy combatants" by definition.

I argued this motion before the military commission on the afternoon of June 4, 2007, immediately following Mr. Hamdan's arraignment.

To my great surprise, that very morning the military judge in the case of Omar Khadr had relied on the exact same arguments we had advanced in our motion to dismiss the charges against Khadr for lack of jurisdiction. In doing so, the judge acted *sua sponte,* as Mr. Khadr at that point was without counsel representing him before the military commission. In the afternoon session in the Guantánamo Bay courtroom, I argued that the government had failed to make the showing of personal jurisdiction necessary to allow the case to proceed. The military judge delivered an oral ruling in favor of the defense, dismissing all charges against Mr. Hamdan without prejudice.

Thus began a roller-coaster ride that was to last at least through the end of 2008 (and that indeed, as of this writing, is not entirely over). Later in 2007, the newly appointed Court of Military Commission Review overturned the trial judge's decision and reinstated the charges. Ultimately, the military judge ruled that Mr. Hamdan's capture in proximity to a battlefield, with evidence of weapons in his possession, was sufficient to establish his unlawful combatant status and permit the case to move forward. He rejected defense arguments that there was no showing of participation in hostilities and that, even on the evidence adduced by the prosecution, under Article 4 of the Third Geneva Convention, Mr. Hamdan should be entitled to prisoner-of-war status as a civilian authorized to accompany armed forces.

There followed seven months of intense litigation over legal flaws with the charges, the government's evidence, and the military commission system itself. The defense also renewed efforts (largely unsuccessful) to obtain adequate discovery from the government, including, for example, the right to interview the so-called high-value detainees (HVDs) who were alleged co-conspirators of Mr. Hamdan. Direct access to those detainees was never afforded to the defense, though the military judge did permit written questions—duly screened by a security officer—to be submitted. Ultimately, several of the HVDs responded in writing, providing exculpatory evidence that was later submitted at trial.

By early February, the defense also filed a motion seeking relief for Mr. Hamdan from the harsh conditions of confinement that were interfering with his ability to assist in his own defense. The debilitating conditions under which Mr. Hamdan was being held were on display most dramatically during a hearing in late April 2008. The parties had gathered at that point to address a number of defense motions, including most notably a motion to dismiss due to "unlawful command influence" and a motion seeking a ruling on the date of the start of the "war," which would have the effect of excluding evidence and dismissing specifications based on "pre-war" conduct. Although we got through the unlawful command influence argument, we never made it to the start of the war issue. Instead, on the second day of proceedings, Mr. Hamdan leaned forward and spoke into the microphone at counsel table: "Your Honor, this is Hamdan. . . . May I speak to you for a few minutes?"

The military judge readily assented. Mr. Hamdan continued:

> Last night I told you that I did not want to come to this court, be-cause there is no such thing as justice here. The law is clear. The law in America is clear. The international law is clear. If you ask me what the color of this paper is, I will tell you the color is white. You say, no, it's black. I say white. You say black. I say, fine, it's black. Then you say, no, it's white. This is the American government. Do you understand what I have just said, your Honor?

Thus began one of the most remarkable events I have ever witnessed in a courtroom: a colloquy between the prisoner and the military judge that lasted thirty to forty minutes, characterized by the utmost courtesy, personal consideration, and restraint on both sides. Mr. Hamdan asked how, despite winning a case in front of the Supreme Court, he could still be subjected to a legal proceeding that deprived him of basic rights:

> These words are not directed to you personally; I am talking about the American government. . . . If you want to try me, you can try me be-fore the civil law, with any law that is recognized. It has been four years now that we are in this court. . . . We fought to the Supreme Court and the Court made a decision. Then the government went to the Con-gress, and they changed the law. Why did they change the law? Just for my case?

The military judge responded to this appeal for justice with great hu-manity, expressions of understanding, reassurances about the right to a fair trial, and explanations about the procedures that would play out over the coming weeks:

> I understand your frustration, Mr. Hamdan. I know that you have been held as a detainee for six or seven years now. I know that the

government has tried three times to try you for the offenses it believes you committed. Twice they have done it wrong. . . . I believe you are entitled to a fair trial. I want you to have a fair trial.

The military judge also urged Mr. Hamdan to allow his lawyers to defend him before the commission:

Mr. Hamdan, I think you should have great faith in American law because you have already been to the Supreme Court of the United States, . . . and the Supreme Court of the United States said to the president: "You cannot do that to Mr. Hamdan." And you were the winner. Your name is printed in our law books. You beat the United States once, in our system with these attorneys here with you today.

At the end of this extraordinary exchange, however, Mr. Hamdan respectfully told the Court that he would not return and that he would not permit his defense team to defend him in his absence. In addition, he initially refused to speak with defense counsel following that hearing. We flew back to the United States not knowing whether we would be allowed to continue our efforts on Mr. Hamdan's behalf. At that point, trial was one month away.

There followed a period of great uncertainty as to whether any meaningful trial would occur. Would the government present its case unopposed? Would it forcibly compel Mr. Hamdan to attend the trial? Would defense counsel be required to sit mute in the courtroom? In the face of these questions, we were able to obtain a continuance of the trial to await the Supreme Court's decision in another case, *Boumediene v. Bush*, which could have significant implications for Mr. Hamdan's case. In the meantime, I returned to Guantánamo with my co-counsel and partner, Harry Schneider. Thankfully, we were successful in our objective of persuading Mr. Hamdan that his best interests required that we be permitted to defend him.

Ultimately, after a three-week trial at Guantánamo, Mr. Hamdan was acquitted of the more serious conspiracy charge and convicted of one count of material support for terrorism. The commission members, after hearing all the evidence (including an unsworn statement from Mr. Hamdan during the sentencing phase in which he apologized if, unwittingly, he had done anything to injure anyone), imposed a sentence of sixty-six months' confinement, having been informed by the military judge previously that Mr. Hamdan would be given credit for pretrial confinement of sixty-one months and eight days. Thus, the sentence amounted to less than five additional months of confinement. The military judge addressed himself to Mr. Hamdan at the end of the last day of trial, after the commission members had been dismissed. He said, in substance, "I do not know what is going to happen, Mr. Hamdan. But I hope that after you serve your sentence you are able to return to Yemen to be reunited with your family, to live peacefully, and to support your wife and daughters."

"*Inshallah*," said Mr. Hamdan, standing at counsel's table.

"*Inshallah*," said the military judge, from the bench.

After the commission members and judge had retired, and as three U.S. marines escorted him from the courtroom, Mr. Hamdan turned one last time to address those still in the courtroom (defense counsel, the prosecution team, the press, and others). Waving both hands in the air and smiling broadly, he said, "Bye-bye, everybody!"

The question then became whether the government would in fact release Mr. Hamdan after the completion of his sentence, or whether it would continue to hold him as an alleged "enemy combatant" in the "war on terror." Our inquiries to the government on that point were not answered until, in late November 2008, we were abruptly told that Mr. Hamdan would be returned to his native Yemen, "to serve the remainder of his sentence." Within seventy-two hours of our receiving that message, and after one hastily arranged phone call with us, Mr. Hamdan was on a flight to Yemen.

In the second week of January 2009, Mr. Hamdan was released from the custody of Yemeni authorities, and reunited with his family, including the seven-year-old daughter he had never met. His ordeal at Guantánamo is over, but there remains for him the challenge of recovering his health and rebuilding his life and relationships in his native land.

David H. Remes: Confessing to Freedom

Ironically, as a result of being convicted for aiding terrorism, Salim Hamdan left Guantánamo sooner than he would have if the government had charged him with a terrorist offense in federal court. When I visited my clients at the prison in December 2008, they told me that the prisoners were delighted for Salim but outraged that they, who were charged with no offense, remained imprisoned, while Salim, who was convicted of aiding terrorism, was set free. One client remarked that if he had known things would turn out so well for Salim, he too would have confessed to being Osama bin Laden's driver.

David Frakt: The Circus

I am a law professor and a JAG officer (military attorney) in the U.S. Air Force Reserve. In January 2008, I received an e-mail from Air Force JAG headquarters. The Department of Defense was looking for volunteers to defend detainees at Guantánamo facing trial by military commission. I decided to volunteer and in late February was selected for the position. I was assigned to take over two clients' cases that had already been referred to trial. The military judge was eager to get the cases moving again and set arraignments on both cases for the following week.

I met Mr. al Bahlul for the first time on May 2. From the beginning, he made it clear to me that he had no intention of accepting the assistance of an American military lawyer. He was al Qaeda; I was the enemy. Although he was cordial when we met, more often than not he refused even to meet with me when I went to the detention camps. After his initial refusal, I would prepare a letter to him and have it translated by my interpreter. The prison officials would then bring the letter in to him. Sometimes this would work, and he would then allow us in. Sometimes he would refuse even to accept the letter.

Mr. al Bahlul refused to see me prior to his arraignment. He was in a holding cell outside the giant new courtroom that had been constructed especially for the trial of the alleged 9/11 co-conspirators. His arraignment was to be the first test of the multimillion-dollar, high-tech "Expeditionary Legal Center." In the holding cell, he told me that he wanted to represent himself, that he intended to boycott the proceedings, and that he did not wish me to sit with him or say anything on his behalf. The new courtroom had six rows of defense tables, so I told him that I would sit at the second table and that he could sit in the front row by himself, unless the judge ordered me to sit with him. I informed the judge of this arrangement prior to the hearing, and he gave me permission to sit apart from my client.

The test of the new courtroom turned out to be a complete flop. The arraignment was plagued with technical difficulties with the audio and video equipment. The microphone at the judge's bench was working only intermittently. The judge got so fed up with it that he rose from the bench and wandered around the courtroom looking for a functioning microphone. He found one in the first row of defense tables at the opposite end of the table from Mr. al Bahlul. While he was conducting the hearing sitting at the table with Mr. al Bahlul, there was a complete power failure and blackout in the windowless courtroom. Undeterred, the judge continued with the hearing using the dim light provided by a couple emergency lights. The prosecution did not have a copy of the charges in Arabic and was forced to read the multipage charge sheet in English while the court interpreter translated. My limited role in the hearing consisted of asking the court to advise Mr. al Bahlul of his right to self-representation and urging the judge to allow Mr. al Bahlul to proceed *pro se*. Mr. al Bahlul indicated that he wanted to represent himself but intended to boycott and remain silent. The judge granted Mr. al Bahlul's request for self-representation and assigned me as "standby counsel," a role that would require me to be ready to step in and defend Mr. al Bahlul on a moment's notice if either he or the judge changed his mind about self-representation.

Mr. al Bahlul had been requesting the right to represent himself since 2004. Under the military commission rules established under the presidential order of November 13, 2001, which was later invalidated by the Supreme Court in *Hamdan v. Rumsfeld*, the accused had no right of self-representation. Both times that Mr. al Bahlul was charged and arraigned by military commissions under the old system he attempted to reject his appointed military defense lawyers and proceed *pro se*. It should not have been a surprise that Mr. al Bahlul still wanted to represent himself under the new system, but although the Military Commissions Act authorized detainees to represent themselves, the government was ill prepared for a detainee to do so. There were no procedures in place for detainees to have access to their case files, much of which were classified and therefore off-limits to the detainees. Little, if any, legal materials were available to facilitate a detainee's right to represent himself. Even basic resources such as the court rules and procedures had not been translated into the native language of the accused. Detainees were not allowed access to a phone or a computer; even such basic office supplies as pens and paper were strictly limited. The prosecution therefore spent the rest of the summer trying to persuade the court to revisit the *pro se* issue and revoke Mr. al Bahlul's right to represent himself. After the judge who granted Mr. al Bahlul's request was forcibly retired and a new judge was appointed to replace him, the prosecution succeeded.

Mr. al Bahlul was completely disgusted with the process, which he termed "a circus." He believed that the commissions were simply for show and that the outcome of his trial was predetermined. He did not recognize the legitimacy or legality of the commissions. When his right to self-representation was revoked in August 2008, he directed me to waive all pretrial motions and demand a speedy trial. He also requested that I ask to be excused from representing him, which I honored. The judge rejected my request and ordered me to stay on the case.

Mr. al Bahlul was the second detainee, after Salim Hamdan (Osama bin Laden's driver), to be tried by a military commission. At the commencement of the trial, in accordance with Mr. al Bahlul's directions, I requested once again to be excused from representing him and requested that the judge grant Mr. al Bahlul's request to represent himself. The judge once again denied Mr. al Bahlul's request, claiming that the request was "untimely" despite the fact that Mr. al Bahlul had been requesting to represent himself for over four years. I was ordered to continue representing Mr. al Bahlul and to remain in the courtroom. Upon denial of the request, I announced that I was boycotting the proceedings and sat mute throughout the rest of the trial. Mr. al Bahlul never spoke to me, much less consulted me, throughout the trial. The trial resulted, not surprisingly, in Mr. al Bahlul's being confined to prison for life (the maximum punishment authorized and a grossly disproportionate punishment for the conduct that Mr. al Bahlul was proven to have committed), after less than forty-five minutes of deliberation by the jury of nine air force, marine, and army colonels and navy captains. The trial concluded on Monday, November 3, the day before the historic election of President Obama, meaning a possible end to the military commissions. Mr. al Bahlul's primary offense was creating a propaganda video used to spread al Qaeda's political and religious views, a video that is available to purchase and view legally in the United States.

I was struck by the fact that there was no apparent legal reason to try Mr. al Bahlul before a military commission. Some of the rationales advanced in support of military commissions are that the offenses are uniquely military in nature or that the evidence and statements available to prove the charges would not meet the stringent requirements of the federal rules of evidence because they were obtained under unique wartime constraints. In my view, as a former special assistant U.S. attorney and as a law professor of evidence and criminal law, there was absolutely no reason that Mr. al Bahlul could not have been tried in federal court. Equivalent crimes covering all of Mr. al Bahlul's alleged acts are available under federal criminal statutes. Numerous other al Qaeda terrorists have been tried and convicted in federal court for similar offenses. In fact, three American citizens convicted of "material support to terrorism" in federal court (one of the crimes of which Mr. al Bahlul was convicted) testified as witnesses for the prosecution against Mr. al Bahlul. There was no evidence that Mr. al Bahlul engaged in active combat or personally harmed any U.S. or allied military personnel. According to the testimony of the agents who interrogated Mr. al Bahlul, his statements were entirely voluntary. No evidence from battlefield interrogations or evidence obtained by coercive methods was offered. All the evidence offered at trial was gathered by experienced federal agents in compliance with standard evidence-collection protocols, so there was no problem with the chain of custody of the evidence. No classified evidence was offered, and no closed sessions were held. Although the government did convincingly prove that Mr. al Bahlul created the videotape, the rest of the case against him was very flimsy and circumstantial. I am convinced that if Mr. al Bahlul had been tried in a federal court with competent representation, he would not have received a life sentence.

In mid-June 2008, I returned to Guantánamo to meet with my other client, Mohammed Jawad, prior to his upcoming hearing to address motions I filed on his behalf in challenging his prosecution before a military commission. Mohammed was under eighteen when he was arrested in Afghanistan, making him a child soldier and his prosecution illegal under the laws of war. (The Afghan government says he was as young as twelve.) Mohammed had also been tortured both in Afghanistan and at Guantánamo, where he was subjected to the "frequent flyer program." The program, which was meticulously documented in prison activity logs, consisted of moving a detainee from cell to cell approximately every three hours for days on end. During a two-week period in 2004, Mohammed was moved 112 times, an average of eight times per day. Other prisoners were subjected to the program for even longer periods.

The judge in Mohammed's case, Colonel Stephen Henley, had a reputation as a very fair judge who was protective of the rights of defendants. Colonel Henley was also an experienced former defense counsel. One concern that I had was that Colonel Henley was close personal friends with the chief prosecutor, Air Force Colonel Lawrence Morris, and had even been in Colonel Morris's wedding party. But I feared that if I tried to have him disqualified, I would end up with someone far worse, so I decided not to make an issue out of it.

By July, Lieutenant Colonel Darrel Vandeveld, the lead prosecutor in the case, started to believe that the case against Mohammed was not as strong as he originally had thought. The more that he learned about Mohammed's treatment, the more disenchanted he became with the prosecution. Lt. Col. Vandeveld is a deeply religious man with a strong moral and ethical compass. He was disturbed that Mohammed had not been treated as a juvenile and had been offered no rehabilitation. He made concerted efforts to convince his superiors to pursue a negotiated resolution to the case that would enable Mohammed to receive rehabilitation and return to his family, but he could not convince the chief prosecutor even to consider any reasonable terms, and the negotiations foundered. To Lt. Col. Vandeveld's great credit, he sought diligently to discover and provide to the defense exculpatory and mitigating evidence, including evidence of abuse at Guantánamo and Bagram. Ultimately, Lt. Col. Vandeveld became so disenchanted with what he perceived to be systemic problems with the military commissions that he decided he could no longer ethically serve as a prosecutor and resigned, requesting reassignment to other duties and later testifying as a defense witness in Mohammed's case, even though he knew that it would be harmful to his military career. Vandeveld has since become an outspoken and highly credible critic of the commissions. He is a true patriot and hero.

A hearing that August focused on our motion that Mohammed could not be subjected to prosecution because he was a child soldier. We also challenged the use of statements from Mohammed that had been derived from torture. I had planned to call as a witness a military psychologist who had been part of a Behavioral Science Consultation Team (BSCT) at Guantánamo in 2003. In that capacity, the psychologist had conducted an assessment of Mohammed's mental state and provided it to the interrogators along with recommendations about how to exploit his psychological vulnerabilities. The assessment was one of the most outrageous and chilling documents I have read, and I wanted desperately to expose its contents; but the document was classified, and I could not release it. I therefore decided to call the psychologist as a witness. Just before the psychologist was scheduled to testify, the prosecution informed me and the court that the psychologist (whose name is protected by court order) had consulted a lawyer and, if called as a witness, would invoke the right against self-incrimination provided by Article 31 of the Uniform Code of Military Justice, the military equivalent of pleading the Fifth. The BSCT psychologist's apparent refusal to testify became a major national news story and helped influence the outcome of a referendum before the American Psychological Association to bar the involvement of its members in interrogations. The referendum passed by a wide margin.

Although Colonel Henley declined to dismiss the charges, he took the highly unusual step of ordering the Convening Authority to reconsider her earlier decision to refer the charges against Mohammed to trial. Colonel

Henley seemed to be trying to send the Convening Authority a message that the case against Mohammed was weak and that she should voluntarily dismiss it. The prosecutors and Brigadier General Thomas Hartmann, the legal adviser to the Convening Authority, had acknowledged that they were unaware of the abuse of Mohammed or Mohammed's suicide attempt at the time that they recommended the charges against him, and they agreed that these were relevant factors that should have been considered. Judge Henley barred Hartmann from providing further legal advice in the case, finding that he had compromised his objectivity by too closely aligning himself with the prosecution. Things seemed to be looking brighter.

The Convening Authority, however, reaffirmed her decision to refer the charges to trial and ordered the prosecution to press forward. Shortly thereafter, Colonel Henley issued a ruling that was sharply critical of the "frequent flyer" program, finding that "under the circumstances, subjecting this Accused to [the] program . . . constitutes abusive conduct and cruel and inhuman treatment" and stating that "[t]hose responsible should face appropriate disciplinary action, if warranted under the circumstances" for their "flagrant misbehavior." Judge Henley came very close to holding that the United States had tortured Mohammed Jawad, underscoring that "the scheme was calculated to profoundly disrupt his mental senses," a characterization similar to a definition of psychological torture under federal law. Perhaps the most important legal conclusion in Colonel Henley's opinion was this statement: "It is beyond peradventure that a Military Commission may dismiss charges because of abusive treatment of the Accused." This ruling affirmed that judges had the power to dismiss charges on the basis of torture and may potentially serve as a deterrent to such abuse in the future.

Then, in a subsequent decision, Colonel Henley ruled that the self-incriminating statements attributed to Mr. Jawad by the Afghan police had been obtained by torture and suppressed the statements. Colonel Henley later suppressed the statements to U.S. interrogators in Kabul on the day that Mohammed Jawad was arrested, finding that they were "tainted" by the death threats made by the Afghan authorities just hours earlier. The government, realizing that it could not possibly hope to prove the charges against Mohammed without these tainted confessions, filed an emergency appeal in the Court of Military Commission Review, which is still pending at this writing.

I visited Mohammed in December 2008 to update him on the case. We brought him a video that my co-counsel Major Eric Montalvo had taken of his family in Afghanistan. We talked of life after Guantánamo and of Mohammed's plans upon returning home. Mohammed smiled and even laughed a time or two. He said that he wants to go back to school and study, to make something of himself. He is finally starting to believe that he is going to be released from Guantánamo. For the first time in a long time, Mohammed has hope.

Michael D. Mori: Escape from Guantánamo

David Hicks left GTMO in May 2007 as a result of the first U.S. military commission in over sixty years. His release did not come about through a dramatic trial that resulted in his being found not guilty. The irony is that Mr. Hicks escaped GTMO not by fighting his case in the military commission system. His freedom after five years' detention at GTMO in May 2007 came as a result of a guilty plea in a case that had begun over three years before.

Mr. Hicks was the first GTMO detainee allowed to meet with an attorney, in December 2003, and the first person charged in the original military commission system, in June 2004, approximately three weeks before the U.S. Supreme Court ruled in his favor in *Rasul v. Bush*, in which he was one of the original petitioners.

Yet the excitement of a win at the Supreme Court wore off quickly. The reality was that nothing the Supreme Court said would result in Mr. Hicks's release from GTMO or the release of any other detainee designated by President Bush to face a military commission. The practical result of the *Rasul* case was that a detainee could get into the U.S. federal courts to raise a challenge to his detention at GTMO, through habeas corpus. It was only the beginning, not the end, of the process.

It might have been naive to hope that through the military commission system some semblance of justice could be found. Mr. Hicks's legal team worked tirelessly for him. In fall 2004, through the help of academic and legal experts across the globe, the team was ready to expose the system's failure to comply with Common Article 3 of the Geneva Conventions and to show that the offenses created by the government were not valid under the laws of war. We were prepared to present leading experts in the law of war, international criminal law, and human rights law in support of our motion before the military commission in November 2004. The prosecution was unable to find one reputable expert to support the legal positions of the Bush administration. The only recourse for the commission was to ban all experts in an attempt to avoid exposing the foolishness of the administration's fabricated legal positions. Right or wrong, it was clear that the military commission system was not going to provide Mr. Hicks the opportunity to put forth his defense. Justice did not have any part in the commission process.

By the fall of 2004, detainees were being released. It appeared that some detainees were released so that the Bush administration could hide embarrassing situations from the courts or media as well as to curry favor with allies. Yet none of the detainees personally selected by President Bush to face a military commission had been released. That changed in the beginning of 2005, when two British citizens, designated by President Bush, were released because Britain would not tolerate its citizens going through the commission process. In Britain's view, the military commissions did not comply with international legal standards. Additionally, the other Australian besides Mr. Hicks, Mamdouh Habib, was released to avoid the ramifications of his rendition and torture and, potentially, as some people speculate, to hide any U.S or Australian official's fingerprints on his torture. Yet this Australian's release seemed only to cement the Australian government's position that Mr. Hicks should go through the commission system.

With little hope of a fair trial at GTMO and victory in the U.S. Supreme Court leading only to further years of litigation, it was clear that the only way out of GTMO before the end of the Bush administration was through a political solution.

Further litigation was mounted in the United Kingdom and Australia to increase the pressure on the United States. After a win in the British appeals court in 2006, a final hearing was set to be heard in May 2007, which would have involved a British court ruling on the abuse suffered by Mr. Hicks at the hands of U.S. service members. Also, in the first week of March 2007, in a separate suit that we had instituted in Australia to require the Australian government to secure Mr. Hicks's release from GTMO, an Australian judge denied the Australian government's request to dismiss the case, making way for a full hearing.

The Bush administration's trial tactic of delay, and the utter incompetence of the military commission system, had assisted in its own undoing. The years of delay provided the opportunity for members of the Australian public and media to question the process and expose its flaws. This was the culmination of events when the offer that could not be refused came knocking.

In a U.S. court-martial, a person can plead guilty only if in fact that person is guilty. Unlike a court-martial, a guilty plea before the military commission required only that a person admit that he would be convicted before a military commission; in essence, the person had to admit that he would be convicted in the unfair military commission of an offense that had been made up after the fact and was not a valid offense under the law of war.

It was not until the first of March 2007 that a new charge was brought against Mr. Hicks under the new military commission system created in late 2006, after the Supreme Court invalidated the old system in its *Hamdan* decision. Shortly following was an offer guaranteeing that Mr. Hicks would leave GTMO within two months, if he would plead guilty.

Whatever the cause or wherever the pressure originated, an offer to leave GTMO within two months of pleading guilty, after five years of incarceration, could not be ignored, as solitary confinement wears down anyone's will to resist. Fighting the case would have taken us into the next year at the very least. And the Bush administration publicly touted that even if the unthinkable happened and a detainee was acquitted of all charges, that person would still be detained at GTMO as an enemy combatant until the end of the never-ending "war on terror."

A political solution was offered: if Mr. Hicks would admit that he would be convicted at the unfair military commission of the made-up charge, he could leave GTMO. On March 30, 2007, Mr. Hicks pleaded guilty, and he left GTMO that May. His freedom did not lie in fighting the system and remaining in solidity confinement. His freedom was halfway around the world, back in his country with his family.

To fight the system would have left Mr. Hicks in solitary confinement for at least another year, if not more. Another detainee, Salim Hamdan, was predictably convicted in August 2008 on charges that were sworn against him on the same day in February 2007 that Mr. Hicks's charges were made. At the time that Hamdan was released from GTMO in December 2008, Mr. Hicks had been out of GTMO for almost seventeen months.

The military commission system had no credibility and will never be viewed as a fair system embodying the values of the United States. The Supreme Court's decisions had no lasting impact on the military commission process, as the rulings were circumvented by the Bush administration. Delay was on the administration's side, as it led to continuing detention. Years of litigation equaled only years of confinement, which became more solitary and desolate as the years passed.

Although the personal desire for an attorney may be to fight a trial after years of preparation, the responsibility is to the client, not the cause. Over three years of work by numerous lawyers and experts across the globe were put in preparing to defend Mr. Hicks before the commission. It took me to Kosovo, Pakistan, and throughout the north of Afghanistan. There was effort by so many people to prepare to defend an individual in a system designed to offer no hope of success. Yet not employing all the team's preparation was what was best for the client. Knowing that the legal team was on the right path on the legal issues raised in 2004 provides some minor satisfaction, as the affidavits produced for the Hicks commission in 2004 were used by the defense in 2008 during Hamdan's trial. Nothing can compare, though, to seeing your client board a jet and escape five years of questionable detention.

With the end of the Bush administration, detainees remain at Guantánamo, with only three military commissions ever having been completed seven years after President Bush first signed his military order. It is strange irony that two of the three convicted detainees have left and that the freedom of these two men was a result of their going through this unfair system, which has been crumbling since its inception.

Denny LeBoeuf: From the Big Easy to the Big Lie

I went to Guantánamo only three times, for three weeks. Double that, or more, in dream time. It always took a week or more before I could leave the place in my dreams.

My first trip was in September 2008, a latecomer to the tent city called "Camp Justice," built on an old airfield. Big canvas tents, with beds for six women. A plywood floor raised above the cracked and gnarled asphalt, like the shotgun cottages of New Orleans are raised above the floor of the sea-level city, but not far enough, as it turned out.

No running water in the tent, but a refrigerator—which was entirely unnecessary, as the tent itself was refrigerated, kept below sixty degrees. I'd been warned, advised by the veterans to bring my sleeping bag. We'd been told that the chill was required to keep out the insects and banana rats.

"What are they, *man-eating* insects?" I said. But the trim lieutenant in charge of our group did not permit a smile. She sat on the foot of my bed, giving me a receipt for the $100 in cash that promised Internet access in a tent. A promise like all of Guantánamo's promises.

"We no longer torture prisoners." "This is a court of law." "We are officers of the United States military, and our honor is important to us." "This is a tropical island."

Every word true, but only sometimes. And no way to predict when the promise was false. When the truth in that moment was: We tortured Prisoner 63 into madness. We bounced a teenager from cell to cell so many times he cried and talked to the walls and begged for sleep. We are running this courtroom like we ran the interrogations: with no principles to guide us, only results we desire. "This is not Cuba—this is power, planet-killing power."

I was in Guantánamo because for twenty years I had been a capital defense lawyer based in New Orleans, working mostly in the South, and I had been a volunteer lawyer with the ACLU. Those two strands of my life wove themselves together and led me to Guantánamo when the military commissions charged some of the so-called high-value detainees with capital crimes. There had been brilliant and dedicated lawyers and human rights advocates defending the detainees for years. But few had death penalty experience, and it takes a special knowledge to handle capital cases, which I'd accumulated sitting at my mama's kitchen table in the Delta, listening to experts, learning the consequences of trauma and mental illness, and litigating in the byzantine world of death penalty jurisprudence.

There's a song, "Leaving Louisiana in the Broad Daylight," I heard many times in the years I lived in New Orleans. Emmylou Harris sang it to us on the radio, driving down the back roads of some backwoods county in Alabama or Mississippi, looking for a witness or a record or a piece of the truth about my clients' lives. I did that, I left Louisiana: left the city where I'd practiced capital defense and worked for abolition of the death penalty. Left the South, where I never had felt entirely at home, moved back to New York, took this job with the ACLU working on the capital cases at GTMO.

But on the island, I wondered if I'd ever left the South at all. Not because I felt the tropical sun burn through my suit jacket in the five-minute walk past barbed wire into the big metal windowless edifice built to serve as a courtroom. It wasn't that, though the same tropical sun burned outside the parish courts of south Louisiana.

Instead it was the judges and the prosecutors and the rules of the made-up court they called the Military Commissions, and we called the Torture Tribunals.

Not that I ever got inside the actual courtroom. You need a different kind of clearance for that, one I was eligible to get but one no experienced capital lawyer has ever received in the Torture Tribunals. It is almost a full year into capital military commission cases at this writing, and not a single capital defense lawyer has been cleared to go inside the courtroom.

So my first trip I went as an "NGO observer"—an observer from a nongovernmental organization. We were the lowest rank, lower even than the journalists who flirted with the younger women in the bars or sandwich shops at night. We NGOs had to go everywhere together, and we were always escorted. That meant all decisions were group ones: should we work out this morning, go for a walk, stay in the freezing tent and work?

As a group we were escorted to the courtrooms in the morning, allowed to split up only if some were going to the "old" courthouse where the noncapital trials were still to be held. Those of us who came to observe the 9/11 trial of Khalid Sheikh Mohammed and his four co-defendants went to rows of seats behind glass.

The glass was soundproof. The only way we could hear what was going on inside the courtroom was through an audio feed, with a forty-second delay. We could see what was going on, of course. See the five defendants seated at the end of their own table, translators and lawyers next to them. Prosecutors at their own table, the judge straight ahead. A row of uniformed officers, almost all men, backs to the wall stage right, watching the defendants in profile. And then some men and one woman no one in the court ever identified, not even when one of the defense lawyers rose to his feet and requested it.

The people in the back of the courtroom—not in the observation area but inside the court itself—did not react. "They're OGA," we are told by the journalist—Other Governmental Agency. Like the CIA. That's *the* OGA in these cases, because it is the CIA who mostly tortured the defendants in these cases.

And now these trials, "America's secret show trials," one lawyer calls them in disgust. Capital cases with no capital defense attorneys allowed, trials of Arabic-speaking men with no skilled translators available, and all on this island base you can reach only if you have "theater clearance" and special papers. On this tropical refrigerated paved-over island, with its protected iguanas eating garbage from Subway and McDonald's. No Constitution for tortured prisoners, but the iguanas can count on the Endangered Species Act.

The reason for the courtroom glass is the Rule: detainees are forbidden from speaking about their torture. Period. The former vice president said that we Americans waterboarded Khalid Sheikh Mohammed. So did the director of the CIA. There has been testimony about it in Congress. But Khalid Sheikh Mohammed can't say it, and if he tells his lawyers, they can't say it. There are some dark acts at the dark heart of what happened in Guantánamo and before Guantánamo, in Poland and Thailand and other places where the United States conducted and permitted torture of these prisoners. And the detainees cannot say so. That is the core of what cannot be said, what must be interrupted, drowned out.

So there's an audio feed, and a button that interrupts it, makes the audio inside the courtroom inaudible. It's a technique learned from live television in the puritanical 1950s, when the transmission could be interrupted if someone uttered an obscenity.

Different times, and a far different obscenity.

On the second day in September that I attended court, there was a new feature in this new courtroom. A large red light mounted on a pole that rises from what would in a normal courtroom be a witness chair. In this courtroom it's the Security Officer's seat (he sits to the right of the judge), and the red light flashes and rotates whenever he pushes the button that stops the time-delayed audio feed. It is usually the same man, a burly "security guard"—OGA—whose smile doesn't reach his eyes.

The first day of the new device we were treated to premature flashing. Khalid Sheikh Mohammed was addressing the court on a matter of religious bigotry, and apparently meant to cite a book by former president Richard Nixon to support his argument. The sound of Nixon's name alone triggered the switch and the light—for nothing, we were later told. That is, the judge told us the interruption of the feed was premature, not necessary, but never told us what the detainee said. It will not be on the transcript, if one is ever prepared.

The contraption is exactly what is wrong with the military commissions. It serves a sinister purpose with a lie, the pretense that if we don't talk about the torture, it didn't happen, or it was all right, or look at who they are and what they did anyway. And the Rube Goldberg aspect of the flashing light and the too-hasty finger on the button captures the sense I frequently had, that the whole process was a movie set, a front, with no substance at all behind it. Some days Torquemada, other days Groucho Marx.

Like the day the judge called the process "a learning experience," as if it was fine to put training wheels on a vehicle lurching toward execution.

Or the many days the interpretation was gibberish. The prosecutor once dismissed that complaint: "What do they need a translation for, they are here all day, they know what went on."

All too reminiscent of Groucho in *Duck Soup*, as the prime minister of Freedonia, a made-up country with silly pomposity and unspeakable cruelty vying for ascendance.

.   .   .

My second and third trips to Guantánamo were not as an NGO but as legal adviser to the 9/11 lawyers, which helped me do my job and freed me from the constraints of an escort. Better for that, but I missed the NGO women.

The third trip was in January. I watched the Obama inauguration from Guantánamo, in the office of the military defense attorneys up on the hill, and found myself thinking of Hurricane Katrina as well as the dramatic events of that day, or what I could see of them given the grainy Armed Forces Network reception.

Why Katrina? Because it was Katrina that first exposed the last administration's abandonment of American principles, Katrina that shocked the world and shocked the conscience of my generous country. Not Katrina the storm but Katrina the criminal indifference to the sufferings of people left on their baking, sinking roofs and in the lightless, stinking Dome for a *week* while people in power had to be roused to act.

For a long time, if you asked me my Katrina story I could only tell you the whole story, exactly the same, every detail. Where I was, how I got away, how we got my sick sister into her car with her medicines and intravenous foods. The fourteen hours on the road. I know from my work with the death penalty, that stuck-memory business is one of the effects of trauma, the disorder of memory.

I don't do that so much anymore. But I can tell you exactly where I was when I heard that white law enforcement officers fired their guns at black storm victims to keep them from crossing the parish line to safety. I said, "But these are storm victims, not inmates." Because, after twenty years in the system, I had come to expect mistreatment of inmates.

I had no idea then, few of us did in August 2005, that at that moment in time Americans, with the written approval of lawyers, and the assistance of doctors, had embarked on a program of systematic torture of prisoners. We were in full flight from our principles.

One of my New Orleans friends left a message on my cell phone on inauguration day: "Okay, I haven't left the TV for twelve hours. I'm staying up long enough to see Michelle's dress, and then we start working to make this America again."

I couldn't watch all day. The Torture Tribunals had held court in the 9/11 case on the previous day, even though it was Martin Luther King Day and a federal holiday in all *real* American courtrooms. Court was in session the next day as well. And of course I didn't get my friend's message till the cargo plane landed at Andrews Air Force Base days later: no cell phones at GTMO. There are landline phones, of course, but we just assume they are monitored, especially when a defense lawyer from the ACLU is using them.

•   •   •

In one of many passionate late-night discussions in the women's NGO tent, I tell them, thirty years of the death penalty set us up for this. The hideous rush to build more and more prisons, put more people in them, set us up for this. Set us up to treat Katrina's storm victims as if they were inmates, treat inmates during Katrina as if they were garbage, or worse. Set us up to believe that color, class, beliefs, or even the deeds of another, no matter how terrible, could somehow exempt us from the obligation to treat them as human. Set us up for the horrifying excursion America has made to "the Dark Side."

I believe that. I believe America's views on the death penalty, on race, and on the treatment of inmates laid a path to Abu Ghraib and Guantánamo, to the dark sites of Afghanistan and Poland and Thailand. And the officers who fired at storm victims on a bridge over the Mississippi in Katrina are brothers under the skin to the scores of officers, lawyers, high government officials, intelligence agents, doctors, and soldiers who have actively participated, who sanctioned, and who still seek to immunize torture in the twenty-first century. And defended it by saying, "Look at what they did, at who they are."

It was President Obama's opponent, Senator John McCain, who gave us the sentence that sums up the revulsion felt by many Americans as the stories emerge from the Black Sites and Guantánamo: This isn't about them. It's about us.

•   •   •

In my Guantánamo dreams I am often expostulating with someone, almost always a man, who is sitting high above me. Sometimes he can't hear me, or just isn't listening. Sometimes he is behind glass, smiling remotely. Sometimes it is hot, hot, and sometimes too cold but never comfortable. When I wake up it takes a long time to shake it, to be where I really am.

Before the last trip I told a friend how I dreaded going back there. Sister Marya, she runs a nonprofit offering Earthhope from a tiny monastery in the lower Big Horn Mountains in Wyoming. "Go to the earth," she said. "Cuba is a beautiful country, and the earth abides." So in the early mornings I would take a yoga mat down to the sea wall and try to meditate.

I rarely could still my thoughts.

Sometimes I would wonder: if it had been my farmhouse that the trains rolled past on their way to Treblinka, what would I have done? If I'd had a family and a small place in Kansas or Kentucky or Vermont in the first half of the nineteenth century, would I have been one of the nameless heroines with a spot in the root cellar for runaway slaves? Or would I have hollered to the slave catchers, "Over here, mister!"

What would I have done about the red-baiting that destroyed so many careers and lives in the 1950s? Segregation? The internment of Japanese Americans during World War II?

Every historical era poses its great moral question, and one way or another, we take a stand. I wonder if the defining characteristic of this coming decade will be how we as Americans respond to the truths about the torture as it emerges. How we figure out what it means about us, and how to stop it from ever happening again.

I hope I never have to go back to Guantánamo, to the fake court or the freezing tent or the yoga behind barbed wire, to the banana rats that look like nutria, aquatic rodents that swim in the bayou outside my little house in New Orleans.

I'll go back in my dreams. In my dreams, that's enough. In all our dreams.

Emmylou sings: "There ain't no way to stop the water." Sang that prophetic line thirty years before the levees failed.

•   •   •

During the December trip the courtroom was very tense. Family members of victims of 9/11 were there, and JTF-GTMO had hung a curtain bisecting the observation seating area so that we couldn't see each other. I told the NGO women I had seen that before.

"At executions. That's what they do with the families at executions— put the defense lawyers and the spiritual adviser behind a curtain, away from the victim's family, so we can't see each other's pain."

I didn't know I was going to do it, but I started talking to the coast guard that day. There were a dozen of them in the anteroom checking our passports and badges.

"Thank you" was all I had to say. "I am from New Orleans." And then, unexpectedly, I teared up, horrified but unable to get my composure back immediately.

The men and women of the coast guard are the reason that Katrina didn't kill 6,000 more people. The coast guard sent boats and helicopters out again and again, perhaps against orders from Washington. They rescued more than twice as many people in Katrina as they'd saved in the entire history of the coast guard.

I told them that once two coast guard officers boarded a New Orleans–bound plane I was on. This was right after Katrina, maybe that November. People on the plane started crying, and clapping.

In the anteroom of the courthouse on Guantánamo where the truth cannot be told and NGOs and defense lawyers have to be curtained off from American families, my shoulder was patted comfortingly and a tissue was handed to me by coast guardsmen who went from Katrina to Guantánamo.

Some of them were unchanged by the journey. Some were not.

Political Maneuvering

Gary A. Isaac: The Great Writ Gets Political: Defending Habeas Corpus in Court, in Congress, and on the Campaign Trail

Most of the attention given to the Guantánamo detainees' fight for habeas corpus has focused on the epic litigation, which as of this writing has been running (or perhaps walking slowly) for over seven years. Three times the litigation has gone all the way to the U.S. Supreme Court for consideration of whether the detainees have a right to habeas corpus—in *Rasul* in 2004, *Hamdan* in 2006, and finally *Boumediene* in 2008—and three times the Supreme Court resoundingly rejected the Bush administration's legal position. But the detainees' fight for habeas has been as much a *political* struggle as a *legal* one, as the Republican-controlled Congress tried not once but twice to overturn the Supreme Court's decisions and strip federal judges of jurisdiction over the detainees' cases. Thus, when the detainees' lawyers argued that the cases were about such fundamental principles as checks and balances and the separation of powers, they were not exaggerating. The struggle surrounding the habeas cases has involved all three branches of our federal government, in which an overreaching president, aided and abetted by a compliant Congress, sought to avoid review by the courts.

Once the battle over habeas entered the halls of Congress, we lawyers needed to become political organizers and lobbyists, to press our case with members of Congress on both sides of the aisle, and to make them understand the importance of this fundamental—but potentially politically thorny—issue and the toll that would be exacted on the rule of law and our constitutional liberties if they made the wrong decisions. We needed also to organize among ourselves, and to reach out to allies, in order to muster whatever was necessary to sway elected officials rather than federal judges.

Round 1 in Congress: The Detainee Treatment Act of 2005

The first indication that an attack in Congress was imminent came on an early November morning in 2005, at the tail end of a newspaper story concerning the Supreme Court's decision to hear the *Hamdan* case. The *Washington Post* reported that Senator Lindsey Graham of South Carolina "hopes to add language to the defense authorization bill"—then up for consideration in the Senate—"that would eliminate habeas rights for detainees captured during the terrorism fight to halt 'the never-ending litigation that is coming from Guantánamo.'" Unfortunately, with the Republicans firmly in control of the Senate, Graham would not be required to introduce his amendment in committee, where it could be the subject of hearings and due consideration; indeed, we learned to our dismay that Graham would not be required even to make the text of his proposal available before offering it on the Senate floor and perhaps ramming through a vote. Our understanding from sympathetic Senate staffers was that there could be a vote on the still-unseen proposal literally that very day.

The *Post* story set off a flurry of activity among habeas counsel as we began to organize to oppose the legislation. This was no easy task—most of us were litigators, not lobbyists, and we had little time to learn the ropes. But we attacked this political threat to the habeas cases with the same tenacity that had characterized our responses to the Bush administration's arguments in court: we hurriedly drafted talking points to distribute to senators and to the press; we rallied our habeas counsel colleagues around the country to contact key senators; we enlisted local bar groups to do the same; we sought to make common cause with the human rights and civil liberties groups that had been outspoken in criticizing Guantánamo; we endeavored to get op-ed pieces written and placed; and we reached out to a number of individuals—particularly the retired military officers and retired federal judges—who had supported the habeas cause in the first place by submitting amicus (or "friend-of-the-court") briefs in *Rasul*.

In fact, two of the people I called first after hearing of the impending legislative threat were retired admirals John Hutson and Donald Guter, both former judge advocate generals of the navy and both signers of the amicus brief that I had coauthored in support of the certiorari petition in *Rasul*. Guter enjoyed a good relationship from his navy days with Senator Graham and, as dean of Duquesne Law School in Pittsburgh, was a constituent of Senator Specter, the chairman of the Senate Judiciary Committee. Hutson had a strong relationship with Senator McCain and with members of McCain's staff. Over the next several days, Admiral Guter engaged in backchannel discussions with Senator Graham to try to persuade him to drop or moderate his proposal, and Admiral Hutson made heroic efforts to rally other retired military officers against the "Graham Amendment"—drafting a crucial letter to Senator Specter in opposition, cajoling other retired military officers to join in sending a letter to Senator McCain, and personally lobbying Senator McCain and his staff to oppose the legislation.

When I spoke with Admiral Guter, he was on his way to Washington for a Duquesne alumni event the next day. Evidently, Senator Graham was just as interested in Admiral Guter's support as we were, because late Wednesday afternoon, I received a voicemail from Guter saying that he'd talked to Graham and that I should call him back right away. The last line of Guter's message gave me a sick feeling: "I'm considering going over to the dark side," he said. That would be disaster for us, because Graham would use Guter's "blessing" to sell the proposal to others. I quickly returned the call.

Guter told me that he had been with alumni in the bar at the Army/ Navy Club when Senator Graham called him there. Up to that point, none of us had seen any draft legislation, so we had no idea what exactly Graham had in mind. But Graham laid out for Guter what he said he was thinking, and Guter had dutifully scribbled as much as he could on the back of some cocktail napkins. Apparently what Graham had described—perhaps some sort of substitute hearing before the highly regarded U.S. Court of Appeals for the Armed Forces, with the detainees even being permitted to introduce new evidence—sounded pretty good to Admiral Guter, so he wasn't sure if he should still oppose the bill. I implored Admiral Guter not to give his approval to Senator Graham just yet and to wait at least until we actually saw whatever Graham was going to propose in writing. Guter agreed, and when Admiral Hutson finally got his hands on Graham's draft amendment the next day, it looked nothing like what Graham had told Guter over the phone. There would be no switch to the "dark side" for Admiral Guter: he was now firmly with us.

The two key senators, it seemed clear to us, would be McCain and Specter. We expected the Bush administration and its supporters to portray opponents of the Graham Amendment as "soft on terror," and Senator McCain's vote against the legislation—if we could get it—would provide invaluable political cover for any senators who might be wavering. Senator Specter's support was vital because he had served for many years on the Senate Judiciary Committee and was considered an expert on legal matters, so his opinion about the wisdom of Graham's proposal was likely to carry a great deal of weight with some senators. In addition, apart from opposing Graham's proposal on the merits, one of our main arguments was that legislation effecting such a dramatic change in the courts' habeas corpus jurisdiction should be enacted, if at all, only after full hearings and careful consideration by the Judiciary Committee. There was no emergency that justified rushing through such a proposal with no hearings and with virtually no debate. Admiral Hutson emphasized this point in the letter he sent to Senator Specter and several others:

> The Great Writ of Habeas Corpus has been at the heart of U.S. law since the first drafts of the Constitution. Indeed, it has been part of Western culture for 1000 years, since the Magna Carta. Creating broad exceptions that would categorically deny the writ to thousands of those subject to the full detention power of the U.S. government should be done, if at all, only with the utmost care, serious debate and consideration, and attention to the practical effects of such a limit. The restriction on habeas contemplated by the Graham Amendment would be a momentous change. It is certainly not a change in the landscape of U.S. jurisprudence we should tack on to the Defense Department Authorization Bill at the last minute.

We expected Senator Specter, as chairman of the Judiciary Committee, to be most sensitive to this argument. We were hoping that Senator Specter would help derail Graham's proposal by arguing that, whatever its merits, it had to be taken up by the Judiciary Committee first.

November 8 came and went with no action by Senator Graham. The next morning, we began to hear rumors that Graham was poised to introduce his amendment that day, just before the Senate recessed for the long Veterans Day weekend. We spent the morning trying to shore up our support, and when Graham finally stood up on the floor of the Senate that afternoon, we were cautiously optimistic that we could beat back the proposal because our intelligence was that Senator Specter and Senator McCain would both vote against Graham's proposal. We did not have to wait long to learn the outcome, though, because the Republican leadership was allowing only two hours of discussion—total—on Graham's extraordinary proposal.

Most of the country was unaware of what was being done to the Constitution that day in the Senate, but habeas counsel around the country anxiously watched the debate—if it could be called that—and roll-call vote on C-Span. Senator Graham took up most of the Republicans' time, delivering an utterly demagogic, but highly effective, speech ridiculing the supposed frivolousness of the habeas litigation and suggesting that some of the habeas lawyers were using the litigation to interfere with the mission of our armed forces. Senator Levin—the ranking Democrat on the Senate Armed Services Committee—took the lead for the Democrats, but he lacked Graham's intensity, and he failed to respond to some of Graham's most blatant distortions of the record. It was exceedingly frustrating to watch.

When the voting began, we still thought that we had a chance, because although the Republicans held a clear majority in the Senate, a number of Republican senators who would have voted against us had already left town for the holiday weekend. Senator Specter not only voted against the Graham Amendment but spoke against it, urging (as we had hoped) that the proposal be submitted to the Judiciary Committee for consideration. As we had expected, the outcome was likely to come down to Senator McCain. Unfortunately, we could see that Senator McCain and Senator Graham were huddled together on the Senate floor—not a good sign. When Senator McCain's name was called, he stood up and voted "aye." It was over: the Graham Amendment passed the Senate by a 49–42 vote. Most surprising, though, was that several Democrats—including some reliably liberal Democrats—had voted with Graham. We clearly had our work cut out for us if we were going to somehow turn this around.

As we talked within the habeas counsel group about our own strategy for the weekend, we were torn. It was conceivable to us that we could garner enough votes to repeal the Graham Amendment *if* the Democratic leadership would really twist arms over the weekend. It was also possible, however, that no amount of effort would turn the vote around, particularly because all the Republicans who had missed the first vote would be back after the holiday recess. If the Democratic leadership genuinely thought that there was no way to bring enough pressure to bear (the Republicans, after all, controlled the Senate), then it would make sense for us at least to explore the possibility of some type of legislative compromise. But if we raised the possibility of some form of compromise, or even suggested that we might be able to live with one, then we could be all but certain that the Democratic leadership would fold. So what to do?

The stakes could not be higher—we were playing for habeas corpus itself and perhaps for our clients' very lives—but this was like trying to solve a single equation with three variables, particularly since we did not have reliable information of our own about how each senator really was likely to vote if the issue came up again. In fact, while we were seeking guidance from Senate staffers about whether there was a chance to win a second vote, the staffers said they didn't know and kept asking what *we* were hearing. This strongly suggested that the Democrat leadership in the Senate had no real appetite for a fight with the Republicans over habeas corpus rights for alleged terrorists. Some of us began to come to the conclusion that our best hope might lie in some sort of compromise.

We decided to proceed along two fronts. On the one hand, we continued to do all we could—writing op-eds, seeking editorial support, and rallying our allies to call or write the senators—to push for the Graham Amendment to be dropped from the Defense Authorization Bill. On the other hand, within our group, we began to debate whether there was any compromise that we could live with. And over the holiday weekend, while the senators were away, Tom Wilner (one of the habeas lawyers who brought the first Guantánamo detainee cases) and Agnieszka Fryszman, another habeas counsel, worked with staffers for a few sympathetic senators—Senator Kennedy, Senator Bingaman, Senator Durbin, and Senator Levin—to vet compromises that might be acceptable to us and that a majority of the senators might support as well. Several ideas were floated: since Senator Graham had suggested in his speech that the habeas litigation was clogging the courts with frivolous objections to conditions at Guantánamo, one idea we kicked around was to offer an amendment stripping the courts of jurisdiction over conditions claims but leaving jurisdiction intact over challenges to the detention itself. Another notion we discussed was to tinker with the language of the effective-date provision, to foreclose future habeas cases but leave pending habeas cases unaffected. That Saturday, we sent the staffers draft language to effectuate a number of these ideas, but we still didn't know what would fly with the senators themselves.

By Monday, as the senators were returning to town, our intelligence was that the Democratic leadership was trying to gauge whether it could win an up-or-down vote to strip the Graham Amendment from the Defense Authorization Bill and that Senator Levin was pessimistic. One of the issues we faced was that other Democrats were deferring to Senator Levin as the ranking member of the Armed Services Committee, and although we were in touch with his staffers, we were unable to get a meeting with Senator Levin himself. We were hearing from his staff that Senator Levin was interested in pursuing an amendment to the effective-date provision, but he wanted to know whether we really thought it would work: if he got the new language we were talking about, was the Supreme Court likely to hold the Graham Amendment inapplicable to the habeas cases that were already pending, therefore at least keeping our current cases alive? Tom Wilner was convinced that it would and said so to Senator Levin's staffers.

As Monday wore on, the situation was still very much in a state of flux. We did not know just what the Democrats planned to do, but it began to look like a straight up-or-down vote on the Graham Amendment wasn't going to happen. It was against this backdrop that Senator Levin quietly negotiated with Senator Graham several changes in the wording of the Graham Amendment. The most significant change was to the amendment's effective-date provision, which had previously made clear that the amendment was intended to apply retroactively, to oust the courts of jurisdiction even over cases that were already ongoing. The new wording that Senator Levin negotiated injected ambiguity into the provision, giving us at least an argument that the change meant that the Senate intended the Graham Amendment to apply only to *future* habeas cases and had ultimately decided to leave jurisdiction over the pending cases intact. On Tuesday, November 15—just one week after the *Washington Post* had reported on Senator Graham's plans— the Senate passed a "compromise" version of the legislation, now known as the Graham-Levin Amendment, by an 84–14 vote.

This new ambiguity in the effective-date provision was an awfully slim reed on which to rest our hopes, but it was all we were going to get. We immediately set to work to bolster our legal position in the litigation that was sure to follow; we worked with Senator Levin and other Democratic senators to prepare statements for the *Congressional Record*, explaining that the change in the effective-date provision had been intended precisely to preserve jurisdiction over the pending habeas cases. Interestingly, we heard at the time that part of the deal that Levin had cut with Graham was that Levin could make a statement regarding the purpose of the change in the effective-date provision, and Graham would say nothing to the contrary.[1]

We then turned our attention to trying to make sure that the changes negotiated by Senator Levin were not eliminated when the House-Senate Conference Committee took up the Defense Authorization Bill.[2] We desperately wanted to meet with Senator Levin to urge him to stand firm in the conference, but we still could not pin him down for a personal meeting.

On Capitol Hill, access is critical, and we began thinking about how to get it. As an Illinoisan, I was represented by one of the most progressive members of the House, Congresswoman Jan Schakowsky ("Jan" to her supporters, and I was one), and perhaps the two most progressive members of the Senate, Senator Dick Durbin and then-Senator Barack Obama; if any members of Congress could be enlisted to help out on the habeas battle, it should be them, we believed. When I called Jan's office and scheduled a meeting with her, I thought I would get perhaps fifteen minutes to make my case. But talking through this constitutional crisis was not something Jan wanted to rush: we ended up discussing Guantánamo for two hours. And when I mentioned to Jan that we had been frustrated in our efforts to get Senator Levin to meet with us, Jan knew just what to do. "Let's call Barack," she said. That sounded good to me; I had actually spoken with Senator Obama about the Guantánamo litigation twice before, during his 2004 Senate campaign, and I had been impressed then with his obvious interest in the issues.

Jan proceeded to whip out her cell phone to call Senator Obama on his cell phone. Sure enough, he answered. Jan explained that she had been meeting with me about Guantánamo and that we needed to talk with him; would it be okay if she put him on speakerphone? Senator Obama said that would be fine, but before we got started, he apologized for any noise in the background because he was home for the weekend, and his two young daughters were climbing all over him at that moment. Jan, Barack, and I proceeded to talk for half an hour about the Guantánamo litigation and our concern about the new legislation, and when Jan mentioned that I had been trying, unsuccessfully, to secure a meeting with Senator Levin, Barack said that he would ask Levin to meet with me as a matter of "senatorial courtesy." Jan and I didn't want to keep him away from his family any longer, so we both thanked him and left it at that. Sure enough, several days later, I had an e-mail from Senator Obama's legislative director, Chris Lu, saying that Senator Levin had agreed to a meeting.

Tom Wilner and Agnieszka Fryszman, who had been taking the lead in our meetings on Capitol Hill, went with me to the meeting. Senator Levin was angry because he was being condemned for compromising with Graham, and he felt that given where the votes had lain, the compromise he negotiated had been the only way to salvage the pending habeas cases.

We listened politely and urged Senator Levin to oppose any backtracking in the conference. Tom thanked the senator profusely for all his help.

We continued with other advocacy efforts as well. Admiral Hutson, Admiral Guter, and General David Brahms (who had also signed our *Rasul* amicus brief) sent an open letter to members of Congress, urging that the jurisdiction-stripping provision be dropped from the Defense Authorization Bill, so that the issues it raised could "be subject to hearings and be given the kind of consideration and debate that any amendment to the Habeas Corpus Act deserves." But the letter also argued, "If the Congress is bound and determined to enact some form of an amendment to curtail the Habeas Corpus Act, at the very least, the application of any such amendment must be prospective only so as not to require dismissal of the Guantánamo-related cases pending in the Supreme Court (*Hamdan*), in the D.C. Circuit [Court of Appeals], and in the D.C. District Court."

When the Defense Authorization Bill emerged from the conference committee, the effective-date language from the Graham-Levin Amendment was unchanged, so at least that much of a "victory" had been secured. But several other provisions pertaining to treatment of the Guantánamo detainees had been substantially watered down. And although at last the Defense Authorization Bill was attracting attention, it was not for reasons we had hoped, exactly. The focus was now on the McCain Amendment to the bill, which barred "cruel, inhuman, and degrading" treatment of detainees in U.S. custody. The White House vigorously opposed the McCain Amendment and even threatened to veto the entire Defense Authorization Bill if the ban on cruel, inhuman, and degrading treatment was part of it. Senator McCain drew widespread praise from the media and from human rights groups for his opposition to torture, since he seemed to be putting principle before politics in this instance.

Habeas counsel were obviously supportive of any antitorture legislation, but many of us argued that Senator McCain—and his cosponsors, Senators Warner and Graham—had crafted a hypocritical and dangerous subterfuge with this amendment. At the same time that they were drawing widespread praise for standing up to the White House over the inhumane treatment of detainees, they were also aiding and abetting such ill treatment by stripping the courts of jurisdiction over the detainees' habeas corpus cases. If detainees at Guantánamo continued to suffer abuse notwithstanding the McCain Amendment, they would have no way to challenge their mistreatment because they would no longer be permitted to go to court. Indeed, it was only because of the habeas cases that many of the abuses had even come to light. We thought that the Democrats were making a tremendous mistake by giving McCain—who was likely to run for president in 2008—a free pass on his support for Graham's attempt to oust the courts of jurisdiction over the detainees' habeas cases. Two other likely candidates for president in 2008 were Senator Clinton and Senator Obama, and I urged staffers for both senators to try to derail the jurisdiction provision by calling out McCain for his hypocrisy. But the idea never seemed to gain any traction with the senators, and on December 30, 2005, President Bush signed into law the Detainee Treatment Act of 2005 (DTA), including Senator Graham's provision stripping the courts of jurisdiction over habeas claims brought by detainees at Guantánamo.

Round 2 in Congress: The Military Commission Act of 2006

After President Bush signed the DTA into law, the fight for habeas corpus moved back to the courts and, in particular, to the Supreme Court. In a sense, we were fortunate, because we would not have to wait years to resolve the issue of whether the DTA applied to the pending habeas cases. The Supreme Court had only recently granted certiorari in the *Hamdan* case challenging the president's military commissions, and the threshold question that now confronted the Court was whether it still had jurisdiction to hear the case at all. Tom Wilner and Neil Koslowe at Shearman & Sterling quickly drafted an amicus brief on the issue to submit on behalf of other Guantánamo detainees, and when the Court issued its decision in *Hamdan* at the end of June 2006, it held—relying principally on the change in the effective-date provision negotiated by Senator Levin—that Congress had intended the statute to apply prospectively only. We had won the battle over the DTA.

The war, on the other hand, was far from over. After the Court affirmed its own jurisdiction in *Hamdan*, it went on to strike down the Bush administration's military commissions, holding that Congress had never authorized them. The administration was beside itself, so its friends in Congress went to work on new legislation to authorize the president's military commissions. What we didn't know, however, was whether the Senate Republicans would try to pass new legislation to endeavor to strip the courts of jurisdiction, yet again, over the detainees' habeas cases. The Republicans ended the suspense in early September, when they released a draft of the proposed Military Commission Act of 2006. Most of the bill concerned the new military commissions, but tucked away at the very end of the eighty-page bill was another provision to take away the federal courts' habeas corpus jurisdiction. And *this* time, the Republicans left no room for doubt as to their intention: the provision was expressly applicable not just to future cases but to pending cases as well.

We again sprang into action, and in many ways, we were better positioned this time around to fight the legislation. We had more time to organize opposition because the bill was not likely to come up for several weeks. We had more resources at our disposal because the habeas counsel group itself had grown, so we had more attorneys around the country whom we could call on to organize opposition in the senators' home states. And we had the benefit of our prior experience from the fight against the DTA.

In fact, we returned to many of the organizing tools that we had used the previous fall. We again called on prominent supporters—including Admirals Hutson and Guter, and General Brahms—to send letters opposing the legislation to members of Congress. We again drafted talking points and op-eds and called on our habeas counsel colleagues to contact their own senators and representatives. And we again reached out to local bar groups and worked directly with organizations such as the ACLU, Human Rights Watch, Human Rights First, and Amnesty International to forge a broad coalition in opposition to the legislation.

One of our most effective organizing tools, however, was new: what we came to call "lawyers letters." These were open letters to members of Congress—essentially petitions—urging preservation of habeas corpus, and we used all our connections at big firms and throughout local legal communities to organize as many lawyers as possible to sign on to the letters. Many of us knew from our own personal experience that elected officials rely heavily on lawyers, and particularly on well-heeled corporate law firms, for support, and we now had dozens of the country's largest and most connected law firms working on the habeas litigation. This was a way to put real pressure on members of Congress to do the right thing.

I worked with Jeff Colman, David Bradford, Pat Bronte, and others at Jenner & Block in Illinois to organize the first of the lawyers letters, and in little more than three days, we managed to get over 600 attorneys—including retired judges, bar officials, and even a former U.S. senator—to sign on. Jeff Colman then sent the letter to Senator Durbin, Senator Obama, and the other members of the Illinois congressional delegation.

We fully expected Senator Durbin and Senator Obama to vote with us, but we were looking for more from them—Senator Durbin was the Democrats' deputy leader in the Senate, and Senator Obama was the party's rising star and a likely presidential candidate in 2008. When we decided to organize the Illinois lawyers letter, we were hoping to leverage our Illinois connections to Durbin and Obama to get the Senate's Democratic caucus as a whole behind us. We figured that sending Senator Durbin and Senator Obama a letter with hundreds of Illinois lawyers' signatures not only would help assure that we got their attention but would give them ammunition to help convince their Senate colleagues that supporting us was not only the right thing but also the politically smart thing to do.

Jeff Colman, his Jenner partner Tom Sullivan, and I followed up on the Illinois lawyers letter by flying to Washington, D.C., to meet with Senator Durbin, Senator Obama, and anyone else on Capitol Hill who would see us. We managed to secure a meeting first with Senator Specter, and Tom Sullivan—a former U.S. Attorney and a "pillar of the bar"—spoke so eloquently about the importance of habeas and the real injustice being inflicted on his detainee clients that Senator Specter decided to hold hearings in the Judiciary Committee the following week concerning his proposed amendment (later called the Specter-Leahy Amendment) to delete the jurisdiction-stripping provision from the MCA. We then trooped off to Senator Durbin's office—the huge office that had been Lyndon Johnson's when he was "master of the Senate"—to meet with Senators Durbin and Obama together. Senator Obama was running late, so we began the meeting without him.

Senator Durbin was, as we expected, very supportive personally, but he was not optimistic about our chances of defeating the legislation, and I recall being very frustrated that the Democratic leadership still seemed unwilling to have a knock-down-drag-out fight with the Republicans over the habeas issue.

Just as we were finishing up our meeting in Senator Durbin's office, Senator Obama strode in with his legislative counsel, Ruchi Bhowmik. Senator Obama apologized for being late and suggested that we repair to Senator Durbin's anteroom next door so as not to take up more of Senator Durbin's time. The meeting with Senator Obama turned out to be just the meeting I had been looking for.

It is impossible to run a "whip" operation to win a difficult legislative vote without an accurate vote count. Ruchi brought that to our meeting, identifying all the senators who solidly supported us, all who clearly opposed us, and all whom we needed to work on. Those of us working the issue for the habeas counsel group had our own list, so we compared notes with Ruchi and divided up responsibility for reaching out to the undecideds. Not only that, but now we had a powerful ally joining our efforts to lobby the legislators: Senator Obama, telling us he regretted his vote in favor of the DTA in 2005 more than any vote of his legislative career, pledged to "personally whip the [Democratic] caucus" to support the Specter-Leahy Amendment.[3] We had never gotten this type of commitment from any senator during the fight over the DTA, and no other senator made such a pledge during the fight over the MCA. Indeed, from that point forward, we worked closely with Ruchi and others on Senator Obama's staff to collect enough votes to defeat the jurisdiction-stripping provision. There were several days when we used a conference room in Senator Obama's office as the staging area for our Senate visits, and I can recall at least one occasion when Senator Obama stopped by to touch base and to offer his encouragement.

Over the course of the next week, lawyers in our habeas counsel group scrambled to reach out to as many uncommitted senators as possible. We searched for every personal or professional connection to the senators that we could possibly use—through our firms, through our friends, through our college roommates—to help us get access. We made progress securing commitments from senators we had pegged as undecided, but the situation remained very fluid, and with the Republicans in the majority, we would clearly need virtually all the Democrats in the Senate to support us, and we would need at least some of the Republican moderates who had voted for the DTA—Lugar, Hagel, Snowe, Collins, Coleman, and DeWine—to switch sides. In our meetings with the staff members for these senators, our basic pitch was the same: we talked about the importance of habeas corpus to the rule of law; we explained why the Combatant Status Review Tribunals set up by the Bush administration were a sham and why the detainees, no less than anyone else facing possible life imprisonment, should be given a day in court; we argued that a vote to fundamentally alter habeas corpus was not like a vote on an earmark or a highway bill; and we implored the senators to cast a vote that would not make them ashamed when they looked back on it in thirty years. In a number of meetings, the staffers seemed almost physically discomfited by the idea that their senators might vote to gut habeas corpus. Several asked if there was any way that some compromise might be found.

In fact, a few of the senators, and at least one of the human rights groups involved in the ongoing debate, began to float ideas for a possible compromise. There were details to be resolved and language to be worked out, but the basic outline of the proposal that seemed to gain the most traction was as follows: (1) the courts would not be permitted to consider any challenges by detainees to the conditions under which they were being held, and (2) any detainee held longer than one year would be permitted to bring one—but only one—habeas petition to challenge the basis for the detention. Some human rights activists vehemently objected that the government should not be permitted to detain *anyone* for such a length of time before the detainee could seek habeas review. That was obviously a legitimate concern. But since all the detainees at Guantánamo had *already* been imprisoned for years, and since our chances of defeating more onerous legislation seemed iffy at best, those of us doing the lobbying for the habeas counsel group would have supported such a compromise, provided that the detainees' prior years of detention would "count," so they could pursue their habeas petitions without waiting. Most important, it seemed clear to us that the compromise being floated would attract the votes of enough moderate Republicans to pass. That must have been clear to the Bush administration as well, so Senator Frist, the majority leader, essentially refused to allow the compromise even to be introduced. The only amendment to the jurisdictional provision that Frist would permit to be introduced was the Specter-Leahy Amendment to delete the jurisdiction provision from the MCA altogether; Frist obviously believed that *that* amendment would never gain enough votes to pass.

That, in fact, also seemed to be the consensus view. Tom Sullivan and I had returned to Washington on September 26 for another round of visits on Capitol Hill, and when we saw Senator Durbin, he told us that he didn't think we would have the votes to pass the Specter-Leahy Amendment. That was obviously discouraging, and I came away from the conversation convinced that we had to try to get a meeting with Senator Graham, and we had to keep searching for a compromise we could live with. I called Admiral Guter and asked him to do whatever he could to get us a meeting with Senator Graham.

Several of us were meeting in Senator Obama's conference room late that afternoon, trying to figure out what needed to be done next, when Admiral Guter called me to say that Senator Graham would meet with us but only if we got over to his office within the next five minutes. Graham's office was in a completely different building, and I was afraid that we might get lost on the way over and miss our chance with Senator Graham, so I asked one of the Obama staffers we were working with to walk us over. We got there just in time. Graham was gracious, but he clearly believed that "enemy combatant" determinations should be the province of the military and not of federal judges sitting in habeas cases. Tom Sullivan and I tried hard, but Graham simply wouldn't budge. There was no compromise to be had here.

We kept pushing every button we could, pressing feverishly for support up until the roll-call vote on the Specter-Leahy Amendment began the morning of September 28. When it was all over, forty-three of the forty-four Democrats voted to preserve habeas corpus, with Senator Ben Nelson of Nebraska the lone Democrat to vote the other way. Unfortunately, only four of the fifty-five Republicans who voted (Sununu, Chafee, Specter, and Smith) supported the Specter-Leahy Amendment, and none of the Republican moderates whom we had needed to change their votes did so. When we began our advocacy against the MCA, we had been told by sympathetic Senate staffers that we were unlikely to get more than thirty or so senators to support us. But we had come excruciatingly close. The final count was 51–48. We had fallen short by two votes.

Until my experience lobbying against the MCA, I had resisted seeing the habeas struggle in partisan political terms. After all, the Democrats in the Senate had hardly covered themselves in glory during the fight over the DTA. But the MCA fight made me reconsider. There had been a clear and unmistakable difference between the way the Republicans and Democrats had voted on the Specter-Leahy Amendment. More fundamentally, I was appalled not just by the way the Republicans voted but by the way they ran Congress. It seemed to me that as run by the Republicans, Congress had ceased to function as an independent branch of government and as a check on the president, as the Founders had intended. I thought to myself that this is what it must have looked like in Germany in 1933, when the members of the Reichstag voted to hand power to Hitler and presided over their own funeral.

It was clearly time for change.

Signs of Hope and Change

Congress's passage of the MCA plainly implicated the Constitution's Suspension Clause, and our focus turned to obtaining Supreme Court review of the statute's constitutionality as quickly as possible. In early April 2007, however, our hopes were dashed when the Supreme Court declined to hear the issue. Desperate, our thoughts turned once again to Congress, where the Democrats had won control of both houses during the 2006 midterm elections. But even with the change in control, we faced two formidable—and perhaps insurmountable—obstacles: the Senate Republicans' ability to filibuster, and the president's ability to veto any stand-alone habeas bill.

We decided to try to avoid these obstacles by using the same strategy that Senator Graham had used so effectively during the DTA fight in 2005: attaching the habeas legislation as an amendment to the new Defense Authorization measure or another "must-pass" bill that the Republicans could not oppose. We planned to bring habeas counsel from all over the country to Capitol Hill on May 1 to press the new House leadership and the members of the House Armed Services Committee to pass "habeas restoration" legislation. Over seventy habeas counsel attended the meetings, and we came away with commitments from a majority of the committee members to support the legislation. But the Democrats decided not to move forward, apparently concerned that a vote for habeas could make it tougher for some of their colleagues to win reelection in 2008 and therefore put at risk the Democrats' control of the House. With the Democrats in Congress unable or unwilling to act, and the Supreme Court declining to hear our challenge to the MCA, we seemed to be running out of political and legal options.

Then, suddenly, our fortunes started to change. Our hopes were revived on the legal front when the Supreme Court astonishingly reversed itself in late June in the *Boumediene* case and agreed to hear our Suspension Clause challenge to the constitutionality of the MCA. And we were to have at least one more turn in the political arena as well.

From the courts to Congress and now to presidential politics: if habeas were to be restored, it was evident that change had to come at the highest level of our government. Clearly, with President Bush on his way out, some sort of change was inevitable. But the Democrats in Congress had frequently acted as if they wished that this whole habeas issue would just go away, and the Democratic presidential contenders might have chosen to ignore the issue as well. One of them—Barack Obama—did not. During the candidates' debates in 2007, I was struck by how Obama often seemed to go out of his way to bring up the rule of law and the importance of habeas corpus. As Tom Wilner and I discussed the difference between the candidates and what we knew of their history on habeas, we both became convinced that, on this issue, Barack Obama was the candidate that we needed to see in the White House. And this was more than just a personal commitment—we felt it necessary to involve our habeas counsel colleagues in this and to utilize the habeas issue to enlist broad support for Senator Obama's candidacy. But how, exactly?

First, Tom and I decided that we should share our experience working with Senator Obama during the MCA fight to counter his opponents'
refrain that he lacked substance. Obama was one of only a few senators in
2006 who had actively endeavored to assist us, and that support, I argued
in an open letter, revealed a good deal about him:

> Some politicians are all talk and no action. But we know from first-
> hand experience that Senator Obama has demonstrated extraordinary
> leadership on this critical and controversial issue, . . . continuing to
> raise Guantánamo and habeas corpus in his speeches and in the de-
> bates. . . . The writ of habeas corpus dates to the Magna Carta, and was
> enshrined by the Founders in our Constitution. The Administration's
> attack on habeas corpus rights is dangerous and wrong. America needs
> a President who will not triangulate this issue. We need a President
> who will restore the rule of law, demonstrate our commitment to hu-
> man rights, and repair our reputation in the world community. Based
> on our work with him, we are convinced that Senator Obama can do
> this because he truly feels these issues "in his bones."

We enlisted other habeas attorneys to add their names to the letter,
and, of course, the more signers we could get, the more force it would have
once we made the letter public. But we weren't just looking for numbers.
We wanted to show that the habeas counsel supporting Senator Obama
were from all over the country, so we noted their states of residence. We
also sought to include colleagues whose military or judicial backgrounds—
such as Admiral Hutson, Admiral Guter, and Judge John Gibbons, who
had argued *Rasul* in the Supreme Court—made their participation particularly worthy of attention. And to maximize its potential impact, our
goal was to release the letter before the critical "Super Tuesday" primaries,
which might well decide the Democratic nomination. When we released it
on January 28, one week before Super Tuesday, the "Habeas Lawyers For
Obama" letter had over 80 signatories, and ultimately 130 habeas lawyers
around the country signed on to publicly endorse Senator Obama.

As we had hoped, the Habeas Lawyers letter got noticed. The *Miami
Herald, Boston Globe,* and *Wall Street Journal* ran stories about it, and it re-
ceived extensive—and overwhelmingly positive—play in the blogosphere.
As one poster noted on Daily Kos, "Forget the Kennedys, Kerrys, NOWs
etc. This to me is one of the most meaningful endorsements anyone can get."
The Obama camp also gave the letter prominent emphasis, featuring it for

several days on the home page of the Obama campaign website. This again underscored for us that the habeas issue was not one Barack Obama was ducking—in fact, he was highlighting it whenever he had the opportunity.

Through the habeas work, we had essentially built a network of lawyer-activists around the country, and the letter became an organizing tool we could use to garner support for Obama beyond the habeas counsel group. During the critical primary campaign, we encouraged Obama supporters in our group to circulate the letter as broadly as possible within their law firms, local legal communities, and otherwise, and to use it to organize support in their own states. And again during the general campaign, we used our nationwide network of habeas counsel to organize and recruit lawyers for critical "voter protection" work on behalf of Senator Obama in the battleground states on Election Day. Hundreds of habeas lawyers raised money or volunteered for the campaign, and some even took leaves of absence from their day jobs to help elect President Obama.

Our work felt validated as we moved forward, since Obama campaign staff repeatedly sought the advice of habeas counsel as they devised policy regarding Guantánamo, a stark contrast with the outgoing administration. We had provided the campaign with talking points concerning various possible outcomes in *Boumediene*, and the moment the decision became public on the morning of June 12, the campaign's Deputy Policy Director called to get my take on the decision and my help in preparing a statement for Senator Obama to issue in response. And after the election, we had a number of meetings with the Transition Team to share our views and recommendations concerning how the new administration should deal with Guantánamo.

In a sense, then, we had come full circle when President Obama, in one of his first official acts as president, issued an Executive Order acknowledging that "[t]he individuals currently detained at Guantánamo have the constitutional privilege of the writ of habeas corpus," providing that the executive branch would undertake "a prompt and thorough review" of whether the "continued detention" of the men at Guantánamo "is in the national security and foreign policy interests of the United States and in the interests of justice," and ordering that "[t]he detention facilities at Guantánamo . . . shall be closed as soon as practicable, and no later than 1 year from the date of this order." The photograph of the White House signing ceremony that flashed over the newswires moved me to feeling of great pride and profound patriotism: standing over the president's left shoulder as he signed the Executive Order was Admiral Guter, and over the president's right shoulder, Admiral Hutson; General Brahms was there too.

Much work remains to be done to implement the president's Executive Order, and the Guantánamo story's ending is still unwritten. As of this writing in March 2009, a number of habeas counsel—including some who actively supported the Obama candidacy—are disappointed that the Obama administration has not moved more quickly to implement the Executive Order and release or transfer some of the detainees. But however the individual cases unfold from here on out, we can take satisfaction that what was initially a little band of habeas lawyers—that later grew into a brigade—took on two branches of government, over a seven-year period, and won the fight to preserve habeas corpus. We learned, while we were at it, that upholding the "Great Writ" required all the talents we could muster, inside the courtroom and out: legal theory, brief writing, political organizing, strategic maneuvering, and outreach to many constituencies. Our Constitution defines the individual liberties we cherish. Preserving and defending those rights, though, necessitates the vigilant attention and the determined efforts of many people, working together.

NOTES

1. I don't know if the report was true, and I'm not sure why Senator Graham would have agreed to such a compromise, unless he too was unsure whether he had the votes to win a second up-or-down vote on his original amendment. But the fact remains that Senator Graham did not do anything to take issue with Senator Levin's statement in the *Congressional Record* until months later, *after* the legislation had been signed into law and *after* the significance, if any, of the Senate's change in the effective-date provision had become a hot issue in the litigation.

2. A conference committee was necessary to reconcile the different defense authorization bills passed by the House and Senate. Ultimately, the Republicans tacked the Graham-Levin Amendment onto the Defense Appropriations Bill as well, so as to have two chances to get it passed.

3. In 2005, Senator Obama had voted against the initial Graham Amendment prior to the change in its effective-date provision that Senator Levin negotiated with Senator Graham. Senator Obama was one of the eighty-four senators who then voted for the compromise legislation. Senator Durbin voted against both the initial Graham Amendment and the compromise version.

Boumediene v. Bush: The Death Knell for Prisons beyond the Law

In June 2008, the Supreme Court issued its landmark ruling in Boumediene v. Bush, holding that Guantánamo detainees had a constitutional right to habeas corpus and finding that the substitute Congress and the Bush administration had created violated that core right. More generally, the Court rejected the Bush administration's argument that it could evade habeas corpus simply by holding people outside the United States, ruling that habeas corpus could extend to U.S. detentions beyond Guantánamo and rejecting the idea of a lawless enclave on which Guantánamo was based. Yet, ironically, the Boumediene case was almost never heard by the Supreme Court.

Mark C. Fleming: A Stunning Reversal

On February 20, 2007, I was working out of the Washington, D.C., office of my law firm, WilmerHale. There was a Supreme Court argument the next day in a case involving our client, AT&T, and I was helping Seth Waxman, the chair of our Appellate and Supreme Court Litigation practice group, prepare for it. In the midst of preparation, I started getting e-mails announcing that the U.S. Court of Appeals for the D.C. Circuit would be issuing its decision in *Boumediene v. Bush*, the case in which we represent six Algerian-Bosnian nationals who had been detained at Guantánamo Bay since 2002.

Boumediene had been before the D.C. Circuit for nearly two years. The D.C. Circuit had received five rounds of briefs and heard two oral arguments. Congress had passed two laws attempting to strip the federal courts' power to hear habeas corpus cases from Guantánamo prisoners. Now, finally, we were getting a decision.

Shortly after 10 a.m., we learned that the D.C. Circuit had ruled against us by a 2–1 vote, holding that the Military Commissions Act of 2006 validly stripped jurisdiction to hear our case. There was only one question in our minds: how quickly could we get before the Supreme Court?

On February 21, as we drove to the Supreme Court building for the AT&T oral argument, Seth commented that if we wanted the Court to hear and decide the Guantánamo case before the summer recess in June 2007, we would have to walk the walk ourselves and get our papers on file very quickly. The team was hard at work on our papers before we even got back from Court.

Within thirteen days of the D.C. Circuit's decision, we filed a complete request for the Supreme Court to take the case (called a Petition for

Certiorari, or "cert")—a process that is normally allotted at least ninety days. We also moved to expedite consideration of the petition, hoping that the Court would order accelerated briefing and oral argument in time for a decision before the summer.

On April 2, the Court stunned us by refusing to take the case. In a very unusual move, five justices issued statements explaining their positions. Justices Stevens and Kennedy said that they wanted to wait to see how the newly created procedures under Congress's Detainee Treatment Act (DTA)—a very limited procedure that we argued was not a constitutionally adequate substitute for habeas corpus—would play out. Three others, Justices Souter, Ginsburg, and Breyer, dissented outright, saying the Court should have taken the case.

As April wore on, the broader habeas counsel group started considering the possibility of asking the Supreme Court to reconsider. One major reason was the government's position that, because the habeas cases were technically "over," we had no right to continue to communicate with or visit our clients at Guantánamo. The government also argued that all the classified information that we had accumulated during our three years as counsel to Guantánamo prisoners—including notes of our interviews with our clients—would have to be destroyed.

In late April, we started preparing a "Petition for Rehearing," the document that asks the Supreme Court to change its earlier refusal to take the case. We did not ask the Court to take the case right away; we simply asked the Court to keep the case open, so that our files would not be destroyed and so that we could resume the case once the DTA process had run its course.

Our first step was to file a motion with Chief Justice Roberts, who is responsible for cases originating from Washington, D.C., asking for an extension of time to file the rehearing petition and for an order keeping the case open. On April 26, the Chief Justice denied our application, taking the rare step of issuing an "Opinion in Chambers," in which he wrote (among other things) that the arguments we had raised "can hardly provide a basis for believing this Court would reverse course and grant certiorari."

The next day, we filed our petition for rehearing. We recognized that it was a very long shot. There are varying estimates of the number of times the Supreme Court has decided to take a case after first refusing it, but all agree it is a very low number.

Two months later, on June 29, the last day before the Supreme Court's summer recess, the Court announced that it was not only keeping our case open but was granting cert and taking the case immediately. The Court did not explain why it had changed its mind. This began yet another intense period of time, as we at WilmerHale, other detainee counsel, and numerous supporting "friends of the Court" put together our written briefs explaining why our clients had a right to a fair habeas corpus hearing in federal court.

On December 5, 2007, scores of people were lined up outside the Supreme Court building in bone-chilling temperatures and snow to try to get in to hear the argument. Some had been there overnight, giving the whole event the feel of a rock concert. Seth gave one of the finest arguments I have ever heard. And on June 12, 2008, the Supreme Court reversed the D.C. Circuit and ordered the case back to the district court for prompt hearings into the legality of our clients' imprisonment. *Boumediene* marked the first time in American history that the Supreme Court had invalidated an act of Congress as an unconstitutional suspension of habeas corpus.

Lakhdar Boumediene remained at Guantánamo for more than a year after the Supreme Court's decision, during which time U.S. District Judge Richard Leon (an appointee of President George W. Bush) granted his habeas corpus petition. Mr. Boumediene was released to France on May 15, 2009—the first time a European country accepted a Guantánamo prisoner who was neither its citizen nor its former resident. Three of our other clients returned to Bosnia in December 2008. The two others—one of whom was also ordered released by Judge Leon—are well into their eighth year at Guantánamo.

Thomas B. Wilner: A Stunning Reversal—Another Perspective

Attorneys on behalf of the various detainees were extremely disappointed when the Supreme Court denied the petitions for certiorari in the *Boumediene* and *Al Odah* cases. We believed, however, that the opinions issued by the individual Justices left a small sliver of hope. Accordingly, we decided to file petitions for rehearing from the denial of certiorari. We filed those petitions on April 27, 2007. None of us at that point had much hope of prevailing, but we wanted to keep the issue open to take advantage of any possible developments that might occur. In retrospect, that was a wise decision.

The Court requested that the government respond to our petitions. The government filed its response late in the afternoon of June 19. Neil Koslowe, my colleague at Shearman & Sterling, and I quickly decided that, although the Supreme Court rules did not provide for it, we would file a reply to the government's opposition on behalf of the *Al Odah* petitioners. To have any effect, we believed we had to file the reply brief almost immediately. We spoke to Seth Waxman and Paul Wolfson at WilmerHale, and they decided to do the same on behalf of the *Boumediene* petitioners. The briefs we ended up filing, however, were very different.

Neil and I decided to file a very short, hard-hitting brief asking the Court to reverse itself and to grant certiorari. Our brief made three points to demonstrate that it was useless to wait to exhaust the alternate DTA remedy because the government had already demonstrated that the DTA remedy was inadequate. First, the government had argued that lawyers did not need full access to their clients at Guantánamo because, unlike in habeas proceedings, the DTA (which solely relied on the record compiled during the sham CSRT proceedings) did not allow petitioners to present facts to the courts. Second, the government had also acknowledged that, unlike habeas corpus, the DTA did not allow the courts to order the prisoners' release from imprisonment, even when that confinement was unlawful. Third, there was also no reason for the Supreme Court to delay determining whether the detainees had constitutional rights because the D.C. Circuit had already made a final decision on that issue, concluding that they had no such rights.

In addition to making those three points, Neil and I attached to our brief the declaration of Colonel Steven Abraham, which lawyers from the firm of Pillsbury Winthrop had just obtained and filed in a pending DTA case. David Cynamon of Pillsbury Winthrop explained to me in an e-mail that the Abraham declaration "was a truly serendipitous find." Abraham was the brother of an attorney in the real-estate group in Pillsbury's northern Virginia office who had seen a presentation that David Cynamon and others had given at the firm on the Guantánamo cases. Abraham had seen the CSRT process from the inside. Neil and I decided that we should refer to the Abraham declaration and attach it to our reply brief.

Boumediene was one case, and WilmerHale was really the sole law firm involved in it. By contrast, what was known as the *Al Odah* case (which had been consolidated with *Boumediene*) was really eleven separate cases combined under that one name, with fifteen separate sets of lawyers and law firms. Although we were counsel of record in the *Al Odah* case, we had to act with the concurrence of the other lawyers involved. Getting that concurrence could, at times, be very difficult and time consuming. All the counsel liked the arguments made in the brief. Some, however, questioned whether we should refer to or attach the Abraham declaration. The majority agreed with us that we should go for broke and file the declaration and ask the Court outright to reverse its prior denial of certiorari. We therefore filed the reply brief in that form with the Abraham declaration on June 22.

The reply brief that WilmerHale filed in the *Boumediene* case took a different approach. In its brief, it did not ask the Court to reverse its prior decision and to grant certiorari. It asked only that the Court defer consideration of the petition for rehearing for now and hold open the possibility of considering it later. Also, the WilmerHale brief did not attach or refer to Abraham's declaration.

Interestingly, a few days later, on June 26, the government sent a letter to the clerk of the Supreme Court objecting to our filing of Abraham's declaration because it had not been part of the record in the lower courts. The government asked the clerk to distribute another declaration, by Admiral McGarrah, to which Abraham referred in his declaration, asserting that McGarrah's declaration "would assist the Court in understanding" the CSRT process. Early the next morning, we sent a letter to the clerk in response saying that we had no objection to the filing and distribution of the McGarrah declaration and pointing out that the Abraham declaration would also "assist the Court in understanding" the CSRT process. We asked the clerk to circulate our letter to all the members of the Court.

Two days later, on June 29, 2007, the Supreme Court reversed itself and granted certiorari in the cases. I understand that it was the first time in fifty years that the Court had reversed itself on a decision to deny certiorari.

Stephen E. Abraham: Preserving Habeas Corpus

Looking back, it is a source of considerable wonder to me that I should have had any role in the Guantánamo habeas corpus litigation. In 2004, I was a retired lieutenant colonel in the U.S. Army Reserves and a former JAG officer. Shortly after the *Rasul* decision, I was assigned to the Office for the Administrative Review of the Detention of Enemy Combatants (OARDEC) in Washington, D.C., which had responsibility for the CSRTs to review the DOD's previous determination that all detained at Guantánamo were enemy combatants. There I served as liaison with various intelligence agencies, reviewed evidence possessed by the DOD that inculpated the detainees as enemy combatants, and examined evidence that might exculpate detainees. However, I was denied the access necessary for me to perform my duties. To this day I do not know if there was any exculpatory evidence, only that there may have been. Anyone who could have known was willing to swear that exculpatory evidence did not exist. I protested, but the process was not changed.

I also served on a CSRT panel. Such panels were employed to determine whether the detainee was classified as an enemy combatant. The hearings I attended were particularly memorable, not only because it was one of the few instances in which an individual was not properly classified as an enemy combatant but more so because of the utter incompetence of the preparation of the case against the detainee. These hearings demonstrated the problems endemic to the entire tribunal process. Surprisingly, I later learned that detainees who were not classified as enemy combatants were subjected to new tribunals, presumably to reverse prior decisions.

In April 2007, the Supreme Court declined to grant the petition for writ of certiorari in the *Boumediene* case. The Court appeared to rely on the depiction of the CSRTs that had been painted by the government, and it seemed to believe that the CSRT functioned as was described on paper. An important indication to the contrary had been a report published in November 2006 by researchers at Seton Hall Law School demonstrating that there were serious defects in the CSRT process. Their report revealed at least three instances in which detainees were originally found not to be enemy combatants but were retried until their status as enemy combatants was confirmed. In one instance, a detainee was found not to be an enemy combatant twice before his third tribunal found him to be one.

On June 11, 2007, attorneys at Pillsbury Winthrop were scheduled to give a webcast presentation on their efforts in representing certain detainees at Guantánamo. The presentation had an impressive title: "Guantánamo: An Overview of the Judicial, Legislative, Diplomatic and Human Aspects of the U.S. Government's Experiment in Fighting 'a New Kind of War.'"

Pillsbury Winthrop sent out an announcement about the presentation on Wednesday, June 6, 2007. My sister Susan, an attorney, received the announcement and e-mailed David Cynamon to inform him that she would like to attend the presentation. She mentioned that I was part of the organization about which they would presumably speak. My sister forwarded me the string of e-mails between David and her, asking if I would speak with David about presenting to a group of attorneys in Washington, D.C. I accepted. It became clear that what outsiders knew had no resemblance to what was happening on the inside. I was the first CSRT member they had ever spoken with, so the attorneys had no concept of how the tribunals were conducted beyond the stories told by the excerpts of tribunal records to which they had access. I explained how the CSRT relied on generic and unreliable information and was prevented from obtaining the true facts about detainees by other agencies even when it tried. My presentation also commented on a declaration submitted by the director of OARDEC, Rear Admiral McGarrah, and challenged McGarrah's depiction of the CSRT as a fair and legitimate process. This presentation was later used as the basis for a sworn declaration that was submitted to the U.S. Supreme Court before it reversed its initial denial of certiorari in *Boumediene*. Had I not attended that presentation and been given an opportunity to speak out, the truth about Guantánamo might never have been made known.

Thomas B. Wilner: Ending Prisons beyond the Law

To win the *Boumediene/Al Odah* cases (which were consolidated under the name *Boumediene v. Bush*), we had to convince the Supreme Court on two issues: (1) that the Guantánamo detainees had a constitutionally protected right to habeas corpus (or, more precisely, that the Suspension Clause in Article I, Section 9, of the Constitution applied to the detainees at Guantánamo) and (2) that the review process provided under the Detainee Treatment Act (DTA) was not an adequate and effective substitute for habeas corpus.

The second issue posed the greatest risk. Justices Anthony M. Kennedy and John Paul Stevens had originally voted to deny certiorari so that the DTA review process could be pursued. Although Kennedy had clearly joined in the June vote to grant certiorari, it was by no means certain that he was convinced that the DTA review process was inadequate. His opinions in other cases showed that he was likely to dig deeply into the process to decide the issue. We could not rely on rhetoric but had to demonstrate through a detailed, down-and-dirty analysis what habeas would require and why the substitute provided under the DTA was inadequate.

The greatest strategic challenge, however, was structuring the first part of the brief dealing with the constitutional rights of the detainees. Disagreements over how to structure that argument—basically, whether to push the Court for a broad or narrow ruling—ended up dividing many lawyers on our side.

The cases involved only detainees held at Guantánamo. We believed there was a very good chance, based on the earlier decision in *Rasul*, that a majority of the Court would find that the Constitution protected the fundamental right to habeas corpus at least at Guantánamo, which, as Justice Kennedy had said in his separate concurring opinion in *Rasul*, was for all practical purposes American territory. However, if the Court decided the case on the basis that Guantánamo was uniquely like American territory, it would leave open the question whether prisoners held elsewhere had the right to habeas corpus or, indeed, to any constitutional protections. The government was still holding prisoners at Bagram Air Base in Afghanistan as well as at secret prisons across the globe. Given the Bush administration's past performance, we believed there was also a risk that if the Court held that constitutional protections extended to Guantánamo, the government might simply transfer the Guantánamo prisoners elsewhere and claim that they, as well as any other prisoners held outside the United States and Guantánamo, lacked legal rights or access to the courts. A number of us felt that it was essential, therefore, to try to obtain an opinion from the Court that would at least offer the possibility of court review and constitutional protections to prisoners held outside Guantánamo.

In other words, although it is traditional for lawyers to seek the narrowest ruling from the Court—that is, not to push the Court further than necessary to win the case—we believed that this case was different and that there was a need to push the Court beyond the facts of the particular cases before it.

To do so, it was necessary to attack the central premise of the argument that the government had made since it had established the Guantánamo prison site: that there were strict territorial limits on the reach of the Constitution to aliens. Understandably, that seemed to some other lawyers to be a very tall order. But we believed that the case offered an opportunity to push for a broader ruling, and our analysis of the Court's opinions persuaded us that we had a real chance to achieve it. Most observers believed that Justice Kennedy's was the crucial vote. In his concurring opinion in *Rasul*, Kennedy had concentrated on Guantánamo as essentially American territory. But other, broader themes emerged from Kennedy's opinions over the years—most importantly, an abhorrence of rigid, categorical rules and a faith in judicial review embodied in the principle of separation of powers and the ability of judges to act flexibly to dispense justice. In one prior opinion, for example, Kennedy adopted what has been called a "global due process" approach, under which the application of constitutional provisions abroad depended not on rigid rules but on the "particular circumstances" and "practical necessities." That was the rationale we wanted the Court to adopt.

We wrote the brief with that as our goal. We emphasized that the government was seeking to establish a categorical rule that would allow the executive to disregard any constitutional restraint on its actions in dealing with aliens abroad; such a rule would allow the executive to manipulate a court's jurisdiction and avoid the law and judicial review simply by stepping across a geographical line. By doing so, the executive could preclude courts from examining its actions whether in time of peace or war, no matter how egregious those actions were. Such a rigid rule would violate the essential purposes of habeas corpus and the separation of powers.

On June 12, 2008, the Court issued its decision in *Boumediene v. Bush*. The majority opinion was written by Justice Kennedy and was largely what we had hoped for. It explicitly rejected the Bush administration's claim that constitutional rights are limited strictly by constructs such as sovereignty over a given territory. It thus repudiated any "rigid and abstract rule for determining where constitutional guarantees extend" and emphasized instead that "questions of extraterritoriality turn on objective factors and practical concerns, not formalism."

In doing so, the Court not only restored the right of habeas corpus for prisoners at Guantánamo but also made clear that the executive could no longer bring prisoners across a geographic line and argue that, by doing so, it had escaped the law.

5

Tortured

At Guantánamo, illegal detentions and sham military trials were part of a larger cruel and dehumanizing prison system—a system built on torture and other abuse. The mistreatment of detainees in turn helped drive the Bush administration's effort to keep everything at Guantánamo secret and to avoid any scrutiny of its actions including its use of harsh interrogation methods to extract information.

A Product of Torture Culture

Torture and other mistreatment took a variety of forms. While some of the abuse was physical, the mental torture was often as bad if not worse. Among the most pernicious aspects of this psychological cruelty were the prolonged and near-complete isolation and the indefinite nature of the confinement itself. Guantánamo, in short, was designed to break the human spirit by creating a sense of total fear, hopelessness, and despair.

George M. Clarke III: Letter from Tawfiq II

The following is the second portion of a letter written by my client Tawfiq. It appears in its original form.

> After we reached Afghanistan, they threw us into a vehicle; they threw us the way somebody would throw trash in a truck. Then they took us to a prison in Kabul area called Wazir Akbar Khan. It was underground and we were interrogated as soon as we reached there. It was done in a very savage manner. Then they put us in a very small cell, there was no bed in the cell. We were unable to breathe and sleep, the area was very tight. Even the food was not enough and it was of very poor quality. It was one of the most difficult prisons I have been through.

When the representatives of the Red Cross would come, the authorities there would hide us so that the Red Cross would not see us as the authorities wanted to interrogate us and after they wanted like to kill us. This was told to me by one of the prisoners who had good relationship with one of the guards. However, with the blessings of the Almighty, who saved us from these criminals, one of the other prisoners who met the Red Cross representative informed them that there are some Arab prisoners here who have been brought from Iran around three weeks ago and that they are being hidden from you [the Red Cross] in some very dirty bathrooms.

The Red Cross representatives found out about us and recorded our names in a log book. Once we were discovered, the guards lost their mind and started hitting all the prisoners. Some of the hitting showed that there was no mercy in their violence. Then the American FBI agents came to question us.

They took [me to] another building in the same prison, I was handcuffed behind and they put a hood on my head so that I could not see anything. When I entered the interrogation room, the American guards pushed me down to the ground in a very savage manner. They started to cut my clothing with scissors. They undressed me completely and I was nude. They made me sit on a chair and it was very cold. I was also afraid and terrorized because the guards were aiming their weapons towards me. The interrogator put his personal gun on my forehead threatening to kill me. He asked me, if I belonged to the al Qaeda organization. I told him no, and he hit me on my head. I told him to believe me that I do not belong to al Qaeda and that the Iranian government has fooled you. My interrogation lasted for almost three hours. They took my photographs and gave me clothes to wear and I was taken back to the room.

I stayed in the prison for approximately two months and two weeks. Then they moved me to another prison with solitary confinement. Here I spent approximately five months and ten days. There were some poisonous scorpions. The guards were from Afghan armed forces and the watch was very strict and with very bad treatment. The interrogation was also very savage.

Then they moved me to another prison in a very strange manner. While I was in the vehicle, they started to hit me and strangle me, they would put a rope around my neck and I was about to die. They were American soldiers, I heard their laughter. When we reached the prison, there were Afghan guards. This was absolutely the worst prison. It was a very dark prison and there was no light, no bed or a carpet, the floor was semi cement.

The restraints on my feet were very tight, they put me into a cell and kept me hanging tied to the wall for almost ten days.

The meals were one meal every two days and the portion was very small. They would untie me from the hanging positon for half an hour for meals. I would try to sleep during this half an hour but I was unable to sleep because of the extreme cold in Kabul. The irritating music 24 hours a day was very loud and hard banging on the door. When I used to go for interrogation, I was unable to walk because of the restraints on my legs and tightness on my feet. I would fall down to the ground and scream that I cannot walk. They would pick me up from the ground and I would walk with them while they are hitting me on the way to the interrogation until I would bleed from my feet. When I would fall to the ground, they would drag me while I am on the ground. Then they would bring me back to the cell and sprinkle cold water over me. Sometimes they would put a weapon on my head threatneing to kill me using some provocative statements which I cannot mention in this letter.

After ten days, they brought me down from the hanging positon and made me sit on the floor. Then they tied my hands upwards for approximately one month so that I could not lie down on the floor for comfort, therefore I was unable to sleep except for quarter of an hour every day. Whenever I was able to sleep for half an hour a day, I would feel as if I have slept for the whole day.

After one month and ten days, they removed all my restraints, however I was unable to rest or sleep because of extreme hunger and cold and the loud irritating music and the banging on the door. I stayed in this prison for approximately two months and a half and I had no idea whether it is day or night as it was extremely dark and oppressive conditions.

After this they moved me to Bagram base by helicopter. As soon as I reached there, the treatment was very bad there as well. They put me in a solitary confinement for ten days, however after the previous prison of darkness this place was like heaven for me.

Then they moved me to a group prison, but it was almost like a solitary confinement because we were not allowed to talk to each other.

I spent approximately two months in this base. There were some American male and female soldiers for whom I have nothing in heart except love and respect and I will never forget them. They were good to me, I still remember them and I wish I could return the favor to them for what they did to me. This is a fact and I will not deny it as long as I live. I do not hold any grudge in my heart against anybody in spite of all that has happened to me. I wish from humanity that they resolve the hatred that exists between them, as some have oppressed others for no reason. A human is always punished for oppression; the oppressed might be in the situation because of some circumstances. These soldiers proved to me that they are different from the other American soldiers that I have met.

I have very fond and good memories of these excellent soldiers and I was very sad when I left them and moved to Cuba. They came to say goodbye to me. I saw sadness in their eyes for leaving me. Each one of them came to see me and say goodbye and shook my hand. I will never forget those moments which made me forget everything that had happened to me in the past.

Then my trip to Cuba began. When I reached Cuba and until now, you might know the rest of the story of Cuba. You have heard about the oppression of innocent people here who do not carry weapons or have any evidence. There is no evidence to implicate anybody or any reason to imprison them here, except for a very few, and many of those have already been released. This is all that I remember of my story.

Joshua Colangelo-Bryan: Habeas on the Gate, Part II

My interpreter, Karim, and I walked into Jumah's room. Jumah smiled broadly and shook our hands.

"How bad was your night?" I asked.

Jumah smiled, suggesting an appreciation for my choice of words. "I was okay. How was your night?"

I wondered if there was an appropriate answer. "It would have been better if you'd been with us, but it was fine."

I put some food on the table, including candy bars Jumah had requested. We chatted about nothing in particular while eating. Jumah had just rebuffed my first attempt to have him eat some fruit when he said, "I want to tell you my story."

I had not expected this and reached immediately for a notepad.

"I was trying to get home from Afghanistan. I went to a checkpoint on the border with Pakistan and asked to be taken to the Bahraini embassy. The Pakistanis laughed and took me with other Arabs to a prison.

"I was in the Pakistani prison for sixteen days. They served food in a bucket and the bread was inedible. I had shackles on my legs. They were not connected to each other with a chain like here but with a steel bar. It was very painful.

"I was interrogated by the Pakistanis many times. There were no beatings, but there were threats. In the last few days there, two American men questioned me. One of them spoke Arabic fluently, but not as a native speaker. They did not use violence, but they did use abusive language. One cursed in Arabic.

"On our last day in that prison, the Pakistanis put us in blue uniforms, handcuffed us, and made us wear blindfolds. We were taken to a military airport, where there was a plane with an American flag."

"How did you see the plane if you had a blindfold on?" I asked.

"The blindfold was not very good. You could see through it. And they took it off to put sacks over our heads. They shackled us to the floor of the plane with chains around our thighs, waists, and shoulders. The chains were pulled so tight, they pushed us forward. It was very painful to my stomach. I had surgery on my stomach six years ago because I was obese—I weighed about 115 kilograms.

"There are tubes in my stomach now, and I tried to tell a soldier that the chains were hurting me. He hit me in the stomach, and I vomited blood. After a couple hours of flying, they took us off the plane in Kandahar."

"The soldiers at the American base in Kandahar put everyone on the ground. We were connected to each other by a wire that was around our arms."

I glanced up from my notes and saw that Jumah had pulled himself away from the table—away from us. He wasn't looking in our direction anymore either but off to the side of the room.

"The soldiers were walking on people. It felt like someone urinated on me. They beat people. One of them hit my head into the ground. Someone put his boot in my mouth. This all went on for over an hour."

Jumah's voice had become quieter.

"We were taken to a tent that had barbed wire around it but no sides. It was open to the elements, and Afghanistan in winter is very cold. The soldiers continued to hit people. If you screamed there was more beating.

"I was taken somewhere else, where there were many soldiers and a translator. I think he was Lebanese. He cursed at me very badly. He called me 'Al Qaeda, terrorist, dog.' They tore my clothes off and put their fingers in my anus. They took photographs of me.

"The next morning they took me for an interrogation. They made me walk barefoot on barbed wire to get there. They hit my head against a metal hangar and said it was an accident. They pushed me to the ground, where there was broken glass."

Jumah pointed to a scar on his knee and looked in my direction. "This is from the glass." He looked away again. "The interrogator was black. I told him that I would sign anything, and there was no need to beat me. He said that beatings were not allowed and left. A soldier called me a terrorist and poured hot liquid on me. I said I needed to see a doctor. The soldier spit on me and said, 'We brought you here to kill you.'

"Another soldier put a cigarette out on me," he said, pointing to a small circular scar on his wrist. "The soldier said that he did it in the name of God and Christ.

"I was in Kandahar for two weeks. One night, they took me to another tent with my hands and legs tied and a sack on my head. They plucked some of the hairs of my beard, and they shaved my moustache. They used a scissors to cut off my clothes and took me to a different tent with other naked detainees. They put us in orange clothes and tied us with chains. I had to crouch for hours with my hands tied in front of me. It was very cold."

Jumah's words came more slowly now, but in an unrelenting rhythm.

"Then they put very tight goggles on me through which I could not see. They placed something on my ears so that I could not hear. They took us to an airplane and chained us to the floor. I said that the chains made my stomach hurt. Beating was the response. When they saw that I was in great pain, they brought me sleeping pills.

"Somewhere, after many hours, they dragged us off the plane as if we were little boxes. They put us on a second plane. It seemed we were on that second plane for a whole day. The goggles were so tight that they made my nose bleed. They gave me more sleeping pills.

"When we arrived in Cuba, they tied us together on the ground for many hours. They took me to a concrete building in which they took off my clothes and took photographs of me. They gave me a very cold shower and very tight clothes.

"They took me to Camp X-Ray." Camp X-Ray was the original detention facility at Guantánamo, which had been built in a matter of weeks. There were photographs showing that it consisted of a series of open-air cages. It looked like a kennel.

"We were forbidden to move. We had to sit still. If you even turned around in your cage to look at someone, there would be a punishment. Sometimes we were forbidden to pray. Later, they allowed us to pray but not to face Mecca. Then we were allowed to face Mecca. But whenever there were new detainees, we were again prohibited from looking at each other or praying.

"We had rats, snakes, and scorpions in the cages but no bathrooms. When we left the cages to use the bathroom, they always chained us and pushed our heads down hard. It was too painful, and the chains caused injury. We refused to get chained to go to the bathroom, so they gave us buckets to use in the cell. I was in X-Ray for three months. At the end, I tried to kill myself by breaking a metal piece from my cell and swallowing it. I was in the hospital for three days."

Jumah put his elbows on his thighs and his face in his hands. He pulled back even more from the table, although the shackles kept him from going far.

"When I came back from the hospital, the head of the shift took everything out of my cage. He pushed me on the floor and cursed me. I yelled at him, and he told the staff sergeant to get the IRF." Jumah pronounced "IRF" as if he was saying it in English. IRF was shorthand for Immediate Reaction Force—a team of five soldiers, wearing helmets, face masks, chest protectors, and shin guards, tasked, supposedly, with subduing unruly detainees.

"A lieutenant came and told me to get on the ground. I went down and put my hands on my back. I saw the IRF coming, but it had six people instead of five." Jumah was crying softly.

"The staff sergeant opened the door, and a very big guard, wearing all of his gear, ran in. He jumped in the air and landed on my back. He held my neck, and two others held my legs. A female guard hit my head on the floor repeatedly. The staff sergeant said, 'Don't leave until he bleeds.' The guard kept choking me, and I thought I was going to die. Blood gushed out of my nose, and I lost consciousness. Other detainees told me later that the female guard held my face up for the camera." I had read that all IRF interventions were videotaped.

"I woke up in the naval hospital—the one that they use for the military, not for detainees. I saw the same staff sergeant holding a video camera. They gave me an IV and a CAT scan. While I was in the hospital, a female interpreter, who said that her name was 'Alin,' came and asked me about the incident. It was the first beating like that. Everyone knew about it."

Without making eye contact, Jumah raised his head and pointed to a scar on his nose. "I have this from the beating."

He buried his face again in his hands. He choked back tears. Karim was ashen and looking down. His eyes were wet.

A moment or two passed. Jumah kept his face in his hands and didn't say a word. We didn't have tissues, so I put a few napkins in front of him.

"I am so sorry to hear about what you experienced," I said very softly as Karim translated. "I cannot imagine how painful that must have been— I cannot imagine how painful it is now. No human being should have to endure those things. I don't know if you've ever been able to tell those stories to anyone who cared. I want you to know that we care very much."

I paused. Jumah didn't move.

"We will do everything we can to make sure those kinds of things never happen again. I promise. You are not alone in that way anymore."

Jumah didn't respond. The world seemed to have fallen silent around us.

"I am so sorry. Nobody should ever be subjected to that kind of abuse." I couldn't help repeating myself. He still hadn't looked up.

Karim leaned over and whispered, "May I speak to Jumah in Arabic?"

I nodded. Karim spoke in words I didn't understand, but with an unmistakably gentle tone. Jumah remained silent and motionless.

I worried that the trauma Jumah was experiencing as we sat there might not let go of him. He had already tried to kill himself. He would be spending the rest of that day and the night alone in his cell. For the first time—but certainly not the last—I wondered if Jumah would be better served by a therapist than an attorney.

"Jumah, I would like to ask you some questions. I just want to make sure I understand everything you've told us. Is that okay?" I asked very quietly.

I hoped to bring him back to the present, which seemed crucial, without making it appear that I wanted to ignore what he had told us, which I certainly didn't. The lawyer in me also needed more details.

But there was something else at work that I didn't want to admit to myself. I don't trust people easily, especially when I don't know them. To me, there's nothing worse than trusting someone who later takes advantage of that trust. There had been conviction behind each of Jumah's words. His pain and horror were so stark that they seemed to take on a physical presence in the room as tangible to me as his shackles. But what did I really know about Jumah after one day? How could I know if he was or wasn't some kind of bad guy? Was he telling me the truth or just using me to spread anti-American propaganda?

Still, it felt right to be purely compassionate with Jumah. It also was the right thing to do as an attorney who was trying to develop a relationship with a new client under the worst conditions.

Jumah looked up and wiped his eyes. "We can talk about your questions."

"I appreciate that very much. I can only imagine how difficult this must be. I just want to make sure that I understand everything that happened." He nodded. I continued, "Do you know the name of the head of shift who called for the IRF?"

"Collins," he said, very quietly. (All names of Guantánamo personnel are pseudonyms.)

"Do you know the name of the staff sergeant?"

"Williams."

"How about the female guard who hit your head?" I spoke as calmly as I could.

"She was Thomas."

I stayed quiet for a moment, and so did Jumah. "You said that Williams told the IRF, 'don't leave until he bleeds.' I assume he said that in English. How did you understand what he said?"

"I am able to speak some English, and I could hear that he said something like that." I wasn't entirely surprised. At times, Jumah seemed to laugh at my jokes—weak as they were—before Karim translated them completely.

"Is your English good enough that we can talk without translation?"

"It has gotten better since I've been here," Jumah said, "but I am not always that comfortable with it."

I looked through my notes for other questions. How did you know that you were in Kandahar when you got off the plane there? Did you ever sign a statement in Kandahar after you said you would? What did you mean that you and the other detainees were connected by "wire" that was around your wrists in Kandahar? Do you know what date you arrived in Cuba? Where were you when you had the surgery on your stomach?"

As Jumah answered, his voice became stronger. He started looking me in the eye again. I nibbled on a biscuit, hoping he might follow suit. He did, although not with the same gusto.

Jumah said the surgery had been performed at a hospital in Jeddah, Saudi Arabia.

"I have to say, it's really hard to imagine you overweight, Jumah." I would have called him gaunt.

"I was fat."

"Amazing. Does that mean I shouldn't bring food here? I don't want you to lose your figure."

"I am on the Guantánamo diet." His expression eased somewhat. "You have to bring food."

"OK, I promise."

It was nearly noon, and we had to leave. I was very concerned about how Jumah would manage alone in his cell.

In a now familiar ritual, guards knocked on the door, abruptly. I gathered my things. Karim and I both gave Jumah little hugs. Guards surrounded him, shackling his hands. Jumah looked very small.

H. Candace Gorman: Arrogance

Al-Ghizzawi was first taken prisoner in Konar, where he was staying with his wife and daughter at his in-laws'. The local thugs sold him to the Northern Alliance, and he was then moved to Kabul. When Al-Ghizzawi heard that American troops were coming to Kabul, he tried to get himself turned over to them. As Al-Ghizzawi later told me, he thought he would be safe with the Americans "and have rights" and be treated "with respect." Al-Ghizzawi convinced the Americans to take him when they learned he spoke English. That was all the troops knew about him. Ignorance of who he was or why he was there, however, proved no impediment to torture.

In the early years, "the Americans treated me very brutally and disrespectfully, worse than the Northern Alliance, . . . and the Northern Alliance was very bad," Al-Ghizzawi recounted to me. "But now the torture is much different. Now the torture is my life every day in this prison, alone without my family, dying, with no rights and no charges."

His American jailers spared him the very worst of the worst in the long list of torture techniques now in use. He was not murdered or waterboarded. He did not have a razor blade taken to his penis, nor was he hung from the ceiling by his arms. One might describe Al-Ghizzawi's torture as a "kinder, gentler" torture.

In American custody, Al-Ghizzawi was *only* beaten with chains, bound to chairs in excruciating positions for endless hours, threatened with death and with rape, stripped and subjected to body-cavity searches by nonmedical personnel while men—*and women*—laughed and took pictures.

Among many other brutalities and indignities, Al-Ghizzawi was also posed naked with other prisoners, terrorized with dogs, forced to kneel on stones in the searing heat, left to stand or crouch for extended periods, deprived of sleep, subjected to extreme cold without clothes or covering, denied medical attention, and kept in isolation for years.

A kinder, gentler torture.

John A. Chandler: Cancer on the Body Politic

Sent to Guantánamo in 2003, sixty-year-old Abdul Razzaq Hekmati, a hero of the war against the Taliban, died of colon cancer nearly five years later on December 30, 2007. Hekmati never had a colonoscopy, which might have detected the cancer and saved his life; indeed, colon cancer is entirely preventable if doctors detect and remove precancerous growths. Instead, in 2007, Hekmati was given painkillers, the treatment of choice for men in Guantánamo. And he died in Guantánamo never having been charged with a crime, never having had a fair hearing, and despite the fact that several prominent men in Afghanistan were willing to travel to Guantánamo and testify that Hekmati had been improperly detained.

A detainee at Guantánamo Bay does not have the option of deciding to visit a physician for age-appropriate routine health examinations that might detect the presence of cancer; he has no choice about who treats him and how; he never even gets to give his informed consent to the treatment he does receive.

We do not know what type of treatment Hekmati received for his cancer other than painkillers, nor do we know whether, with proper medical care, the disease could have been diagnosed earlier. What we do know is that Hekmati died from this highly treatable disease while in the care of the U.S. government.

Similarly, one of our clients, who is starting his seventh year in Guantánamo, has his blood pressure regularly clocked at numbers like 168/120 and 207/103. For a forty-five-year-old man, 120/80 is normal. Does he have serious heart disease? Well, by any measure he has dangerously high blood pressure. He takes Zestoretic for high blood pressure and Lipitor for high cholesterol (plus sixteen other medicines, some of which are contraindicated).

The doctors at Guantánamo have suggested procedures such as a cardiac catheterization for him, but he refuses. Why? Would you agree to be treated by a doctor who would not tell you his name? Are you willing to trust yourself to a doctor who covers his name so you cannot see or figure out anything about his skills?

Our client has asked the military to tell us (not him) the doctor's name and credentials so we can investigate and advise him. Guantánamo is a small naval base with an unsophisticated hospital. Guantánamo, of course, refuses—why do anything for these terrorists? We have alternatively asked that the client be treated at a U.S. military hospital, that we be permitted to send a cardiologist to see him, or that he be sent home to Yemen. Answers: no, no, and no. Guantánamo just says, "Trust me."

George Brent Mickum: Madness

At the start of Bisher al-Rawi's fifth year in prison, it pains me to report that the once healthy and extremely articulate man is failing. He is no longer able to withstand the most insidious form of torture being used by the U.S. military: prolonged isolation coupled with environmental manipulation that includes constant exposure to temperature extremes and constant sleep deprivation.

Bisher al-Rawi is slowly but surely slipping into madness. Gradually, over time, Bisher simply has worn down. He no longer has the power to withstand the ravages of psychological isolation and the constant abuse he suffers at the hands of the Bush administration, allegedly in the name of freedom. To be sure, Bisher is not the only affected prisoner; attorneys representing other prisoners at Guantánamo report that clients who are being kept in isolation are going insane. But many of those prisoners have spent much less time in solitary confinement than Bisher.

Bisher's world is a six-by-eight-foot cell in Camp Five, where alleged "noncompliant" prisoners are incarcerated. After years and hundreds of interrogations, Bisher finally refused to be interrogated further. Despite the fact that Guantánamo officials have publicly proclaimed that prisoners are no longer required to participate in interrogations, Bisher is deemed noncompliant and tortured daily.

Solitary confinement is but a single aspect of the torture that Bisher endures on a daily basis. While in isolation, Bisher has been constantly subjected to severe temperature extremes and other sensory torments, many of which are part of a sleep-deprivation program that never abates. Frequently, Bisher's cell is unbearably cold because the air conditioning is turned up to the maximum. Sometimes his captors take his orange jumpsuit and sheet, leaving him only in his shorts. For up to a week at a time, Bisher constantly shivers and is unable to sleep because of the extreme cold. Once, when Bisher attempted to warm himself by covering himself with his prayer rug, one of the few "comfort items" permitted to him, his guards removed it for "misuse." It has never been returned.

On other occasions, the heat is allowed to become so unbearable that breathing is difficult and labored. Again, for up to a week at a time, all Bisher can do is lie completely still, sweat pouring off his body during the day when the Cuban heat can reach 100 degrees Fahrenheit, and the temperature inside Camp Five is even higher.

Bisher is allowed no contact with fellow prisoners. Bright lights are kept on twenty-four hours a day. Bisher is given fifteen sheets of toilet paper per day, but because he used his sheets to cover his eyes to help him to sleep, his toilet paper (considered another comfort item by his beneficent constabulary) has been removed for "misuse." Accordingly, he no longer receives his daily ration of fifteen sheets of toilet paper. Imagine being in the position of having to make a choice between using your tiny allotment of toilet paper for the purpose for which it was intended or using it to sleep, and then having it removed altogether.

Dinner never arrives before 9:30 p.m. and sometimes comes as late as 12:00 a.m. It is almost always cold. Changes of clothing take place at midnight, when prisoners are given a single thin cotton sheet for sleeping. Thereafter, a noisy library cart is dragged through the corridors; Bisher has been denied library privileges for some time, but the library cart and the noise are constant reminders that he is afforded no intellectual stimulation. Prisoners are unable to sleep until close to 1:00 a.m. They are awakened at 5:00 a.m., when each is required to return his sheet. All of Bisher's legal documents and family photographs were seized months ago and have never been returned.

Bisher's treatment is designed to achieve a single objective: to make him lose his psychological balance and, ultimately, his mind. Every aspect of Bisher's prison environment is controlled and manipulated to create constant mental instability. What is so ineffably sad about all this is that

Bisher realizes he is losing his mind. He is constantly stressed and tired. He has told us that he knows that he is no longer normal. He reports talking to himself all the time in his cell. He reports, Guantánamo Bay "has taken an extreme toll on my body—even more on my mind." Some of his descriptions are so heart-wrenchingly sad: "Sometimes you are so hurt by what is done to you, by the conditions, that you lose your balance." The damage to Bisher's psyche is, therefore, not unexpected; it is the natural and expected result of prolonged isolation and the elimination of all stimulation and human contact, other than guards and interrogators. The ravages of extended isolation and sensory deprivation leave no marks, but they destroy the mind.

Jamil, my other client in Guantánamo, is also suffering. His diabetes, which abated during his early imprisonment due to the fact that he was starved and lost more than 100 pounds, has manifested itself again. Unfortunately, Jamil is not being properly treated, primarily because he refuses to trust the medical staff at Guantánamo. That mistrust is the direct result of the Guantánamo medical staff's active and direct involvement in the interrogation and torture of prisoners. He is experiencing constant pain in his legs and reports that his eyesight is deteriorating. Although the medical staff at the prison has ordered that Jamil be provided with a special diet, the guards who dispense food refuse to provide it. Apparently no one on the medical staff ever thought it was important enough to bring the necessity of the matter to the guards' attention.

Jamil reports that although he continues to meet with his interrogator, he talks little. His interrogator constantly baits him, trying to turn him against his friend Bisher. Jamil says his interrogator claims that Bisher has accused Jamil of being a terrorist and supplying money to terrorist organizations. Jamil dismisses such accusations with a wave of his hand. He knows Bisher would do no such thing. The friendship between my clients is truly touching. Each feels genuine affection for the other, and each has told me he would gladly remain if the other were released. Neither wants to leave unless his friend is able to leave as well.

As part of a general pattern of mistreatment, mail from prisoners' families is heavily censored, generally for no reason other than as part of a calculated program of cruelty. The military routinely redacts portions of letters in which a family member tells a prisoner that he or she loves or misses him. This has happened to Jamil. Among other things, the medical personnel at Guantánamo have determined that Jamil's weak point is his young family. Unable for a time to have children, Jamil is now the father of five young children, the eldest of whom is ten. Jamil has never seen his youngest daughter, who was born after he was arrested in Gambia in 2001 and sent to Guantánamo. I have seen letters from Jamil's youngest children on my visits to Guantánamo, one-page letters with drawings that are heavily redacted by military censors. What is the offending language that the military has seen fit to redact? Language like "Daddy, I love you" and "Daddy, I miss you." How do I know? Because on my instructions, Jamil's wife has saved copies of the letters her children sent.

Melissa Hoffer: Beaten Down

Shortly after arriving at Guantánamo in early 2002, Lakhdar Boumediene was subjected to a thirteen-day period of extreme interrogation and near total sleep deprivation. He was interrogated from midnight until 5 a.m. and for several hours during the day.

After interrogations, he was returned to his cage, his wrists cuffed and his feet shackled to an anchor on the floor. Several times, while incapacitated in this position, guards repeatedly lifted him up and threw him to the floor. When I first met him in May 2005, he showed me a scar on his knee from one such incident.

His captors threatened to send him to Jordan, where "they could make him talk," and to a U.S. prison, where he would be raped. They threatened to shave his beard and apply lipstick to him. He was violently choked by a Jordanian interrogator. Each time Lakhdar made a request, he was told to ask his interrogator. Access to medical treatment was granted or denied based on the interrogators' assessment of his cooperation.

In April 2005, my colleagues and I filed a Freedom of Information Act suit seeking records concerning the treatment of Lakhdar and our other clients at Guantánamo. As a result, the U.S. government produced thousands of documents, including one confirming the involvement of medical personnel in interrogations. Lakhdar himself has been interrogated between 100 and 200 times.

One of our other clients, Mustafa Ait Idir, was alone in his cell when guards said they wanted to search it. The guards instructed him to sit on the floor and secured his hands behind his back. They slammed Mustafa's body and head into the steel bunk. They threw him on the floor, pounding his body and banging his head into the floor. They banged his head on the toilet. They stuffed his face down the toilet and repeatedly pressed flush. Mustafa feared he would drown. The guards carried him outside and threw him on the ground. They held him down and stuffed a garden hose into his mouth. They opened the spigot. Mustafa began to choke. He could not breathe. The guards took the hose out of his mouth and sprayed his face. This violent assault was wholly unprovoked.

A few days later, guards again came to search his cell. An officer ordered Mustafa to sit on the floor with his hands behind his back, which he did. The officer sprayed chemical irritant into his face. Two or three guards entered the cell. One forced Mustafa's body onto the steel floor and jumped on his back. The second guard did the same thing. They secured his hands behind his back, carried him outside, and threw him onto the gravel. An IRF member jumped on his head.

After this beating, half of Mustafa's face was paralyzed for several months. He was in constant pain. When he tried to eat, food and liquid leaked from his mouth. The guards simply mocked him.

Mari Newman: We Are All Damaged Forever

Ahmed works hard to get along with the interrogators and guards, and his life at Guantánamo is better because of it. But it is just this compliance that got him where he is. When the apartment where he was staying was raided by Pakistani police, Ahmed immediately surrendered. He had nothing to hide. Despite his unfettered cooperation, Ahmed was whipped and told to confess to possessing weapons he knew nothing about. Then, with his long shirttails pulled up over his head, he was beaten so severely with a Kalashnikov rifle that one can still feel the divot in the back of his head. This beating (like the others to come) was directed by Americans, who took videos of Ahmed's blood-saturated clothing. Call me a cynic, but I'm betting we will never see these videos, although the beatings had the desired outcome: Ahmed confessed to whatever the Americans suggested, regardless of the truth. Ahmed was then sent to a dark prison in Afghanistan and then to Bagram, where he continued to tell his torturers everything and anything they wanted to hear.

When Ahmed describes the torture he endured, his voice becomes monotone, and his sparkling eyes go flat. It is impossible to recount these events without it seeming like a bad movie. But this script was directed by our own government. For some forty days Ahmed was chained to a wall in a freezing, dark cell, in a position that did not allow him to sit down. If he fell asleep, he was beaten. No one spoke a word to him. Thugs burst into his cell at random to beat him over and over. Then, to complete the manipulation, Americans would take off Ahmed's handcuffs and massage his hands and give him water. But the torture would always resume. He was unchained intermittently for brutal beatings or to be placed under a tidal wave of filthy freezing water from a large pipe. This, they said, was not to torture but rather to "clean" him.

Periodic "medical" examinations were humiliating to the point that he would not even describe them. But these "doctors" allowed the beatings to continue. Ahmed was recuffed so tightly that his wrists bled. He screamed for two days until, mercifully, he passed out. He was suspended by his handcuffs for hours on end. The sparse food was repulsive and the water worse. "Scary" music was played at an excruciating volume, but the space between the tapes was worse, filled with the screaming of other men. I think guiltily about Ahmed's description of cacophonous music filled with the voice of the devil; I wonder if it is music I listen to, in the comfort of my life, thinking such music makes me "edgy."

Sometimes Ahmed was dragged to the interrogation room by his neck. Sometimes a hood was yanked over his head, and he was charged by vicious snarling dogs that barked so close to his face that he could smell their breath. Sometimes a gun was held to his head while interrogators demanded information. At first Ahmed tried to tell the truth, but the interrogators were never satisfied. Between the beatings, Ahmed listened carefully to the interrogators' questions with the hope of divining what it was that they wanted him to say, what confession would cause them to stop. He learned to lie in order to confess to whatever it was that the interrogators were seeking. He confessed to all that and more. And those "confessions" are the basis for his continued detention.

One of my other clients, a poetic man named Faez, says that the treatment of the men imprisoned at Guantánamo is akin to putting a bird in a cage and then banging on the bars with a baseball bat.

My worst fear is that even if these men are released, they are ruined. How can they ever participate in normal relationships when they have seen the utter darkness of humanity? How can they ever love when they have been so profoundly betrayed? I do not believe that most of the interrogators and guards who participated actively in this perversity started out so devoid of compassion. Surely they have engaged in considerable mental contortions to somehow justify the dehumanization they perpetuate. And what of us? Are we not complicit, going about our lives as if our own government is not perpetrating this most fundamental injustice? We are all forever damaged.

Amrit Singh: Freedom of Information

In 1966, Congress enacted the Freedom of Information Act (FOIA) to guarantee public access to government records and promote government accountability. Then House representative Donald Rumsfeld welcomed the legislation, declaring on the floor of the House that the law would "make it considerably more difficult for secrecy-minded bureaucrats to decide arbitrarily that the people should be denied access to information on the conduct of government." Ironically, Rumsfeld went on to become, as defense secretary, a key figure in the Bush administration's campaign to mask from public view the truth about the widespread and systemic torture of prisoners held in U.S. custody overseas in connection with the so-called "war on terror." President Bush himself led this campaign, declaring that the United States was leading the fight against torture by example and repeatedly assuring the world that the United States does not torture. Other senior officials, including Vice President Dick Cheney and CIA directors George Tenet and Michael Hayden, echoed those public disavowals of torture.

Federal agencies, taking their cue from high-level officials, played their own role in blocking the disclosure of information relating to the treatment of prisoners held in U.S. custody abroad. In October 2003, the American Civil Liberties Union (ACLU) and its partners filed a FOIA request with a number of agencies, including the CIA, the FBI, the Department of Defense, and the Department of Justice, seeking records relating to the treatment of such prisoners and the U.S. practice of "rendering" prisoners to countries known to employ torture. Government agencies largely ignored the ACLU's FOIA request. The Department of Defense declined to expedite the request, claiming there was no "compelling need" for release of the requested information.

In late April 2004, when photographs of U.S. military police abusing prisoners at Abu Ghraib were leaked to the press, it became all too apparent that the Bush administration had all the while been withholding records responsive to the ACLU's FOIA request. Soon thereafter, the ACLU filed suit in federal court. In September 2004, Judge Hellerstein of the Southern District of New York issued a strongly worded opinion, observing that "[n]o one is above the law" and that "FOIA, no less than any other law, must be duly observed." Noting that the information requested was of "significant public interest," the court chastised the government for the "glacial" pace of its response, which, according to the court, displayed an "indifference to the commands of FOIA, and fail[ed] to afford accountability of government that the Act requires." "If the documents are more of an embarrassment than a secret," the court said, "the public should know of our government's treatment of individuals captured and held abroad."

Notwithstanding that opinion, for years into the FOIA litigation, key records documenting the Bush administration's torture policies continued to be withheld by agencies claiming that their disclosure would harm national security. The CIA—by far the most secretive of federal agencies—barely made any substantive disclosures in the FOIA litigation during the Bush years. Indeed, the threshold legal battles against the CIA were fought over that agency's refusal even to confirm or deny the question of whether documents responsive to our FOIA requests existed. In particular, for more than two years, invoking what is known in FOIA parlance as the "Glomar" doctrine, the CIA refused to confirm or deny the existence of a 2001 presidential directive authorizing it to set up secret overseas detention facilities. Nor would the CIA disclose the existence of an August 2002 Office of Legal Counsel (OLC) memorandum authorizing it to use torture methods, including waterboarding, a technique designed to induce a drowning sensation by pouring water from a height onto a prisoner strapped to an inclined bench with his feet elevated and a cloth covering his nose and mouth. The CIA claimed that it would jeopardize national security even to admit that it had an interest in detainee interrogations—a fact that had been publicly reported countless times and that President Bush himself admitted in a September 2006 press briefing when he confirmed the existence of secret CIA jails or "black sites."

The CIA, however, was not the only agency to use national security as a pretext for withholding documents that could prove embarrassing, if not incriminating. The Defense Department fought tooth and nail to suppress the disclosure of photographs of U.S. personnel abusing prisoners at overseas locations, including at U.S.-run detention facilities other than Abu Ghraib in Iraq and in Afghanistan. It claimed that the disclosure of these images could lead to violent outrage and propaganda directed against the United States. In other words, the images should be withheld from public view precisely because they depict government misconduct. Moreover, even though the ACLU sought disclosure of the images only after individually identifying information had been deleted from each of them, the Bush administration also argued that disclosure would expose the prisoners to "insults and public curiosity" in violation of the Geneva Conventions. Ironically, the administration took this position while vigorously arguing that the Geneva Conventions did not apply to detainees seized in the "war on terror."

All of these arguments were soundly rejected both by the district court and a three-judge panel of the Second Circuit Court of Appeals. Following the Second Circuit's denial of the government's petition for rehearing by the full appeals court, the Obama administration initially agreed to release a substantial number of prisoner abuse images. But two weeks before the scheduled May 28, 2009, release date, the administration reversed course. Obama announced that publication of these photos "would not add any additional benefit to our understanding of what was carried out in the past by a small number of individuals" and "may only have a chilling effect on future investigations of detainee abuse." In doing so, Obama essentially ratified the Bush administration's position, and significantly undermined his promise to "creat[e] an unprecedented level of openness in Government."

The FBI was not as recalcitrant as other agencies in observing its obligations under FOIA. Early on in the litigation, it turned over numerous records describing its conflict with the Defense Department over the latter's use of abusive interrogation methods at Guantánamo Bay.

One can certainly speculate as to the reasons why the FBI made these records public. One FBI e-mail, dated December 2003, describes an incident in which Defense Department interrogators at Guantánamo Bay impersonated FBI agents while using "torture techniques" against a prisoner. The e-mail concludes, "If this detainee is ever released or his story made public in any way, DOD interrogators will not be held accountable because these torture techniques were done the [sic] 'FBI' interrogators. The FBI will left [sic] holding the bag before the public." Regardless of whether or not the FBI released its records to insulate itself from liability, those records were undoubtedly among the most significant early disclosures in the FOIA litigation. They were particularly important for informing the ongoing debate about the effectiveness of abusive interrogation methods for producing intelligence. Proponents of the use of torture have framed this debate by employing a hypothetical "ticking time bomb" scenario. This scenario purports to justify the torture of a prisoner believed to possess intelligence relating to a live bomb on the grounds that the torture would surely elicit information that could be used to defuse the bomb, thereby saving countless innocent lives. But FBI documents received through FOIA confirm that the FBI objected to the abusive SERE

(Survival, Evasion, Resistance, Escape) interrogation methods used by the Defense Department at Guantánamo Bay and argued that these methods were not effective at producing valuable intelligence. One FBI e-mail complains that these "torture techniques" had "produced no intelligence of a threat neutralization nature to date and . . . ha[d] destroyed any chance of prosecuting this detainee." Indeed, the documents showed that the FBI preferred "rapport-building" techniques to abusive techniques in interrogating detainees at Guantánamo and that the Defense Department continued to employ abusive methods over the FBI's objections.

The FBI documents also confirmed the truth of Guantánamo prisoners' claims of abuse. On numerous occasions, Rumsfeld publicly dismissed those claims, declaring, "[The prisoners are] taught to lie, they're taught to allege that they have been tortured, and that's part of the training that they received." But eyewitness FBI agent accounts of prisoner abuse at Guantánamo Bay confirm that those dismissals were unfounded. In one such account, an FBI agent at Guantánamo reports,

> On a couple of occasions, I entered interview rooms to find a detainee chained hand and foot in a fetal position to the floor, with no chair, food, or water. Most times they had urinated and defecated on themselves, and had been left there for 18–24 hours or more. On one occa[s]ion, the air conditioning had been turned down so far and the temperature was so cold in the room, that the barefooted detainee was shaking with cold. When I asked the MP's what was going on, I was told that interrogators from the day prior had ordered this treatment, and the detainee was not to be moved. On another occasion, the A/C had been turned off, making the temperature in the unventilated room probably well over 100 degrees. The detainee was almost unconscious on the floor, with a pile of hair next to him. He had apparently been literally pulling his own hair out throughout the night.

The FBI documents were not only significant for vindicating accounts of prisoner abuse at Guantánamo in the face of official denials that such abuse had occurred. They were also significant for documenting details of the severe mental and physical damage caused by interrogation methods that were specifically approved for use at Guantánamo by Rumsfeld—details hard to discern from clinical descriptions of those methods contained in interrogation directives.

Defense Department documents further demonstrate that the ticking-time-bomb hypothetical is inapposite for the added reason that the vast majority of prisoners held in U.S. custody, at least in Iraq, were not individuals who possessed intelligence of any value but were innocent bystanders swept up in military dragnets. A military commander in Iraq reports in a sworn statement,

> It became obvious to me that the majority of our detainees were detained as the result of being in the wrong place at the wrong time, and were swept up by Coalition Forces as peripheral bystanders during raids. I think perhaps only one in ten security detainees were of any particular intelligence value.

The FOIA records clearly and unambiguously show that the torture and abuse of prisoners at the hands of U.S. personnel was not confined to Abu Ghraib, or indeed to Guantánamo, but occurred at countless other locations in Iraq and Afghanistan. Numerous autopsy reports describe in gruesome detail the homicide deaths of prisoners in U.S. custody by "strangulation," "asphyxia," and "blunt force injuries." One such autopsy report records the homicide death in Al Asad, Iraq, of a forty-seven-year old Iraqi male who was shackled to the top of a door frame with a gag in his mouth at the time he lost consciousness and became pulseless and died. Other autopsy reports confirm that in December 2002, U.S. interrogators at Bagram Collection Point in Afghanistan killed two prisoners by subjecting them to "blunt force injuries."

Perhaps most importantly, the records obtained through FOIA litigation showed that senior Bush administration officials caused the widespread and systemic abuse and torture of prisoners held in U.S. custody by authorizing departures from long-established legal prohibitions against torture and cruel, inhuman, and degrading treatment. Four OLC memoranda released in April 2009 by the Obama administration demonstrated how senior Justice Department officials sanctioned the CIA's use of waterboarding and other torture methods. Each of the memos concluded that such methods were legal even though after World War II the United States had prosecuted Japanese accused of waterboarding for war crimes, precedents the memos neglected even to mention. Such legal contortions confirm that the memos were designed not to render objective legal advice but to provide legal immunity for the CIA's use of torture.

The earliest of these four memos, dated August 1, 2002, was authored by then Assistant Attorney General Jay Bybee and addressed to John Rizzo, then Acting General Counsel of the CIA. The memo concluded that ten interrogation techniques—including methods such as "waterboarding," "insects placed in a confinement box," "walling" (slamming individuals into a flexible false wall), and "cramped confinement" in small dark boxes—did not violate the federal statute criminalizing torture. In a previously released companion memo authored on the same day, Bybee supplied a more general legal analysis granting the CIA carte-blanche authority to torture. The latter memorandum adopted a definition of torture so narrow that it encompassed only those methods that result in pain akin to that associated with "death, organ failure or the permanent impairment of a significant body function." Much of the legal analysis of the latter memorandum was repeated in a March 24, 2003, memorandum authored by Deputy Assistant Attorney General John Yoo addressed to the Defense Department's general counsel, William Haynes, that also gave the Defense Department carte-blanche authority to torture.

The remainder of the three OLC memos released by the Obama administration in response to the FOIA lawsuit were authored by Principal Deputy Assistant Attorney General Steven Bradbury in May 2005, long after the details of prisoner abuse at Abu Ghraib had become public, and as Congress moved toward enacting legislation prohibiting the "cruel, inhuman and degrading treatment" of all prisoners in U.S. custody. These memos followed the same legally and morally bankrupt approach of the August 2002 Bybee memos. One went so far as to argue that techniques like waterboarding did not even amount to "cruel, inhuman and degrading treatment" within the meaning of the Convention Against Torture and Other Cruel, Inhuman and Degrading Treatment or Punishment, a treaty signed and ratified by the United States along with more than 150 other nations.

Since the ACLU first filed its FOIA request in 2003, more than 100,000 pages of government documents relating to the torture and abuse of prisoners have been disclosed. But most of those disclosures were significantly delayed and came only after protracted litigation. Moreover, key records relating to the Bush administration's illegal policies governing prisoner treatment and interrogation still remain secret. Some observers would therefore rightly question the value of the FOIA as a tool for promoting government accountability. Yet, partial and delayed though these disclosures are, they have played an important role in exposing, through the Bush administration's own documents, the critical role played by senior officials in spawning the torture and systemic abuse of prisoners held in U.S. custody abroad. Whether the political will exists to hold those officials accountable is of course a separate question, one that remains to be answered in time to come. But these documents helped confirm what detainees and their lawyers had long been maintaining in the habeas corpus litigation: that the Bush administration had deliberately sanctioned torture and other abuse in creating a network of lawless prisons at Guantánamo and beyond.

In addition to torture, detainees were subjected to harsh disciplinary measures, often arbitrarily. They were also subjected to various forms of religious abuse and other mistreatment.

Marc D. Falkoff: This Is to Whom It May Concern

"This is an island of hell," Adnan tells me, when I ask him to explain what life is like in Guantánamo.

He tells me about his arrival in Cuba. After deplaning, he was chained hand and foot. He was still wearing black-out goggles and ear muffs. Soldiers kicked him and hit him. They dislocated his shoulder.

He spent his first weeks in Camp X-Ray. He was kept in an open-air cage, exposed to the tropical sun. There was no shade. There was no shelter from the wind, which buffeted him with sand and pebbles. His only amenities in X-Ray were a bucket for water and another for urine and feces.

During one of his first interrogations at Guantánamo, he was questioned with a gun to his head.

Adnan then explains to me some of the punishments for disobeying the arbitrary disciplinary rules inside the wire, such as the rule against squirreling away some food from your lunch: solitary confinement. No comfort items. No mattress. No pants.

"No pants?" I ask. "What do you mean?"

"They take away your pants," he explains, "and leave you wearing only shorts. This is to prevent the brothers from praying. It would be immodest to pray uncovered. They do it to humiliate us."

I get it now, and I find it chilling. The punishment makes no sense except as a religious humiliation.

Another typical punishment? They shave the detainees' beards, a form of religious and cultural degradation.

George Brent Mickum: Comfort Items

Bisher wrote me two letters on November 5 and 6. I was allowed to read his letters on December 17. He complained of being placed in solitary confinement without "comfort items."

Bisher was being punished for having a short list with the names of prisoners who wanted to be represented by counsel and asked him to write to me on their behalf. He apologized for bothering me, conceding that he "needs a shoulder to cry on."

I wrote a letter to the military, complaining about his treatment. I never received a reply.

Ellen Lubell: A Penalty

Aziz told us after our first visit that he'd been denied sunlight as a penalty for meeting with us. "For your sake, they punished me," he had told us. "They made me walk in darkness for four months."

Richard Grigg: Naked

My client talked dispassionately and unemotionally about the cruel methods that had been used to interrogate him. He never changed expressions until he talked about being forced to strip naked in front of women—his voice broke and his eyes filled with tears. This made me realize that as horrible and despicable as we think the photos from Abu Ghraib are, we have no appreciation for the effect they have had in the Muslim world.

Maya D. Curtis: Learning English in Guantánamo

In our meeting, Samir painted a vivid picture of the treatment endured by some Guantánamo prisoners unfamiliar with the English language. Consider the experience of Amar, who ripped his trousers to seek respite from the sweltering Guantánamo prison cells. Although Samir did not witness everything that happened to Amar, he was within hearing distance and generally could learn of incidents happening in the same prison area almost contemporaneously.

Since prisoners are forbidden from altering their uniforms, a guard came to Amar's cell and ordered him to stand behind the black line painted on the floor so that he could pass him new trousers. Amar misunderstood the command and thought that the guard was asking him for his trouser size. An absurd exchange ensued; instead of standing behind the black line, Amar continued to repeat his pant size, "3XL? 3XL?" while gesturing to his trousers. The guard left the cell.

Samir, who knew the guard, told his neighboring prisoners to warn Amar that the guard would probably return with pepper spray, but his fellow prisoners were afraid to become involved. The guard returned with pepper spray, as predicted, and apparently used it against Amar. Samir was told that after screaming in pain and coughing, Amar lay down, unconscious. Neighboring cellmates then heard the familiar footsteps of the Immediate Reaction Force (IRF) team. Clad in riot gear, IRF teams are used to subdue "noncompliant" prisoners at Guantánamo. Samir was told that despite Amar's being in a prone position, the IRF team beat him. Samir then saw Amar being removed from the cell and taken to a different area of the prison.

Samir learned that Amar was isolated for forty-eight hours. Every ten minutes, he was forced to verbally acknowledge a knock on his door. Failure to respond resulted in another visit from the IRF team. When Samir saw Amar being returned to his cell, Amar wore only shorts, although he had worn pants when he was taken.

It thus appears that Amar was pepper-sprayed and spent two days in isolation for misunderstanding a shouted command. However, a language barrier cannot provide the only explanation for this altercation. Behind this beating lies a system in which guards may have been trained to identify the prisoners as the "worst of the worst," to lump them all together as Muslims or Arabs, and to avoid seeing the common humanity that binds us all together.

After Samir related the story, we both lapsed into momentary silence. I reflected on the fact that prisoners in Guantánamo are denied access to most written materials. Although prison officials cite security concerns as the reason for denying such materials, I often wonder whether the real reason is to prevent the empowerment that comes from understanding a captor's language. One habeas attorney had the temerity to submit *Dr. Seuss's ABC* for his client, in the hope that a children's book might pass the scrutiny of the prison officials who must approve all nonlegal materials given to prisoners. Dr. Seuss failed the test, as have other written materials. The one book that the U.S. government has deemed appropriate is the Quran, written in Arabic.

It is curious that our government will give only the Quran to prisoners, many of whom had never read the Quran closely prior to their years of imprisonment. Although the Quran has given mental solace to many prisoners at Guantánamo, Amar's experience demonstrates the important role that the English language plays on a day-to-day basis in these men's lives. Providing Arabic-language Qurans to prisoners cannot and should not obscure all the fundamental things denied them: an ability to understand their captors, knowledge of the evidence against them, and an ability to defend themselves.

Reactions

Indefinite detention, isolation, and abuse all took a devastating toll on prisoners at Guantánamo. Prisoners responded in different ways. The only three aspects of their lives over which the detainees continued to exercise control were representation by an attorney, whether they would continue to eat, and whether to take their own life. Although the habeas attorneys were important advocates for their clients' release, some detainees exercised one of the only rights they still possessed: rejecting their attorneys.

Jim Nickovich: Waiting

The military official goes into his office and then emerges and tells you the prisoner is refusing to meet with you. Can you blame him? The military will not tell him ahead of time that you are not a military official. They will not explain to him who you are. He just knows that in the seventh year of his imprisonment some American wants to meet with him. You have it on good authority that his experiences with Americans since his capture and imprisonment have not been pleasant. You accept that building trust with the prisoner is a difficult process and an integral one. So you wait again. You write a note and hand it off to a military official to pass along to the prisoner. You hope the military translator on the inside of the prison translates the note correctly. You are not allowed to see the prisoner yourself. You are not allowed to have your translator directly translate the note to the prisoner. You are not even allowed to have your translator present when the military translator translates your note to the prisoner. Still, through the note, you ask the prisoner to meet with you and tell him you will be back again.

Frustrated at having been shut out in your first trip to GTMO, you wonder what to do. Everyone representing a prisoner tells you the same thing: GTMO takes time. So you go to GTMO again a month later. The same ordeal. The same flights. The same ferries. The same buses. The same waiting.

Muneer I. Ahmad: On Being Fired

When Omar Khadr, my former client at Guantánamo Bay, fired me in April 2007, it was not for the first time. By my count, it was at least the third, but, finally, the last as well. For me, it was the formal end of nearly three years of the most challenging client representation in which I have engaged. For Omar, it was just another day in the dim, nearly forgotten hole in our collective conscience known as Guantánamo.

This disparity in how Omar and I experienced the firing mirrors a broader set of differences between us in life experience and world perspective. Ultimately, Omar's decision to fire me and my co-counsel reflected a judgment not only about our efficacy but also about the ability of law and legal process to bring meaningful change at Guantánamo. Whether that judgment was correct is something about which I feel deeply ambivalent, and I suspect that Omar does as well.

Like other prisoners, Omar was brought to Guantánamo based on a unilateral and superficial designation by the executive that he was an "enemy combatant." But Omar's case was unique in several respects. First, when he was captured by U.S. forces in Afghanistan in July 2002, Omar was only fifteen years old. He remains the youngest prisoner at Guantánamo. Second, Omar is a Canadian citizen and the only Westerner still imprisoned at Guantánamo. Finally, whereas the vast majority of prisoners at Guantánamo have never been charged with any crime and, by the government's admission, never will be, Omar is one of the handful of individuals there who has been charged with alleged war crimes, to be tried before the substandard military commission system. The charges against Omar arose from allegations that at the end of a U.S. assault on a house in Afghanistan where he was living, he threw a grenade that killed a U.S. service member. In addition, members of Omar's family are alleged to have terrorist connections, and the notoriety of his family has figured prominently in how he has been perceived, both in Canada and by the U.S. government.

My colleague Richard Wilson and I began representing Omar in July 2004, after the Supreme Court's decision in *Rasul v. Bush* recognized the right of Guantánamo detainees to habeas corpus. Over the next two and a half years, we met with Omar more than a dozen times, filed mountains of paper in federal court, and represented him in preliminary military commission proceedings.

The first time we saw Omar, in November 2004, he looked very much the teenager: gangly, awkward, and with a disarming smile. He had lost most of the vision in one eye from the shrapnel he received during the firefight in Afghanistan. He showed us the scars on his chest and back where he had been shot, multiple times, and let us feel the shrapnel still embedded in his forearms. He told us of the interrogations that began almost immediately after his capture in Afghanistan and continued at Guantánamo. He was threatened with rendition to Afghanistan and Egypt, where, his interrogators told him, he would be raped by older men. On one occasion at Guantánamo, interrogators refused to permit Omar to use the bathroom, and so he urinated on himself, after which two guards lifted his hog-tied body, poured pine solvent on him and the floor, and used him as a human mop to clean the mess. We told Omar we were there to help, and he smiled in appreciation.

The last time I saw Omar, in November 2006—the second-to-last time he sought to fire me—was the most extraordinary of all my visits with him. On the first day, he refused to see me. I wrote him a note that military officials took to him, but still he refused. I left a second note, saying I would come back the following day. When I returned, I was told that Omar had agreed to see me this time and that he had been taken to Camp Iguana for the meeting, a short drive from his solitary confinement in Camp Five.

We had never met in Iguana before, and there was a deep irony to our doing so now: Camp Iguana had been established to house a group of children, some as young as twelve years old, who, like Omar, had been brought from Afghanistan to Guantánamo as "enemy combatants." There, they lived in dormitory-style rooms on the ocean's edge, received educational instruction and psychological counseling, played soccer outdoors, and were allowed ice cream and viewings of various movies, such as *Castaway* (Tom Hanks stranded on a desert island) on DVD. Eventually, they were all sent home. Although Omar was only fifteen at the time he was captured, he was never taken to Iguana because an arbitrary Pentagon policy, without any basis in law, reserved Iguana for those who were fifteen or younger *at the time of arrival* at Guantánamo; Omar had turned sixteen while in custody at the U.S. base in Bagram, awaiting transfer to Guantánamo. Only now, at the age of twenty, when he had grown to over six feet tall and his peach fuzz had given way to a thick beard, was he being allowed in Iguana.

I arrived at Iguana and waited as guards prepared Omar for my visit: removing the goggles and headphones prisoners must wear while being transported to keep them disoriented, unlocking his wrist shackles, and attaching his ankle shackles to an eyehook in the floor. Just when I was getting ready to enter the room, a guard told me that Omar had changed his mind about meeting with me and was being transported back to Camp Five. I walked outside to intercept him, and as I emerged from the bunga-low-style building in which I had been waiting, I saw two guards on the other side of a fence escorting Omar to a white van. "Wait!" I shouted and hurried toward them. Omar turned and stared impassively, waiting for me to speak. It was late morning and already uncomfortably warm. "Assalaam aleikum, Omar," I said. "Waleikum assalaam," he replied. I asked him to meet with me, but he demurred, saying he wanted to go back to Camp Five. I asked that he sit with me for fifteen minutes, so that I could update him on his case. "You're not my lawyer anymore," he said. "I fired you. I don't want you representing me anymore." Guards stood on each side as this transpired, holding Omar by the arms, and a lawyer from the Staff Judge Advocate (the military lawyers for the base) stood beside me. So much for attorney-client privilege, I thought.

I asked Omar why he wanted to fire me, and at this he glowered, say-ing that I was doing nothing to help him and that I was of more benefit to the government than I was to him. I knew immediately what he meant, in part because I harbored the same concern: as a lawyer at Guantánamo, my mere presence and ability to meet with my client signified the exis-tence of some law and legal process at Guantánamo, even as I attempted to demonstrate the lack of both. By participating as a lawyer at Guan-tánamo, I risked unwittingly legitimizing Guantánamo. And yet, with so little to show for our efforts—Omar was still detained indefinitely and still faced a trial before a sham military commission—this legitimizing of Guantánamo threatened to overwhelm any good we could do on Omar's behalf. It did not help that, though Muslim, I was American, as Omar had come to mistrust all things American, which is hardly surprising given his experiences in Afghanistan and Guantánamo.

As I pondered Omar's argument, and how to respond, I felt myself momentarily departing my body, rising, and gazing down on what felt like a scene out of a movie. There we stood in tense confrontation, star-ing face-to-face through chain-link fence, the sun bearing down, guards flanking Omar, shackled in his khaki jumpsuit, and me, an accordion file of legal papers under one arm, shielded from the glare and hiding from Omar's accusatory stare behind sunglasses, secretly panicked as to how to negotiate myself back into his confidence. I finally broke the silence and told Omar that I worried he might be right. I told him what I believed to be true—that his position was not unreasonable and that perhaps the costs of legitimizing Guantánamo were greater than the benefit gained of trying to challenge it through legal process. But I also told him that this was worth discussing and that even if in the end he decided not to keep his lawyers, I could help him to think through how best to proceed without us, because whether he liked it or not, legal process was being thrust on him in the form of military commissions.

For whatever reason—persuasion, exhaustion, pity—Omar relented, and eventually we sat down together. It was a long and often difficult meeting, lasting five hours, and in the end, my co-counsel and I were tentatively "unfired." But within a matter of months, we were fired again, this time permanently.

That day in November was one of accounting, and of accountability. It forced me to speak candidly with Omar about what law and lawyers could do to help him and, perhaps more important, what they could not. This, in turn, forced me to confront anew these questions for myself and to think seriously about the contradiction of using legal process and legal identity—that is, my standing as a lawyer—to prove the lawlessness of Guantánamo. And it dramatized, not for the first time, how vastly different are the worlds that Omar and I inhabit—mine a world of ideas bounded only by imagination and time, his a world of concrete and steel, circumscribed by concertina wire, in which time is the one thing in abundance. When these two collided, the question was posed, could my world penetrate his, and his mine?

Over the lifetime of the Guantánamo litigation, events that have been momentous for the lawyers often have been mundane, or even meaningless, for the prisoners: court victories, congressional maneuverings, condemnations of Guantánamo by world leaders, publication of favorable editorials. For the lawyers, these were all victories. Moreover, because only in brief, delusionary moments did we believe that a single blow would destroy Guantánamo, because we were committed to a longer view of history and a gradualist view of change, we became all the more invested in the small gains. We knew that we were not just litigating individual disputes; we were trying to create political consciousness and shift cultural understandings of Guantánamo, on the part of the courts and the public, so as to enable fundamental change. We were educating as we were litigating, and the education process is often imperceptibly slow.

It was, then, frequently jarring to meet with Omar and to learn of what little consequence these developments were in his life. The Supreme Court's decision in *Hamdan v. Rumsfeld*, and Omar's reaction to it, exemplify this phenomenon. *Hamdan* was an unexpected and significant victory in the Guantánamo litigation, not only invalidating the Bush administration's military commissions but rejecting its claim that prisoners could be held without any protections under the Geneva Conventions. Yet, despite my enthusiasm for the legal victory, despite the fact that the decision had halted his own military commission proceedings, Omar was unimpressed. In retrospect, his reaction proved more sanguine than my own, because he understood intuitively—*viscerally*—that while the theoretical foundation of Guantánamo might have shifted, the material fundamentals remained the same. Omar's captivity, in solitary confinement, continued, unmodified by Supreme Court jurisprudence. The guards and interrogators wielded essentially the same power over him as before, and he was, once more, detained indefinitely and without charge. The law may have changed, but the will of the administration had not. As the lawyers hailed a new legal landscape, for Omar, life the day after *Hamdan* looked, smelled, tasted, and felt unmistakably and unrelentingly like the day before.

To the lawyers, *Hamdan* mattered not only because it halted ongoing, deeply flawed proceedings but also because of what we believed it to signify: it was, first and foremost, a rebuke of a central pillar of the Bush administration's Guantánamo policy and, more broadly, of the administration's claim of expansive, and unfettered, executive power. We believed that it signaled a willingness of the courts to serve as a meaningful check on the executive and that although it did not itself resolve Omar's plight at Guantánamo, it augured well for future court proceedings. But beyond the courtroom, *Hamdan* was significant because it delegitimized the administration's strategy of using military commissions, thereby increasing the political costs for continuing to use them, and further delegitimized Guantánamo, which already was an international embarrassment for the administration. Relatedly, it raised the political costs for Canada's acquiescence to the commissions, by implicitly adjudging Canada to have placed its faith in an illegal system by failing to press for Omar's repatriation. Our hope, and our belief, was that these consequences of the *Hamdan* decision might erode the political viability of the commissions, for both the administration and Canada, and thereby open the way for an alternative, bilaterally negotiated resolution to Omar's case.

Thus, in order to explain to Omar the significance of the *Hamdan* decision, we had to make explicit our assumptions about how law operates and how it produces change. Providing context for the decision meant engaging Omar in political education, articulating a political theory, and explaining our theory of social change. Moreover, our lawyering theory— our vision of how change is effected through law and our self-conception in that process—was deeply implicated in our relationship with Omar. As there is in every lawyer-client relationship, whether openly acknowledged or not, there was a specific politics to the representation, and with Omar, we often tried to make that politics plain.

But it is not only the lawyers' politics that are brought to bear on the relationship, and despite his youth, Omar had developed a politics, too. His was not a politics of religious ideology learned in the madrasahs (indeed, he had never attended one) but a theory and understanding of power, the brute force that undergirds politics, grounded in the excruciating, lived experience of Guantánamo. For his lawyers, power was an abstraction, soft and diffuse, transmitted through a blurry, bureaucratic membrane, a sophisticated, nearly invisible form of social control. For Omar, power was the barrel of a gun.

What emerged, then, was a difference in the metric for success that Omar and his lawyers used. For Omar, observable, experienced change in his physical and psychological condition—that is, not merely his material well-being but his *materiality*—was the measure of success. For his lawyers, removed from the lived experience of Guantánamo, we saw incremental progress even when none was felt by Omar. But the fact that our professional judgment was unimpeded by the daily degradation of Guantánamo was both an asset and a part of the problem.

It would be a mistake to say that Omar was concerned merely with short-term relief (improved living conditions, more exercise time, better medical treatment) while we were concerned with the long-term goal of his release. The difference between us was rather more profound and concerned competing judgments about how best to achieve the long-term goal. In the beginning of our relationship, Omar gave law, and us, the benefit of the doubt. But over time, he developed a theory of social change far different from ours, and in light of how little material gain his lawyers had been able to achieve for him over the course of two and a half years, placed significantly less weight on law and lawyers.

As much as we viewed litigation as one part of a multiprong strategy to shift the politics around Guantánamo, it was, predictably, legal process in which we were primarily engaged. For Omar, the solution did not lie in law. His daily existence at Guantánamo was, in his eyes (and, increasingly, in mine), an indictment of law, and with every passing day, the case against law got only stronger. So, too, did the case against us, his lawyers.

Without any formal legal training, and without even a high school diploma, Omar achieved a keen understanding of law's potential limits. His experience of law at Guantánamo and of legal process in habeas corpus and military commission proceedings led him to view law as a series of infinitely manipulable categories (enemy combatants versus prisoners of war, detainees versus prisoners), whose master is not merely politics but power. Omar came to see law as the government's tool of oppression rather than his and the other detainees' instrument for liberation. And he saw that no matter what the legal victory—the granting of habeas rights in *Rasul,* the invalidation of the military commission system in *Hamdan*— the government could simply readjust its legal position, choosing once more from the infinite pool of legal categories, and achieve the same practical result as before the supposed victory.

Since early on in the litigation, I wondered about the will of the courts (as distinct from their authority) to remedy the injustices of Guantánamo. At the same time, I threw myself into the litigation, fueled by an understanding that law has at times, in my own career and over the course of American history, proven an effective means for change. So long as we were in federal court, I held out hope that Omar's case would be heard and that, once heard properly, justice would be dispensed. Of course, politics was evident there, too, as the outcome of identical motions filed on behalf of multiple prisoners varied, predictably, depending on who had appointed the judge. But it was my brief participation in the military commission system that most severely undermined my belief in the integrity of law, at arm's length if not wholly separate from politics, and it was in the course of representing Omar in the commissions that I unwittingly may have bolstered the argument for my firing.

David Marshall: Impersonations

Things did not go according to plan for us. An official met us at the ferry with the news that our client, a young Syrian, had refused to meet us.

Our first order of business was going to Camp Five, where our client was imprisoned, so that we could write him a request to reconsider.

Prisoners at Guantánamo sometimes refuse to meet with their lawyers. My client eventually changed his mind, so we did meet that day. I have learned that there are a few reasons that often motivate refusals at Guantánamo.

Prisoners find it hard to believe that the lawyers are not really working for the government. They come from countries in which a prisoner could never count on a lawyer to be loyal to him.

Guantánamo prisoners also often consider the legal process futile. Why participate in a process that will raise their hopes and then surely dash them? When one looks at the record, most victories in court have been quickly nullified by an act of Congress.

There are reports that some interrogators have impersonated lawyers for the prisoners. I don't know whether that has happened, but even an untrue report like that will discourage cooperation with attorneys.

If a prisoner is moved to another camp to meet his lawyer, he will undergo shackling and placement of a hood over his face. This could be distressing to anyone. If the prisoner has undergone "harsh interrogation" in the past, it will probably be much more distressing. (How many of the prisoners at Guantánamo suffer posttraumatic stress disorder?) A prisoner thus may refuse to meet with his lawyer because he is unwilling to undergo transportation to the meeting.

The tendency of prisoners to refuse to meet their lawyers is just one of many features of Guantánamo litigation that distinguishes it from the rest of my twenty-two years of representing prisoners. Almost all these features complicate the work.

Gordon S. Woodward: A Climate of Despondency

I offered to represent a young man imprisoned at Guantánamo Bay. Toward that end, I met with him twice. However, after our second meeting he asked me to stop and take no further action on his behalf.

After six years he had a dim view of our justice system. As far as he was concerned, lawyers could do nothing for him. The American justice system was hypocritical and corrupt. He felt that by participating in this system he would only lend credibility to the charade—that participation merely perpetuated the myth of American justice.

To say his story is tragic really does not do it justice. He did not want to go to Afghanistan. He went with his family because his father made the decision for him. He went because he was told to go. Unfortunately, within two months of arriving, al Qaeda attacked the United States; not long thereafter Kabul was under attack, and the family fled to Pakistan.

This young man was a foreigner—an Arab—in a place where Arabs were being hunted down and sold for bounties, and somewhere along the way locals turned him and his father over to Pakistani authorities.

His treatment on the way to Guantánamo was brutal, including beatings, threatened electrical shocks, sleep deprivation, temperature extremes, and isolation. It is difficult to say whether, in his view, the circumstances were any better in Guantánamo. What can be said, however, is that conditions remained oppressive, coercive, and bleak.

I argued that he should not give up on the legal system. Even if he did not want to fight for justice, he could just let me keep his case open. The courts might rule in his favor, and if they did, it would be important for him to have access to a lawyer.

He responded by saying, "You can't tell me what is right for me—I'm the one who is living this nightmare."

What do you do in this situation as an attorney? It is difficult to stop representing someone when you firmly believe that to stop is a bad idea. Some attorneys have argued that a client's decision to refuse help cannot be made rationally in the environment of Guantánamo because the government has specifically pursued a strategy of breaking prisoners down, creating a climate of despondency and hopelessness—a climate in which the prisoner feels he has no power, is helpless, and is dependant on his captors. Perhaps this young man's decision is no more than the intended consequence of the government's interrogation program. Perhaps the government has succeeded in convincing him that seeking justice is futile.

Despite these compelling arguments, it feels hypocritical to advocate for justice and dignity yet refuse to honor a client's choice. Arguably, we are little better than the system we oppose if we refuse our clients the freedom to choose whether and how to advocate for themselves.

There is no easy answer. I wished him luck as I left.

Mark Muoio: Caged Animals

We had been rejected again, the third time in three days. While the other lawyers were meeting with their clients, five of us—three habeas lawyers, our interpreter, and our military escort, a young airwoman— were sitting in the shade of a large shed in between Camp Echo and Camp Six. The conversations varied. In an off moment I retold a story I had only half heard the day before while buying postcards at the Naval Commissary and Exchange (NEX).

The story as I remembered it recounted by the armed forces radio was about a domesticated chimpanzee on Xanax mauling an innocent person. I recounted to the group as much as I could remember. Everyone was disturbed and disgusted. Our escort was particularly disturbed by the story. She said, "Ya know, it's no wonder the poor chimp attacked a person—it's away from its home, it's been put it in a cage and drugged up. It has no one to be with, and it's probably pretty sexually frustrated. It's really no wonder the animal would hurt someone—look how they treat it." Nervous laughter and yelps of victory erupted from the habeas lawyers. Our escort, realizing the implications of her statement, rolled her eyes and put her head into her hands with an unsavory smile.

Hunger Strikes

Hundreds of prisoners went on hunger strikes over the years as a means of protesting their inhumane treatment. Hunger strikes provided a voice to those who had been denied justice for so many years, the only way of exerting control in an environment in which they otherwise had none. Many prisoners were willing to risk dying rather than silently endure the injustices of Guantánamo. The government's response not only was cruel, if not brutal, but also failed to acknowledge that the underlying problem lay in its treatment of the prisoners.

Julia Tarver Mason: "Medical Treatment"

In July 2005, I visited Yusef. I had not seen him for over two months, and I was amazed at what I saw. He had lost a distressing amount of weight in a relatively short period of time. When I asked him about it, he explained that he, along with hundreds of other prisoners, had been engaged in a hunger strike. Understandably, the detainees were losing faith in the ability of their lawyers to do anything to affect their situation. Because there was no real progress regarding their case or detention, the prisoners seized on the only thing in that environment over which they retained control: their willingness to eat.

While they viewed the hunger strike as their only form of protest to the terrible conditions of their confinement, I saw it, rightly or wrongly, as a symptom of their deteriorating mental health. I spoke to Yusef about the strike, and I urged him not to give up hope and not to do anything that would jeopardize his physical well-being. But Yusef said to me with a reassuring and hopeful tone, "Don't worry, don't worry, Ms. Julia" (as he calls me), "I started eating yesterday because the government promised me that things were going to get better, and I believed them." He explained to me how the head of the camp, "the man with all the stars on his shoulder," had come to him and told him that he was finally going home. As Yusef said those words, his big brown eyes began to well up with hopeful tears, and I started to feel my eyes welling up as well. Yusef said to me, "So don't worry about me. I'm going home. I won't see you again until I am with my parents, and then maybe you can come visit us in Saudi Arabia." Yusef was very excited.

Less than three months later, in early October 2005, I could hardly recognize Yusef when I walked into the room. Nineteen-year-old Yusef now looked closer to age ninety. He was gaunt and feeble—sitting in chains—behind a walker. We had to turn off the fan in the room so we could hear Yusef's soft whisper. He could barely speak. He had a tube taped to the side of his nose that went through one of his nostrils and down into his stomach. We soon learned that the U.S. government had broken its promise to send Yusef home. He had resumed his hunger strike and was now being force-fed by the military, in order to preserve his own life. To be fair, I didn't want Yusef to die either. I did not think he had, under those circumstances, the mental capacity to make the decision to die, so I supported the government's attempt to preserve his life.

But what I came to learn from Yusef about this forced feeding made everything else I had heard about treatment at Guantánamo pale in comparison. Yusef told me about his so-called medical treatment from the physicians at Guantánamo. He described how it began at first with IVs, through which the military doctors would poke around for veins in an attempt to force enough nourishment into the hunger strikers' bodies so they would not die. Ultimately, the military concluded that the IVs were not working. So they instituted a strict regimen of brutal forced feeding that ultimately became a form of torture in its own right.

This so-called medical treatment bears little resemblance to what you and I have come to think of when we think of the Hippocratic Oath. Yusef described how six or more military guards, equipped with riot gear, would rush into his cell. Four guards would hold down his arms and legs; one guard would hold his chin in place, while another guard pulled his head back by his hair so that someone else could violently insert a tube up his nose and down into his stomach. He described how tubes were reused from one detainee to another without sanitation. He would see a tube with another detainee's blood and stomach bile all over it. Yusef said that often, when the tubes were removed from his body, he vomited up blood and then passed out. The violence of this assault—all supposedly in the name of medicine—left Yusef unable to speak for two days.

During our last meeting, nineteen-year-old Yusef gave me his Last Will and Testament. He told me that he could no longer go on living the life that he was living at Guantánamo. All he wanted to do was to die.

When we raised our concerns about the treatment of Yusef and the other hunger strikers with the military and the courts, all the military would tell us was that they were providing "safe and humane" medical treatment at Guantánamo and that our clients' attempts to kill themselves were just another attempt at "asymmetric warfare." The military and the courts seemed determined not to see these prisoners as human beings. The military also refused the help of experienced medical personnel from the United States who volunteered to assist—medical personnel with experience in dealing with prison hunger strikes. Instead, the military appeared determined to make the force-feeding process so excruciatingly painful that the prisoners would stop their strike.

It has been difficult to see my country doing things that violate the core principles we stand for as a nation; it has been equally, if not more, painful for me to imagine that members of the medical community might be participating in such atrocities. Perhaps even higher than the values we share as a nation are the fundamental, civilized values that we share as fellow human beings. Embedded in those values is the settled assumption that medical-care providers are there to provide caring treatment to those who are wounded, regardless of their country's military objectives. Therefore, even when individuals are captured in war, once they reach that place, that tent—perhaps on the battlefield—with the big red cross or the big red crescent on it, they know they are safe, and they will be treated as human beings, not as enemies. People around the globe seem to know and expect this. It is sad to imagine that in fighting this "war on terror," we may have lost sight not only of who we are as Americans but of who we are as human beings.

One of my other clients at Guantánamo is Abdul Rahman Shalabi. Abdul Rahman, at age thirty-one, seems like an elder statesman at the prison. He is one of our few clients that is out of his teens or twenties. But when I met with him during the height of the forced-feeding program, he had to be brought into the room on a stretcher. He was too weak even to walk. In the faint voice that he could muster while he had a tube inserted from his nose to his abdomen, Abdul Rahman tried to explain the situation to me:

> These detainees are young. They are innocent. The United States thought they had information. These people do not have information. Now the situation is more severe. It has been four years now. People on the island have lost trust in any human being. In the beginning, the interrogators used to say, "Trust us." Delegations from other countries said, "Trust us." All the promises we have been given are lies. We lost trust. There is no law here, only injustice.

Abdul Rahman Shalabi was force-fed, twice a day, every day, for the duration of his hunger strike. Rather than guards holding down his every limb, he was placed in a "restraint chair" (called the "execution chair" by detainees). Even though he no longer resisted feedings, Abdul Rahman, like the other long-term hunger strikers, was forced to sit in that chair, with his limbs and his head completely immobilized, while the military forced fluids through his nose. And although the feeding only takes about twenty minutes to complete, Abdul Rahman was forced to remain in that chair for hours, sitting—despite desperate pleas for help—in his own excrement.

John Robert Holland and Anna Cayton Holland-Edwards: The Only Means of Protest

Mohammed told us over the course of his imprisonment at Guantánamo how he had engaged repeatedly in hunger strikes. These he described in painful detail and with great poignancy. His words filled us with horror. He told us about the medical abuses and torture inflicted on him in a relentless effort by the government to break his will and make him stop striking. Eventually, he had resolved to stop only when freed or dead. It was, as he eloquently explained, his only means of protest against his outrageous confinement.

He described being tied so tightly into restraint chairs that he could not move. Overly large feeding tubes were very painfully forced down his nose and into his stomach. He would be kept like this for hours at a time. He told us how they would deliberately position the tube into his stomach and then repeatedly yank it out, stating that they had not gotten it into the right location. This too would cause him great pain and make his nose bleed. They recycled tubes that had been used on other prisoners, caked with remnants of human blood and bodily fluids. They would overfeed him through the tubes until he vomited, defecated, and urinated on himself. Then he would be thrown into his cell covered in his own feces, blood, urine, and vomit and left there. Mohammed also talked about doctors who taunted him, warning that this treatment would not stop until he gave up his hunger strike.

Mohammed also described being abused with IV needles. Trainees working with medical personnel subjected him to medical experimentation, sticking him repeatedly with needles, allegedly unable to find his veins. They would stick him dozens of times, one person after another—for no valid medical reason.

For us, the sincerity and believability of his accounts was overwhelming. They were delivered to us with the vividness of reliving his experience and with that raw indifference to any listener's disbelief that marks credible people who are witnesses to the truth. His accounts shamed us. Yet we remained powerless to stop the abuse. If our courts care about what is going on, from the prisoners' standpoint, it doesn't matter because those courts have not acted. The government has thus been entirely free to carry on in these and hundreds of other pernicious ways.

Marc D. Falkoff: "Voluntary Fast"

January 26, 2005. Today I'm scheduled to visit with Adnan. Just two days ago, the Department of Justice refused our request to bring a doctor down to Guantánamo to evaluate the health of our clients, almost all of whom have lost significant weight while at the camp.

I enter the interview cell. Adnan is slouched in his folding chair. He is painfully thin. His eyes are rheumy, and he can barely speak. When I ask, he tells me in a weak and scratchy voice that he's been spitting up blood, has problems hearing, and has suffered from an excruciating headache for weeks. He gets no rest because they've confiscated his mattress, leaving him to sleep on the steel of his bunk. Adnan had apparently violated some disciplinary rule, but he waves off my questions about it.

I call the guards on the intercom and ask them to come to the interview cell. They arrive and ask if I am okay. I say that I am but that my client needs to be taken to the infirmary at once. Their faces immediately turn to stone.

"A corpsman visits regularly, sir," one of the soldiers tells me. He spits out the "sir" like an insult. A corpsman, I learn, is a soldier who has been given some rudimentary medical training—not a nurse and certainly not a doctor.

I insist that Adnan be seen by medical personnel at the infirmary immediately. They refuse, so I try to work my way up the chain of command at Guantánamo. That doesn't work, so I call our law office in Washington, D.C., and they call the Department of Justice. Someone from the DOJ must have called someone at the DOD who called back down to Guantánamo because the soldiers finally agree to take Adnan to the infirmary.

•   •   •

April 15, 2006: We've won some legal victories, and we thought we'd finally get our day in court. Then in December, Congress stripped detainees of their habeas corpus rights. I've come to Guantánamo to discuss these legal developments with Adnan.

"I've lost hope of being released," he told me in a weak voice.

I listened, but it was hard to concentrate. Adnan looked like he'd just been in a car accident. One eye was swollen shut; the other was a sickly black-blue. There were cuts on his head and contusions all over his body. He was slumped in his chair and could barely keep his head up. He could not swallow. He could talk, but it hurt and he had to stop frequently.

Three days ago, he explained, he'd been visited by an IRF team. A half-dozen men in body armor, carrying shields and batons, forcibly extracted him from his cell. His offense? He had stepped over a line, painted on the floor of his cell, while his lunch was being passed through the food slot of his door.

"Suddenly the riot police came. No one in the cellblock knew who for. They closed all the windows except mine. A female soldier came in with a big can of pepper spray. Eventually I figured out they were coming for me. She sprayed me. I couldn't breathe. I fell down. I put a mattress over my head. I thought I was dying.

"They opened the door. I was lying on the bed, but they were kicking and hitting me with the shields. They put my head in the toilet. They put me on a stretcher and carried me away."

He'd stepped over the line, you see.

"Perhaps you can kill yourself without realizing it," Adnan ruminated. "If you don't realize what you're doing, maybe you won't end up in hell."

•   •   •

THREE GUANTÁNAMO BAY DETAINEES DIE OF APPARENT SUICIDE
By Sgt. Sara Wood, USA
American Forces Press Service

Washington, June 10, 2006

Three detainees at U.S. Naval Station Guantánamo Bay, Cuba, died of apparent suicides early this morning, military officials reported today. . . .

[Navy Rear Adm. Harry B. Harris] said the joint suicides were clearly planned by the detainees as a way to advance their cause in the war on terror.

"I believe this was not an act of desperation, but an act of asymmetric warfare aimed at us here at Guantánamo," he said. "We have men here who are committed jihadists. They are dangerous men and they will do anything they can to advance their cause."

•   •   •

September 7, 2006. I've been collecting poems from the Guantánamo detainees, and now the University of Iowa Press is interested in publishing them as a book.

For months now, Adnan has included poems in his letters to us. The Pentagon refused to declassify most of them, including one called "The Shout of Death." But for some reason, they cleared his poem about the hunger strikers, which I have decided to include in the volume. Here is part of Adnan's "Hunger Strike Poem":

They are artists of torture,
They are artists of pain and fatigue,
They are artists of insults and humiliation.
. . . .
Where is the world to save us from torture?
Where is the world to save us from the fire and sadness?
Where is the world to save the hunger strikers?

But we are content, on the side of justice and right,
Worshipping the Almighty.
And our motto on this island is, *salaam*.

•   •   •

February 27, 2007. Adnan has been on a hunger strike for more than a
month. The military refers to the hunger strike as a "voluntary fast." This
is in keeping with their Orwellian tendencies. They long ago redefined
suicide attempts as "manipulative self-injurious behavior" and "hanging
gestures."

Twice a day, they force-feed Adnan a liquid nutrient by inserting a
tube up his nose and into his stomach. His arms and legs are strapped to a
special restraint chair during the feedings. His head is immobilized.

Another of my colleagues, Brent Starks, visits with Adnan for the first
time. In his notes from the meeting, he writes, "Still on hunger strike. Incredibly thin. Looks incredibly weak and broken. Horrible."

Later, he observes scars on Adnan's wrists.

•   •   •

FROM: Henry, Terry (CIV)
SENT: Monday, March 26, 2007
TO: Marc Falkoff
SUBJECT: RE: Allal ab Aljallil Abd al Rahman Abd, ISN 156
We have raised with DoD your request that a psychiatrist of your
choosing be permitted to visit petitioner [Adnan] Abd with you to
assess Mr. Abd's mental and physical condition and encourage him
to take medication. . . . Guantánamo is not in a position to accede to
your request for intervention by an outside medical professional.

•   •   •

May 14, 2007. Adnan tells me he's now been on hunger strike for four and
a half months and that he has been force-fed for three months. The force-
feeding, he says, "is like having a dagger shoved down your throat."

Sitting across the table, shackled as always, Adnan seems more se-
date than usual. Or maybe, I think, he has simply been sedated. I wonder
whether the military has silently slipped some meds into the liquid nutrient they force-feed him.

Of course, there is no way for me to know if they're sedating him or
feeding him antipsychotics or antidepressants since the military refuses to

share his medical records. We could try to go to court, but Congress tried to take away the power of the judges to intervene. And the DOJ is right—the courts don't like to micromanage our prison camps.

Maybe, I think to myself, it's for the best that they're feeding and medicating Adnan by any means necessary. Maybe this will keep him from trying to escape from Guantánamo by the only way that seems possible to him. It's growing hard for me to keep his faith in our legal system alive. Right now, it's hard for me to keep *my* faith in the legal system alive.

As I prepare to leave, Adnan has one last thing to say.

"Death," he tells me, "would be more merciful than life here."

Thomas B. Wilner: A Measure of Control

I met with my clients in Guantánamo in September 2005. First, I met with Omar Amin, with whom I had met on all my previous trips to Guantánamo. Based on my observation, Mr. Amin had deteriorated significantly from our last visit. He was extremely thin, weak, and depressed. I observed bald patches on his arms where the hair had fallen out. He reported that he had been on a hunger strike but had stopped because he was too weak. He said that his other health problems had grown worse. He said that he reported his conditions to the authorities at Guantánamo but had not received treatment. He reported that he was told that the doctors at Guantánamo will not treat his medical conditions until the hunger strike ends. He had been given only aspirin for his problems. He said that the medical care at Guantánamo is "atrocious" and the doctors at Guantánamo are "terrible."

Mr. Amin said that a number of the Kuwaitis were refusing food. He said that Abdulaziz al Shammari and Fawzi al Odah have been refusing food for many weeks and that he heard they were hospitalized and in dire physical condition.

In the afternoon, I met with Mohammed Al Daihani, who was also participating in the hunger strike. Mr. Al Daihani appeared weak and gaunt and clearly had lost significant weight since our last visit. We tried to encourage him to end his hunger strike, telling him that we believed there had been positive developments before the courts and that we hoped he would be granted a hearing soon. Al Mr. Daihani told us that he had no faith in the U.S. courts. We had brought him a pizza from the local Subway on the base,

---

This excerpt is based on a motion filed on behalf of Tom Wilner's clients in Guantánamo.

which he refused to eat. Pointing to the pizza box, he said, "The American justice system is like this pizza box. It looks very good on the outside, but it is empty on the inside. It is nothing but air." He said that the only control he has at Guantánamo is over what he eats and that he would not eat again until he is released or charged and tried so that he can defend himself and prove his innocence. Mr. Al Daihani informed us that he had written us a letter at the end of July and asked why we had not responded. We had not received his letter as of September 12, when we left for Guantánamo.

I then met with Saad Al-Azmi. Mr. Al-Azmi is the youngest of the Kuwaiti detainees; he was twenty-six at the time of our meeting. Although thin, he had always appeared healthy. He had changed significantly. He was participating in the hunger strike and had lost substantial weight. His shoulder bones were sticking out of his prison uniform. He was pale with circles under his eyes. He told us that the doctors had informed him that he had lost more than 30 pounds in the past few weeks and now weighs only 140 pounds.

Mr. Al-Azmi told us the origins of the hunger strike. He said that there had been a hunger strike that began in July with the prisoners asking to be charged and tried or released, to be treated in compliance with the Geneva Conventions, to be provided with adequate and proper food and water and medical care, and to be accorded respect for their religion and, particularly, for the Quran. Mr. Al-Azmi said that the prior hunger strike ended as a result of a negotiated agreement under which the U.S. authorities at Guantánamo agreed to the last three conditions. He said that conditions improved for several days but that the interrogators then sabotaged the agreement by abusing him and a Tunisian detainee. Mr. Al-Azmi said the interrogators had opposed improving the conditions at Guantánamo and wanted to undermine the agreement.

Mr. Al-Azmi reported another incident that he believed helped precipitate or reinforce the renewed hunger strike. He said that in August a congressional delegation had visited Guantánamo. He believed it was led by Senator Kennedy. He said the delegation passed close to "Whiskey Block" in Camp Four on its way to go into the Guantánamo hospital. Several detainees in Whiskey Block who spoke in English yelled out the window that the delegation was not seeing the real picture of Guantánamo and that it should visit Camp Five and talk to detainees there. Mr. Al-Azmi was in Whiskey Block in Camp Four at that time. He said that two days later the guards came and took all sixty people from Whiskey Block and put them in different cells scattered throughout Camp Delta and removed items of their clothing and other comfort items. Mr. Al-Azmi said that the guards expressly told them that they were being taken from Camp Four and punished because they had spoken out to the congressional delegation.

Mr. Al-Azmi also explained that the hunger strike takes many forms. Some people accept the food that is given them but then flush it down the toilet. The government, according to him, does not know these people are on a hunger strike until they collapse in their cells. Other people skip only some meals each day or only meals on some days. Other people openly refuse food, and other people openly refuse both food and water.

Two of our other clients, Fouad Al Rabiah and Fayiz Al Kandari, were also participating in the hunger strike. Mr. Al Rabiah couldn't join the hunger strike fully because of health reasons but skipped two of three meals a day. Mr. Al Kandari joined the hunger strike for six days and then ate one meal a day to renew his strength. Mr. Al Kandari described the underlying reasons for the hunger strike to be the hopelessness of the situation at Guantánamo and the distrust of receiving any justice from the government or the courts. He had always been one of the healthiest and most optimistic of our clients. Abdullah Al Kandari was a member of the national volleyball team of Kuwait and was a superb athlete. He had previously been detained in Camp Four, where limited socialization is permitted, and although he had limited room to exercise, he had kept himself in superb condition. He had also always been cheerful and optimistic. I was absolutely shocked when I walked into the cell this time to see him. He was a completely different person. He looked terrible—bleary eyed, very weak, and emaciated—and he was barely able to conduct a conversation. He reported that he not eaten for fifteen days. He said that he had been one of the people in Whiskey Block in Camp Four who, after some of the people in that block had yelled out to a congressional delegation, had been taken to other cells and other camps and punished. He said that he has been treated with "absolutely no dignity; like an animal, not a human being." We tried to encourage him to stop the hunger strike and reported recent developments in the U.S. court system that we thought were positive. He said that although he appreciated our efforts, he had lost any patience and any belief in the U.S. courts. He told us that his file of our confidential legal papers had been searched and documents removed. He also said that the guards had taken his pen so that he could not write us. I have never seen a greater change in a person over a short time, both mentally and physically.

We met briefly with Fawzi al Odah, who had been on a hunger strike since August 8. He had lost a significant amount of weight and told us that he weighed only 113 pounds. He had a plastic tube protruding from his nose that was secured with tape. During the interview, he bled intermittently from his nose.

Mr. al Odah said that he was among twenty detainees then being force-fed under a new method supervised by doctors flown to Guantánamo. He said that the new method involves the use of a larger feeding tube that forces a larger quantity of food into the detainee, but that causes nausea and vomiting. Mr. al Odah said that he has been experiencing constant nausea, vomiting, and diarrhea. Instead of gaining weight under this feeding method, he had lost an additional four pounds. He also said that, presumably to cause pain and encourage detainees to stop the hunger strike, the medical staff at the hospital had been removing the tube after each feeding and then inserting it again for the next feeding without using an anesthetic. He also said that there is no use resisting the insertion of the tube, because the medical staff would just strap you down and force the tube in and keep you strapped down during feeding.

Mr. al Odah said that he has vowed not to eat or drink anything until he is either released or dies. He said that he is innocent, and "if the United States thinks I am guilty of something, then charge me so that I can defend myself." He also indicated that he had heard of reports of U.S. congressmen coming back from Guantánamo and saying that the detainees were all being well treated and eating very good food. He said, "I can no longer be part of this lie. If I eat, I condone the lie." We tried to encourage him to begin eating again, but he said that he would not and that this was a personal decision he had made.

The government had not originally told us that another client of ours, Mr. al Shammari, was on a hunger strike. However, he had been on a hunger strike since August 4, 2005, longer than anyone else at Guantánamo. He was transported in a van to Camp Echo from the detainee hospital. Six people assisted him to the interview. He was skin and bones and could sit in a chair only with the aid of a walker. He looked like the pictures one sees of starving people in the Sudan. He was being force-fed in the same manner as Fawzi al Odah. Like Mr. al Odah, he had a plastic tube protruding from his nose that was secured with tape. He was not kept at the hospital with Mr. al Odah but at a special ward in the prison camp. We also tried to encourage him to begin eating and reported what we thought were positive developments in the court cases. Mr. Al Shammari expressed the same opinion as the others that the court system had not provided relief and that he had no faith that it ever would. He emphasized to us that what he is doing is a very personal act. He said that the only control he has at Guantánamo is over what he eats and drinks and that he simply will not voluntarily eat or drink again until he is home in Kuwait.

Agnieszka Fryszman: Wrong Side of History

One day last summer, our office got a call from the secure facility in Crystal City, Virginia: "You have a letter." My colleague Abby volunteered to take the trip and get it. It was from our client, a young man named Mohammed Al Amin from sub-Saharan Africa who'd been living and working in Pakistan in 2001. He'd never even heard of al Qaeda until the Twin Towers fell. Nonetheless, he was picked up by Pakistani authorities in exchange for a bounty and ended up at Guantánamo. Mr. Al Amin had been there for five years. We had been his lawyers for two.

We sent his letter to be translated by one of our volunteer translators. "To my Attorney," it begins.

> Warm Greetings. This is the first letter I was able to write for over three months, for I am forbidden to write both legal and other letters as the result of my hunger strike. . . . I am confined to isolation in an ugly location where I can't recognize days from nights and I am going through deep suffering.

The letter wasn't long, but it was difficult to read. Mr. Al Amin had started a peaceful hunger strike to protest his fifth year of detention without charge. He described being strapped into a chair that he at first took to be an electric chair, and how he was force-fed by a tube through the nose. Mr. Al Amin described how the tube was inserted and removed for each feeding, sometimes repeatedly, and jabbed into his stomach and sinuses. The feeding mixture was pumped into him, until he vomited, at which point he was fed again, until he vomited again. He was left in the restraint chair for hours at a time. When the tube was yanked out, he would lose consciousness from the pain and shock. He would be doused with cold water and locked in a freezing-cold room where there was a steel bunk but no mattress and no blanket. He wanted us to know what was happening.

I am urging you, as soon as you receive my letter, to take the necessary
steps. . . .

Peace is the best ending. Mohammed.

The letter was dated February 25, 2007—it was about four months old.
Abby and I called other lawyers representing Guantánamo detainees, representatives from human rights groups, and reporters we knew. But one
big advantage for the government of running an island prison where all
outgoing information is classified "secret" is that no one knew for sure
whether our client was still on a hunger strike or what was happening to
him. The lawyers at the Department of Justice could not, or would not,
give us any information about our client's condition.

We made plans to go to Guantánamo, but it takes months to get approval from the Department of Defense and to get the stars to line up on
the same day: a translator, a room at the base, and plane tickets on one of
the two tiny airlines that schedule inconvenient flights to and from Guantánamo from Fort Lauderdale.

In the meantime, we got a curt e-mail from the Department of Defense. It had rejected our submission on behalf Mr. Al Amin to the Administrative Review Board, the DOD procedure set up to evaluate each year
whether a detainee still remained a danger to the United States. Why? No
submission was necessary. Mr. Al Amin wasn't scheduled to receive his annual review. He had already been "approved to leave Guantánamo." Franz
Kafka couldn't have written it any better. In fact, it turned out later that
Mohammed Al Amin had been cleared for release for quite some time.

Although Mr. Al Amin he had been "approved to leave," he remained
in solitary confinement, in the dark and cold, and was being force-fed.
Amnesty International took up Mr. Al Amin's case and began a letter-writ-
ing campaign on his behalf.

By the time we were able to see Al Amin, it was more than six months
after he had written to us. He told us that getting the letter to us was a
stroke of luck—the guard had made a mistake and let him have paper and
pencil. But it didn't feel like a stroke of luck to me. It took the letter four
months to get to me, and once it did, there was really nothing I could do
other than visit, months later, and tell him that the government had long
ago cleared him for release, yet there he was, still.

•   •   •

I was thinking of that visit to Mr. Al Amin one day, not long ago, because I had been asked to accompany a group of human rights activists tasked with visiting members of Congress to try to explain what was happening at Guantánamo and to try to stop Congress from stripping away the detainees' ability to challenge their continued detention in court.

We were sitting in a conference room near the Senate floor, and the staff asked about our clients, so I told them this story. "Your client is just collateral damage in the war on terror," one staffer said. A senator I like and respect asked me, "How can we let them go now, even if they were innocent before? What if they've been radicalized?" Another yelled at us for placing in his hometown newspapers op-eds by military leaders who supported the rule of law. We were repeatedly asked if there was a chance for compromise, so as to avoid a recorded vote in an election year.

One of the interest groups advised us, "Don't talk about the detainees. The polls show that no one cares about their plight, that it is too hard to humanize them. Talk about American values," they advised. "What does this say about us?"

I gave a copy of Vladimir Bukovsky's *Washington Post* op-ed, "Torture's Long Shadow," to one member of Congress. It described Bukovsky's experience of being force-fed by KGB agents and the pain of being forced to sleep on an iron frame night after night after night in the cold. "What Vladimir Bukovsky described," I said, "happened to my client," I heard the congressman read Bukovsky's piece later to his colleagues. "I don't want to be on the wrong side of history," a senator told us.

We went to a lot of meetings, and many members and their staffs worked very hard to try to balance the competing pressures. But in the end, it was the Supreme Court that stopped us from being on the wrong side of history. And although my client never got his day in court, he was unceremoniously returned home in September 2007.

Mari Newman: A More Vital Sustenance

I think our client "Mohammed" must survive on fury alone. Several months into a punishing hunger strike, his sustenance is pure outrage. I find it impossible to blame him. Mohammed, along with many other prisoners, began his hunger strike as a protest against the guards' persistent desecration of the Muslim holy book. For these men of faith, the Quran is the only solace. I am an agnostic at best and an atheist most days—especially days when I contemplate the unthinkable human cruelty of Guantánamo—so I must admit I have no frame of reference for this point, an assault on and injury to one's faith. But I do not for a moment doubt our clients' sincerity in their assertion. Mohammed and many others had ceased eating in order to make the point that the abuse of this holy book must end. Their refusal of one kind of sustenance mirrors their forced starvation of another sustenance, one that they hold to be more vital. Thus, the majority of prisoners had made the impossible decision to relinquish their holy books rather than to have them defiled by guards who seem to believe that God by one name is somehow more deserving of their respect than God by another.

The Bush administration, which could not even allow these men to assert power over their own bodies, had responded to this humble protest with a brutal force-feeding regimen. The prisoner was strapped to a chair, his feet shackled. With back hyperextended and head cranked up at an unnatural angle, his nose was plugged, and a tube was shoved down his throat in order to pump him full of gruel. The image of the chair evokes visions of execution, but the Bush administration would not allow these men to die. In fact, the interrogators and doctors told the prisoners that they had no real concern about their well-being but would not risk the bad publicity of another Guantánamo death.

Whether by orders from the top or individually motivated sadism sanctioned by administrative neglect, the guards seemed to relish the opportunity for subjugation that the force-feeding presented. Prisoners reported that the guards were intentionally brutal when shoving the tubes in place and that they were treated as human guinea pigs for officers in training. Although the striking prisoners were told that they were supposed to be "fed" every six hours, the guards force-feed them every three hours. Since the prisoners were subjected to twenty-three and twenty-four hours of solitary confinement in small cells, they had no opportunity to digest the "food" from the last "feeding," so the "food" came up through their noses while the tube continued pumping. Men who vomited were left in their filth.

Suicides

For some detainees, Guantánamo simply became too difficult to bear. In 2006, three prisoners killed themselves, and another prisoner took his life the next year. Rather than recognize that the suicides were the inevitable result of cruelty and injustice, the Bush administration blamed the prisoners, claiming they had engaged in "asymmetrical acts of warfare." The response, however, only demonstrated how out of touch administration officials were with the reality of Guantánamo.

Alan Sussman: Asymmetric Warfare

The term "asymmetric warfare" was first used in reference to Guantánamo immediately after three inmates committed suicide in 2006. Guantánamo's commander, Rear Admiral Harry Harris, said of the men who hanged themselves with clothing and bed sheets, "I believe this was not an act of desperation but an act of asymmetric warfare against us."

"Asymmetric warfare" can be used to describe any hostility, ancient or modern, in which the weaker force employs guerrilla or terror tactics to inflict death and injury on the more powerful on a scale that far exceeds its relative conventional weight. Perhaps Admiral Harris thought he might use a fashionable phrase to explain what was asymmetrical to him: the fact that there was so much international concern about a bunch of terrorists who did not deserve even the slightest degree of decency with which they were being treated at Guantánamo.

We cannot know for certain what motives propelled the Guantánamo suicides. Handwritten notes the three men left behind were never disclosed by their keepers, but the fact that the suicides occurred simultaneously suggests a political purpose. Even if the motives were solely psychological, occasioned entirely by personal pain or despair, the "message" was nonetheless political because the solemnity of the acts could not be perceived by an outsider in any manner other than that conditions endured at Guantánamo overwhelmed the desire to remain alive.

It is more likely that the suicides were intended to be political statements of the gravest sort. These detainees were expressing, when all other methods of expression had been forbidden, the fact that conditions were so dreadful and hopeless that one's own life was less important than the public attention its extinction would bring to bear on the situation.

The suicides were far from acts of war, asymmetrical or otherwise. Suicide bombers in Sri Lanka, Iraq, or Israel hope to take with them to their death as many people as possible. But the Guantánamo detainees harmed only themselves. They were not conducting military acts but were appealing to the moral sense in others who, upon learning of the acts, would be forced to conclude that *something must be wrong*. They raised memories of the monks in Saigon who were seen by millions on television immolating themselves in stunning acts of protest, which contributed in an immeasurable way to the moral sensibilities of a world audience that something was not right in Vietnam.

Neither the psychological nor the political message was what the Bush administration or Guantánamo officials wanted the world to hear, of course, and the immediate Orwellian label to the suicides suggests that in their view *any* response to the inflexible logic of the "war on terror" was to be termed an act of war itself.

George Daly: Don't Take It Personally

It took us nine months to get permission to visit our client. When we were finally cleared to visit, Jeff Davis and I decided that I would make the first trip. There are rampant tales of CIA agents trying to and sometimes succeeding in tricking information from prisoners by falsely posing as their lawyers. I am well beyond the age of being a CIA agent, and what hair I have is white, so we thought I would have a marginal advantage in convincing the client that I was truly his lawyer and not a government spy.

The next morning we were met by a navy chief, a pleasant enlisted man from the south side of Chicago who was to be our military escort for the day. He said he would take me to get my identification badge before we went to the prison. I knew the chief was charged to stick close by us all day, so I started talking trash with him, hoping to get on his good side.

"Now, Chief, if you're from the south side of Chicago, you must be a bad dude."

"No worse than all the rest down here."

"Does that include the lawyers?"

"Hey, what is this, am I on trial? Come on, I got to get you badged."

"What's all this badge crap about?"

"They got to keep track of you while you're down here."

"But Chief, I don't like badges. I don't like having my picture taken. What if I just refuse to get a badge?"

"Well, 'refuse' must be the word for the day, because your detainee has refused to meet with you." Then he added, "Don't take it personally. This has happened before."

It was like being told a friend had died. I felt numb, and we all were silent for a while.

Then the chief said, "Maybe he'll agree to see you tomorrow. That happens sometimes. Send him a note asking him to."

The chief took us to get a cup of coffee and let us talk things over. After a few minutes' discussion, I took my translator's advice—he was a veteran down there—and we sent the prisoner a short letter asking him to see me the next day.

The next day he did not show up. Three weeks later he committed suicide. I don't even know if he ever received the note I tried to send to him. I don't know if anyone told him he was on the verge of being released and sent home. I'm still trying to find this information via a FOIA request—which of course is dragging on and on.

Jeffrey Davis: Pending Release

Our client's name was Mane Shaman Al-Habardi, also known as Manei al-Otaibi and Manei al Utaybi. I have never known why there was so much confusion over his name, but there was, though we can be certain who we are talking about because of his prisoner ID number, 588. His case is far and away one of the most tragic of all the Guantánamo cases because he committed suicide on the eve of his scheduled release, apparently not knowing he was going to be released.

Mr. Utaybi died with two other prisoners. When the government announced that three prisoners at Guantánamo had committed suicide, I immediately inquired whether any of the three were my clients and was told no. Later that same day, I was told that indeed one of the suicides was my client Mr. Utaybi and that he had left a suicide note. I immediately asked for a copy of the note, as well as a copy of the videotapes from the surveillance camera that monitored him, but that request was denied.

Because of the information that the government did release and because of its refusal to release the suicide note, my co-counsel George Daly and I were initially skeptical that his death had actually been a suicide. I made a broad FOIA request but was denied access to anything at all. I sued in federal court, and the government subsequently released over 3,000 pages of documents to me. From an examination of those documents, George and I have concluded that Mr. Utaybi's death was indeed a suicide and that he had been one of the hunger strikers who was force-fed. Again, Mr. Utaybi had been cleared for release just before his death.

At the same time that George went to Guantánamo to see another client, he also attempted to see Mr. Utaybi. The government prohibited us from telling him of his impending release, but George's goal was to ask in the abstract if Mr. Utaybi wanted to return to Saudi Arabia, his home country, if given the chance.

When George arrived at Guantánamo and asked to see Mr. Utaybi, he was told by the guards that Mr. Utaybi refused to see him. We do not know whether this was true because we are aware of many instances when guards reported to other lawyers that a client allegedly refused to see his lawyer that turned out to be untrue. We were also aware that Mr. Utaybi's condition had deteriorated because of the hunger strike.

In any event, what we do know is the following:

1. George did not see him.
2. He had been cleared for release.
3. We were forbidden from telling him that, so we suspect that nobody had told him.
4. He died days later of suicide.

Joshua Colangelo-Bryan: Habeas on the Gate, Part III

On October 15, 2005, I was at Guantánamo again. Jumah's normal energy and gallows humor were notably absent during our first session. He said that he had been at the detainee hospital after my prior visit in June 2005 because of his participation in a hunger strike. At the hospital, he had been able to convince other hunger strikers to voluntarily accept nasal tube feeding; the alternative was to be restrained and painfully force-fed. In a nod to these efforts, a major had told Jumah that if he ended his hunger strike, he would be moved from Camp Five to Camp One. That meant going from solitary confinement to a camp where detainees could see and talk to one another. There was nothing Jumah wanted more, so he ate. The military sent him back to Camp Five anyway.

The isolation in Camp Five was so unbearable that Jumah had talked to a psychiatrist. "Please, I need help," he had pleaded. "I'm a human being."

I had seen Jumah depressed, but never like this before. He could barely smile, let alone laugh. At the end of our first day, I said, "I don't mean to sound stupid, considering where we are, but it seems like you're in a really bad mood."

"I am," he replied, looking as tired as I'd ever seen him.

The next day, I met with Jumah again. After about an hour, he gave me a sealed envelope and said it had something in it that he wanted to talk about, but he needed to use the bathroom first. "Give me ten minutes," he said.

To get Jumah into the bathroom was anything but routine. I had to call guards who would shackle Jumah's hands, unshackle his ankle from the bolt in the floor, and move him to the tiny cell next to the meeting area, where there was a toilet. The cell was separated from the meeting area by a steel mesh wall that, although very solid, could be seen through. After the guards came, I went outside to give Jumah privacy. The guards came out as well after moving him.

In pouring rain, I chatted with one of the guards about nothing in particular. We waited to hear Jumah yell that he was finished. Several minutes passed. Running out of small talk and noticing a vague anxiety in myself, I decided to check on Jumah. I cracked the door open a few inches, hoping just to hear him say that he needed a minute.

The first thing I saw was a large, dark puddle on the white floor. My mind was scrambling, trying to make sense of things. Within a split second, I realized it was blood. "God," I thought, "Jumah made himself throw up blood because he thinks I didn't believe him." He had told me about a few episodes in which he had vomited blood, and maybe I didn't react strongly enough. But then, I looked up and saw something hanging from the cell side of the steel mesh wall. Whatever this thing was, it absolutely did not look like Jumah.

I took two steps and was at the mesh wall. I saw that the hanging figure was Jumah. His body and face were covered in blood. There was a gash in his arm. His eyes were rolled back in their sockets. His lips and tongue were swollen. He looked demonic. I yelled Jumah's name, but he didn't respond. He was unconscious and did not seem to be breathing.

I was an inch or two from Jumah, but I couldn't reach him because the mesh weave is tight and the door to the cell was locked. I yelled for help. Guards arrived quickly. After initially trying the wrong key, they were able to get into the cell. One started hacking at the noose around Jumah's neck. I yelled to the second to hold Jumah's body up to ease the tension; he did. Within seconds, the guards had cut Jumah down and laid him on the floor in front of me. Jumah still didn't seem to be breathing. A guard ordered me out of the room. I didn't want to leave but realized that an argument was the last thing Jumah needed. As I walked out of the room, I thought I heard Jumah gasp for air.

I walked in the rain across Camp Echo's gravel compound to another hut with a cell and meeting space, which served as an attorney waiting room. Karim, the interpreter, was already there, having left the area around Jumah's cell when he heard my yell for help. We exchanged looks of shock. I paced around the room, flush with anger—not anger at Jumah but anger at the circumstances that had driven him to do this. I cursed under my breath a few times—"motherfucker"—then stopped so that Karim wouldn't think I was cursing at him.

I remembered the envelope that Jumah had given me. I took it from my bag and began to open it, sickly certain that I was about to see a suicide note. I pulled out several pages of Arabic writing that were marked by dried blood. I felt chills as I showed the letter to Karim, not really wanting him to read it. He looked at it and just said, "I can't."

I wanted to see what was happening across the compound, so I cracked open the door even though doing so blatantly violated Camp Echo rules. After a few minutes, corpsmen walked toward Jumah's cell with a stretcher. Ten minutes later, they carried Jumah out on the stretcher, which was now bloody. I closed the door and waited.

Two officers came into the room and said they were with Behavioral Health. "Do you have any idea why he would do this?" one asked. Was this guy serious? Did he think this was a college campus where a normally cheerful student inexplicably had taken too many sleeping pills? This was goddamned Guantánamo Bay. There were a thousand reasons why someone would try to kill himself here. Instead, I said, "Isolation can do terrible things to people." The officer nodded with more sympathy than I had expected—maybe I had misjudged the question—and that was the end of our conversation.

Next, a beefy colonel whom I knew to be the head of day-to-day operations at the camp came in. He said that Jumah had been taken to the hospital for treatment and that they expected him to be okay. I asked if I could see Jumah later, and the colonel said that it shouldn't be a problem. He seemed genuinely concerned.

A military lawyer offered Karim and me a ride to the ferry. "That's not how you want your client to greet you, huh?" he said to me with a smirk, as we walked out of the camp. As we drove, he said, "I've seen the files on your clients. It would be a mistake to think that they're goat farmers." I wanted to spit in his face.

By the time we got to the Combined Bachelors' Quarters, it was dark, and the rain was coming down in sheets. Karim offered me scotch, which

I don't drink. Still, I gladly accepted, in part for medicinal purposes but also because the idea of sitting alone in my room made me a little sick. We worked our way through a couple glasses and talked a bit about what had happened.

When I finally went to my room, I immediately turned on the TV to break the silence. Despite my best efforts to focus on whatever show was playing, the picture of Jumah's hanging body and bloodied, unconscious face came into my mind time after time. I also imagined that face was lurking just outside the darkened windows that were being battered by the rain, waiting to look right at me.

At 10:00 p.m. the telephone rang. The military lawyer who had given me a ride told me that Jumah had undergone surgery on his arm and was sedated. When I asked if I could see Jumah, he said that might be arranged if Jumah woke up and asked for me. Perhaps, I suggested, someone could ask Jumah if he wanted to see me. The lawyer would not promise anything.

I turned off the light late that night and had only a couple hours of very fitful sleep. By 4:00 a.m., I was writing a statement about the incident, as I'd been asked to do by the military lawyer. At 6:40, I got on the bus to go to Camp Echo for a day of meetings with other clients.

Throughout the day I asked the military about Jumah, including whether I could see him. All I heard was that he was still sedated. At the end of the day, I turned over my client interview notes and Jumah's suicide note to my military escort, as is required at the end of each trip; the escort would send them to the "secure facility" in the States where classified information relating to the detainees is kept. The next morning, I flew back to New York.

Several months later and after a fair amount of wrangling, I was able to get Jumah's suicide note declassified. When people ask me why Jumah tried to kill himself, I usually just show them the letter:

> Josh, . . . I feel very sorry for forcing you to see—it might
> be the first time in your life—to see a human being who suf-
> fered too much dying in front of your eyes. I know it is an awful
> and horrible scene, but there was no other alternative to make
> our voice heard by the world from the depths of the detention
> centers except this way in order for the world to re-examine its
> standing and for the fair people of America to look again at the
> situation and try to have a moment of truth with themselves. . . .

Josh, . . . I hope you will always remember that you met and sat with a "human being" called "Jumah" who suffered too much and was abused in his belief, self, in his dignity and also in his humanity.

When you remember me in my last gasps of life before dying, while my soul is leaving my body to rise to its creator, remember that the world let us and let our case down. Remember that our governments let us down. Remember the unreasonable delay of the courts in looking into our case and to side with the victims of injustice. Remember that if there were people who are actually fair and who defend justice and defend the victims of injustice and if there are judges who are fair, I wouldn't have been wrapped in death shrouds now and my family—my father, my mother, my brothers and sisters, and my little daughter—would not have to lose their son forever.

Take some of my blood, take pieces of my death shrouds, take some of my remains, take pictures of my dead body when I am placed in my grave, lonely and send it to the world. Send it to the judges, to people with live consciences, to people with principles and values, "the fair-minded."

Josh, . . . at this moment, I see death looming in front of me while writing this letter. . . . Death has a bad odor that cannot be smelled except by people who are going through the agony of death.

Josh, farewell. Farewell with no hope of your seeing me again. I thank you for everything you have done for me, but I have a final request. Show the world the letters I gave you. Let the world read them. Let the world know the agony of the detainees in Cuba.

Prisoner of Deprivation
Jumah Abdul Latif Al Dossari
Guantánamo Bay, Cuba
Friday, 10/14/2005

6

Alternative Forms of Advocacy

With the Bush administration determined to block legal challenges from going forward, a Congress twice willing to eliminate habeas corpus, and the courts failing to act swiftly in the cases before them, attorneys turned to alternative channels of advocacy on behalf of their clients. Those alternative channels included advocating with a detainee's home government, pressing the United States for repatriation, and lobbying other countries to accept detainees who could not be returned home because they would be tortured or persecuted.

John Robert Holland and Anna Cayton Holland-Edwards: Representing the Rightless

Nouakchott is the capital of Mauritania, a large but mostly unpopulated Islamic republic of about three million people on the western side of Africa, next to Morocco. The largest city in the Sahara, Nouakchott spreads for miles across a large swatch of brilliant orange desert near the Atlantic Ocean. The people there speak both Arabic and French. Mauritania is a very poor country with an average income under $400 a year. Despite bans, it is reported that slavery is still practiced. There is still a castelike system, with black Africans on the bottom rung. Eight hundred thousand people live in Nouakchott; many are without running water and depend on donkeys pulling barrels on carts for their supply.

At the time we went, Mauritania was just returning to democracy. As a result of a bloodless coup in August 2005, General Ely Ould Mohamed Vall became president and was running the country with a promise to restore democracy through free elections. Those elections were in full progress as we arrived.

In Mauritania, much political work is done through press conferences. We had barely left the airport when our first press conference occurred. Family members from all the Mauritanian detainees held in Guantánamo, politicians, and many members of the media were at the conference.

Although we had traveled to Mauritania with the express purpose of meeting with government officials, there was no certainty that such meetings would occur. Nevertheless, we felt compelled to act at all times as if this was a certainty. So we made media splashes in the first few days, hoping we would be called by the government to come and meet with the minister of justice or with President Vall. We were only going to be there for five days, and we absolutely needed to meet with the government.

We told the assembled media that we were grateful to the government of Mauritania for having arranged our mission and allowing us to come. We explained to them our honest regret as attorneys that the U.S. courts were completely closed to these wrongs. We told them we had come to request the assistance of the Mauritanian government to secure justice for their citizens held without rights at Guantánamo Bay.

As American and British attorneys, it was embarrassing to travel to an impoverished, fledgling democracy in West Africa to request that the government there act in a humanitarian fashion and work for our clients' return by promising fair and just proceedings to investigate and determine the guilt or innocence of our clients—proceedings we have been completely unable to secure in the United States.

We went to a television station in downtown Nouakchott and were invited to join a panel discussion about Guantánamo that was being broadcast live to many millions of people in several different cities. We still had not been invited to meet with the government, nor had we been assured that we would get to do so. This troubling fact was very much on our minds. We told the watching audience that we were very grateful to the Mauritanian government for having allowed us to come to their country to discuss the plight of their fellow countrymen and to seek their assistance in securing justice, something we were unable to do for our clients without their help, as proven by the years of legal futility that we had experienced in the United States. Once again we stressed that we were very much looking forward to meeting with the top government officials and were hopeful that this would occur very shortly.

Later that same night, we prepared a letter to President Vall in our hotel, and Anna persuaded a pilot from Air France to help her translate it into French. So as not to alienate our own ambassador, and to make sure U.S. officials and diplomats were in the loop, we also decided to hand deliver a copy to the American ambassador in Nouakchott.

The next day we were invited to meet with Mauritania's minister of justice, Mohameden O. Bah O. Hamed. We also met with Koita Bamariam, the director of the Mauritanian Commission for the Rights of Man. Although these Mauritanian officials were welcoming, our meetings with them were pretty brief and to the point. We explained why we had come. We asked for the president to intervene with the U.S. government and request the return of Mauritania's citizens. We also asked that he assure the United States that if our clients were returned home, there would be a sufficient effort on Mauritania's part to investigate and detain our clients further if necessary. This was a difficult request to make as lawyers, but we understood that it was essential. Because Mauritania was in the midst of an election, we realized we should not depend solely on the present acting government. Mauritania is an ally of the United States in the "war on terror," and these decisions affecting Guantánamo detainees raised political questions for its government.

We decided that we had to try to meet with every major candidate running for president in March 2007. We prepared letters for all the candidates, requesting that they take a positive position on the plight of the prisoners and that they meet with us. Our host, Hamound Ould Nebagha, the president of the Mauritanian Detainees Support Committee, arranged to drive us all over Nouakchott, ever on his cell phone locating these candidates.

We met with six candidates. The meetings were intense. We presented our clients' situations, and we urged them all to become directly involved. We obtained commitments by most of them to do so, some more heartfelt than others. One of the candidates, Sidi Ould Cheikh Abdallahi, told us that he would make these prisoners' fates one of the focuses of his campaign.

We held a farewell press conference, thanked the government for meeting with us, and expressed our fervent hopes that President Vall would soon act to request the return of the Mauritanian prisoners. We attended an outdoor dinner, and as the sun set, we heard the call to prayer echoing across the desert dunes about an hour outside of Nouakchott.

About a month after coming back from Mauritania in February 2007, we received notice from the U.S. government that Mohammed "has been approved to leave Guantánamo." However, he was to be held for another seven months.

We traveled to Guantánamo to see Mohammed. We got pictures of our trip to Mauritania cleared and were very excited to show them to him. The joy he had in seeing his family and hearing of our efforts in Mauritania was wonderful to see. But he was still on a hunger strike and remained deeply committed to it until he was released.

In March 2007, Sidi Ould Cheikh Abdallahi was elected president of Mauritania, and Mohammed determined that he wanted us to write to him, quoting him in his own words to the newly elected president. After our notes containing these words were found unclassified, we wrote to President Abdallahi. The following is from the letter John wrote:

> The Honorable Sidi Ould Cheikh Abdallahi
> President of Mauritania
>
> Dear President Abdallahi:
>
> Since I wrote you last I was just in Guantánamo to see your citizen, Mohammed Al Amin. Clive Stafford Smith, my distinguished colleague who you met with during the election, recently saw Ahmed Abdel Aziz.
>
> Mohammed Al Amin was clearly declining, both physically and mentally, and we feel there is now a burning need to fairly resolve his situation.
>
> As you know, Mohammed is one of the prisoners who our country has cleared for unconditional release. This means that he has been found to be no threat to anybody—the U.S. or Mauritania. It also means that no charges have or ever will be filed against him by the United States. The U.S. has now effectively conceded the truth of what he has been saying all along—that he should not have been imprisoned at Guantánamo.
>
> Although a very young man, he has aged enormously due to his mistreatment by the U.S. military. Because of his concededly unjustified confinement, Mohammed has engaged in a long, peaceful hunger strike in which he is daily tube fed on multiple occasions. I know you are aware of this approach. He also reports being victimized by shocking abuses during the course of this strike. As he has stated, he is hunger striking "to protest my detention, to ask for my freedom out of this place after staying here for six years without guilt." You can imagine my meeting with this young man.
>
> After I told him all of the news of our trip to Mauritania, including our very encouraging meeting with you, I had to tell him that there were continuing delays in his being returned home and that I did not know when this would change. I told him that you had told us personally that you would actively seek his return and that you said this publicly during the elections.

I told him I did not know or understand why this had not happened or what had changed.

My notes from this astounding meeting have just been returned to me, and while they are not completely verbatim to what Mohammed said to me they are sufficient for me to fairly paraphrase what he asked me to write to you from him directly about his plight.

Dear President Abdallahi:

I told my attorneys there is a poem that you would know that expresses my feelings. My homeland and my people are still very dear to me even if I do not receive enough support from them.

You are the father of our country. Please do not forget that our religion imposes a duty on the father to advocate for your children.

Those who imprison me say and know that I am innocent and yet I am now told that my country is causing the delay in my return. If this delay was from the Americans I could better bear it but hearing it is from our country makes my condition so much harder. If my freedom were in the hands of the Mauritanian people they would not delay my release one moment.

Mohammed Al Amin

President Abdallahi, while keeping up his morale, Mohammed is personally asking you to end this nightmare of injustice and to intervene to secure his prompt return. We, and Mohammed as well, have no doubt that you are fully aware of the will of the Mauritanian people as you expressed it to us when we met. He is looking forward to coming home and eating again normally with his beloved family in Mauritania.

In late September 2007, we found out that Mohammed had been placed on a government plane and flown to Nouakchott. Upon his arrival, he was held for a few days in comfortable accommodations. His mother was allowed to visit him. President Abdallahi was in the United States. Immediately upon the president's return, Mohammed was released without restrictions and allowed to go home to his family. President Abdallahi kept his word.

Mohammed Al Amin is now living free.

Cori Crider: Tunisian Heroes

For me, the *real* heroes of the Guantánamo detainee litigation are not the American or European lawyers. Many are not lawyers at all. They hail not from London or Boston or New York but from places such as Tunisia, where a lot of our clients were born. Standing up to injustice in Tunisia requires more than late nights polishing a brief in a swank (or even a dingy) office. Standing up to injustice as a Tunisian risks a hell of a lot more than "random" stops at the airport or agents listening in on your phone calls. It can get you killed.

Tunisia was the first place, though by no means the last, that I encountered heroes like this. The activists I met in Tunis risked their liberty and their very lives to help a team of Western lawyers they scarcely knew protect a group of marked men they would never meet.

We first met Lotfi Hidouri loitering outside our hotel on the Avenue Bourguiba. A tall, lanky man with a thin mustache, his leather jacket was too big for him and too heavy for Tunis in March. He wasn't sweating, nor were several men who passed by clad, inexplicably, in puffer vests.

Avenue Bourguiba is Tunis's Champs-Elysées and does a fair impression of it for a stretch, except for the police infestation and President Ben Ali's grinning mug plastered everywhere.

Lofti strolled over and briskly shook our hands. He cast an eye up and down the Avenue Bourguiba and asked—just a little sharply—whether we'd left any papers in the hotel. We shook our heads in unison like rapt schoolchildren.

He cracked a sardonic smile and relaxed. "Good. Don't leave any documents in your room, ever, because"—he gestured to a couple men behind us sporting dark glasses, earpieces, and leather jackets of their own—"of '*les flics*.'"

I asked in a tone that I'd hoped would be neutral but came out terribly earnest and American, "Are they *following* us?"

"Always." He grinned again, shrugged, and loped without the slightest sign of concern down the avenue.

Chris and I shuffled after Lotfi for about ten minutes. In a pretty unconvincing show of bravado, we vocally admired Ben Ali's many outfits and poses on the massive billboards ("the man likes his pastels"; "dig those cartoon-villain *eyebrows*!") and tried, with mixed success, to limit ourselves to looking over our shoulders just once every couple minutes. After Lotfi's offhand remark, every man looked like the police to us. About one in three probably was.

Eventually we ducked into a dusty, tiled hall on the ground floor of a nondescript building. A wooden plaque advertised the offices of something like a doctor or a dentist, named Ben Sedrine—which was the surname of one of the activists we were supposed to meet.

Lotfi pressed the buzzer. We heard murmurs and waited for a few tense moments until the door cracked open. A woman peered through. She seemed about half Lotfi's height.

"*Salut,* Sihem!" Lotfi cried in his singsong French.

This unleashed the tiny tornado that is Sihem Bensedrine. She flung open the door, seemed to sweep all three of us into a hug at once, and ushered us over to a small living room. We plonked down on a leather couch in their office/flat and asked whether anyone lived there. Sihem explained that the official use of the building is as a "residence" because the authorities don't permit her organization, the Conseil National pour les Liberties en Tunisie, or indeed any human rights organization, to operate in the country.

After a few minutes, we gathered around the meeting/dining table and explained, while Sihem plied us with mint tea and figs, why we were there. I said there were twelve Tunisians in Guantánamo, many of whom had not had a chance to meet with an attorney. We were afraid that a number of them might not want to go back to Tunisia branded Islamists and terror suspects, but we needed to get information from the families and local lawyers to be sure and to see them for the first time in Guantánamo.

Later I learned that everyone at the table except Chris and myself had been to prison for what they believed.

Later I met another man named Lotfi who had spent around twenty years in Tunisian jail. His crime? Participating in a political protest. This failed to crush his spirit, and he now spends most of his time speaking out against torture. He took us to the family member of a prisoner who had reached out to us for help. There was Sami, an eager man who wrote prison studies, and Samir ben Amor, a haggard underdog of an attorney who is one of the only people who represents suspected Islamists in Tunisia. The circles under his eyes are not just dark—they are black. He showed us files on our clients, files that showed that they had been convicted in absentia in military tribunals in Tunis during their time in Guantánamo. If there were any doubt about what they would face, those doubts were put to rest. "You didn't get these from me," he said.

We met families. Some signed authorizations so that we could represent their loved one in Guantánamo and gain access to him. Some told background stories about our clients.

Chris and I were with the families one day when three plainclothes police came up to us and insisted we go to the station for a "controle de papiers." Since I had never been arrested before, this was a frightening proposition for me. The two men sitting in the police office who actually spoke played a very obvious, and mild, version of good cop/ bad cop.

But I also realized that this was only a small taste of what it was like to be a human rights advocate in countries such as Tunisia.

Wesley R. Powell: Preserving Our Image

In May 2008, fourteen U.S. lawyers and I visited Yemen. After years of seeing the GTMO litigation stalled in federal court pending the outcome of various appeals, many of us reached the conclusion that, though we must continue to fight in court, our clients' most likely route to release would be through a diplomatic resolution between the United States and their home countries. This already had happened for most of the European detainees; for example, all the French detainees were released by early 2005. But the progress for detainees from countries such as Yemen, with far less favorable relationships with the United States, was much slower. We realized that one of our most important roles as lawyers was to serve as a conduit for communications between our clients and their families. We also realized that there is strength in numbers. So the fifteen of us traveled together to Yemen to meet with families, to publicize the plight of our clients in the Yemeni press, and to meet with government officials in an effort to spark more focused efforts to negotiate with the United States for the release of the Yemeni detainees.

What stood out most about our trip was this: having realized on my first trip to Guantánamo that this case was about securing for our clients fundamental fairness and due process, I found myself having to explain to dozens of Yemenis how it could be that these Yemeni men could be denied those basic rights by the U.S. government. I learned that even in the most remote parts of Yemen, there is an image of the United States as the land of freedom and fairness. How could it be that these men had been singled out for treatment so inconsistent with that image? We had to answer that question again and again, in Sana'a, in Hadramout, in Houdeida, and in Menakkah. I'm not sure I gave a very good answer, but at least by making the trip, looking people in the eye, and pledging to continue representing their sons to the best of our abilities, we took a shot at preserving that image of the United States.

Bernhard Docke: Lost and Found

At the end of 2005, I wrote a letter to Germany's new chancellor, Angela Merkel, requesting help and assistance on behalf of my client, Murat Kurnaz. Angela Merkel answered within three days: "Yes, I will do it." And she did, in January 2006. She put the Kurnaz case on President Bush's table and explained that she wanted Kurnaz sent back to Germany. In August 2006, Kurnaz was released.

It is an irony of history that it was a conservative chancellor who opened the door for Murat Kurnaz after Gerhard Schröder, as the head of the red-green government, had allowed him to languish in Guantánamo for years. It is sad but true that Germany was complicit from the beginning.

Murat's release received incredible media hype. As the media focused more and more on Germany's role, many journalists did a great investigative job to dig out the truth. Under public pressure, the Bundestag set up two investigative committees examining whether the former government had missed a chance of releasing Kurnaz years earlier and whether German soldiers beat Kurnaz while he was in U.S. custody in Kandahar, Afghanistan, before his transfer to Guantánamo. The reports of these investigations have not yet been published, but some facts are clear.

The German Army and Secret Service informed the government in Berlin in January 2002 of Kurnaz's detention in Kandahar. The Bundeskriminalamt (federal police) supplied the FBI with a file on Kurnaz compiled by the police of Bremen, which contained later-disproved suspicions that Kurnaz might have intended to join the Taliban forces. Information transfers of this kind require a request for legal assistance and proof by the prosecutors' office that if the demanding state assures a fair trial, this information will not be used to impose a death sentence. In this case, Germany rushed ahead and supplied the information without any check or assurance. Not all the detainees from Kandahar were sent to Guantánamo, and the United States had caught just five percent of the prisoners in Kandahar. The United States obviously had no information about Kurnaz or whether he fit its criteria for transfer to Guantánamo. According to the German information, the United States had the wrong impression that Kurnaz was a terror suspect. The German information could have caused Kurnaz's selection for Guantánamo. It would be highly interesting to have access to the U.S. documents about the motives to bring Kurnaz to Guantánamo. It seems that Germany was responsible from the beginning.

In September 2002, three German agents interrogated Murat Kurnaz in Guantánamo. After two days of intense questioning, the agents came to the conclusion that Kurnaz had chosen a bad time to travel and that he seemed to be a naive young man without links to terrorists or involvement in criminal plots. Kurnaz would not pose any threat toward American, Israeli, or German interests. After talks with the CIA, the agents informed Berlin that the United States considered Kurnaz innocent and that he was to be released approximately six to eight weeks later.

In October 2002, the prosecutor in Bremen suspended the investigation into Kurnaz and his fellow suspects because of a lack of evidence.

On October 29, 2002, the Kurnaz case was discussed by the presidents of the German security services, top officials of the Interior Ministry, and the Chancellor's Office. Despite the fact that all German and U.S. services stressed Kurnaz's innocence, his torture and imprisonment were not ended through steps that German officials could easily have taken.

Germany excommunicated Kurnaz and blocked his return. In October 2002, the door was half open to his return, but Germany slammed it shut again. According to disclosed documents, the United States was not amused and was instead irritated because the release was planned as a diplomatic favor to Germany. But instead of releasing Kurnaz to Turkey, the United States kept him in Guantánamo for four more years, a decision that it later justified through fabricated allegations.

By joint action of Berlin and Kurnaz's hometown, Bremen, his residency permit was revoked. According to German law, a foreigner's permission to stay is cut off once that foreigner stays abroad for more than six months. We appealed this decision successfully. A German court decided that Kurnaz's stay in Guantánamo was not of his free will. It found Kurnaz had intended to go back to Germany with a return ticket from Pakistan. Germany had tried to avoid any responsibility by annulling Kurnaz's right to stay in and to return to Germany. This court decision helped change Germany's attitude toward Kurnaz.

After Kurnaz was released, he claimed that he was beaten by German special forces while in U.S. custody in Kandahar. Defense Ministry officials denied the claim: First, they said that Kurnaz was a liar because in January 2002, there were no German troops in Afghanistan. Then, they admitted Germany had troops there but that they did not know Kurnaz was in U.S. custody. Weeks later, the officials said that German soldiers knew about Kurnaz's detention but had no contact with him. Finally, officials admitted that they saw and talked to Kurnaz but that no one had beaten him. After the questioning of about twenty German elite soldiers, the prosecutor had doubts that the witnesses told the full truth. He had the impression they coordinated their response beforehand.

The key to the case was the existence of a truck in the camp. According to Kurnaz, the beating took place behind a truck with a tank for emptying human waste. All the soldier witnesses denied the existence of such a truck in the camp. No truck, no mistreatment was the formula.

It was easy to check this story with U.S. witnesses who served in the camp. The German news magazine *Der Spiegel* interviewed American soldiers in the United States. They all confirmed that the fecal matter was taken out of the camp and incinerated using a two-and-a-half-ton military truck driven through the camp's main gate. The prosecutor requested permission from the U.S. government to allow U.S. military personnel to testify concerning activities by German military personnel relevant to the investigation. The embassy answered,

> After careful consideration of all aspects of this matter, the United States has determined it cannot provide the assistance you have requested. The United States appreciates Germany's important contributions to the Afghanistan mission and is confident that any reports of abuses will be appropriately investigated and addressed through existing law enforcement and judicial processes.

When information about Germany's role was published, it caused a political crisis. Two parliamentary inquiries were established and Germany's foreign minister, Frank Walter Steinmeier, the former chief of the Chancellor's Office, came under fire for his role in preventing the release of Murat Kurnaz. Steinmeier defended his decisions with two arguments: First, there had been no formal offer to release Kurnaz in fall 2002. But since Guantánamo is a lawfree zone, offers to release are not sent by sealed letters but must be initiated by talks between the secret services. And since clear U.S. intentions for Kurnaz's release had been documented, it was simply a lack of political will on Germany's part to give a positive response. Second, Steinmeier insisted that Kurnaz represented a possible threat to German security interests. That claim, however, is inconsistent with the findings of the prosecutor, the German secret services, and the U.S. investigation at that time. And even if it were true, Germany is not allowed to use a lawless torture camp as a tool of its security interests. Germany was obliged to get Kurnaz out. If there were serious allegations, Kurnaz could have been charged in Germany and afforded a fair trial.

Steinmeier's arguments were a dirty blaming-the-victim strategy to avoid political pressure. Some reports in the media recycled old and invalidated allegations that Kurnaz had terrorist intentions and that he posed a security risk. Some papers asked why Germany should sacrifice its foreign minister for a Turk. Even Kurnaz's long Guantánamo beard was exploited to create fear and inflame prejudices.

Up to now there has been no remorse on the part of the German government and no compensation for Kurnaz. Indeed, Steinmeier has said that he made no mistakes and would do the same thing again.

Mark Wilson: Private Diplomacy

David McColgin and I arrived in Kabul in the last week of March 2007. Having recently learned that four of our clients at Guantánamo had been "cleared for transfer" (although they each still bore the "enemy combatant" designation), we were puzzled about the reason for any delay in transferring our Afghan client. He had not had an Administrative Review Board hearing for two years, so it was easy to infer that he had been cleared for transfer for that period of time. Our plan in Kabul was to investigate our innocence claim, to find out why our client had not been transferred to Afghanistan, with the hope that the transfer might be expedited, and to meet with members of the local press who we hoped would build pressure on the Afghan government to push for the return of the "cleared" Afghans. For a week we would meet with our client's family and with any government official who would see us. A U.K. organization, Global Strategies Group, provided us with lodging, sustenance, and an extraordinary "fixer" named Shakoor. We also had enlisted the services of the Afghan Human Rights Organization (AHRO) and its director, Lal Gul.

On our third day in Kabul we sat in a book-lined office, befitting the reputation of Sibghatullah Mojaddedi as a Sufi scholar. When the opportunity for an audience with Mojaddedi arose, we quickly said yes. He had briefly been the president of Afghanistan in 1992 (and still is the only person in modern Afghan history to have voluntarily surrendered leadership of the country), and he had been instrumental in the writing of the current constitution. At the time of our meeting he held two important posts. He was the elected leader of the upper house, the Meshrano Jirga, of the parliament, and he had been appointed by President Karzai to chair the National Peace and Reconciliation Commission. He had a reputation as a mediator not unlike that of Jimmy Carter. His was the largest office we were to see in Kabul, but it was packed with a dozen assistants, who were not introduced and did not speak. There was also a television film crew with lights and the camera rolling. I felt uneasy about the situation. What had we gotten ourselves into?

After the customary tea was set before us, Lal Gul, who had arranged the audience, launched into a colloquy with Mojaddedi in Dari, while our interpreter sat mute next to me. I had been nervous about the AHRO director's agenda and anxious about how we were going to convince Mojaddedi that our client should be brought back to Afghanistan and released. I leaned close to the interpreter and asked what was being discussed. The eighty-year-old Mojaddedi heard my whispered question. Imposing with his long white beard and weathered face, he looked at me and in unaccented, fluent English began to address me. He knew our client. He knew his story. He expressed his belief that our client was innocent, one of the Afghans spirited into the custody of the U.S. military on the false word of a villager who coveted the promised bounty. The anxiety melted away, and I looked at David with a raised eyebrow that was meant to signal, "Okay, this works." I knew right then that the Afghans were not the cause of the delay in Muhammed's transfer. Mojaddedi promised his assistance in gaining his release.

Seven months later Muhammed was transferred to the new American-built wing at the Soviet-era Pul-e-Charkhi prison on the eastern outskirts of Kabul. We never heard directly from Mojaddedi again, but persistent phone calls to his staff and various other officials in Kabul over the following five months ultimately brought the call from Kabul that Muhammed had been released to his village.

Charles H. Carpenter: Playing Politics

My firm represents, among other Guantánamo detainees, Hani Saleh Rashid Abdullah, a Yemeni who was arrested in Pakistan by Pakistani authorities in September 2002. We filed a habeas petition in January 2005, and my first visit with Hani was in June of that year. Since then, I've been to Guantánamo nine times. He's a delicate, birdlike man. But he has a sense of humor and patience that has carried him through torture at the notorious "prison of darkness" in Kabul when he was first arrested and then through the long years of mostly solitary imprisonment at Guantánamo.

I was not without trepidation, then, when I decided to attend the January 2008 "Imam's Conference" in Yemen. Hani's brother attended as well, and I planned a trip to Aden to meet with others in his family. I bought a guidebook, which said that the biggest surprise about Yemen is that it is safer and friendlier than wherever you live. My assistant hired a guide for me, and off I went.

Always paranoid, I arrived at the airport about ninety minutes early. My guide had other business, so I had to make do with the ten or so words of Arabic I know. There was a problem with my ticket: I had not come to the airport the day before to confirm in person, and my seat had been reassigned. The polite woman at the counter told me that there were no additional seats, and I would need to go to the airline's business office. It was outside the security area, and so it was clear that I would have to wait in the chaotic line again. I was naturally a little steamed. I was even more angry when the clerk in the business office told me that the flight was sold out. Perhaps I could come back in three days. I explained that I had checked out of my hotel, had booked a room in Aden, and was only staying one day. Suddenly, it occurred to him to ask if I would like to upgrade to first class. How much? $50. Soon he was processing the paperwork.

Just then, a clerk from the immigration office came in to talk about some people they would be deporting. He looked straight at me and asked why I was going to Aden. I explained about meeting Hani's family. The airline clerk, the immigration clerk, and two other airline passengers asked a number of questions. They became very animated and were excited that American lawyers would represent one of their countrymen, saddened that their president had been unable to get the American president to release the Yemeni prisoners, and very disappointed in the United States for allowing the whole thing to happen. I heard this over and over in Yemen; people could not believe that the United States, which they had grown up regarding as a beacon of human freedom, would hold people without trial. As the airline clerk completed the paperwork, he announced that the upgrade only cost $40. The immigration clerk walked with me to the security line and explained to the guards who I was. They quickly sent me through.

It was nearly 10 p.m. by the time I got to the hotel restaurant for dinner. There were only two other men in the restaurant, and they recognized me from the first-class cabin on the flight. They invited me to dine with them, and I was happy to do so. We had a lively discussion about politics, history, religion, and business. By around midnight, we had become quite familiar with one another—and they with my mission. One of the men asked if I would like to meet the governor of the state of Aden. I said no thank you and that I did not have an interpreter. But they would not take no for an answer, and the second man, from Dubai, offered to interpret. After some argument, I agreed to let them call the governor. He was awake, and after some discussion, he agreed to meet me.

The next day we went to Governor Al-Kohlani's office. We had a long wait in the anteroom. Eventually, the governor's assistant called us in, and we sat at the end of a long table. I explained who I was, what I was doing, and who the client was. The governor thanked me and my law firm on behalf of the people of Aden. He then had a series of questions about the conditions at the camp and about my client's family. We discussed rehabilitation of terrorism suspects, and he described a somewhat ham-handed attempt by an American official—someone from the White House—who came to give him a lecture on how to do it. Governor Al-Kohlani was engaged and interested and told me, at the end of the conversation, that return of the prisoners was his government's top priority. He also told me, in broken English, that he could barely believe that the United States had engaged in a detention policy such as the one at Guantánamo. He expected much better of us.

Back at the hotel, as I got on the elevator, a tall Yemeni man saw my suit and tie and said that he hoped my business had gone well. I told him that it had. He told me that he was the oil minister, that the Cabinet was getting ready to act, and that he too viewed the return of the prisoners as a top priority. He also thanked me for our efforts.

I have since corresponded with Governor Al-Kohlani and his successor and have received follow-up inquiries from the Foreign Ministry. I cannot say that this diplomatic initiative was a success, but I think some groundwork has been laid for my client's successful reintegration into ordinary life.

Gaillard T. Hunt: Letter to Fidel

The following are two letters sent by Gaillard T. Hunt on behalf of his client in Guantánamo. The letters appear in their original form.

June 3, 2006

Su Excelencia
Dr. Fidel Castro Ruz
Presidente de la República de Cuba
La Habana, CUBA
Re: Correspondence from Mr. Saifullah Paracha
    Detainee of U.S. at Guantánamo Bay, Cuba

Dear Mr. President:

Saifullah A. Paracha, a citizen of Pakistan held by the United States at Guantánamo Bay, Cuba, has written a letter addressed to the President of the Republic.

I represent Mr. Paracha in the United States courts. I must operate under a "protective order" which makes communication with Mr. Paracha very slow and sometimes impossible. The protective order forbids me to describe the content of Mr. Paracha's letter. The letter has been seized by U.S. officials who refuse to release it.

It would be altogether proper for your government to approach the diplomatic representatives of the United States and to request delivery of the letter directly and without further delay. I do not know how many other prisoners at Guantánamo may have written to Cuban authorities, but we can assume that all such letters have also been impounded.

Respectfully yours,
Gaillard T. Hunt
Attorney for Saifullah A. Paracha

•

May 2, 2006

Ministro Felipe Pérez Roque
Ministerio de Relaciones Exteriores de Cuba
la Habana, CUBA

Re: Mr. Saifullah Paracha
    Detainee of U.S. at Guantánamo Bay, Cuba

Dear Sr. Pérez Roque:

I represent a prisoner named Saifullah A. Paracha, held by the United States at Guantánamo Bay.

Mr. Paracha is a 58-year-old Pakistani businessman who was seized July 5, 2003, at the airport in Bangkok, where he had gone believing he had an appointment with representatives of K-Mart, the large American retailer. He is not typical of the Guantánamo prisoners. He lived in the United States for 16 years and still has an American green card, a permanent residence visa, although he returned to Pakistan some years ago. He has numerous relatives in America and had an exporting business with a partner in New York. Many people have sent me numerous statements on Mr. Paracha's behalf, all agreeing that Mr. Paracha did not support terrorism. He was very active in business and charitable affairs. He came into contact with some businessmen who the United States believes were secretly supportive of terrorists, and because of this guilt by association, the United States has confined him under the strictest conditions for nearly three years now.

The Government of Cuba has taken the view that the occupation of the mouth of Guantánamo Bay by the United States as a coaling station is a relatively minor irritant in the context of the major problems such as the trade boycott. Beginning in early 2002, however, the placement there by the United States of prisons to hold without judicial hearings several hundred nationals of countries at peace with both Cuba and the United States raises serious problems under international law and the law of human rights. I understand the Government of Cuba recognized these problems in a statement issued around January 19, 2005. Constructing prisons was probably also a breach of the lease, under which the United States is to use Guantánamo Bay as a naval base only.

The Guantánamo Bay lease reserves the ultimate sovereignty over the base to Cuba. The Detainee Treatment Act's withdrawal of judicial responsibility for these prisoners from the United States courts implies that they are to seek review of their confinement from the courts of Cuba, the nation with ultimate sovereignty. I would therefore like to contact an appropriate lawyer, or law firm, or bufete, to learn how to go about this. Could someone please refer me to the proper place to start this process?

Thank you very much,
Gaillard T. Hunt
Attorney for Saifullah A. Paracha

Other forms of advocacy included efforts to increase public awareness about the illegal detention and treatment of prisoners at Guantánamo both at home and abroad.

H. Candace Gorman: Blogging Guantánamo

What does a lawyer do when the rule of law is abandoned and the courts refuse to do their job? When I am not filing court papers or taking the long trip down to Guantánamo, I blog.

Since I have not been allowed to meaningfully represent my clients in the courts, I have turned to different kinds of advocacy. As I see it, my role is to get the word out, to educate and agitate my fellow citizens. I can only hope that the decency of the American people holds the day and that public outrage will pressure our government to reinstate habeas corpus and restore the rule of law.

Before I started my newfound blogging career, I started giving talks about Guantánamo. I knew the media was giving Guantánamo little coverage, and what I learned was that people really wanted to know more. They wanted to know what the military base was like, what my clients were like, and what was really going on in the courts. When I gave talks, people were always coming up to me afterward and telling me how ashamed they were about what our country was doing. They wanted to know what they could do to help put an end to our country's lawlessness. I would always tell them the same thing: donate to nonprofit organizations working on these issues, tell everyone you know to pay attention to this issue, and contact Congress and tell them to close the place, every day if you can.

In addition to giving speeches to community and church groups, I turned to the Internet, and, like many activists in recent years, I discovered

the blogosphere. In September 2006, I submitted an article to *The Huffington Post*, explaining why I was representing a Guantánamo detainee. The
article tried to shed some light on a little-reported aspect of the U.S. campaign in Afghanistan: the bounty leaflets our military scattered over the
Afghan countryside following the U.S. military invasion in October 2001.
I asked the readers of *The Huffington Post*,

> Imagine if someone dropped a thousand leaflets over your city that
> said, "We will pay you enough money to support you, your imme-
> diate family and your extended family for the rest of your life if you
> turn over individuals who are 'murderers and terrorists.'" Imagine—
> your immediate family and your extended family taken care of for the
> rest of your life and all you have to do is turn over "murderers and
> terrorists."

This debut post was followed by other pieces about my client, Abdul
Hamid Al-Ghizzawi, and the injustices at Guantánamo. As interest in the
prison camp increased, other blogs began picking up my articles. It is safe
to say that Internet media has followed Guantánamo more diligently than
the "old media."

In December 2006, my law clerk decided to set up our own blog.
We have regularly posted on all kinds of developments related to Guantánamo, not just on my own activities. Although not many people leave
comments on the blog, we keep track of the traffic and regularly get visitors from such far-flung lands as Guinea Bissau and Brunei. My posts have
run the gamut from indictments of the odious Military Commissions Act
to ruminations on what the FBI's surveillance of singer John Lennon tells
us about the government's abuse of "state secrets." The encouragement
and goodwill of bloggers has been heartening. After I was interviewed on
a NPR program, an anonymous listener left this message on my blog:

> I came from a communist ruled country and knew exactly what was
> going to happen if you are charged by the government. If the govern-
> ment want[s] to make you a criminal, all they need to do is to find
> the excuse. Many people in my country had fought for democracy and
> freedom and dreamed that one day we will be as free and democratic
> as the United States. And most of them ended up in jail with the simi-
> lar fate of your clients or worse. Maybe the power of corruption exists
> everywhere? Maybe we as humans, even with noble aspirations and

speeches, the fear and hatred will ultimately drive our actions? Everything else is just like window dressing?

Although I may not share my anonymous friend's bleak outlook, I certainly agree that power corrupted the Bush administration and its lackeys in Congress.

When I am not blogging, I have other creative ways to bring attention to Guantánamo. Earlier in the year, in honor of International Human Rights Day, I joined activists around the nation and world and wore an orange jumpsuit to work (the kind worn by some of the Guantánamo detainees). I dressed the jumpsuit up with a belt and turtleneck (I don't know why—maybe I was thinking it would be more lawyerlike). I wore the jumpsuit hoping that people would stop and ask me about it. However, it didn't happen quite that way. As you might imagine, people that know me were forced to listen to my explanation, but the "masses" were keeping their distance. Most people turned their heads or averted their eyes when they saw me coming. Some crossed to the other side of the street. It might have had something to do with the headache-inducing orange color, or maybe the fact that there is a federal metropolitan correctional center a few short blocks from my office. Anyway, now I am thinking about sporting a giant button that reads, "ask me about Guantánamo."

Richard Wilson: International Fora

In my thirty-five years of practicing law, the Guantánamo detainee litigation has been the single most difficult and complex case with which I have ever been involved. I read more background material and learned more new areas of law than I had in any of my hundreds of other cases. More lawyers were involved in this litigation than any other with which I have ever been involved. The legal and nonlegal strategies employed in this litigation were broad and included domestic and international litigation, legislative proposals, diplomatic interventions in both the United States and Canada, and extensive and high-profile public education and advocacy. The extraordinary security precautions taken around this litigation and the lawyers involved in it were like few others in U.S. history.

As early as February 2002, just after the U.S. military began placing detainees in Cuba, I joined the Center for Constitutional Rights and other human rights organizations in filing a request to the Inter-American Commission on Human Rights. These groups sought protection for all Guantánamo detainees, whose identities were withheld by the government, through a request that the United States take precautionary measures to assure them fair treatment and legal process under international humanitarian law and human rights norms. These standards were made obligatory on the United States by virtue of its participation in the Organization of American States.

The decision of the Commission on Human Rights was issued on March 12, 2002, and was the first statement by any international body dealing with the legal situation of the detainees. It served to provide an international-law-based legal framework for the detainees' claims, while forcing the U.S. government, for the first time, to articulate some rational and legal basis for the detentions. We continued to submit periodic updates to the commission regarding the situation of all detainees at Guantánamo, and the commission continued to call on the United States to comply with its obligations under international law. That these decisions are uniformly ignored by U.S. courts (and by most lawyers representing detainees) speaks to my primary observation in this reflection: the almost total absence of judicial recognition of international legal obligations within the U.S. legal system. This failure is one of the primary reasons why the international community looks with such scorn and disdain on the U.S. responses, legal and political, to Guantánamo, an ignominious national shame and scandal.

Matthew Darby: Just the Facts

As a senior member of the Center for Policy and Research at Seton Hall University School of Law, I coauthored reports that reveal a number of embarrassing truths about the detainees at Guantánamo Bay. These reports have proven useful both for defense lawyers representing the detainees and for causing the general public to question the way our government has handled Guantánamo. We did not begin this project with the intention of writing the reports. Rather, we were simply trying to assist Mark Denbeaux with his legal defense of two detainees. Thus, we came to analyze piles and piles of government documents. By producing statistics and noting patterns, we hoped to give Mark an idea of where his client stood with respect to the rest of the detainees. It wasn't until we saw how the statistics and bigger patterns showed that the government might not be holding the right people that we decided to write the reports. The reception of these reports has been both hot and cold: hot in the sense that they have received a lot of attention from the press, cold in the sense that many people think that such reports are unbecoming of an American citizen. The latter reception is the one that puzzles me.

When I first told my granddad about my work, he responded with an e-mail forward depicting the Twin Towers falling. "Do you remember?" the page asked. The implication, of course, is that I was being unpatriotic. Whenever I mention these reports at parties or at job interviews, there is always a moment of awkward silence as I wait for the other person to respond. Sometimes I hear a positive "Oh, that's cool!" Other times I get a less-than-approving "Ah."

As if it were unpatriotic for a citizen living in a democracy to question his government! I see things differently. I consider my work with Seton Hall's Center for Policy and Research to be very patriotic. Our mission is to provide the general public with a glimpse of what the government would prefer not to disclose.

Because of my work and the work of my colleagues, we know, not just suspect or believe, some frightening facts—facts that are based solely on the *government's* own data. Although we have not seen any of the classified evidence against the detainees, we know that over half of all detainees are not even accused of having committed a hostile act against the United States or its allies. We know that the detainees were not allowed to present any evidence of their own during the kangaroo courts known as the CSRTs. We know that most of the detainees were not captured by the United States but, rather, were turned over to the United States by foreign powers, in many instances for a financial reward. Even though the government has certainly withheld much information, it has revealed enough to allow a partial audit. The results of this audit are extremely disturbing.

At Guantánamo, our government has shifted off our foundations of justice and onto the sinking silt of so-called military necessity and false patriotism. It is the patriotic duty of all Americans to question those actions.

Alan Sussman: Teach-In

If more than a hundred lawyers armed with a Supreme Court ruling were unable to force the Bush administration to obey the law, it seemed to me that an additional approach could be taken. This was the genesis of the Guantánamo Teach-In. My thought was simply that if the administration could ignore the pleas of lawyers and disobey orders of the courts, it could not as easily withstand the opinion of the public.

On October 5, 2006, the Guantánamo Teach-In took place at Seton Hall University Law School. Some of the speakers at the event were attorneys who represented inmates at Guantánamo, but most were professionals whose confrontation with Guantánamo significantly challenged their usual practice, professional ethics, or personal judgment.

What the public lacked was information. There had been little discussion of the pertinent legal issues in the media, and when questions were raised, deference was given to Defense Secretary Donald Rumsfeld's self-justifying quotation that the men detained at Guantánamo were "the worst of the worst," with little, if any, inquiry by journalists. Even among my acquaintances and those who shared my political views, few knew the degree to which the Bush administration had transgressed centuries-old legal standards of due process at Guantánamo.

The idea that a Teach-In could provide information and mobilize public opinion was based on a number of assumptions. The first was that a significant number of students would be interested in learning more about the situation at Guantánamo. The second was that once the students were aware, they would become so offended or enraged by what they learned that they would insist that the government alter its course and honor the law. The third was that the government could not withstand the force of this outcry and would be compelled to change its ways.

Such assumptions are common. Anyone who plans an event of public protest imagines that the course of history can be changed if everyone possessed his or her level of passion and, moreover, that everyone would share that passion if they had the same information he or she had. Although this assumption is almost never the case, such illusions are necessary. Few protests would occur were they not indulged.

But the Teach-In was not intended to be a protest. Its purpose was to disseminate information and to educate. "Students" were to be the audience, and the "teachers" were people who knew something about the topic. We were able to persuade both the lawyers closely connected with the cases and "the best of the best"—those with incomparable knowledge and experience in the fields of law, medicine, psychology, religion, and human rights—to participate. We spent most of the summer finding and convincing professors, students, and administrators of various universities of the value of hosting the Teach-In on their respective campuses. By the date of the event, we had signed up over 200 colleges, seminaries, and law schools, where perhaps 20,000 to 50,000 students heard all or part of the day's proceedings in college auditoriums connected to Seton Hall Law School's Internet simulcast.

Although the Teach-In was not a protest, it was a dissent. As in judicial opinions, a dissent has strength because it is both reasoned and, by definition, contrary to prevailing policy. Dissent should not be merely tolerated; even some dictators do that. To be tolerated is to some degree to be patronized. Nor should a dissent, in a democratic society, be considered a simple irritant. It is an essential element of the democratic process. Free speech guarantees it, but self-government demands it. It is the mechanism by which decision-makers are informed that they are not infallible, the process by which a polity educates itself and acquires maturity.

President Bush, when asked how we should treat our adversaries in the "war on terror," was fond of saying that we have an obligation to "bring these men to justice." The Teach-In was proposed to explain what justice has meant at Guantánamo.

7

Leaving Guantánamo

The obstacles to leaving Guantánamo are tremendous, even for those prisoners whom the United States says it no longer wishes to detain. For example, many detainees who have been cleared for release still remain at Guantánamo, facing a seemingly endless cycle of failed efforts to repatriate them. Other detainees who have been released continue to face hardship and in some cases imprisonment in a new country. And even those fortunate enough to have been returned home continue to suffer the effects of years of unlawful detention and separation.

Stuck in Limbo

One of Guantánamo's singular failings is how it handles prisoners who cannot safely be returned home or for whom there is no longer a home after years of unlawful imprisonment. Men who the U.S. government concedes are innocent or present no threat thus remain at Guantánamo year after year because the United States refuses to allow them to live temporarily in its country after imprisoning them by mistake and branding them "terrorists," so other countries are fearful of accepting them. The United States has also persisted in trying to send prisoners it has "cleared for release" home even though their return would probably result in their torture or continued detention. In some instances, it has simply dumped prisoners in third countries with which the prisoners have no ties and whose language they do not even speak.

Elizabeth Gilson: Looking for a Home

In spring 2007, I got a notice that the military had cleared my clients Arkin and Bahtiyar (and the other Uighurs) for release but that it still considered them "enemy combatants." Try finding asylum for enemy combatants. The U.S. government has acknowledged that they will be in danger of torture or death if they are sent back to China. However, every country that has been approached diplomatically has been unwilling to help the United States solve the Uighur problem at the risk of jeopardizing their relations with the

Chinese government. So I, and other Uighur counsel, continue to work on legal, legislative, and diplomatic fronts to try to find a place for these men. The government has since admitted that it detained the Uighurs by mistake, but it nevertheless continues to hold them at Guantánamo until a home may be found.

Kent Spriggs: The Tallahassee Uighur Settlement Project

The Uighurs are an ethnic group of about twenty million persons in Xinjiang, a province in the extreme west of China. That they are Muslims and have aspirations of independence from China has led to their being treated in a very hostile manner by the Chinese government. Substantial numbers have fled from China as a result of persecution. Twenty-two men who had been in a refugee camp in Afghanistan when the U.S.-led invasion commenced in the fall of 2001 were picked up and taken to Guantánamo.

Under international law, the United States cannot repatriate persons to countries that it believes will torture them. Five of the twenty-two Uighurs were subsequently sent to Albania after several years of incarceration.

In late August 2007, there was a hearing before District Judge Ricardo M. Urbina on the habeas corpus cases of the seventeen Uighurs who remained at Guantánamo. The judge indicated that he believed he had the power to release the Uighurs into the United States as a part of his habeas jurisdiction. At that point, realizing that the Uighurs might be released into the States, an "APB" went out among the GTMO habeas lawyers asking for communities that could settle some of the men.

Tallahassee, Florida, was a natural fit. The community had experience in settling refugees. I was deeply involved as a GTMO habeas lawyer, knew the general story of the Uighurs, and had a sense of the people to contact to put together a plan.

I called Brant Copeland, pastor of First Presbyterian Church. He had convened an interdenominational forum in the days after 9/11. It was clear that he was the kind of person who would be invaluable in putting together a plan. He spoke of the value of multiple clergy involvement to set the proper social context. I suggested that he do that in writing. As the cochair of Tallahassee Clergy, a large group of progressive religious leaders, he said he could e-mail them. We drafted a statement through which the clergy would welcome the Uighurs and pledge to urge their congregations to do the same. In a few days, Brant had six to eight signatures.

I then turned to Salah Bakhashwin, a Saudi national who had lived in Tallahassee for twenty-five years and who had been my Arabic translator for my first GTMO client. He is concerned about human rights generally and is passionate about justice for the prisoners at GTMO. The Islamic Center of Tallahassee, the larger of the two mosques in the city, was the logical spiritual home for Uighurs, and it was clear that Salah was the way into that community. As a member of the Shura Council, the governing board of the Islamic Center, he reached out to the council and broached the idea.

In the meantime, Brant wrote a sermon telling the story of the Uighurs, urging his own congregation to support the project. He also followed up his e-mail to the clergy with calls to a number of recipients who had not responded to the initial e-mail. He ended up with nineteen signatures. Both the sermon and the clergy statement proved important in the process. Meanwhile, I wrote a first draft of what was to become the Uighur Settlement Plan.

I was invited to meet with the Shura Council. I took with me the clergy statement and the sermon that Brant was delivering. The response of the Shura Council was very positive. The sermon and clergy statement were very valuable in the exchange at that meeting.

Several members told of slights and injustices that they and others in the congregation had suffered solely because of their Islamic faith. Some of the injustices were substantial. It was good to be reminded of the isolation and ostracism that Muslims often face in the United States. The fact that the "majority" religious community was enthusiastic about welcoming the Muslim Uighurs sent a message that for once they were not alone.

The Islamic Center contributed by finding housing near the center. They promised jobs and pledged money. All these were integral parts of what became the Uighur Settlement Plan.

All the documents we collected were transmitted to the lawyers for the Uighurs. They liked the sermon so much that they had it translated into Uighur to be distributed to their clients and others. They were very surprised and impressed at the outpouring of support by the clergy. In preparation for the momentous hearing of October 7, the lawyers decided to present the settlement plans for their seventeen Uighur clients to the court. The Lutheran refugee agency for the greater Washington, D.C., area was to take fourteen of the Uighurs, and Tallahassee was to take three. The plans of both groups were proffered to Judge Urbina and became part of the record.

Although Judge Urbina in a courageous order ruled that the Uighurs could be settled in the United States, that order was stayed and then overturned on appeal.

A copy of the sermon follows.

Brant S. Copeland: A Sermon
23rd Sunday in Ordinary Time
Romans 13:8–14
September 7, 2008

Ever hear of Uighurs? If the answer is "No," don't feel bad. Neither had I until a few weeks ago.

Uighurs are an ethnic group who live in what is now the Xinjiang region of China—way up in the northwest of that vast country, with Mongolia to the east, Russia to the north, and Afghanistan, Kyrgyzstan, Pakistan, and India to the west. Uighur country is sparsely populated. It's mostly deserts and mountains. I think it's fair so say that most Americans have never heard of it.

Uighurs speak Turkic, and many of them are Sufi Muslims. Like their neighbors in Tibet, the Uighurs have been persecuted by the Chinese government for decades, but unlike the Tibetans, they don't have a spiritual leader like the Dalai Lama to tell their story and keep their plight in the international headlines.

The U.S. State Department officially lists Uighurs as the victims of state persecution on account of their religion, and that status is a sticking point in Chinese-American relations.

Now this is a sermon, not a social studies talk, and in any case I've told you just about everything I know about Uighurs. Now I'd like you to meet a few Uighurs—in your imagination at least. Each has a slightly different story, but I've learned enough to give you a general picture.

Turn your calendar back to the year 2001. Having fled China to escape persecution, some Uighur men were living in a refugee camp in the mountains of Afghanistan—the Tora Bora mountain range, to be precise. It seems they were in that settlement on September 11, 2001, when, faraway in cities they had never heard of called New York and Washington, D.C., planes crashed into the World Trade Center and the Pentagon.

We all remember what followed.

- The declaration of a "war on terror"
- The invasion of Afghanistan
- The hunt for Osama bin Laden and the bombing of the Tora Bora caves

The men in this story made their way across snow-covered peaks into Pakistan, where they hoped to find refuge. Some local tribesmen took them in, fed them a feast, and then betrayed them. They turned them over to the military authorities in order to collect the $5,000 bounty per person the Americans were paying for allies of Osama bin Laden. The problem is, these Uighurs had never heard of Osama bin Laden.

Twenty-three Uighur men were caught in that snare and were eventually hooded, shackled, and flown to the U.S. prison in Guantánamo Bay, Cuba.

That was seven years ago, and they've been there ever since. They're not "terrorists." What they are is refugees who were caught in the wrong place at the wrong time. They're certainly not "the worst of the worst," as we were once told was the case with all the prisoners at Guantánamo. What they are, in biblical terms, is the "least of the least."

There are now seventeen Uighur men being held in Guantánamo. I've told you a bit of their story because there's a chance that in October a federal judge in Washington, D.C., will be ordering their release—or in legal terms, their "parole." If that should happen, these Uighurs will have no place to go. Return to China is impossible, and it appears no other nation in the world will risk China's displeasure by showing hospitality to Uighurs.

The volunteer attorneys who represent these men are hoping that there might be some communities around the country who would agree to take a few of them in—give them housing, find them jobs, teach them the skills they will need to make new lives in the country that has imprisoned them for so long.

A few weeks ago I was approached by someone close to these men's case and asked if I thought Tallahassee might be a place where three of these Uighur men might find hospitality. "I'm asking you," this person said, "because I've heard of First Presbyterian Church and thought that if any congregation would be willing to work on a project like this, it would be yours."

I thought about that. I thought about the welcome our session gave to the family of John Spenkelink, back in 1979, when Florida reinstituted the death penalty, and John's family needed somewhere to hold John's funeral. I remembered the time refugees from El Salvador occupied our chapel, living there during Holy Week to raise awareness of their nation's plight. I thought of the Vietnamese families we have embraced through the years and of the folks fleeing hurricanes Katrina and Rita three years ago. I remembered all that Cajun food being cooked in our kitchen, and how I didn't eat anywhere else for a whole week.

More than that, I remembered how the faith communities of Tallahassee pulled together to minister to those 700 Katrina victims who found themselves in Tallahassee. I remembered sitting around the table with Christian pastors and clergy from Temple Israel and Masjid Al-Nah, one of the two local mosques, planning pastoral care for the folks at the Red Cross Center. I thought about the conversations I've been having with colleagues in the organization called the Tallahassee Interfaith Clergy, which is co-chaired by me and Rabbi Jack Romberg.

I put all that together in my head, and I told that person, "Yes. I think the congregations of Tallahassee would be up to that challenge."

In the past few days, the momentum has been picking up. I sent out an e-mail to my ministerial colleagues explaining the situation. Every time I check my e-mail I get another message saying, "Yes, we'll help." We're talking with a local Presbyterian pastor who worked for three years resettling refugees up in northern Virginia. He is an expert. He says he'll show us how it's done.

And as we worship the triune God this morning, a conversation is taking place with the governing body at a local mosque. "If you'll take the lead," we're telling the Muslim community, "the other faith communities in Tallahassee will help. We'll stand with you, and together we'll follow God's call."

I said this was a sermon, and it is. It's a commentary on today's reading from Romans. I didn't know it at the time, but all week long the Holy Spirit has been writing my sermon for me, putting into context these words from the Apostle Paul:

> Owe no one anything, except to love one another; for the one who loves another has fulfilled the law. The commandments "You shall not commit adultery; You shall not murder; You shall not covet"; and any other commandment, are summed up in this word, "Love your neighbor as yourself."

For Christians, the meaning of the word *neighbor* is found not in a dictionary but in a story. You know that story well—the parable of the Good Samaritan. Neighbors, that story implies, are not just the folks who live nearby; they're the folks whose need cries out from a ditch on the road to Jericho or from a Red Cross Service Center or even from a prison in Guantánamo Bay.

Seldom does that cry arise at a convenient time, and it almost always involves crossing some kind of boundary. That's the nature of *neighbor* in the Christian tradition. Jews and Muslims have different traditions, but I suspect they would arrive at much the same conclusion when it comes to the story I've been telling you.

A patriot might say that what our nation has done to these men is shameful and ought to be put right in order to restore our nation's honor. A prophet might say that they have suffered a great injustice. A Christian might well agree with both the patriot and the prophet, but when it comes right down to it, these men are simply our neighbors, and Christ commands us to love our neighbors.

The story of these Uighur refugees is far from finished. The congregations of Tallahassee will be writing the next chapters. Let us pray that when their story is told to our children, they will give thanks to God for our faithful response to God's call.

Jeffrey Davis: Fear of Torture

Our client, Abdul Ra'ouf Zalita, was originally from Libya. He was serving in the Libyan Army years ago when he deserted and fled Libya because of religious persecution. He then lived in several different countries before settling in Afghanistan, marrying, and fathering a child. When the fighting in Afghanistan moved close to his home, he took his family and fled to Pakistan. Sometime while in Pakistan, he was turned in to authorities for a bounty and ultimately ended up in Guantánamo.

Mr. Zalita has been cleared for release, but the U.S. government has announced that it intends to return him to Libya, not to his home in Afghanistan or to Pakistan, where he was arrested. Mr. Zalita fears that if he is returned to Libya, he will be imprisoned, tortured, and ultimately killed, so we have asked the government to change the destination country. The government has refused.

Based on this refusal, and Mr. Zalita's very reasonable fear for his safety, we asked a federal district court to block his transfer to Libya. The court initially refused to act, saying it had no power to intervene. The court of appeals affirmed, and the U.S. Supreme Court declined to act, without an opinion.

During the court proceedings, I called the then general counsel of the Department of Defense, Jim Haynes—whom I knew from his days as a U.S. federal district court law clerk in Charlotte, North Carolina, where I live. I told Haynes about Mr. Zalita's plight and explained that if Mr. Zalita were returned to Libya, we intended to tell the story to the press. We said we believed that it would be an embarrassment to the Bush administration, given that Mr. Zalita was determined to be deserving of release but was instead being sent home to almost certain torture and death. I also urged Haynes to read the classified parts of Mr. Zalita's files.

Haynes listened attentively, thanked me for the call, and never got back to me. However, over a year and a half later, Mr. Zalita has not been returned to Libya and remains in Guantánamo. During this time, we have been attempting to obtain permission from other countries, including Pakistan and Switzerland, for Mr. Zalita's release there. So far we have not succeeded.

Mark P. Denbeaux: A Fate Worse than Guantánamo

In February 2007, I was advised by the DOJ that the DOD had determined that Mohammed Abdul Rahman was no longer an enemy combatant. They referred to him as "NLEC" (no longer enemy combatant) status. They gave no reason why Mohammed's status had changed, did not suggest he had been cured, and did not admit that his original status was a mistake. Mohammed continued to be held under exactly the same terms and conditions—chained to the floor during interviews, shackled hand and foot when he was moved. And he was to be held in that manner until a country was prepared to accept him after his release. In April 2007, I arranged to see him with Joshua Denbeaux, my son and co-counsel.

Before I left for this meeting, I attended a conference in London. That conference was a dazzling experience for me in that another habeas attorney, Clive Stafford Smith, walked up to me and said, "We have found your client's brother."

I said, "Which client?"

Clive said, "Rafiq Al Hami," one of my other clients from Tunisia.

"Rafiq does not have a brother. In fact he has no family that I know of, and he has told us never to try to contact anyone in Tunisia. He lived in Germany his entire adult life," I replied.

He said, "Well, he does have a brother. His brother is in Tunisia. In fact, his brother is in Tunis, and his brother is a lawyer in Tunis."

I was totally dumbfounded. The idea that my client had a brother who was a lawyer in Tunis was really quite stunning. In the course of the conversation, I stammered and asked questions. I found out that human rights contacts in Tunisia had found his brother while looking for Rafiq.

They also advised me that Rafiq had been convicted in absentia of violating the Tunisian "Patriot Act."

It turns out that in 2003, Tunisia passed an act parallel to the U.S.A. Patriot Act, enacted by Congress in the aftermath of 9/11. In 2005, Rafiq was found guilty of violating the 2003 Tunisian Patriot Act. Upon hearing that, I said, "Well we have a great alibi, because he has been incarcerated in Guantánamo since 2002." I then was told that in Tunisia, there was no prohibition against ex post facto application of law. Even though the law was passed in 2003, when Rafiq was in Guantánamo, he was still found guilty of violating a law that did not yet exist at the time he was picked up and taken to Guantánamo.

Tunisia is not an open or democratic country; hence, it was difficult to absorb that this group found Rafiq's brother there. It is even more remarkable that it happened when neither Rafiq nor I knew they were doing this investigation. This network of human rights activists around the world worked together informally and anonymously. I was not told and did not ask how their connections and contacts were made. They arranged to have Rafiq's brother contact me, and eventually he did.

I told him that Rafiq had no hope, had given up, and would rarely see me. He said he would try to send some communication to him to encourage him to talk to me. In the meantime, he gave me the names and biographies of some of his brothers and sisters. I mentioned that it was possible for Rafiq to get back to Tunisia, but his brother was adamant that if he returned to Tunisia, he would die there.

After gathering this information about Rafiq and Mohammed, I visited them in April 2007. It was unclear how they would react. I met first with Mohammed. I told him that he had been approved for release but that there was no country for him to go to. He was adamant that he could never return to Tunisia because it would actually be worse than Guantánamo and that with his serious health problems he would die there. I then was told that his wife and son were living in Khartoum. But he said he did not want to go to Sudan either. He wanted to go to Italy, where he had lived as a young man, after leaving Tunisia.

I told Mohammed that the United States would send him to any country it thought was suitable and that was likely to be Tunisia, where he was picked up. He said he would refuse to sign any document authorizing him to go there. I was stunned that he believed that he had control over where the United States would send him. This was a man who had no control over what he could eat, who he could talk to, what he could read, or any other decision. Nonetheless, he refused to go.

I then visited Rafiq. I explained that I spoke to his brother and gave him an update on his family. He said that he specifically directed me not to communicate with them. He was extremely distressed and angry. He said, "Don't come see me anymore. It is too painful. I would rather stay alone in my room without hope than I would talk about my family or anything else."

I told him that Tunisia had convicted him in absentia. He said that it was to be expected: "The Americans must have done this." He explained, "So my only trial on United States evidence has happened in Tunisia. The American government knew about it, did not tell me, did not allow me to appear or have a lawyer, and I was still found guilty."

He then told me that the Tunisian government sent its own interrogators to Guantánamo. Those interrogators kept twisting his words and were very abusive. He refused to describe the abuse in any detail; he simply said it was horrific, though not as bad as the treatment he received in the "prison of darkness" outside Kabul.

In mid-May, I received notification that after thirty days Mohammed was to be returned to Tunisia. Our judge, like some other judges, had issued an order requiring the government to provide advance notice before rendering detainees to other countries. I arranged another visit to Guantánamo.

My meeting with Mohammed was eerie from the start. He still refused to return to Tunisia and believed he could refuse to sign the release papers. He was very concerned about his health and was deeply concerned that he would die if he were sent back to Tunisia. It was both poignant and pathetic that he could believe that he had any control over any of this.

I advised him that Rafiq, his compatriot from Tunisia and a man he had never met, was also tried and convicted in absentia under Tunisia's equivalent of the Patriot Act. He nodded. I told him that the United States' retroactive laws could not justify convictions, but apparently that was not true of Tunisia. He shrugged.

On that trip I attempted to see Rafiq twice, but he refused to see me.

I went back to my room and discovered an e-mail from Cori Crider of Reprieve, the organization that had connected me with international human rights intelligence investigators. Cori advised me that she had come across another judgment in absentia convicting a Tunisian of violating the Tunisian Patriot Act. That man was Mohammed.

I called my co-counsel Joshua; he immediately determined that we had to get an injunction to prevent Mohammed's removal to a place that was very likely to kill him. However, the Court of Appeals for the District of Columbia Circuit had previously decided that the Military Commissions Act stripped all federal courts of any jurisdiction to hear Guantánamo detainee cases.

We immediately filed a motion with the district judge. As we began the proceeding, the government lawyers handed us a document, which they said they had an obligation to give to us. The Supreme Court had granted certiorari to review the appeals court's decision and decide the constitutionality of Congress's efforts to strip the federal courts of jurisdiction. I looked at it quickly and said to Joshua, "What does this mean?" He said, "It means we win, they lose, and they are screwed."

Our first point was obvious; our government had attempted to deceive us because they knew Mohammed was not just simply returning to Tunisia but was being transferred to a prison there. The government claimed that there was no obligation even to tell us this information.

Our second point was that given Mohammed's serious health problems, he would die in that prison. We had been able to take the equivalent of a medical history from him during our interviews. We sent that medical history to Physicians for Human Rights to be evaluated by a doctor. The doctor's evaluation found that, if the facts were true, Mohammed faced significant dangers. The doctor was unwilling to speculate about the consequences but recommended that Mohammed have a full physical by a neutral doctor before any transfer.

The judge was profoundly concerned. She asked, "Do you mean to say that he would rather stay in Guantánamo then return to the Tunisian facility?" Everybody in the courtroom was also shocked to learn that this information about Mohammed's conviction had been obtained by an informal human rights intelligence network and had not been provided by the U.S. government. The judge granted a temporary restraining order preventing the transfer.

We later learned that the DOD had had an airplane with one empty seat waiting on the tarmac. They were assured that Mohammed would be in that seat. To our immense relief, that seat remained empty. However, those detainees that were on that plane arrived in Tunisia and disappeared. Their lawyers never saw or spoke to them again.

Emi MacLean: "Somalia? You're Going to Be Here a Long Time"

The day after the inauguration of President Barack Obama, I sat on a patch of grass beside a barbed-wire fence at Guantánamo. Beyond the barbed wire was an airport, and on the other side, an ocean.

An airplane rested on the tarmac in anticipation. One or two, or maybe more, prisoners were scheduled to be released. If history repeated itself, at some moment that night, some fortunate men would be bound, hooded, shackled, and transferred out of Guantánamo in much the way that they were transferred in. Good fortune is relative at Guantánamo.

One young released detainee told me he feared the guards lied to him when they told him he was going home. How could the United States be releasing him to freedom, he thought, when the guards were strapping cuffs on his hands and feet, draping a hood over his head, and treating him like a time bomb about to explode? He felt guns pointed at him on the plane. Once the plane landed, officials made him deboard, while still hooded. They told him to walk. In the blindness, uncertain where he was, he felt certain his executioner walked behind him. It was only when his country's security forces told him, in his own language, to put his head down into the police car that he knew that his life had been spared. He was, indeed, "home."

Why would the government make the transfer home of a Guantánamo prisoner, whom the government had no right to detain in the first place, as brutal and dehumanizing as the imprisonment itself? Wouldn't it serve the national interest to give these individuals a different parting memory?

When a prisoner leaves Guantánamo, there is at least the sense that freedom is closer, and the brutality of Guantánamo is nearing its end. The person will have a name again, not just an "internment serial number" (ISN). "I don't want to know the names, ma'am," a prison guard once told me when I asked him if he knew our client's name, not just his ISN. "Why?" I asked. "It's all about attachment. It's like when you're a kid on a farm and you're told not to name the animals that you're going to eat in the future."

Seeing an outbound plane at Guantánamo is bittersweet. Even the process of a transfer to "freedom" from the prison is traumatizing.

But getting released in the first place after so many years in the prison is not so easy either. This much I knew even from sitting on that patch of grass by the Guantánamo airport: the plane was not waiting for the nighttime departure of any of our clients. Their imprisonment continued.

For many of those who remain in Guantánamo in 2009, there is no certain end point to their ordeal. Their fate rests not solely on a unilateral decision by the United States to release them, but it is also tied up in geopolitics as much as it was when they were first imprisoned. The single most important determinant of their fate is their country of nationality.

The prisoners in Guantánamo figured out long ago the key that unlocks the prison gate. Many predicted that their fate would not rest with the law but with politics. We are lawyers, but we would be naive to ardently disagree. Our clients are right: it has been politics that more often won (or lost) the day. For the men at Guantánamo, the key to freedom lay in having a country to take them in and to demand their return.

A few examples prove the point.

The families of the British detainees traveled around the United Kingdom and the United States to advocate for their brothers and sons. Not long after, the British government leveraged their "special relationship" with the United States to demand the return of the British nationals and, later, the British residents.

All the Europeans were released relatively early on, thanks in large part to the pressure exerted by their governments. Almost all Saudi prisoners were released soon after.

The Australian government eventually intervened on behalf of an Australian military commission defendant imprisoned for years and tried through a sham tribunal. The Australian prime minister and the U.S. vice president apparently negotiated his plea agreement outside the earshot of the prosecutor charged with trying his case. Sentence: a yearlong "gag order" and detention for nine months. He was released, coincidentally, right before the Australian election.

Yet virtually all the Yemenis remain. In 2009, almost half the prison population is Yemeni—nearly one hundred men. Their continued imprisonment has nothing to do with the seriousness of the allegations against them, or the strength of the evidence. They want to return to Yemen, and the Yemeni government has stated its willingness to receive them. But the United States refuses to send them home. Some Yemeni prisoners were told years ago that the U.S. government cleared them for release, but they are in effect held hostage because the U.S. government does not trust the security of their country. Because theirs is a poor country with some internal strife and its own problems with terrorism, the men still call Guantánamo home.

One Somali prisoner remains at Guantánamo because his country, the newly formed independent republic of Somaliland, has no diplomatic relations with the United States and hence cannot negotiate his release. Years ago, he fled the Somali civil war and sought refuge in Pakistan, where the United Nations High Commissioner for Refugees (UNHCR) recognized him as a refugee. He married, he worked, and he built a life far from any battlefield. The allegations against him can only be described as baffling: at one point, he was told that one of the reasons for his imprisonment was that he traveled from Somalia to Pakistan.

Somaliland is stable, and he wants to return there. But it is little surprise that such a transfer is not a diplomatic priority for either Somaliland or the United States. Moreover, the UNHCR—obligated to protect him— effectively abandoned him and others; the politics of Guantánamo is uninviting. When early on, our client told a guard his country of nationality, the guard said, "Somalia? You're going to be here a long time." The guard was right: he remains seven years and counting.

Internationally, diplomacy works only insofar as a country has power that it can, and wants to, wield with the United States in the service of imprisoned men.

Then, there are those who have no country to which they can safely return: they are in effect Guantánamo's refugees.

Prisoners from China, Libya, Syria, Tunisia, and Uzbekistan languish in Guantánamo, unable to return to their home countries and with no third country that will accept them, abandoned on the far side of Cuba. In 2009, sixty men from these and other countries are in the unenviable position of fighting to stay in Guantánamo, rather than face torture and persecution in their home countries. The United States would violate domestic and international law to repatriate these men. But that may not be enough to protect them from repatriation.

Seven years of imprisonment at Guantánamo has left them marked with an indelible stigma. Without evidence, or even nuance, the United States has called them all the "worst of the worst." As often happens with injustice, this strategy backfired. The United States is now finding it very difficult to secure allies who are willing to help resettle these wrongly stigmatized men.

I have traveled to foreign ministries to seek a reprieve for our clients. Foreign officials challenged the U.S. detention regime and other aspects of U.S. government counterterror policy and hoped that a new president would repair some of the damage caused by the old. They often spoke eloquently about the travesty of U.S. executive detention—but they nevertheless did little. They have been slow to share the burden and provide relief for those remaining at Guantánamo.

When asked to take in some of the men without a country, foreign government officials have been skeptical. "Wasn't there some reason that these men were in Guantánamo? What did they do?" It did not matter that the United States picked up virtually all of them in exchange for bounty and far from any battlefield, that few have been charged, and that U.S. intelligence experts and government officials have acknowledged that the U.S. government made many mistakes. Foreign officials also wanted to know why they should intervene if these men were not citizens. "Why should we care?" Neither the international prohibition against transfer to torture nor the humanitarian plea carried much weight. So in 2009 these men are left uncharged—fearing a transfer to torture and forced to try to secure safe haven in some unknown country. Stranded, stigmatized, and forgotten.

Over the years of the Guantánamo litigation, reams of paper were spoiled with battling legal arguments and occasional judicial decisions. Lawyers trade in ideas, arguments, and heated rhetoric. In the Guantánamo litigation, none of those has ever been in short supply. At times over the course of the past seven years, the battling legal arguments appeared decisive.

There were tremendous victories, won by a slim margin. In 2004, in *Rasul v. Bush*, the Supreme Court said that the men imprisoned at Guantánamo have a right to challenge their detention through habeas corpus. Lawyers immediately began to seek, simply, a day in court for their clients. But Congress intervened and tried to strip the men of that right; Congress passed the Detainee Treatment Act.

So in 2006, in *Hamdan v. Rumsfeld*, the Supreme Court said that Congress did not thwart the right of the men at Guantánamo to contest their imprisonment. In response, Congress geared up to try again to strip them of the right to know the reason for their imprisonment and to dispute the government's allegations against them. Lawyers and others highlighted the humanity of the men and the need to protect their rights as we protect our own. When that failed, as it often did, we targeted the lawmakers' appreciation for "fair process." But Congress passed the Military Commissions Act, a second congressional attempt to thwart the prisoners' right to challenge their detention through habeas corpus.

The right had to be won (again) through litigation. In 2008, in *Boumediene v. Bush*, the Supreme Court said a *third* time that the right remains. Days later, in *Parhat v. Gates*, the D.C. Circuit Court of Appeals mocked the evidence relied on by the government to justify the imprisonment of one man. Quoting a Lewis Carroll nonsense poem, the court declared that "the fact that the government has 'said it thrice' does not make an allegation true."

But the heady days of major litigation victories related to Guantánamo have always been short-lived. How many times can you tell an imprisoned man that a major court decision was decided in his favor but that he must nevertheless remain behind bars? These momentous legal decisions are only meaningful if they translate into remedies. The remedies have been slow to come, and when relief is granted, it is distributed once again in an arbitrary fashion, subject to chance and diplomatic developments. The first habeas hearing began in November 2008. The first prisoners to be released as a result of a court order were three men released in December 2008 to Bosnia, nearly seven years after the opening of the prison.

In the middle of 2009, these three releases remain the *only* releases resulting from a court decision. In April 2009, twenty-four out of the twenty-eight prisoners who have had their cases heard in court have won, and yet twenty-one of these "victorious" men remain behind bars. Indeed, Lakhdar Boumediene, the "victor" in the last great Supreme Court victory, shares prison space behind barbed wire in Guantánamo with Huzaifa Parhat, the "victor" in the last great D.C. Circuit Court victory. The litigation victory for these men has been meaningless because they still seek a safe country willing to accept them and demand their release—and the U.S. has refused thus far to be that country. That has consistently proven to be what is truly decisive.

·   ·   ·

The day after the inauguration of President Obama, I was sitting in Guantánamo watching a plane on the tarmac. The following day, I was on a fourteen-seater flying out of Guantánamo Bay. I was mistaken about the purpose of the plane I spied the day before. It was still sitting there, on the tarmac. No further transfer of prisoners from Guantánamo was imminent.

President Obama's Executive Orders promised the eventual closure of Guantánamo and bought him some time to sort out the new administration's policies. The prisoners continued to wait. As policies were debated yet again, the value of the prisoners' liberty appeared inconsequential.

Weeks and months passed. The new administration's lawyers embraced legal positions not substantially different from those of the previous administration regarding the legality of preventative detention, detention conditions at Guantánamo, and transfers to countries despite a risk of torture.

I returned to Guantánamo three months after President Obama's inauguration. Our Somali client was still there, but he was reluctant to meet. He wrote, "There is no justice here. Men captured on the battlefield have been released, and men kidnapped out of their homes remain. The only question is whether they have a country to go to, and whether their country has the power to get them home."

Only one Guantánamo detainee left the prison in President Obama's first three months in office. That man was a British resident, released to the United Kingdom. The trend still holds: a detainee's country tie is the most important determinant of his fate. The government can assert that the ones in Guantánamo in 2009 remain because of threat assessments, but that is mere propaganda. Those left at the prison in Guantánamo in 2009 are there because of the vagaries of their nationalities.

The transition of presidents—from one whose administration epitomized expansive executive power to one who promised to curtail it—has thus far not produced the change we need in national security policy. The liberty of a Guantánamo prisoner has been so devalued that the president's Executive Order permitting one year more of detention without charge—after seven years already—produced jubilation from allies.

The role of the Guantánamo lawyer is somehow significant but also greatly limited. The role of the detainee is much grander. He was at first a pawn to justify expansive executive power. He is now a powerful political tool to signify cautious change. His abuse at the hands of the government will forever leave an indelible mark—on him and on his captors.

Out but Not Free

For some detainees, release from Guantánamo has not meant return home.

P. Sabin Willett: Exile

A sullen rain thrums the taxi roof. The car labors along a dirt road stitched with gravel and mined with stupendous potholes. In the wet, the holes have become pools—ponds, some of them—and our driver creeps around them the way a teen in the family Ford negotiates his first driveway. Beside the road, earth movers loom from the fog, alongside heaps of earth, rubble, and exploded garbage bags. The rain grows fiercer, rattling the roof. Outside, on a donkey cart, a boy hunches against the storm. The rain seems to bounce off him, and then I realize it isn't rain at all. The woman with whom I've shared the last cab at the airport shrugs. "It's normal," she says. I had imagined every sort of ending for Guantánamo except a hailstorm.

On Friday, May 5, 2006, at four o'clock in the afternoon, the telephone rings in my Boston office. It is Bob Loeb. At the moment his call comes in, I am looking at stacks of legal cases on the desk. I wonder, are his stacks as high? Has he read every case, read it again, underlined and highlighted and annotated and read it yet again? In my firm we have mapped and plotted Scalia dissents and Stevens majorities and Kennedy concurrences, but by rights, Bob ought to be more worried. We represent only two unfortunates from Central Asia, swept up by mistake in the so-called "war on terror." As a high-level DOJ attorney representing the U.S. government in the Guantánamo detainee litigation, Bob has the most powerful client in the world.

On Monday morning, we are bound for the U.S. Court of Appeals for the District of Columbia Circuit. It is a great court. Chief Justice John Roberts, Jr., of the U.S. Supreme Court sat there not so long ago. At 9:30, three distinguished judges will take the bench. The green light will come on. For the next half hour they will hear about Adel and Abu Bakker, two Uighur men from Turkestan, which is controlled by Communist China. The men are refugees from communism, and if returned to China, they face persecution, further imprisonment, and possibly death. While waiting in Pakistan for Turkish visas in late 2001, they were sold by bounty hunters to U.S. forces. For more than four years, President Bush refused to release them, claiming the power to imprison them until some other country agreed to take them off our hands.

Except they were neither soldiers nor wrongdoers. They were mistakes. Everyone admitted this—even the military. It seems that our mistakes are for the Old Europe to remedy. So they sat in cages in Guantánamo.

But Bob has news. The Justice Department has just filed a motion to dismiss the appeal. "They're not there anymore."

"Where are they?"

After he answers, I say, "No, Bob, where are they *really*?" And he tells me again.

When the call is over, it is past 10 p.m. in Europe. My secretary has an instinct for phone calls like this and is standing in the doorway, waiting for the explanation.

"Kris," I say, "how do I get to Albania?"

•   •   •

I reach the Sheraton Tirana at midday Sunday. The hotel is clean, with shiny marble floors inside and mown grass outside. Upstairs is a room, also clean, with the same minibar you'd find in Cleveland. The same Internet. The same television. In an hour, another cab arrives. The driver frowns at the name I give him.

"*Babrru?* Why?"

We strike off past the rusting soccer stadium, past the university, through Parliament Square, with its creaky monoliths of the Communist era and piles of cobblestones and rubble. Was that the wiring for the street lights hanging from tree boughs? Women in high heels and tight skirts walk briskly in the road, avoiding dogs and rubbish and puddles and Mercedeses. We pass the Parliament building, pass Soviet-style apartment blocks now painted in pastels. Then things deteriorate. We leave the main road, and now there are great piles of rubble interspersed between shops. Children play beside a hill of rubbish in a schoolyard. A goat picks at something in the weedy verge of the road. Asphalt gives way to dirt, now thick with pedestrians, dogs, carts, scooters. No pastel is on the glowering gray walls here. Sometimes there are no walls at all. Then we reach the bridge.

It is narrow, and in spots the cement has crumbled to rebar. A ravine falls away beneath it, and the ravine is coated as far as one can see with garbage. Acres of garbage spread—hills of it—for miles. The garbage is along the banks and in the stream, which runs the color of a pale cement. The vista is of a vast, filthy shantytown clinging to the shoulders of garbage.

"Babrru," says the cabbie. He turns and repeats the word. *I told you.*

For a while we cannot find the refugee center. This is not the sort of place where there are street addresses. The cabbie asks passersby, and they shrug or point in the direction opposite to the last point. We find it in an hour or so: a small sign in English, hung outside a walled compound with barred windows and barbed wire running along the roof. "United Nations Refugee Center," it says.

A little window in the metal gate slides open. Questions are put in English and, when that fails, halting Italian. The responses are curt and in Albanian.

"What's he saying?"

"He say, 'go away,'" the cabbie explains.

But I have clients—five Uighur men, just arrived from Guantánamo! It doesn't matter. Could I visit them just for a minute? I couldn't. Could he confirm they were there, they were safe? Go away. Could I send in a note? No. The little window in the gate slams shut. The cabbie shrugs.

Babrru—told you.

But I have a fallback strategy, the electronic kindness of a stranger received just hours before I left the United States. "Try Eri," her e-mail said. "He knows everyone."

Erion Veliaj runs Mjaft! (Enough!), a sort of Albanian Moveon.org. He is tall, handsome as a film star, quick witted, insistently generous, charismatic, energetic, a polyglot. He is in a hurry; one almost believes his impatience can seize the country by the ears and drag it from its chaos of rubble into the future. His organization rallies Albanian youth through the Internet and is forcing a draught of public service on the old guard of Albanian politicians. Mjaft's website is hit by many Albanians. A lot of them vote.

Eri answers half a dozen text messages while listening to my story.

"You need a meeting with Olldashi," he says.

Olldashi is the interior minister of Albania. Eri is twenty-six.

"Sure. Him and George Bush, too."

"I can't help with Bush."

"How do I get a meeting with the interior minister of Albania?"

"No worries." It is Eri's favorite phrase. He punches a number into the phone and starts speaking in Albanian. In a few minutes he rings off.

"All set," he says. "He'll meet you."

"That was . . . ?"

"Of course."

"Eri, thanks, that's tremendous. But I have only a couple of days. Do you think maybe tomorrow, we could . . ."

"He'll meet you *now.*"

"Now? Where is he going to meet me at nine o'clock on a Sunday night?"

"At his office. Let's go. After coffee."

On the way to the Interior Ministry, Eri drives the wrong way down a one-way street. Two cops pull Eri over. Then they recognize him, exchange pleasantries, shake his hand, and wish him a good evening, smiling broadly. As we pull away, he nods at me.

"No worries."

We are in a set from a James Bond picture: the one where M's Soviet counterpart has his Louis XIV desk beneath a slowly turning ceiling fan: pillars, latticed windows, a minister with an inscrutable half smile, cigarette smoke wreathing to the ceiling. Outside, men in blue uniforms (Are they police? Soldiers? Is there a difference?) tote automatic weapons. It is the first of several meetings with Albanian ministers that span the next twelve hours. The result is that by early afternoon on Monday we are back in Babrru. The gate opens, and the head of the refugee center is there to welcome the attorney for the five former Guantánamo prisoners who on Friday sought political asylum in the Republic of Albania and also to explain to him the rather delicate matter that seems to have arisen with the Chinese ambassador, which is why it would be prudent to avoid publicity.

I barely hear all of this, looking for the guys. The last time I had seen Adel and Abu Bakker, they were wearing white GTMO pajamas, in isolation cells, and Adel was saying to me, "This last year has been the worst. It is over a year since they told us we were innocent, but we have had to stay here anyway."

Adel has bright brown eyes, a ready smile, a handsome Caucasian face, a calm endurance. He is thoughtful, his demeanor gentle and soft-spoken. His friend Abu Bakker is more compact, his features more Asiatic and his manner sometimes intense. He speaks earnestly about what Communist oppression has meant to his people and is quick to recite the mass sentencings in the square, the fire-hosing of peaceful demonstrators, the jailing of poets, the torture of his own father. (Two weeks later a journalist asked him if he was angry with United States. "I would say the better word is disappointed," he said. "In Turkestan, we had always admired America before.")

Now Adel and Abu Bakker and their three buddies Ahmet, Akhdar, and Ayub come out of their small flat across the courtyard, smiling broadly. No more pajamas! They wear new blue jeans, rolled up about six inches, and new sneakers. They are living behind barbed wire in a compound in the middle of a slum, in one of the poorest countries in Europe, a country where not a single human being speaks their language. They are far from their home and friends in China, with little hope of again embracing their wives or seeing more of their children than photographs. It seems that their odyssey has only begun.

But they are out of Guantánamo at last. And those smiles! Across the courtyard they shout the Uighur greeting: "*Yahshimusiz!*"

"Albania! *Al-hem dilillah!*"

What happens *after* Guantánamo? The "detention facility" (the government prefers "detention" to "imprisonment" because it sounds less permanent) is years past any feeble intelligence value that, for appearances' sake, we'd all better pretend it once had. One can almost sense the nervous question being asked by the Bush administration. A few cases have been resolved the way Adel's and Abu Bakker's have: days before a court date, the prisoner is spirited away. Rather than let a court hear an actual case, the government hustles the prisoner out of the jurisdiction.

Unwinding Guantánamo is a problem. After the most penetrating voice in the world has for years branded them as terrorists, who wants the prisoners? We don't want them. The United States' quiet blandishments to our allies (whoever they still may be) that *they* should want them ("It turns out these fellows are not so harmful after all! Trust us!") are greeted with a diplomatic half smile. So nobody wants them.

By Monday afternoon, things have become tense. The Chinese are demanding that the five "terrorists" be extradited to China. (In China, *terrorism* is a one-size-fits-all word. Writing poems is "spiritual terrorism," for example). The Albanians issue vague statements. They will consider the asylum applications, and the Chinese charges, in due course, and in accordance with law, and so on. Behind the scenes, the U.S. embassy is administering heavy doses of restorative. Journalists are clambering onto the roof of the U.N. center, trying to get photographs.

But I am determined that the men should walk in the open air. I ask the center director to drive us back to town. The embassy is particularly concerned that the U.S. lawyer not return to advise the Court that the men are just in a new prison, and so this request, to the great consternation of the director, is granted. The van bursts like a thoroughbred from the center's gates and leads the local press on a merry chase to town, shaking them briefly and reaching a restaurant near a park, while the Uighurs simply look alarmed, staring out the windows at the rubble careening by. For the first time in five years they sit down in a restaurant, but no one is hungry. We walk in the park. Surely freedom will feel good. But the Uighurs by this point are terrified that they might be snatched by Chinese agents. The park is full of trash. A little gypsy boy of about six tugs on their sleeves, asking for money. When we return, there is a report that an Albanian MP had sided with the Chinese. "This will all blow over," says one of the Albanian officials. Eri seems to agree. "No worries," he said. "Give it time."

Maybe. Or maybe not. Who can say what will happen in Albania? Now it is an American client, whose participation as one of the "coalition of the willing" in Iraq secures desperately needed foreign aid. But not so long ago it was a Chinese client. And it remains the case that there is no one in the country who can even translate the asylum applications into Uighur.

What happens after Guantánamo? For the United States, it is a matter of staying the course. The government will delay by writing briefs and taking appeals. It will avoid a trifling number of actual hearings by sending a trifling number of prisoners to client states such as Albania.

For the Uighurs, no one knows what lies after Guantánamo. Adel finally spoke by telephone to his wife and to his small son. After four years in Guantánamo, that blessing was indescribable. The practical reality is harder. They are ten thousand miles away. In Albania he has no language, no job, no friend.

The notion that resettlement in Albania made any practical sense was as absurd to the Albanians as it was to anyone following the case. The United States has a Uighur expatriate population (Uighurs have often received political asylum and are a favorite of our State Department) in which resettlement would have worked. Albania doesn't. It was humiliating to the Albanians to see how easily their emerging nation could be exploited by the United States. The Albanian journalists quickly cut through all the legal and political chaff. To them, it was simply shameful.

Still, your country is like your family: you don't like to hear it criticized outside the home. Which is why, when the local press asked, "Why don't you Americans act honorably?" I so very much wanted to contradict them.

Anne Castle, Trip Mackintosh, and Scott Barker: Stateless

Without any warning at all and after our client had spent more than four years at Guantánamo, we received a phone call from DOJ lawyers on the Friday before Thanksgiving in 2006. We were told that our client, Dr. Muhammed, had been released from GTMO and was en route to Tirana, Albania, where he was to be offered asylum, even though he had previously informed the authorities that he did not want to be sent there. We later learned that the first attempt to transfer Dr. Muhammed to Albania was aborted when a scheduled airborne refueling failed. Apparently, the U.S. government did not want to risk the political ramifications of landing somewhere to refuel. We also later learned that Dr. Muhammed made the eighteen-hour flight shackled to the floor of the plane.

We quickly determined that someone from our team needed to travel to Albania as soon as arrangements could be made to assist Dr. Muhammed in dealing with the United Nations and the Albanian government. Scott Barker left Denver on Tuesday, November 21, and arrived late on November 22. Scott was there through Saturday, November 25. The entire city, even the central plazas, looked tired, with visible Muslim and Christian influences.

Dr. Muhammed was confined to the United Nations Refugee Center in the Babrru district, a half-hour cab ride from the city center. He was told that he could not leave the center until he had officially applied for asylum. Babrru is a slum, and the Refugee Center is minimally basic. It consists of a central cracking concrete courtyard about half the size of a football field, surrounded on all four sides by fifty-year-old one-story barrack-type buildings. Dr. Muhammed's room was about twenty feet by ten feet, with no central heating, although he did have a space heater that functioned on and off. The room was furnished with a single bed, a small table, and two chairs. He shared a bathroom with the person across the hall. Meals were cafeteria style in a small dining room in the compound.

Scott met with Dr. Muhammed on the morning of November 23 (Thanksgiving Day) at the Refugee Center. Dr. Muhammed speaks Arabic, French, and decent English, which he claimed to have learned at GTMO. He had been given a cell phone and had spoken with his family in Algeria already. Dr. Muhammed is a man who has learned to live in peace with his surroundings. He greeted Scott warmly and was all smiles. Dr. Muhammed was, however, deeply troubled by his predicament. He said that he had told the GTMO guards who put him on the plane and the Albanian border police that he did not want to go to Albania and did not want asylum in the country. He had no family or contacts in Albania, did not speak the language, and knew it would be nearly impossible to find housing or a job there. He expressed a continuing desire to get to France or an Arab country, but not Algeria, where he feared persecution. He had not lived in Algeria since 1989 and was granted refugee status in Pakistan after he left Algeria. Scott told him that his task was to meet with the Albanian government and with U.N. representatives to assess the situation. However, Scott warned him that he probably had no choice but to seek asylum in Albania and then try to go somewhere else.

For the next day and a half, Scott trundled around Tirana. Scott met with Drita Avdyli, the Albania minister for refugees; Mohammed Hossein Kheradmand, the director of the United Nations High Commission for Refugees (UNHCR); and Veronique Brumeaux, first consul at the French embassy. The net result of these meetings was that Dr. Muhammed's only choice was to seek asylum in Albania and then mount an effort to get to France or some other country. Dr. Muhammed's "release" from GTMO left him, in effect, a stateless person. Without a connection to some country, no other nation would deal with him in any fashion. Despite his U.N. refugee status, the UNHCR would not intervene on his behalf because it had concluded that Albania was a "safe environment" for refugees.

Scott returned to see Dr. Muhammed on Friday, November 24, and delivered the news that his options were reduced to one: ask for asylum in Albania. He agreed, and we so informed Ali Rasha, the Albanian who was the director of the Refugee Center. An Arabic translator was rounded up, and Dr. Muhammed signed the papers that day in my presence.

Dr. Muhammed remains in Albania, still separated from his family. Despite his medical training, he still has no job, because there is no employment in Tirana for those who cannot speak the language, which Dr. Muhammed is studying daily. We have located a new French lawyer, and efforts continue to get Dr. Muhammed and his family reunited in France.

Kent Spriggs: The Conundrum of Latter-Day Afghan Repatriates

The route to repatriation and release is all politics. Guantánamo Bay habeas lawyers have learned that prisoners are rarely transferred out by court order. The pattern of the DOD transfers has been largely undecipherable to those seeking to decode who gets repatriated and who doesn't. Counsel for the Yemenis, the largest national contingent at Guantánamo, visited the home country and met with politicians, families, and the press hoping to move politics in the right direction. They discussed their findings with other habeas lawyers. As a result, a plan to replicate the same kind of strategy for the Afghans, the second-largest national contingent, was developed. Of the counsel for Afghans who were invited, a delegation of eleven members was formed. Our departure date was set for early December 2007.

We were counseled on whom to meet. We were mindful that those Afghan prisoners repatriated from Guantánamo after April 2007 had not been freed but were detained at the Afghan National Detention Facility (ANDF), built with U.S. dollars and standing on the grounds of the most infamous prison in Afghanistan, Pul-e-Charkhi. We urged repatriation of all Afghans still at GTMO, as well as a speedy process for those repatriated to Afghanistan and incarcerated at the ANDF.

In Afghanistan, we had an important dinner engagement at the Intercontinental Hotel. Members of parliament, Professor Gulrahman Qazi, president of the Lawyers Union of Afghanistan, and a very interesting mix of others who work on human rights issues attended. Qazi spoke of the importance of exchanges between countries and the development of long-lasting friendships.

We also met with numerous government officials, including First Vice President Massoud, the younger brother of Ahmad Shah Massoud, the famous "Lion of Panjshir," who is considered the greatest national hero of the past generation and a brilliant and relentless mujahedeen leader against the Soviets and the Taliban. We met with Second Vice President Kahlili, who was slow to disclose his point of view. What is striking is that most of the government officials with whom we met have strongly held points of view on the repatriation of Afghan prisoners from Guantánamo and the treatment of those detained at the ANDF. They can be loosely characterized as hawks and doves.

Human rights is a passion for Najibullah Mojadidi, special adviser to the president and a member of his Security Council. Mojadidi said he had "converted" 5,000 Taliban to the new government. He also said that he had secured the release of 600 persons from the U.S. detention centers at Bagram and GTMO. The more we talked about the evils of GTMO and the importance of a speedy process for those at the ANDF, the more engaged and excited he became. At one point he turned to the president of the bar, Qazi, and said that "President Karzai needs to hear what they are saying." Others, such as First Deputy Minister of Defence A. Yusuf Nuristani, were visibly angry that repatriates were being detained at the ANDF. He stated that there was no reason to hold them and that doing so put the Karzai government "in conflict with [its] own people." The Ministry of Defense was in charge of the custody of prisoners at the ANDF, but Nuristani was clearly not pleased that his ministry was the jailer. The president of the parliament was also strongly supportive of our message.

We also met with Deputy Minister of Justice for Legal Affairs Mohammad Qasim Hashimzai, an attorney who is fluent in English. Early in his discourse, he talked about the prisoners being "captured on the battlefield," adding that they are "serious criminals." He talked about those released as having returned to the battlefield and about the fact that others are a "potential threat." This characterization of the detainees is a red flag, signaling his point of view about the repatriation of those still at Guantánamo and a speedy process for those at the ANDF. He said that when Afghans are repatriated from GTMO, the government is faced with blackmail, strongly implying that he would prefer to leave Afghan detainees in Cuba. He has little faith in the ability of the legal system to separate out the enemies of the government from those who are not.

A lawsuit filed in federal court in Washington, D.C., *Razatullah v. Gates*, challenged the legality and detention of two persons at Bagram, the U.S.-run prison in Afghanistan. When Razatullah was transferred to the ANDF during the litigation, the DOD suggested the case was moot because the petitioner, Razatullah, was now under the sole custody and control of the Islamic Republic of Afghanistan. Hence, the government argued, there was no basis for a U.S. court to assert jurisdiction. However, Ahadullah Azimai, a human rights lawyer for the International Legal Foundation, tried unsuccessfully to see Razatullah and concluded that some detainees at the ANDF were being treated differently and in violation of the Afghan constitution because of "the involvement of the American military."

We entered a noncontact (glass barrier) visiting room but were led through that room into a smaller room. There were our clients and Afghan guards. My client Omar seemed shocked to see me nine time zones away from GTMO but was also gratified. While at GTMO, he had expressed an interest in adding English to his existing repertoire of four languages. I had been prohibited from bringing him books at GTMO for that purpose. This time I was allowed to bring him a book to learn English through pictures and a Holy Quran with the English text next to the Arabic.

The visit was all too brief. The men talked about their frustration at still being incarcerated after liberation from GTMO. One said that the ANDF was "just like" GTMO: all the hands-on guarding was by U.S. personnel, something we had never heard about. As the interviews progressed, the Afghan guards listened very intently and seemed very sympathetic to the plight of the detainees. One guard produced an official-looking paper that purported to be his permission for release. I promised to contact our clients' Afghan counsel.

Commenting on the trials of some former Guantánamo prisoners in Afghanistan, a human rights worker observed that the prosecution seemed to be working from a U.S. script. In that sense, these prisoners still remained at GTMO.

Sahr MuhammedAlly: Speaking through Holes in Glass

One of the memorable moments in my conversations with Afghan family members was when they described their first meeting with their brother or cousin five or six years after his detention by the Americans. In 2007, family members heard through the media and habeas counsel that their relative had been transferred to Block D in Pul-e-Charkhi, Afghanistan. Family members were jubilant because their relative had been returned to Afghanistan, but they were confused as to why he had not returned home and instead remained imprisoned with the possibility of prosecution by the Afghan government. Nevertheless, this was an opportunity for family members to make live contact with their relative for the first time after a long separation.

Mohammed Qasim's brother Jameel described seeing his brother for the first time in six years:

> Two weeks after he was brought to Block D I saw him. . . . The room was divided by a glass panel. It had small holes. I shook hands with my brother with two fingers through the holes. When I entered the room and saw him, it was unbelievable. It was sad to see my brother. He was limping. He had chains on his ankles. He is younger than me but looked older. I could not believe it was him.

Abdullah Wazir's brother Zahir Shah recalled the emotional reunion with his brother: "We spoke through the holes in the glass. I put two fingers through the hole. I was crying. He was crying."

Ghulam Rohani's brother Hayatullah described his brother, who he had not seen for six years: "My brother looked thinner than when he was captured. I was happy to see him. We both cried. I saw a chain attached to my brother's feet. We could not talk much. It was for only fifteen minutes. But I touched him through the biggest hole in the glass wall. With two fingers we shook hands."

Abdul Wahid, whose brother Izatullah Nusrat had been in Guantánamo since 2003, described meeting his brother in Pul-e-Charkhi: "When I saw my brother I found him weaker—mentally and physically. I could see the signs of his being imprisoned for a long time. He was happy to see me. I spoke to him through the small holes in the glass but could not hear him well."

The family members of Guantánamo detainees have tried to show their relative's innocence by obtaining letters from village and tribal elders, as well as from members of their local government. They sent these letters to habeas counsel in the United States to be submitted to U.S. authorities. These letters were also relied on by the Afghan National Commission for Peace and Reconciliation to negotiate with coalition forces to procure the release of detainees in Afghanistan.

One of the family members, who did not wish to be identified, described his efforts to release his brother:

My brother is not Taliban or al Qaeda. Imprisoning an innocent person for six years is persecution. No one cares about them. When I talk about my brother, everyone says, "sorry." I have struggled so much. I have gone to the National Security Council, the Peace and Reconciliation Committee. They say, "yes, it's sad," but no one can help us. I have all the guarantee letters signed by district governor and the elders, and I took them to the Reconciliation Committee. They say they don't have the power to release him. Even [Hamid] Karzai has no power.

The past seven years have been marked by uncertainty and the pain of not knowing when families will be reunited. The stories of the families I interviewed give only a small glimpse into the lives of the families who are left to struggle, cope, and hope. The suffering of the families demonstrates the reach of the devastation caused by U.S. policies in Guantánamo and beyond. Guantánamo and Bagram are not only legal black holes but, for those affected, an emotional abyss.

Happy Endings?

Approximately 500 people have been released from Guantánamo since the first prisoners were brought there in January 2002. Yet, even for those returned home, the effects of years of unlawful detention remain. Reunions with families are simultaneously joyous and heart-wrenching, as loved ones are left to grapple with the long years of absence and separation. Prisoners also must continually struggle to overcome the physical and psychological impact of years of mistreatment and unjust incarceration. The issues surrounding the release of detainees highlights Guantánamo's long-lasting human effects.

Allison M. Lefrak: You're Going Home

On a day off before the client meetings, Doug and I sat in the lounge area of the Combined Bachelors' Quarters conferring with one of our interpreters. The phone rang at the front desk. "Mr. Douglas Spaulding?" Doug looked up from his notes. "Yes?" The man behind the desk said, "The phone is for you." We exchanged confused expressions—who could be calling? How did the caller know we'd be there in the lounge? "This is Doug Spaulding." "Yes, we have a meeting scheduled with ISN No. 516 tomorrow." "Yes, we will be on the next ferry to the other side." "Okay, thank you." He hung up the phone. Doug's expression was one of shock. "Ghanim is going to be released." I was stunned. Was it possible? Like kids trying to guess what presents would be under the Christmas tree, we had often discussed which of our clients was likely to be the first to go home. We agreed that surely it would be Ghanim since he was the only one who was a citizen of a country (Saudi Arabia) that appeared interested in getting its countrymen out of Guantánamo. Given the lack of progress in the legal cases we had filed on our clients' behalf, we began to realize that diplomatic pressure was truly their best hope for release. Still, we were completely caught off guard and elated by the news. The fact that we happened to be in Guantánamo and would be able to share the news with Ghanim in person served as the icing on the cake. We hurried back to our rooms to get ready as we mentally prepared to deliver the best possible news imaginable to our client.

Within an hour, we were on the ferry to the other side of the island. We had exactly one hour to talk with Ghanim, who did not yet know that he was going to be released. In addition to being able to give Ghanim the news of his release in person, we could discuss with him his rights with regard to the thirty-day-notice order. Had we been in the United States, we would not have been able to share the news with Ghanim. When a detainee is released, if such an order has been entered in his case, the government must give thirty days' notice of the release, in order to allow attorneys to object if the detainee is being sent to a country where he is likely to be tortured or persecuted. In Ghanim's case, the government was releasing him to his home country of Saudi Arabia. It was likely that Ghanim would choose to waive the thirty-day-notice provision in the hope that he would be sent home sooner. We needed to explain this to him and have him sign a waiver if that is what he decided to do. Although Ghanim's English is good, we knew that he would prefer to have something of this nature told to him in his native language. Mahmoud, our translator, was translating for another team of attorneys, and there were no other Arabic translators available that day. When our military escort picked us up at the ferry, we explained the situation to him. The escort told us that he could put in a request for a military translator. We worried that Ghanim would not want to use someone who had possibly been involved in his interrogations, but we thought it best to offer him the option. We were able to send word into Mahmoud that Ghanim was going to be released and that we would be given one hour to meet with him. Mahmoud immediately understood the situation and offered to translate for us for ten or fifteen minutes so we could cover the thirty-day-notice issue in Ghanim's native language. If Ghanim was not comfortable using the military translator for the remainder of the meeting, we would communicate with him in English.

We anxiously watched the guards search our belongings as we waited to meet with Ghanim. Unlike previous meetings, we brought very little with us. Doug held a copy of the thirty-day-notice order. I had a notepad, but I doubted I would be taking notes in this meeting. We were finally brought in to meet Ghanim. He rose and smiled—always happy to see us it seemed. Doug and Ghanim shook hands and embraced. Ghanim smiled and nodded at me, and I did the same. He asked, "Where is my friend Mahmoud?" We told him that Mahmoud was meeting with another detainee today but that he would come in for a few minutes later in the meeting. Doug explained that we could use one of the military interpreters if Ghanim wanted. Ghanim asked which interpreter it was. We did not know his name, so we asked the escort to bring him in. Ghanim clearly recognized him. He greeted the interpreter in a friendly manner; they exchanged a few words in Arabic, and the interpreter left. Ghanim told us that he did not want to use this man as an interpreter for our meeting. We did not ask questions. We would continue the meeting in English.

We sat down, and Doug finally was able to deliver the news. He said slowly, "Ghanim, you are going to be released. You are going home to Saudi Arabia."

Ghanim put his face in his hands. He quickly removed them and revealed a stunned smile. "You are serious?"

"Yes, you are going home," Doug said, bubbling over with happiness as he said these words to his client—a man he had met only four times but for whom he had clearly developed a deep fondness.

I felt tears forming in my eyes as I watched Doug and Ghanim embrace again. Ghanim turned to me, and I smiled through the tears, "Congratulations!"

We were eager to tell Ghanim the story of how we received word that he was going to be released, but Mahmoud then entered the room. He could tell that we had just given Ghanim the news. The two men embraced, and Mahmoud told Ghanim that he was so happy for him. Mahmoud explained that he must get back to his meeting with another detainee, so we quickly discussed the thirty-day-notice order with Ghanim. He agreed that we should waive notice. We told him that we had no idea when he would be sent home, but we got the clear impression that it would be within the week. This was later confirmed when we left the meeting and saw the Red Cross waiting to go in and conduct an exit interview of sorts with our client.

The rest of the hour was spent discussing what Ghanim would do when he got home. He was well informed about the Saudi repatriation program—the Saudi delegation had met with him the last time they visited Guantánamo. He was told that the Saudi government would help him find a wife, a job, and a home after he successfully completed the program. He was eager to get married and start a family.

Before we left, Ghanim presented us with four beautiful notes—there was one for Doug, Bernie, me, and another attorney who worked on his case. Each note was bordered with intricately drawn vines and flowers. In preparing the notes of gratitude, it seemed almost as if Ghanim knew that his release was imminent.

> Dear Allison,
>   I thank you for all that you have done for me. It is a big support to me in this ordeal. I will never forget it for the rest of my life. I hope you have a nice life full of success.
>
>   Sincerely,
>   Ghanim al-Harbi
>   Guantánamo 2007

Only a few days after our meeting with him, Ghanim al-Harbi returned home to Saudi Arabia.

After Ghanim was released, we refrained from contacting him because we heard rumors that the Saudi government told the former detainees to cut all ties with their American attorneys. But it eventually became apparent that other attorneys were speaking with their released Saudi clients. Six months after his release, we sent an e-mail to Ghanim's brother Mohammed to see if we could get any information about how Ghanim was doing now that he was free. Mohammed responded within days, and a telephone call was arranged. With Mahmoud's assistance, Doug and Ghanim spoke to each other. Ghanim is now married, and his life is returning to normal. He now has a mobile phone and an e-mail address, and we can contact him whenever we want. I immediately sent an e-mail to Ghanim telling him that I was so happy to hear that he is doing well. I attached a picture of my new son. To my delight, Ghanim responded within hours congratulating me on the birth of my son and attaching to his e-mail a picture of himself dressed in a long dark robe with his brother standing beside him—both men smiling and proud. He also attached pictures of the feast his mother prepared for the party she threw in his honor upon his return, and one showing five beaming relatives seated on a couch in a comfortable living room—attendees at the welcome-home party for Ghanim. He wished me and my husband and new baby "a happy and quiet life," and he signed off, "Faithful, Ghanim al-Harbi."

The intricately decorated note from Ghanim is now framed and hanging above my desk. After eight years of law practice, my work on this case is the work I am most proud of, and Ghanim's note of gratitude serves as a succinct inspiration to continue working for the release of our other two clients. Admittedly, it is not at all clear that anything we did directly resulted in Ghanim's release from Guantánamo. A more probable explanation is that the Saudis are gradually working to get their citizens returned home and that Ghanim's name was next on their list. Despite his ordeal, Ghanim truly believes that the United States will find its way back to justice and that the ideals we purport to hold dear will be restored. As I prepare for my next trip to Guantánamo to meet with our remaining two clients, I pray that Ghanim al-Harbi is right.

Joshua Colangelo-Bryan: Habeas on the Gate, Aftermath

In the final months of 2005, Jumah attempted to kill himself two more times. In March 2006, he made another attempt, slashing his leg and throat with a razor. At the time, the military was holding him in the "Mental Health Unit." There, the detainee in the cell to one side of Jumah was a Yemeni who believed he was Jesus Christ and ranted to that effect constantly. The detainee in the cell to the other side spent most of his time running around his cell naked. Jumah was kept in his cell for twenty-two to twenty-four hours a day.

I visited Jumah every few months, and we would sit together for seven hours, often not taking a single break. We always battled his despair. I offered Jumah every argument I could think of as to why he should stay alive, invoking God, family, philosophy, and anything else that came to mind. Always, I spoke to him about the efforts that we were making to pressure the government of Bahrain to bring him home through a diplomatic agreement; such agreements had brought several of our clients home already and were the only clear way out of Guantánamo. Sometimes my words seemed to sink in, and other times Jumah said politely that the reasons I offered for staying alive were simply not good enough.

In June 2007, I saw Jumah in Guantánamo. He said that his cell had started to feel like a hole in a mountain of ice and that he could not go on. Jumah was in obvious physical discomfort, and I stood up to get a better look at him. He had cut an inch-deep gash in his stomach in an attempt to reach a major artery. Knowing that Jumah was in desperate straits, I told him about a then-recent report from the Bahraini government that promised he would be home by Ramadan, which was to begin in September. I hoped the information would buy us a few months. It was all I had.

I woke up on July 16, 2007, to my cell phone and Blackberry buzzing. Jumah had just arrived in Saudi Arabia (where he also had citizenship), and his family was on its way to see him. He had been released through a diplomatic agreement of the sort that I had advocated for during the prior three years. He was home. I felt light-headed and wasn't able to stop grinning. I had worried about Jumah, literally, day and night for nearly three years, and now—without any forewarning—he was home.

Just over a week later, I had my first chance to call Jumah in Saudi Arabia. We spoke for over an hour. No guards watched us. Nobody wore shackles. After twelve visits at Guantánamo, it was astounding to talk under such circumstances. Jumah's voice was strong, and the truest aspects of his personality—warmth, a love of people, humor, and compassion—were clearer than I had ever heard them.

Jumah and I have stayed in regular touch, even adding e-mail to our repertoire. So far, we have not been able to see each other because I can't get a visa to Saudi Arabia, and Jumah is not yet allowed to travel to Bahrain, where I could meet him. Yet neither of us has any doubt that if we were able to get him out of Guantánamo, then we will be able to solve these bureaucratic puzzles and sit together in person as brothers and friends sometime soon.

Baher Azmy: Free at Last

Why did my client Murat Kurnaz spend an additional three years in Guantánamo, despite the recognition of U.S. and German officials of his innocence? First and foremost, the absence of law or legal remedy in Guantánamo permitted the U.S. government to avoid defending its actions before a judge or other neutral authority with power to hold it accountable. But, as my German co-counsel Bernhard Docke explains, the Germans are also culpable for Murat's extended suffering. They could have gotten him out. Instead, the German government repeatedly asserted in public that his well-being was beyond its jurisdiction, while in private it declined U.S. entreaties for his return to Germany. It is a shameful episode, one for which German officials may still yet be held accountable. More fundamentally, it highlights that Guantánamo is a geopolitical cancer; its deceit, secrecy, and brazen hypocrisy is malignant. It also distorts reality and corrupts institutions without regard for the punishment it inflicts on real human beings.

During my last visit with Murat in Guantánamo, when his release seemed inevitable, I warned him that Germans might be scared to see him emerge from Guantánamo with his enormous beard, looking like some kind of mullah. He first reaction was to explain, "I don't care. There are good and bad people everywhere. I do this for my religion. They will understand." Then, with a quick smile he asked, "If they are so afraid of men with beards, why don't they call Santa Claus a terrorist?"

German officials told Bernhard the date that Murat was likely to be released, which gave me enough time to fly to Germany for the occasion. On August 24, 2006, Bernhard and I met the whole Kurnaz family at a gas station outside Bremen for the six-hour drive south toward Ramstein Air Force Base, where we were told Murat would be arriving in the early evening. The day was full of intrigue: secret meetings with German officials to tell us the location of the meeting place for the Kurnaz family reunion; constant, intrusive calls from German and American reporters demanding confirmation of a spreading rumor of his release; and almost overwhelming anxiety. While we awaited his delivery in a Red Cross home for the elderly, through the window we saw a huge C-17 military plane descending from the sky. It was Murat.

From the window, Bernhard saw Murat enter the building along with the affable German Foreign Ministry officials who had earlier told us where the reunion drop-off would be. Murat's mother, Rabiye, his father, Ali, Bernhard, and I all assembled in the hallway on the fourth floor to greet Murat. Despite all my prior descriptions, Bernhard still seemed stunned by his quick glimpse of Murat's beard through the window. Rabiye stood in front of the creaky elevator doors; her anticipation built to an almost unbearable state as the elevator repeatedly started and stopped, huffed and creaked. Finally, when the doors opened, Rabiye latched onto her son as if he might be taken away from her again at any moment. With Murat in her arms, she wept helplessly for a long time.

In the incredible excitement of that very long day, which included a 3 a.m. rush into the Kurnaz home past a swarm of waiting journalists, I remember one thing more clearly than any other. In the many hours that Murat and I had spent together at Guantánamo, his ankle had always been chained to the floor. That day, for the first time, I saw Murat walk.

Christi Charpentier: Bittersweet

We received the following e-mail from the U.S. government about Feghoul, an Algerian:

> Through either the Administrative Review Board (ARB) process or the process DOD had in place prior to the ARBs, your client has been approved to leave Guantánamo, subject to the process for making appropriate diplomatic arrangements for his departure. Accordingly, my prior guidance regarding submission of materials for a 2007 ARB for your client is inapplicable to this detainee. He will not be receiving another ARB proceeding.
>
> As you know, such a decision does not equate to a determination that your client is not an enemy combatant, nor is it a determination that he does not pose a threat to the United States or its allies. I cannot provide you any information regarding when your client may be leaving Guantánamo as his departure is subject to ongoing discussions.

So, we said to ourselves, he can leave. What does that mean? Alas, there was no law to tell us anything about this. There were only questions. Who will make arrangements? How will they go about making them? When will they be made? Can Feghoul go back to Algeria? What's he facing in Algeria? Who do we speak with from Algeria? Can we just call up the embassy and ask for a meeting? Can we trust what we are told? Will he need a lawyer in Algeria?

We worked to answer all those questions. In the meantime, Feghoul withdrew. Isolation and silence worked their destruction. Fear of change, distrust of lawyers. Send me somewhere else, just set it up and let me live in Europe. So, more questions. Can we seek asylum for Feghoul in the United States? Can we seek protection in a third country while he is in custody at the base? What country? Can we just call up a nongovernmental organization and ask it to help us? Can we show up in a putative host country and request an audience with the right ministers? Do we need yet another lawyer? Again, there was no law to tell us anything about this.

We worked to get Feghoul a safe repatriation to Algeria. Then, without any prior notification, we received word that he was already home.

I wrote an e-mail to a translator who had worked with us regarding Feghoul.

Hey, yes, we are aware and have been aware of both some unsavory conduct at the time of transfer, and aware of the talk amongst part of the group. all has been aired. in general, in light of most recent developments, Feghoul's situation is one of the more stable legally. to state the obvious, he is no longer in Camp VI, and, he is home! with mother, eating couscous, probably depressed, as he has been during most of the past 20 years.

Christopher Chang: A Cook, Not a General

A few weeks after we finally got hold of Ahmed's file at the United Kingdom's Home Office, Immigration and Nationality Directorate, we received an e-mail from the U.S. Department of Justice informing us that Ahmed had been released and transferred to Moroccan authorities. I had two feelings: one, happiness that he had finally been given his long-overdue freedom, and two, anger that he had not been returned here to the United Kingdom. Another cause for anger was that, as usual, we had been kept completely in the dark and were told of Ahmed's transfer only after it had happened. We are in practice robbed of all opportunity, legally, politically, and in the media, to challenge any decision made. But there was little time to remain angry, because we had to figure out exactly where Ahmed was.

The U.S. State Department gave me no information. I had human rights organizations on the ground checking with their contacts in the prisons to see if anyone from Guantánamo had recently arrived—nothing! I was calling Morocco from a friend's home telephone at five in the morning to try and find out where Ahmed was. "Is he in prison? Is he in pretrial detention? Where is he being held?" But no one was talking. I had spoken to enough people and done enough research to know about the Moroccan authorities and what their secret police was capable of doing. Ahmed's family knew too, and they were right to be worried and fearful. For a week we had no information. We spent that week on the phone, sending faxes and e-mails. I set a deadline: if by the end of the week I had still heard nothing, either I or someone else from my organization, Reprieve, would travel to Morocco and raise some hell to try and find out where Ahmed was.

That very weekend, I received a call from Ahmed's brother Abdeljabbar. He said Ahmed had been released and was there with them. I couldn't believe it—my heart was racing, the hairs on the back of my neck were up; I was ecstatic. I could hear the sounds of Ahmed's family in the background. I could hear the happiness, the joy. Abdeljabbar thanked me profusely on behalf of the whole family before saying that Ahmed wanted to talk to me himself. Ahmed came to the phone. I was so relieved when he said he was okay, unhurt. He thanked me for all the work that we had done on his case. This was one of the most emotional phone calls I have ever had in my life. I told him how happy I was that he was home, safe, free. Ahmed also told me that he had bags full of letters that people had written to him. He was sorry he had not written back, but because he had spent most of his time under disciplinary sanctions in Guantánamo, he was not allowed to write letters.

So Ahmed is back home in Tangiers, Morocco, with his wife, kids, and other family. He is trying to get his life back after more than five years of unlawful incarceration, ill treatment, and abuse at the hands of the United States. Over five years of his life were stolen from him and from his family. He is a Moroccan, but Morocco is a place he doesn't know, millions of miles away from the world he knew in the United Kingdom, where he lived for eighteen years. The only thing that upsets me is that he wasn't returned there. London was the place he knew. He knew how things worked there, how to make a living. In Morocco he has to cope with learning how to live and learning how things work. I'll always feel ashamed at how my government left Ahmed to rot in Guantánamo. He was one of the longest serving prisoners in solitary confinement. Maybe complicity is a dirty word, but it's most definitely appropriate here. I'll probably never know for sure if the evidence we submitted to the U.S. government on Ahmed's behalf was the reason he was released. But sometimes I look at it like this: we carried out an unpaid investigation for the U.S. military, an investigation that proved that our client was just a cook and not a general. The United States never had any evidence against Ahmed. As our investigation showed, he was just another Pakistani lottery scratch card cashed in for a $5,000 bounty by the Pakistani military.

Paul M. Winke: A Day in Court

Shortly after the Supreme Court's *Boumediene* decision, affirming the Guantánamo detainees' constitutional right to habeas corpus, Judge Richard J. Leon, the federal district judge who had presided over our case since the fall of 2004, set an aggressive schedule: he intended to have all twenty-four open habeas cases on his docket decided by Christmas. As our case was the oldest of his Guantánamo cases by far, our clients were given the first hearing.

Our firm represents six men—Mustafa Ait Idir, Mohamed Nechla, Hadj Boudella, Lakhdar Boumediene, Saber Lahmar, and Belkacem Bensayah—who were arrested by federal police in Bosnia in October 2001 on suspicion of participating in a plot to bomb the U.S. embassy in Sarajevo. All six men were born in Algeria, but by 2001, each was living, working, and raising a family in Bosnia. Although the Bosnian authorities firmly cleared the six men of the unfounded charges against them following a three-month investigation (during which time they were detained in a Bosnian jail), they were effectively kidnapped by the U.S. government upon their release by Bosnian authorities in January 2002, and they were among the earliest arrivals at the U.S. detention center in Guantánamo Bay, Cuba. We filed petitions for habeas corpus for the six men in the summer of 2004, seeking what we finally got more than four long years later, in early November 2008—their day in court.

I traveled to Guantánamo on Election Day to keep our clients informed about their hearings back in Washington and to prepare some of them for possible testimony. During the client meetings the next day, I explained to the men how the habeas hearing would proceed in Washington: both we and the government would have the opportunity to make an opening statement that would be open to the public, but then the remainder of the hearing would be closed so that the judge could discuss the classified evidence that was put forward by the government to justify holding the men and our responses to it. The responses of the men varied: some believed that this would be the first chance to show the judge how flimsy the case against them was, while others believed that the judge had already written his opinion siding with the government, and it was sitting in his desk drawer, ready to be pulled out after he made a show of listening to our arguments.

Following the initial round of meetings with our clients, the next day was spent meeting with the three men who were most likely to testify: Mohamed, Hadj, and Mustafa. Before coming, I had prepared a set of questions for each man. There would be no surprises in any of the testimony—we had submitted multipage affidavits for all six men that recited the essential facts of their lives, from their time in Algeria to the various countries through which they traveled before ending up in Bosnia, and ending with categorical denials that any of them had any affiliation with, or even any sympathy for, al Qaeda or the Taliban. Strictly speaking, the testimony of the men was not necessary given that Judge Leon had ruled that hearsay may be permitted and that the government had no objection to the admission of their affidavits. We believed that it would be important, however, for one or more men to look the judge in the eye (via an unprecedented video linkage) and state that he did not do anything the government accused him of and that he condemned terrorism as an affront to Islam.

I was escorted to the first meeting in a location I had never been to previously. According to the men, it was a room where they met with their interrogators. Unlike any other room I had seen at Guantánamo, it was furnished with more than the bare necessities, even if those were fake plants, hideous paintings, and a threadbare couch. The room also contained a small television with a DVD player, perhaps as some kind of reward for cooperative detainees. (Of course, it was also equipped with video surveillance, cleverly hidden between the fake wood paneling on the walls.) Clearly, the military was treating the hearings differently from ordinary client visits.

Before I could begin to prepare the men, however, they had many questions, the first of which was, how soon will the newly elected Barack Obama close down Guantánamo? I could only repeat his campaign promise to shut down the prison. The next set of questions repeated a theme we had heard from the men for several years: is the hearing before Judge Leon a farce, or can we really expect justice to be done? And, as always, the answer was not completely satisfying: all the lawyers representing the men have faith in the American legal system, a faith that we do not expect our clients to share fully, but in particular cases each judge will feel a strong pull to err on the side of deferring to the Bush administration's view, lest that judge be responsible for letting a supposed terrorist go. Given how both we and our clients see the case, we did not believe that the right decision would be a difficult call, but Judge Leon would necessarily have to take into account the fact that the military has declared for years that all six men are simply too dangerous to release. In addition, and much to our dismay, the judge would also have to contend with a cache of evidence that had been provided only to the judge and not to us as counsel for the men. (The judge ultimately decided, in a special session involving only him and the government lawyers and excluding us, that he would not consider this evidence.)

All three men were able to put their skepticism aside and to work with me on answering the questions for their testimony precisely and clearly. I was impressed with each man's care for detail, even for dates and locations that had nothing to do with the government's case against them. Each one understood his duty to tell the truth and patiently worked with me to present truthful answers in the most direct and persuasive way possible.

The next day was a disaster, but it was not until the end of the day that we realized as much. Opening arguments were scheduled in Washington, D.C., and Judge Leon ordered the government to make it possible for all six men to listen to the proceedings as they were happening. (As they were not testifying that day, the connection would only allow the men to listen and not to speak.) The interpreter and I arrived more than two hours before proceedings were to begin in Washington and also before any of the men had arrived. This was also a first: I had never seen the men brought in while shackled. Every prior client visit started with the lawyers being brought into a room where a single prisoner sat behind a table, having already had his handcuffs and foot shackles removed, save for a single "soft shackle" connecting one ankle to a ring bolt in the floor by a chain about one foot long.

The opening of the hearing marked the first time that five of our clients had been in the same room together since they arrived in Guantánamo in January 2002. For those five, the mere fact of reunion was a happy occasion. (The sixth, Saber Lahmar, had been isolated from the others for years for reasons that were never adequately explained to us.) The room was filled with energetic conversation in Arabic, and I asked the interpreter to fill me on the general gist of the conversation but otherwise not to interrupt the lively discussion. In the meantime, soldiers set up a telephone on a coffee table in the middle of the room. We were told that the opening statements would be heard through this telephone but that we would not be heard in the courtroom, per the judge's request.

As the afternoon wore on, even as the five men were still glad to be sitting in comfortable chairs and conversing with one another, there was no indication that the proceedings were about to begin. I asked the soldier who was patiently waiting with the receiver to his ear what was happening, and he told he me that there must be something going on in court that the men were not supposed to hear. He also told me that someone at the court asked him periodically if he was still on the line, and he told them that he was. It was only in the late afternoon, when someone at the court informed the soldier that the day's court session was at an end and thanked him for his patience, that we realized that we had somehow missed the entire session. When I explained this to the five men, their first thought was that their inability to hear was a deliberate ploy on the part of the military. I promised the men that I would look into what happened.

I was unable to get any information from the soldiers before being driven to the ferry that returned me to the sleeping quarters for habeas counsel. While waiting for the ferry, however, my habeas escort told me that she had been ordered by Commander Martin, the head of the Staff Judge Advocate's office, to bring me to his office. There I found out not only that several hours of opening statements were taking place while the telephone line to the court was apparently open but that we heard none of it—and Judge Leon was very unhappy with what had transpired and wanted a full accounting in the morning. Each of the soldiers on the telephone line was required to submit an affidavit explaining what had happened. We then learned that an audio recording of the entire proceeding had been made and that the Department of Justice was making plans to fly the recordings down to Guantánamo the next day, by Federal Express.

When the recordings arrived in the early afternoon the next day, the five men were again assembled in the same interrogation room. (Because there was only one tape, Saber heard the tapes in the evening.) In the room with us was a lawyer from the other side, an assistant U.S. attorney from northern Florida who was detailed to Washington to assist with the backlog of habeas cases following the *Boumediene* decision and who personally flew the tapes down to Guantánamo to play them for the men. Given that it was his task to advocate that all six men still remain imprisoned as enemy combatants, I was surprised at how gracious the five men were toward him, offering him both chocolate and one of the pillows from their couch for him to use on his metal folding chair.

The tape began with prefatory comments from Judge Leon. An Arab translator in the courtroom was heard on the tape, but he had trouble keeping up with the judge. Following the judge was Nicholas Oldham, the DOJ attorney who was lead counsel for the government on the case. Oldham began with an extended riff on September 11, an event unconnected to the allegations against any of the men. He said nothing specific about the men but stated, "What matters is that the United States had reliable information, credible intelligence that these Petitioners planned to travel to the field of battle." When these remarks were translated, one of the five voiced his disapproval, and another stood and asked the guards to take him out, saying he had heard enough. After some cajoling from the other men, he was persuaded to stay, especially as they had yet to hear from Steve Oleskey, the lawyer from our firm who had met with the men over a dozen times in the past four years. Steve's opening statement was more specific and included a thumbnail biography of each man, in addition to cataloging the absence of credible evidence against any of them. His opening was well received by the men. After the tape was finished, several of the men made a point of thanking the DOJ lawyer who brought the tapes for his efforts. Listening to the tapes in the evening, Saber was similarly appreciative.

Subsequent meetings were devoted to refining the direct examination questions for the men most likely to testify and to ensuring that testimony was both truthful and helpful. But in the background, the question for which the men wanted an answer was, how long will President-elect Obama take to close Guantánamo? The topic was clearly the buzz in all the camps. At night, back in my room, I searched the Internet for any official pronouncements, all of which were circumspect and would provide no great comfort to the men.

The next day, my colleague Doug Curtis and I met with Hadj, Mustafa, and Mohamed, our three likely witnesses. In anticipation of the possibility that any of them might testify, I brought down shirts and ties for the men to wear while on camera before the judge. We spent part of our prep time trying on the shirts and ties. Doug reported on that day in an e-mail to our team:

> As part of the preparation for our clients' possible testimony, [two other attorneys on our team] took responsibility for buying some dress shirts and ties, based on guessed sizes, so our guys wouldn't have to appear before the judge in GTMO prison garb. The good news is that the sizing turned out to be right, and they looked great. The even better news was that the simple act of trying on these shirts in preparation for their testimony was itself a strangely moving and uplifting experience. As the men took the new shirts from us and fumbled to unbutton them so they could try them on, they commented awkwardly—and self-consciously, and jokingly—that it had been seven years since they had used buttons, and they were a bit rusty. And then as they put the shirts on, they suddenly transformed from prisoners at Guantánamo to the men we saw in pictures before they were arrested. It was a brief but striking transformation—and it struck us all that we were looking at their future selves, outside GTMO.

Our team subsequently decided that we would put on only two witnesses, Hadj and Mustafa. Mustafa had the distinct advantage of being able to testify in English, which allowed a directness not possible with translated testimony, and Hadj was the last of the six men arrested, and his decision to travel to the Sarajevo police station voluntarily with the knowledge that his three friends (Lakhdar, Mohamed, and Mustafa) had been brought in for questioning was powerful evidence of his innocence.

After some technical difficulties, Mustafa's testimony finally began. We could see the courtroom through a small monitor, no more than twelve inches diagonally. During Mustafa's direct examination—with Doug asking Mustafa questions while sitting beside him—we could see Judge Leon. Later, when Mustafa was cross-examined by the DOJ lawyer, that lawyer and his podium were visible. In addition, Rob Kirsch—another lawyer from our team who had been part of every visit to the six men since our representation began—was visible in the lower right of the screen. His presence on-screen was, I presumed, a deliberate strategy to show a friendly face even as Mustafa faced hostile questioning. Mustafa's testimony, which was considered classified by default but has since been deemed unclassified, was a straightforward recounting of the facts of his life: growing up in Algeria, working for various charities in Croatia and Bosnia in the 1990s, marrying and having children, and coaching karate. He also made sure to emphasize that he had no part in any terrorist activities and that he condemned the terrorist activities of al Qaeda as opposed to the peaceful teachings of Islam. Mustafa also vouched for his three friends and testified that he had no contact with the other two Bosnian-Algerians, Belkacem and Saber, until they were all brought to Guantánamo together. The cross-examination by the DOJ lawyer was brief and consisted largely in attempting to find inconsistencies in the written declaration that Mustafa had submitted earlier. Because that lawyer did not even attempt to contest Mustafa's lack of involvement in terrorist activities, the cross-examination was, in my view, ineffective.

Hadj's testimony was necessarily halting, as both question and answer needed to be translated. Despite Hadj's low-key demeanor, he was still a highly effective witness. In addition to reciting the mundane facts of his life as an employee at a charity, Hadj told of his daughter who died in 2006 of a heart condition and whom he had not seen since October 2001. His testimony ended, as we had planned, with his account of receiving a telephone call from the Bosnian police on a Sunday morning asking him to come in for questioning and his taking a taxi to that police station, even though he would have had ample opportunity to flee the country once he learned that his friends had been arrested. When Hadj went to the police, he testified, "I thought it was just an ordinary thing that was happening, that [we] were just going to be questioned and then released." Instead, as

Hadj concluded his testimony, October 21, 2001, was "the day I headed to the police station and never returned home." That impromptu response— not part of any prepared exchange—was so simple and so haunting that we closed our questioning there. Our clients had been able to look Judge Leon in the eye and to tell their stories openly and honestly.

After our final meeting with the men, the next day, Doug Curtis again captured the day perfectly in an e-mail to the team:

> In my experience, whenever we meet with all of our clients, one or an-
> other of them is inevitably having a down day or an off day—but that was
> not the case today. Each of them seemed to be buoyed by the fact that
> their cases were progressing, and their testimony had been presented.
> Each of them (yes, literally each one of them) asked us to pass along
> some of the most heart-warming (and heart-wrenching) thanks and ap-
> preciation to each and every member of the team who has been working
> so hard on their behalf. Even more important, each of them seemed to
> harbor some hope that things really might be moving in the right direc-
> tion. We tried not to create false hopes, and we dispensed a healthy dose
> of skepticism about Judge Leon—but even on that score, the folks who
> got to see Judge Leon (by video) were surprised by how fair he seemed
> to be, and how hard he was willing to be on the government.

When Doug and I returned to the United States and heard reports on the closing arguments, we were encouraged by our colleagues' sense that our firm team really had made inroads in convincing Judge Leon that there was no reliable evidence against at least some of our men. That sense turned out to be correct: less than a week later, Judge Leon announced his decision (in a packed ceremonial courtroom) that five of our six clients were not enemy combatants, and he ordered the government "to take all necessary and appropriate diplomatic steps to facilitate the release" of those five. He also took the highly unusual step of asking the government not to appeal this ruling, stating, "Seven years of waiting for our legal system to give them an answer to a question so important, in my judgment, is more than plenty." The government took the judge's words to heart and decided not to appeal the ordered release of our five clients. In even happier news, three of the men—Mohamed, Hadj, and Mustafa—arrived in Sarajevo on December 16. We continue to press the government to carry out the judge's orders and release Lakhdar and Saber and to prepare Belkacem's appeal.

David Grossman: Dinner in Chicago

For me, the Guantánamo litigation was about more than legal principles. It was also about people. Throughout my activities, I had the privilege of working with extraordinary colleagues who continually inspired me. But most important, all of our activities focused upon vindicating the rights of the men being imprisoned at Guantánamo. Although I never traveled to Guantánamo, I had the privilege of meeting with Maha Habib, the wife of Mamdouh Habib, an Australian man who was released from Guantánamo in January 2005. Maha flew to Chicago with her Australian attorney, where we met with her over the course of four days. One of the most memorable events of that week occurred when I drove Maha and her Australian attorney to an Indian restaurant on Devon Avenue, in Chicago, where we had dinner. We chose Devon Avenue because the many Indian and Pakistani restaurants in that neighborhood ensured the availability of halal food. On one level, our conversations were no different than countless conversations I have had with first-time visitors to Chicago. For example, we explained that Devon Avenue was once a thriving Jewish neighborhood, but after the Jewish stores moved further west, Indian and Pakistani merchants and restaurant owners arrived. The cross-cultural dialogue made things unusual, but did not create any insurmountable barriers. Yet the reality of the situation was always present, filling that evening, and indeed that entire week, with a seriousness and sadness that we could never completely escape.

Jeffrey M. Strauss: Family Photo

October 2004. Maha Habib shows us old family photos. In one of them, she and her husband, Mamdouh, and their beautiful children are smiling, sitting on a sofa in what could have been my parents' living room (in fact it was their home in Australia), looking for all the world like my Uncle Howard and his Israeli wife, Gila, two of my favorite people when I was a teenager in Buffalo in the 1970s. In the photograph, Maha is wearing a skirt and makeup; her hair is uncovered. She is beautiful. I say, "Maha, I can see your knees!" She laughs. Today, you see, she is wearing the hijab, a modest long-sleeved blouse, and a full skirt to her ankles. The only exposed part of her skin is her face and her hands. She wears no makeup. Her face is drawn and pale. Her eyes are puffy. We have been meeting with her for several days. I have not seen her smile before.

Maha has traveled from Sydney to Chicago—without her husband or children—to meet with lawyers working on the Guantánamo litigation. The four children—including the youngest, four-year-old Hajer—are home in Australia. Her husband is not. He is at Guantánamo. She has not seen or spoken to him in three years.

I was apprehensive about meeting Maha. We knew almost nothing about Mamdouh. How serious were the government's "charges" against him? Would she trust us? Could we trust her?

When I walked into the conference room, Maha was sitting at the large marble table, her back to the door. I said, "Salaam Aleikem." Peace be with you. She responded, "Aleikem Salaam." We talked, gently, about her life with Mamdouh, who was born in Egypt and whose parents still lived there; about how Mamdouh met Maha, an Australian, when he visited Australia in 1982, and how they married shortly thereafter; about his travels in Pakistan during the summer of 2001; about their children, especially the youngest, Hajer, who was only a year old when her father last saw her. I asked if she needed breaks for prayer during the day. We made sure to serve vegetarian food. We told her about the halal restaurants on Devon Avenue on Chicago's far north side, where there are dozens of Pakistani and Indian shops. We asked hard questions. We understood that there were things that we would never know, that probably could not be known.

Hours passed. We began to feel comfortable with each other. We had been told that we were not to shake her hand, that she could not be alone in the room with us without another woman present. But by the second day of our meeting, when our female colleague left the room and the rest of us—all men—got up to leave, Maha said, "No, that's all right." We could stay. She had a spiral notebook, in which she had neatly written recollections about her husband, things she thought we would need to know, records of their life in Sydney. We went through it all—the details of their daily lives. It seemed almost too intimate a conversation to be having with a woman who was covered head to toe, whose husband was supposedly an enemy of the United States.

We came to be fond of Maha. I think she liked us, too. Several lawyers from our firm, Mayer Brown, took her to a family-style dinner on Devon Avenue. One went out on the last day to buy toys and games for the kids, including the Game Boy that Maha's older daughter had specifically asked her mom to bring back from America, and a stuffed animal for Hajer. There were so many that Maha couldn't fit them all in her suitcase. I gave her my large Mayer Brown tote bag. We chatted more freely. Did she—an Australian—speak Arabic? No. But she was learning, so she could read the "holy Quran" in its original language. I told her how similar some Arabic words are to Hebrew. I showed her how her name looked written in Hebrew and wrote her a note, in Hebrew, wishing her peace and a safe journey home. Before she stepped into the taxi to the airport, I felt like giving her a hug but didn't. She thanked us and shook our hands.

February 13, 2005. The U.S. government had released Mamdouh without charges and sent him back to Australia several weeks earlier. I am at home reading the Sunday *New York Times*. There is a front-page article about Mamdouh. The headline is "Detainee Says He Was Tortured While in U.S. Custody." The article reports Mamdouh as saying that his supposed "confessions" were not true; that he "signed to survive"; that during his detention—including stops in Pakistan, Afghanistan, Egypt (where the United States sent him for "harsh interrogation"), and at Guantánamo—he had been beaten, questioned while wearing a wired helmet that delivered electric shocks, and "forced to look at photographs of his wife's face superimposed on images of naked women next to Osama bin Laden."

"His wife's face." I thought, I have met his wife. When I last saw her she was carrying a Mayer Brown tote bag filled with toys for her children. *His* children. There is a photo of Mamdouh, one arm around one of his sons, the other arm around Maha, who is carrying Hajer. They are walking along a boardwalk by the water in Sydney. None of them is smiling.

It is nothing like the happy family photo Maha had shown us in Chicago.

8

Guantánamo beyond Cuba:
A Global Detention System outside the Law

Guantánamo was never simply a prison but was part of an effort to create a globalwide system of prisons beyond the law. Although these prisons varied in some respects, they shared the core features of Guantánamo: indefinite detention without charge or due process, torture and other abuse, pervasive secrecy, and a desire to avoid meaningful judicial review.

Guantánamo Comes to America

Through three important cases—those of Jose Padilla, Ali al-Marri, and Yaser Hamdi—the Bush administration sought to bring the Guantánamo detention system to the United States.

Donna R. Newman: What the F—— Is an "Enemy Combatant"?

In May 2002, when it seemed that the smell of the debris and smoke from the demise of the Twin Towers had just cleared, I received a call from the courtroom deputy to the Honorable Michael B. Mukasey, then chief judge of the U.S. District Court for the Southern District of New York. He asked me to appear in court the following week for an assignment representing a grand-jury material witness who was being held in connection with the grand-jury sitting to investigate 9/11. As in my practice, I came intending to argue for my client's release pending his appearance before the grand jury.

When I arrived in court, the assistant U.S. attorney handling the case handed me the government's affidavit. I learned that my client's name was Jose Padilla, that he was a citizen of the United States, and that he had been arrested when he arrived at Chicago O'Hare Airport on a grand-jury material-witness warrant issued by Judge Mukasey. Although the affidavit stated that Padilla was involved in what was later publicized as a plot to detonate a "dirty bomb" in the United States, I was not deterred from arguing for the setting of reasonable bail. I didn't think the application was ridiculous because the allegations in the affidavit were based on double and triple hearsay, and the affiant admitted that some of the information on which the affiant relied was procured by torture. I thought (perhaps naively) that bail could be secured. In other words, at first I simply saw this case as one of many cases I have had in which the government exaggerates or takes liberty with some facts. But this was not a run-of-the-mill case.

For the first three or four weeks of my representation of Padilla, no special attention was given to the case by the court. It was not in the public eye. I visited my client on a regular basis at the Metropolitan Correctional Center in Manhattan. I filed motions objecting to his status as a material witness and once again sought bail on his behalf. The court scheduled a hearing on my motions.

The day before the hearing, I was driving to another court when I received a call from the prosecutor informing me that President Bush had just signed an order declaring Jose Padilla an "enemy combatant." When I asked, "What the [expletive] is an 'enemy combatant'?" the prosecutor referred me to a Supreme Court case—*In re Quirin*—from World War II. "Are you serious?" I responded. He assured me he was. He then told me that Judge Mukasey had signed an order vacating Padilla's material-witness warrant. I was informed that Padilla was no longer at the Metropolitan Correction Center because the military had seized him from his cell and was now holding him incommunicado at a military brig. My inquiry as to where my client was being held was met with silence. In dismay and disbelief, I lamely said, "But Padilla is not in the military. How is it possible that he is now in military custody?" The prosecutor told me to turn on the radio and listen to Attorney General John Ashcroft's statement from his press conference in Russia.

I turned on the radio. A replay of the statement that had been given earlier that morning was on the air. Jose Padilla, Ashcroft announced, was found to have been part of a plan to detonate a "dirty bomb" in the United States. As a result, President Bush declared Padilla an enemy combatant. He further explained that Padilla was being held for interrogation. I felt like I was having an out-of-body experience. I was confident that I hadn't slept through the revocation of the Constitution or the Bill of Rights, and I hadn't engaged in time travel to the Middle Ages or the Spanish Inquisition.

In between court appearances, I managed to quickly read the *Quirin* case in the court's law library. I found the Supreme Court's analysis difficult to follow and the opinion strained; first impressions are often correct. I knew nothing of the history of the case. The case referenced law with which I was completely unfamiliar. The only thing I was certain of was that I needed a quick course in military law and the international law of war. I recognized that an enormous amount of work needed to be done in a very short span of time since I needed to file a writ of habeas corpus demanding Padilla's release from military custody as soon as possible.

Out of court at long last, I called my office. "What have you done?!" my secretary screamed through the telephone. Our telephone was ringing off the hook with calls from the press asking for a statement from me concerning my client Jose Padilla. A statement, I thought, are they kidding? What would I say? That the government had acted egregiously and illegally? The remainder of the day and through the night my telephone seemed to be on fire with calls from the press.

My secretary also informed me that Judge Mukasey had asked both sides to appear in court to discuss, among other issues, whether my previously filed motions were now moot. The motions were the least of my concern since I realized that the latest I could file the habeas petition was also the day of the hearing.

I was struck, however, that my client was now completely walled off from me, his family, and the world. I was his only hope. It fell to me to unravel the government's position and successfully argue for his release from military custody.

I felt the weight of the responsibility. In the bottom of my stomach was a pit of anxiety. Nonetheless, after staying up most of that evening researching, I awoke early the next morning angry. I was overcome with what I refer to as "mother hen" anger. How dare the government take my client from me! How dare the government not inform me of his whereabouts! How dare they interrogate him! I didn't care what made-up name the president of the United States gave him. My client was a citizen, and he had protections. It was as clear as day to me that this was an extremely dangerous precedent the Bush administration was trying to establish. Each and every one of us could be designated an enemy combatant and denied fundamental due process simply on the executive's prerogative. Probably the last time I thought about executive prerogative was back in my high school honors history class. As far as I recall, our founding fathers sought to protect us from the very situation unfolding here. Although I had only an inkling of the legal basis for my argument, I knew without hesitation that the assertion of power claimed by the executive branch was an abuse that had to be stopped.

I consulted with several other lawyers about possible legal arguments and precedents. By that evening, I had drafted an extremely rough habeas petition to file, recognizing that it would need to be amended.

I appeared in court the next day. I handed up my petition and asked the court for permission to amend. At the prosecution table sat what appeared to me as a gang of prosecutors: not just the assistant U.S. attorney handling the case, but many others, including Paul Clement, who was then Principle Deputy Solicitor General of the United States. It was rather lonely at my table—not even a client sat beside me. The court set a schedule for the government to respond to the habeas petition. I had at least succeeded in getting the ball rolling. After the judge left the bench, I approached the courtroom deputy. I asked that Andrew Patel be assigned as my co-counsel.

Members of the press were also in the courtroom. It was the first time I had addressed the issue with the public, and I wanted to make sure that I stayed within ethical boundaries and yet got my message across. My message was simple. I represented Jose Padilla. We Americans are blessed with a Constitution that provides protection for all of us. The president, I said, had sought to avoid the precious protections afforded us all by arbitrarily labeling Padilla an enemy combatant. No label can eliminate our Constitution. The Constitution was written to stand as a bulwark against the very abuse of power that was being displayed. If Padilla had committed a crime, he must be charged and tried in a court of law. But neither Padilla nor any one of us can be held incommunicado and interrogated simply because the president has designated him or her as an enemy combatant.

Andrew G. Patel: Accessing Padilla

After we filed a habeas corpus petition challenging Jose Padilla's detention as an enemy combatant, Judge Mukasey issued an order ruling that Padilla had the right to access his lawyer. In support of a motion for reconsideration, the government submitted a declaration from Vice Admiral Lloyd Jacoby, the acting director of the Defense Intelligence Agency. In his declaration, Admiral Jacoby stated, "Permitting Padilla any access to counsel may substantially harm our national security interests." In accordance with this position, Padilla had not been permitted to speak to, receive letters from, or write to his lawyers since his transfer to military custody. Judge Mukasey ruled that the military could hold Padilla on the basis of the allegation that he was an "enemy combatant" but that Padilla had the right to challenge this allegation before a federal judge and had a right to the assistance of counsel in doing so. Both sides appealed various portions of Judge Mukasey's rulings. The Second Circuit Court of Appeals found that Padilla's military detention was unlawful and therefore did not discuss the issue of access to counsel.

In January 2004, the government filed a petition for certiorari to the U.S. Supreme Court. As it was late in the Court's term, a member of the Office of the Solicitor General and I discussed a compressed briefing schedule so that the Court could hear us on the last day of the term. Our jointly submitted schedule included dates and times that all briefs were to be submitted. The government's certiorari petition asked the Supreme Court to review the issues of the president's authority to order Padilla's military detention and the jurisdictional question of whether the writ should have been filed in South Carolina, as the government contended, or in New York, as Judge Mukasey and a unanimous Second Circuit had found.

In our response, we urged the Court to deny review because the Second Circuit's decision was correct. We did say that if the Court were to accept the case for review, it should also consider the issue of Padilla's right to access counsel, which the government had still refused to honor. Since Padilla's disposition as an enemy combatant, he had been denied any communication with his lawyers or the world outside. The government's reply brief was due in mid-February 2004.

I was in my office in lower Manhattan, a block from where the World Trade Center had once stood, clearing up some other matters before the government's reply brief was to arrive. At 1:00 p.m., just two hours before that brief was due, I answered the telephone. On the other end of the line, a gentleman identified himself as a lieutenant colonel. I did not catch his name, but he told me that it had been decided that Padilla could have access to his lawyers and that I should contact Navy Captain Daniel Donovan of Joint Forces Command. When I called Captain Donovan, I learned that he was the JAG for Joint Forces Command. Our conversation resulted in Padilla's meeting his lawyers for the first time in more than a year and a half.

Back in my office that February afternoon, I eventually received the government's brief. The government argued that the Court need not review the issue of access to counsel and other due process issues that we had raised because those concerns were now moot. The brief included a citation to a Web link that provided the transcript of a press conference held at 2:00 p.m. that afternoon, one hour after I received that phone call and one hour before the government's brief was due. At the press conference, the DOD announced that Padilla would be given access to his attorneys.

In the litigation surrounding cases concerning the "war on terror," the executive branch has been willing to abuse and manipulate basic concepts of the American legal system, such as a citizen's right to speak with a lawyer. It has also been willing to jettison its own claims of national security concerns to avoid judicial review of its actions. In this instance, the government's manipulation was successful. The Supreme Court did not review the issue of access to counsel, but for the first time since he was declared an enemy combatant, Jose Padilla spoke with his attorneys.

Jonathan Hafetz: Crossing a Constitutional Rubicon

To the public, Ali Saleh Kahlah al-Marri is a "test case": the last remaining "enemy combatant" held inside the United States, a human guinea pig in one of the most important and contentious struggles over executive detention power in the post-9/11 era. To me, al-Marri is a man who endured more than seven years in one of the most brutal experiments in human isolation ever conducted and did so with his dignity and spirit intact.

As Ali's lawyer, I cannot claim impartiality. But witnessing the grueling and high-stakes litigation fought over the corpus of my client does give me a certain insight into his case and the implications—legal and human—of the virtually limitless claim of executive power that lies at its core.

I began representing Ali in late 2004, when I was a public-interest fellow at the law firm Gibbons, P.C. Although I knew only the basic facts of Ali's case, its significance was immediately apparent. By that time, hundreds of individuals had been detained by the military as enemy combatants at Guantánamo. But Ali was one of only two people held as an enemy combatant who had been arrested in the United States. (Jose Padilla was the other.) Ali's case thus did not involve people seized in connection with the armed conflict in Afghanistan, as a number of Guantánamo cases did. Ali's detention involved something very different: a deliberate effort to extend the so-called "war on terror" to Main Street America and to give the president the discretion to supplant the protections of the Constitution by relabeling criminal suspects "combatants" and imprisoning them indefinitely without charge or judicial review.

Ali came to the United States in September 2001 with his wife and five children to pursue a master's degree at Bradley University in Peoria, Illinois, where he had previously studied as an undergraduate. That December, he was arrested at his home by FBI agents and taken to New York City, where he was detained as a material witness in connection with the investigation into the September 11 attacks. Two months later, Ali was charged with credit-card fraud. A second indictment was filed the following year, adding charges of false statements to the FBI and lying on a bank application. After the case in New York was dismissed, a third indictment was filed, this one in Illinois, where the alleged criminal activity had taken place. On Friday, June 20, 2003, the district judge scheduled a hearing to decide a motion to dismiss the indictment filed by Ali's attorneys, Lawrence Lustberg and Mark Berman, two experienced criminal defense lawyers. Ali's trial was less than a month away.

But the hearing and trial never took place. The following Monday morning, June 23, prosecutors came to court with a one-page order signed by President Bush demanding Ali's immediate transfer to military custody. Ali was no longer a criminal suspect with constitutional rights: he was now an "enemy combatant" in the "war on terror" and thus had no rights at all. Why? Because the president had said so. The trial judge dismissed the indictment, and Ali was taken to the Naval Consolidated Brig near Charleston, South Carolina.

For the first sixteen months at the navy brig, Ali was held incommunicado, and all requests to communicate with him by his lawyers, his family, and the International Committee for the Red Cross were ignored or refused. During this time, Ali was subjected to a brutal interrogation regime that bordered on, and sometimes amounted to, torture. Ali was never physically beaten: there was no rack and screw to leave physical marks. Instead, he was subjected to "touchless torture," subtler but no less devastating in its effect. During a series of seemingly endless interrogation sessions, Ali was chained in a fetal position to the floor of a freezing cell, forced to stand in painful positions for hours at a time, and locked in a tiny, dark cell for weeks on end. Interrogators threatened to send him to Egypt and Syria, where they said his wife would be raped in front of his eyes before he was executed. The goal, according to the Defense Intelligence Agency (DIA), which ran the interrogations, was to break the detainee down by creating a sense of total fear, hopelessness, and despair. Guantánamo had come to the United States.

In June 2004, the Supreme Court ruled that Yaser Hamdi, another "enemy combatant" detained at the Charleston navy brig, was entitled to a lawyer and that indefinite detention for purposes of interrogation was illegal. Mr. Hamdi had allegedly been captured on a battlefield in Afghanistan before he was brought to the brig (after a four-month period of detention in Guantánamo, where he was initially held until the United States realized he was an American citizen). Ali, by contrast, had been arrested at his home in Peoria and had already met with his lawyers numerous times in the eighteen months he was in the civilian system. Surely Ali was entitled to an attorney as well. But the government persisted in denying Ali access to his lawyers for almost four more months while it continued to interrogate him in its South Carolina torture chamber, acting as though the Supreme Court's decision did not exist. When the government finally allowed Ali to meet with his attorneys again that October, it made clear that it did not take this right seriously. DIA agents sat on both sides of Ali, who remained belly- and ankle-chained to the floor, and took notes throughout the meeting, with Ali's attorneys on the other side of a glass partition.

I first met Ali in early 2005. Over time, I learned more about the horrors of his sixteen-month incommunicado detention in the United States' new Guantánamo. But there remained more immediate priorities. Although the government had stopped directly interrogating Ali, it continued to subject him to highly coercive—and cruel—conditions designed to break his spirit. Ali remained totally isolated. He was not allowed to talk to his family; letters to and from his wife and children took up to a year or more to arrive due to the government's purported "security review," and by the time the letters finally got there, they were barely intelligible because so much information had been redacted. Even the common greeting uttered daily by hundreds of millions of people throughout the Muslim world—"As-Salamu Alaykum" (peace be upon you)—was crossed out with a black marker.

Ali, meanwhile, remained locked down in his tiny cell almost twenty-four hours a day, seven days a week, utterly alone. Occasionally he was allowed out into an empty yard for "recreation." The government refused to allow Ali to see or share a meal with Mr. Padilla, the remaining "enemy combatant" at the navy brig. (Yaser Hamdi, once considered too dangerous to speak to a lawyer, had been returned home a free man after the district court ordered the government to present its evidence at a hearing.) Ali was denied books, magazines, or news, heightening his sense of isolation. The one book Ali was allowed—a copy of the Quran—was frequently taken away or defiled as an interrogation tool.

It is difficult to imagine enduring this crushing isolation for more than a few days. But Ali had endured it for two years and had done so, moreover, without knowing when, if ever, it would end. And it was taking its toll. Ali had started hallucinating and was becoming increasingly paranoid about his surroundings. When the roof of the brig was re-covered with tar, Ali believed interrogators were secretly putting noxious fumes in his cell. He also started experiencing unexplained heart palpitations and had difficulty sleeping. Ali nevertheless still had the self-awareness to realize what was happening. "I think I'm losing my mind," he told Andrew Savage, the Charleston-based defense attorney and my co-counsel. "I don't know how much longer I can go on."

We were already challenging the legality of Ali's detention through a habeas corpus petition. But we knew that challenge would take years for the courts to resolve, and Ali did not have years. So in August 2005, we filed a separate lawsuit in federal court demanding an improvement in the conditions of Ali's confinement. The suit provided the first glimpse into the mistreatment of detainees in the United States, right at the time that the abuses at Guantánamo were being exposed to the world.

Over the following months, things started to improve, as the government sought to clean up its act before it had to defend Ali's treatment in court. Ali was allowed some books and more time for recreation. He was given a newspaper, though it remained heavily redacted, sometimes leaving him only the sports page, obituary, and classified advertisements. "Am I supposed to be looking for a job?" he joked. The government also started allowing Ali to practice his religion. It stopped, for example, lying to him about the direction of Mecca and the time of day so that he could pray properly. And whereas before guards had punished him for using his shirt to cover his head during prayer, now they permitted us to give him a kofi, or prayer cap. He was finally permitted to have a mattress and a blanket. Eventually, Ali was to allowed talk to Andy and me on the phone and to watch television. Although news programs were prohibited, brig staff let Ali watch *The Daily Show* and *The Colbert Report* since technically those shows did not count as news. And so Ali joined the long list of Americans who learn about world events from Comedy Central. Yet the government still refused to allow him to read the *New York Times* or other newspapers, claiming that to do so would allow him to learn about the progress of the "war on terror."

The continued improvement in Ali's conditions over time, however, had less to do with the government's fear of judicial scrutiny and more to do with the inherent decency of military servicepersons who refused to be turned to the dark side by a corrupt cabal of high-level Bush administration officials bent on destroying the Constitution in the name of misguided, dangerous, and criminal theories of executive power. Although brig staff believed Ali should be punished if he did something wrong, they understood that locking people up for years in solitary confinement and denying them a trial was wrong. They attempted to work with us, making accommodations when they could (although some critical things such as family phone calls remained beyond their control). Once brig staff were no longer required to implement brutal conditions to soften Ali up for interrogations, they had a chance to get to know him. Many staff members had grown to like Ali and to respect him for enduring so many years of harsh imprisonment without rancor or bitterness. Sometimes they went far beyond the call of duty, including the one official who sat with Ali at night during Ali's darkest hours, when he felt he was losing his sanity. Unlike those who made policy in Washington, D.C., U.S. servicepersons had come to see Ali as a person and not just a piece of paper.

In the end, improving Ali's conditions did not alter the underlying reality: a jail is a jail is a jail. Or, as Ali would say, "even a golden cage is still a cage." Ali continued to be deprived of his liberty, without a trial and without any idea of when, if ever, his detention would end.

After more than five years of litigation, our courts still had not resolved Ali's habeas petition or answered definitively the basic question at the heart of his case: whether he could be held in military custody, potentially for life, without criminal trial. In July 2008, the full U.S. Court of Appeals for the Fourth Circuit ruled in a 5–4 decision that the military could continue to hold Ali as an "enemy combatant" if the allegations against him were true. The court of appeals also ruled that Ali was entitled to more due process than he had previously been afforded in challenging those allegations, and it sent the case back to the district court for yet further proceedings. We appealed to the Supreme Court, arguing that Ali was entitled to a criminal trial if he was going to be imprisoned, just like every other person arrested in the United States on suspicion of wrongdoing, including acts of terrorism. Ali's appeal was supported by former top-level Justice Department and military officials, as well as a range of nongovernmental organizations and legal experts.

That November, while Ali's petition for Supreme Court review was pending, I visited his family. I was joined by Andy and his wife and office manager, Cheryl, who had also become very close to Ali over the past five years and whom Ali referred to affectionately as "the Queen of Charleston." Ali's family had moved to Saudi Arabia, except for his brother Jarallah, who was living in Qatar following his release from Guantánamo that July after more than six years of illegal detention. We had talked to Ali's family many times in the past, and I had represented Jarallah in his habeas corpus case. But seeing them at their homes was entirely different. It put Ali's detention in a new light. Ali was not merely the prisoner present before us in the cell but the human being who was absent from his home and family. Ali's family was not a disembodied voice checking in about the status of his case; they were living flesh and blood, human beings who were struggling to cope with the prolonged—and indefinite—absence of a loved one.

We saw where Ali's family lived, the bank where Ali had worked, and the mosque where he had prayed. We saw the plot of land his brothers had put aside for him in their family village in the desert so that he could build a home beside theirs when he was freed. And we saw the pain of separation that his wife, five children, mother, brothers, cousins, and other family members experienced daily. We learned that Ali's eldest son, Abdulhadi, had been with Ali when he was arrested in Peoria. He had not seen his father for seven years. Now sixteen, he survives on boyhood memories of his father. We saw Ali's youngest son, Abdul Rahman, who was an infant when Ali was arrested. Unlike his older brother, Abdul Rahman does not even have memories. One of Ali's brothers, Naji, told us that he did not believe Ali was still alive until he saw us.

Readers of this story may say that Ali's actions brought these hardships on himself and his family. But how we treat prisoners is about us, not them. Depriving a person of his liberty is the most severe punishment the government can impose, short of depriving a person of life. That deprivation is even worse when the detention is indefinite and the person does not know whether he will remain behind bars for another day, another year, or the rest of his natural life. The United States was founded on the idea that the government cannot deprive people of their freedom simply because it suspects them of a crime, however grave, without first affording them a trial. Criminal trials provide the most rigorous safeguards our system has to offer. They do so not only to prevent the wrongful conviction of the innocent but also to give validity to government action in imposing the severest of all restraints.

After September 11, the United States imprisoned hundreds of men without charging them with a crime or trying them in a court of law. Instead, it called them "enemy combatants" and argued that their detention was not punishment but a simple wartime measure to prevent their "return to the battlefield" in a war of limitless scope and duration. But that was a lie: the men were being punished, and they were being punished severely. Ali's detention, like the detention of others held as "enemy combatants," is built on that lie.

Bush administration policies have destroyed countless lives and families. They have also harmed the United States' credibility throughout the world; only the most arrogant and deluded could think otherwise. Guantánamo has come to symbolize this new system. But as Ali's case makes clear, the Bush administration also intended for that system to include the United States. Ali's case serves as a warning that what happens offshore could one day happen here too.

On December 5, 2008, nearly seven years to the date after Ali's initial arrest, the Supreme Court decided to hear his appeal over the government's objections. When we spoke to Ali that afternoon, he was grateful to learn that the United States' highest court would review his case.

On January 21, 2009, we filed our opening brief in the Supreme Court, making clear that Congress had not authorized and the Constitution did not permit the indefinite military detention of legal residents arrested in the United States. The new administration chose not to defend the lower court decision—recognizing that the prior administration's claim of virtually limitless executive detention power was likely to fail. On February 26, the government, less than a month before its brief was due, indicted Ali in federal court for providing material support for terrorism and rescinded President Bush's order designating him an "enemy combatant." It then moved to dismiss the writ of certiorari in the Supreme Court, claiming that the case was moot because Ali would now receive the civilian criminal trial his habeas corpus petition sought. The Court granted the motion, but it also vacated the lower court's opinion, wiping out the ruling that gave the president unprecedented military detention power in the United States. Ali was transferred to civilian custody to stand trial, ending more than 2,000 days of lawless detention and the United States' failed experiment of military imprisonment without out due process.

Geremy Kamens: No Blank Check

When Frank Dunham and I met Yaser Esam Hamdi for the first time, in a small room at the navy brig in Charleston, South Carolina, he was dressed in an orange jumpsuit, and a heavy chain led from his ankles to a post in the floor. But Mr. Hamdi's broad smile, easy laughter, enthusiastic—if imperfect—use of slang (undoubtedly learned from his guards over the course of the prior two years), and warm regard toward American culture suggested that he was not the terrorist fighter the U.S. government claimed he was.

"I really want to get out of here, because I am just chilling." Those are among the first words that Mr. Hamdi, an alleged "enemy combatant," uttered when we met that day in February 2004. When Mr. Hamdi was shown news articles about his case, he said, "I am a famous boy."

Indeed, Mr. Hamdi was neither a combatant nor a terrorist, and he never fought against U.S. troops in Afghanistan or anywhere else. These basic facts often get lost in the "imprison-first-ask-questions-years-later" detention policy devised by the Bush administration. These facts were also impossible for Frank, the former federal public defender for the Eastern District of Virginia, and I to know during the first two years that we represented Mr. Hamdi in federal court—all while he was held incommunicado and without criminal charge inside the United States.

Frank passed away from cancer on November 3, 2006, but I know that representing and securing Yaser Hamdi's release was one of the proudest achievements of his life.

Until February 2004, three months before Frank argued Mr. Hamdi's case before the U.S. Supreme Court, we did not know whether Mr. Hamdi knew that he had lawyers fighting for his release, or even that our country's highest court had accepted his case for review. By that time, Frank and I had represented Mr. Hamdi for almost two years, argued three appeals before the Fourth Circuit Court of Appeals, received four published rulings, petitioned for Supreme Court review, and were preparing our merits briefs before the High Court.

We also knew only the barest information about our client. The first person held in the United States as a so-called enemy combatant since World War II, Mr. Hamdi was born in Baton Rouge, Louisiana. He spent the first three years of his life in the United States while his father, from Saudi Arabia, worked for an oil company. Raised in Saudi Arabia, Mr. Hamdi began attending a university there. A few weeks before September

11, 2001, he had gone to Afghanistan seeking an ascetic break from his college studies. In late 2001, Mr. Hamdi was handed over to the U.S. military by the Northern Alliance and was subsequently sent to Guantánamo Bay. When it was discovered that he was born in the United States, Mr. Hamdi was flown to Washington, D.C., and then to the naval base in Norfolk, Virginia, before later being transferred to the navy brig in Charleston.

Frank Dunham was appointed federal public defender for the Eastern District of Virginia in 2000. Within two years, Dunham had established offices in Norfolk, Richmond, and Alexandria, Virginia, to represent indigent defendants facing criminal charges in federal court. His first client, appointed by the federal district court in Alexandria, was Zacarias Moussaoui, a mentally unstable French citizen of Algerian descent alleged to be a member of al Qaeda. Shortly after the court appointed the federal public defender to represent Mr. Moussaoui, John Walker Lindh faced criminal charges in the same courthouse for his alleged assistance to the Taliban.

When Frank read about Mr. Hamdi's detention in Norfolk in April 2002, he had every reason to believe that Mr. Hamdi would face charges similar to those brought against Lindh. For that reason, he directed Larry Shelton, the head of the Norfolk office, to write a letter to the commander of the navy brig asking to meet with Mr. Hamdi. Shortly thereafter, Frank asked Shelton to find someone to draft a habeas corpus petition for Mr. Hamdi seeking his release. As the youngest, newest, and least experienced attorney in that office, I was the natural choice.

At the time, Mr. Hamdi was in solitary confinement and the U.S. government had no intention of allowing a lawyer to meet with him. When we filed a habeas corpus petition in May 2002 on Mr. Hamdi's behalf, the government claimed that it alone had the authority to decide whether Mr. Hamdi was lawfully detained. This was an unprecedented and dangerous claim. Had the Supreme Court not rejected it in 2004, it would have stripped away the right of any detainee held as an enemy combatant, either within or outside the country, to contest his imprisonment in a court of law. Shortly after the Supreme Court upheld Mr. Hamdi's right to challenge his detention, we negotiated his release. He now resides in Saudi Arabia. Within a year of his return, he married, resumed his university studies, and had a daughter.

The path, however, was difficult. Prisoners of all kinds have a right to challenge their confinement through habeas corpus by virtue of federal law and the Constitution, but as a general matter, a habeas petition must be signed by the prisoner himself. Mr. Hamdi, of course, was incapable of signing a habeas petition because he was being held by the military incommunicado. The federal district judge assigned to handle the habeas petition, the Honorable Robert G. Doumar of the Eastern District of Virginia, naturally assumed that this was precisely the type of case in which the petitioner's signature was not required. He therefore permitted the case to be filed and promptly ordered the military to allow Frank and Shelton to meet Mr. Hamdi.

Within hours of Judge Doumar's decision, however, the U.S. Office of the Solicitor General filed an emergency interlocutory appeal with the Fourth Circuit challenging Frank's ability to file a petition on Mr. Hamdi's behalf. The Fourth Circuit, remarkably, ordered us to respond within two hours of our receipt of the government's brief—notwithstanding prior case law holding that orders permitting the filing of a habeas petition on behalf of a prisoner are not immediately appealable. The court scheduled oral argument to take place the following week in Richmond, Virginia. The speed with which the court acted was unusual, to say the least, and foreshadowed the Fourth Circuit panel's dim view of our efforts on Mr. Hamdi's behalf. In fact, questioning by the appellate panel was so hostile that as soon as we left the argument, we decided to file a new petition, signed by Mr. Hamdi's father so that a "next friend" petition would be filed before the Fourth Circuit ruled. As expected, the Fourth Circuit in short order held that Frank could not file a petition on Mr. Hamdi's behalf because he had never met him. The fact that the military had imprisoned Mr. Hamdi incommunicado and thus prevented him from meeting with counsel was no excuse.

The litigation thus proceeded on the new petition, and Judge Doumar once against promptly ordered the military to allow us to meet with Mr. Hamdi. The Office of the Solicitor General again filed an emergency interlocutory appeal to prevent Mr. Hamdi from meeting with his lawyers. And once again, the Fourth Circuit scheduled a prompt oral argument— this time by telephone—and ordered us to file a brief within twenty-four hours of receipt of the government's brief.

On appeal, the government argued in a circle, claiming that because Mr. Hamdi was an enemy combatant, he had no right to meet with a lawyer to contest the claim that he was an enemy combatant. The Fourth Circuit then endorsed this view, holding that the district court should have considered the merits of the habeas petition before allowing Mr. Hamdi to meet with a lawyer. Before the district court did anything else, the court of appeals said, it should address whether a two-page unsworn declaration was enough, by itself, to find in favor of the government.

On remand, Judge Doumar held a hearing to determine whether he could decide the merits of the habeas petition based solely on a two-page unsworn declaration by a Defense Department official named Michael Mobbs. On August 16, 2002, Judge Doumar concluded that Mobbs's declaration was not enough to support the detention and ordered the government to produce the basis for its determination that Mr. Hamdi was an enemy combatant.

For the third time, the same Fourth Circuit panel reversed Judge Doumar. This time, however, the court of appeals ordered that Mr. Hamdi's petition should be dismissed. The fact that Mr. Hamdi had purportedly conceded that he was picked up in Afghanistan, the panel reasoned, was enough to justify his indefinite imprisonment as an enemy combatant—even though Mr. Hamdi had not been allowed to meet with his lawyers, much less conceded the location of his capture. This point did not escape the notice of at least a few judges on the Fourth Circuit who dissented from the denial of our petition for rehearing, not least among them Michael Luttig, the conservative jurist who left the bench to return to private practice in 2006. The panel opinion "is unpersuasive," Judge Luttig wrote, "because of its exclusive reliance upon a mistaken characterization of the circumstances of Hamdi's seizure as 'undisputed,' when those circumstances are neither conceded in fact, nor susceptible to concession in law, because Hamdi has not been permitted to speak for himself or even through counsel as to those circumstances."

When Mr. Hamdi's case reached the Supreme Court, two main issues were before the Justices: (1) what authority exists to detain an American citizen as an "enemy combatant" and (2) whether Mr. Hamdi was entitled to challenge the factual basis for his detention. The Fourth Circuit's decision ordering the dismissal of Mr. Hamdi's habeas petition adopted the government's argument that the Constitution vests the president with the authority to detain individuals, including citizens, captured in armed conflict overseas and that any inquiry into the grounds for such detentions would violate the separation of powers.

The oral argument took place on April 28, 2004, and it was Frank's second argument before the Court in less than a month. He told me later that he learned at his first argument that the Justices would remain relatively quiet during his rebuttal. For that reason, he was able to give a remarkable closing statement that actually challenged the Court to honor the Great Writ of Habeas Corpus:

We have a small problem here. One citizen—we're not talking about thousands—one citizen caught up in a problem in Afghanistan. Is it better to give him rights or is it better to start a new dawn of saying there are circumstances where you can't file a writ of habeas corpus and there are circumstances where you can't get due process? I think not.

I would urge the Court to find that citizens can only be detained by law. And here there is no law. If there is any law at all, it is the executive's own secret definition of whatever "enemy combatant" is. And don't fool yourselves into thinking that means somebody coming off a battlefield because they've used it in Chicago, they've used it in New York, and they've used it in Indiana. . . .

Congress tomorrow could take these military regs and they could say, "This is the law. We authorize the executive to detain people and to give them hearings the way the military says," and then it would be lawful. But Congress hasn't done that, and I respectfully submit, Your Honor, that until Congress does that, these detentions are not lawful. And I would respectfully ask this Court to step up to the plate and say so.

It did, reversing the Fourth Circuit's judgment and remanding for a hearing that would allow Mr. Hamdi to contest the claim that he was an enemy combatant. A plurality of the Court, in an opinion authored by Justice Sandra Day O'Connor, concluded that Congress had authorized only the military seizure of individuals allegedly captured in Afghanistan fighting alongside Taliban forces against U.S. or allied troops. It also ruled that a citizen detainee was entitled to notice of the allegations underlying the detention, access to counsel, and a fair hearing before a neutral tribunal in order to challenge those allegations. Justice O'Connor emphasized that Congress's authorization to detain was not a "blank check" and was subject to both judicial review and procedural due process.

Shortly after the opinion was issued, Frank sent a letter to the Solicitor General renewing a request he had made several times before, most recently before the oral argument, to settle the case. This time we received a favorable response and promptly began to negotiate the terms under which Mr. Hamdi would be allowed to return home to Saudi Arabia. Although the government originally sought an agreement that would have prevented Mr. Hamdi from ever returning to the United States, we successfully negotiated a provision that would permit him to return (as long as the secretary of defense and the secretary of the Department of Home-land Security agreed), because Mr. Hamdi hoped to travel to the United States someday as a tourist.

Less than six months after Mr. Hamdi was released from the navy brig and returned to Saudi Arabia, Frank Dunham was admitted to the hospital with a diagnosis of brain cancer. At that time, I called Mr. Hamdi in Saudi Arabia to convey the news. I also wanted to see if he and his father could call Frank, because I thought it would cheer Frank up to hear from his second-most-famous client. (The first, Zacarias Moussaoui, had stopped listening to Frank a long time ago.) I did not want Mr. Hamdi and his father to hear about Frank's illness from anyone else.

My call occurred before Frank's illness became widely known and months before it was reported in the *Washington Post*. It has since occurred to me, however, that my private call may not have been private at all but instead may have been monitored by the National Security Agency, without my knowledge and without a warrant.

The Supreme Court's ruling in Mr. Hamdi's case confirms that no such wartime authority, except from judicial oversight, exists. As Justice O'Connor stated, "Whatever power the United States Constitution envisions for the Executive in its exchanges with other nations or with enemy organizations in times of conflict, it most assuredly envisions a role for all three branches when individual liberties are at stake." The Constitution therefore promises judicial and congressional oversight of the president's actions that implicate civil liberties, not secret surveillance programs.

Of course, the most important consequence of the litigation was the release of someone who was never a threat to the United States, never joined its enemies, and, amazingly, bore no ill will toward this country even after more than two years of illegal imprisonment. "I really appreciate it," he said to me shortly before his release. "I really appreciate you guys."

Black Sites

Perhaps the most notorious aspect of the new global detention system was the network of secret CIA-run prisons, or "black sites," and the rendition of individuals to foreign governments for torture and other abuse. The secret detention and rendition of prisoners resulted in some of the worst abuses of the 9/11 era.

Margaret L. Satterthwaite: Known Unknowns

I first heard about the men who became clients of the International Human Rights Clinic at NYU School of Law, which I co-direct, from a colleague at Amnesty International. "Did you hear about the Yemenis that the International Secretariat interviewed?" she asked me, referring to Amnesty's London headquarters. "They were held in one of the CIA 'black sites'—we think in Eastern Europe." It was mid-2005, and a small group of researchers and human rights lawyers had been working to find detainees who had spent time in the CIA secret prisons, known as "black sites." At the time, we knew little more than the basics about the extraordinary rendition and secret detention program, many facets of which the U.S. government had not yet officially acknowledged. Much of what was known had been gathered from individuals who were rendered to foreign custody and tortured, as well as from detainees who were held by the CIA before being sent to Guantánamo and from leaks by intelligence personnel to the media.

Two famous cases illustrated both what was known and what was unknown at the time that I first heard about our clients-to-be. The significance of Amnesty's discovery of men who had been held and then released from the most secret CIA sites—those set up outside Afghanistan—was extremely important. At that time, no one had reported the firsthand account of a detainee who had been held outside Afghanistan in a CIA-run black site. Although our clinic had been engaged in legal and factual investigation concerning rendition and secret detention for several years, we had not yet taken on the case of an individual who had been subjected to rendition and secret detention. Fitting together the pieces of the puzzle that made up this program, therefore, had become somewhat abstract for us. Whereas much of the human rights work my clinic and I did in other countries—on the right to water in Haiti, for example, or the right to equality for women in Nigeria—involved close contact with individuals directly affected by the policies we sought to change. The "war on terror" work was different because it remained flattened, dead on the page, and largely about principles instead of human beings.

When Amnesty asked if we would take on the representation of the men in Yemen, however, a chill ran down my spine. Here were men who told familiar stories about being abducted and transferred to Afghanistan, where they were subjected to excruciatingly loud music, stress positions, sleep deprivation, and extreme cold. But the familiarity stopped when they were transferred out of Afghanistan, into a final secret facility that Amnesty believed was somewhere in Eastern Europe. This prison was aimed at maximizing disorientation and the sense of being isolated and alone. Theirs was the story of a CIA black site—set up to be off the record, off the map, and outside the law. Taking on their representation seemed important as an embodiment of the work we had been doing to change U.S. policy. But I also knew it would bring us—me, our small staff, and ultimately, my students—face-to-face with the results of our government's policy. It would require us to engage on a human level with an inhumane policy.

Several months later, I traveled with my colleague Jayne Huckerby, research director of the Center for Human Rights and Global Justice, to Yemen to visit our clients for the first time. Anne FitzGerald of Amnesty International traveled with us to introduce us to the men; she had met each of them several times and lobbied the government of Yemen either to try or to release them after they were returned by the United States. Yemeni officials told Amnesty that the United States had instructed the Yemenis to detain the men but said that no evidence of criminal activity or terrorism accompanied that request.

We planned our first meeting with Mohammed al-Asad to take place at the office of a local nongovernmental organization. We hoped that the familiar surroundings might break down some of the distance that was inherent in our representation. The other things—our nationality, our gender, our inability to speak Arabic, and our status as outsiders—could not be altered. When Mohammed arrived, he came into the office with a bright smile. "Welcome to Yemen," he said. "I am very glad to meet you." Touching his hand to his chest, he sat down with us at a desk that the organization lent us for the afternoon. "We are so pleased to meet you," I said, and Jayne and I each introduced ourselves. I had an immediate feeling of wonder: how was it possible that this person, who had been abducted and "disappeared" by my government, could still trust that I came in a spirit of justice, despite what my government had done? I was quite sure that I would not have the same generosity or optimism were the tables turned.

Until this moment, lawyer-client discussions had all taken place by phone, probably monitored as part of the National Security Agency's warrantless wiretapping program. Now, I hoped that through regular human interaction we could create the rapport needed for a successful lawyer-client relationship.

Jayne asked kindly about Mohammed's family. "They are all doing well," he said, "thank God. But it is very hard for my wife to be without her husband and my children to be without their father." Mohammed's wife was Tanzanian, and Mohammed was awaiting a visa to allow him to reunite with his family in Dar-es-Salaam. When he was apprehended in 2003, he had lived in Tanzania for more than a decade, and his family, business, and community were there. Mohammed asked about our trip. "It was long," I said, and we all laughed. I almost commented about my hatred of airplanes, but it seemed petty and irrelevant in light of what this man had been through—an experience that began with a disorienting and frightening plane ride from Tanzania to an unknown country in East Africa.

We soon began the conversation in earnest, reviewing the work we agreed to do for Mohammed. We would begin by investigating potential claims he might have that were associated with his rendition and secret detention, investigating the facts pertaining to his treatment, and filing FOIA requests for documents concerning him.

I pulled out a large stack of forms that my students had prepared and explained that we needed Mohammed to sign each one. Mohammed's forehead furrowed as he eyed the stack of about sixty forms. There were two sets: one declared that he waived the privacy interest that the U.S. government could assert as a reason to withhold documents under FOIA; the other certified his identity. "They should know who I am by now," Mohammed said. "The Tanzanians took my passport when they picked me up, and the Americans had me in jail for a year and a half." When Mohammed was apprehended, his passport and cell phone were confiscated. "They did not seem concerned with my privacy when they took me away," Mohammed said. When he encountered the CIA rendition team, they had grabbed him roughly, sliced off his clothes, forced him to endure an anal cavity search, and then bound, diapered, and hooded him before forcing him roughly onto a waiting plane.

As he signed the forms, Mohammed reminded us that he had seen U.S. interrogators, doctors, psychiatrists, and other personnel write down information when they spoke with him. He had seen video cameras capturing his every move. He believed the United States had his passport and cell phone. There should be medical and psychiatric records, interrogation logs, and basic documents processing him into and out of the prisons where he had been held.

"Will the government give us any of these things?" Mohammed asked. We explained that we would seek all those records through our FOIA requests. But because of certain rules allowing the government to refuse to release documents on the basis of national security, we expected that we would not get even a single record. We explained that the government was likely to claim that it was impossible either to confirm or to deny that they held records pertaining to him.

We next discussed the potential claims we might pursue. Listening carefully, Mohammed asked detailed questions: What facts were needed? What forums might be used? Was his case a good one? Jayne and I took turns answering, trying to ensure that Mohammed understood that though we had solid legal arguments, his case was at best an uphill battle, no matter the forum we chose. We explained that cases similar to his own had been thrown out of U.S. courts on the basis of something called the "state secrets" privilege, that cases against the countries that participated in his rendition and secret detention would depend on having factual evidence of where he was transported and held, and that the international human rights courts and tribunals were potential venues but that the United States had either refused to subject itself to their reach or ignored their rulings. We assured him that we had already begun factual investigation and had many leads, that his human rights claims were very strong, and that we—and our students—were prepared to put in long hours to get the work done. We explained that much depended on what his goals were and what he sought through our representation.

When we were finished talking about the potential claims and forums, our client chuckled and shook his head. "What you have told me is that it will be easier to go after the weakest countries and hardest to go after the strongest one—the one that was actually responsible for what was done to me, that the strongest country has shielded itself from courts that protect human rights, and that its own courts are not available to those it has wronged. You are saying that I might have a better chance of obtaining justice outside the courtroom, through the press or international organizations. And you are asking if I want to accept all of this and proceed anyway, despite the possibility of failure. Am I right?"

"Essentially, yes," I said, and Mohammed laughed.

"Well then," he said, "let us begin." We all laughed together then. At that moment I realized that Mohammed had a sense of justice that outweighed his concern about winning or losing.

We met in the conference room of our hotel the next day. Over the course of six hours, Mohammed told us the story of his rendition and secret detention by the CIA. Apprehended by Tanzanian officials in Dar-es-Salaam while he was eating dinner with his family, he was soon placed on board a plane and flown a few hours to an unknown country. For a number of specific reasons, Mohammed believed this country was in East Africa or the Horn of Africa. He was held in what appeared to be a local facility, but he was questioned by Americans. After some days, he was handed over to a team of U.S. officials that was familiar to us as a CIA rendition team. He was taken to Afghanistan, where he was held in two different CIA prisons before being transferred in the spring of 2004 to a final facility. There, he was housed in a small cell with the walls and ceiling painted the same drab color, stainless-steel bathroom fixtures, and an ankle shackle that was attached to a hook affixed to the wall. He was supervised by guards who wore all black and communicated in hand signals. He was never allowed to see other prisoners, and the white noise that was piped into his cell prevented him from hearing even the voices or footsteps of other prisoners, except for during short, unexpected moments when the electricity would go off. Mohammed was shuffled by black-clad guards to meetings with psychiatrists, medical doctors, and interrogators. He was taught a bizarre protocol: whenever he heard the outside door to his cell opening, he was expected to stand in a corner and wait for the guards to handcuff and escort him out of the cell. His every move was captured by the video cameras that were prominently affixed in his cell and other rooms. The isolation was the worst part, Mohammed said, the sense of being utterly alone in an unknown place for an unknowable period of time.

When we asked Mohammed to estimate the size of the interrogation room, he answered by referring to the conference room we were all sitting in: "Not so much smaller than this room." When we asked him to describe the interrogators' approach, Mohammed answered flatly, "It was just like this—they would ask a question; I would answer truthfully. They would write down my answer and then ask another question." When we asked about the type of clothing the interrogators wore, the comparison was again to me and my colleagues. "Not unlike the outfit that she has on," he said, pointing to one of us, "only a different color. There were women interrogators there also, both women and men." Hair color, eye color, and even writing instruments and pads were all compared to what we used. Accents in particular were like mine. As the only American on our team, it was both appropriate and telling that I became increasingly associated with the interrogators whom Mohammed had encountered in the secret prison.

At the end of the day, Mohammed stood up and thanked each of us. Although he smiled at us, it was plain that this day of questioning had renewed Mohammed's memories and made him despondent. As he left, I realized that something had changed for me also. No longer was the rendition and secret detention program something theoretical or distant. It was now a program with a very tangible human toll. And suddenly, all the work I had done in other countries to document torture and disappearances, to take witness statements, to understand the mechanics of repression, were directly and horribly relevant. It was a relevance I had never hoped for. But it was a relevance that I hoped would serve me—and my client—well.

Jayne C. Huckerby: Endless Questions

Our questions for the clinic's clients Mohammed al-Asad and Mohamed Bashmilah were endless. Both men had been rendered to multiple secret U.S. prisons that traversed the globe, before being wordlessly released to their home country of Yemen, never once having been charged with a crime. Where are these prisons? On what basis are individuals being detained? Why are particular detainees sent to particular locations? Is there anything significant about the dates on which detainees are transferred? Who else is the United States secretly detaining? Are there others who have been released? What deals have foreign governments made in exchange for handing detainees to the U.S. government, allowing it to use their airports and territories, and accepting prisoners emptied from the so-called black sites?

More than two and a half years later, we are still waiting for the full answers. A slew of official acknowledgments made by the United States about its rendition, secret detention, and coercive interrogation programs have helped to fill in some of the gaps. But for our clients, the significance of these acknowledgments is mixed. On the one hand, it gives them (and us) hope that one day the U.S. government will reveal the full extent of what has been happening for the past seven years. On the other hand, it is difficult to explain or grasp the government's selective approach to disclosure.

Why, for example, will the government acknowledge the names of some of the individuals it held in CIA custody and not those of others, such as al-Asad and Bashmilah, who it has released? If the government believes, as it claims, that its program is legal, why does it attempt to shield scrutiny of its activities in the nation's courts? Why does the government ask for a privacy waiver alongside our clients' Freedom of Information Act requests when the very reason we have to file these requests is because it violated our clients' privacy without permission? Why is it that when we sit down with Mohammed al-Asad and trace on a world map where he was held for eighteen months of his life, our fingers still cannot draw a definite line of where his plane went when it left Afghanistan?

Alongside these questions that we continue to ask of the U.S. government, we also ask a lot of our clients. There are the dizzying factual questions that span hundreds of hours and attempt to uncover every minute detail, from flight lengths to the air temperature on tarmacs, from their cells' color, sizes, and layout to the types of bread and rice they were served, from interpreters' accents to the shape of drinking bottles, from prison protocols to toilet types, cell camera positioning, directions walked from cells to interrogation rooms, and much more.

Beyond asking our clients to dig through these excruciating memories, we also require a lot in regard to the conditions under which our clients share these details. We ask our clients to trust us even though we cannot guarantee their safety. We ask them to communicate freely with us, even as we explain that our phones are probably wiretapped and that the notice with which we preface all calls ("For the purpose of NSA wiretapping, this is a privileged communication between attorney and client") is probably ineffectual. We ask them to relive painful experiences blow by blow after we have told them that redress is a long way off. We are prolific note-takers, documenting questions asked and answers given. We have explained why we do this and have our clients' consent, yet the lines that distinguish us from their former interrogators—particularly the female interrogators, who, similar to our team in Yemen, are described as predominantly white-skinned and young—often feel painfully thin.

Sometimes our questions are forced to track those of the American interrogators. I particularly regret that we have to ask al-Asad and Bashmilah about the subject of the Americans' interrogations and what they told them. We can, and do, brace ourselves and our clients for the inevitable testing moments, while knowing that we can never fully guard against the ever-present risk of retraumatizing them. For al-Asad and Bashmilah, the experiences associated with secret detention have turned the ordinary into the ominous. Airplane travel, something commonplace that each did before their experience in U.S. custody, now has a wildly different connotation. The lobby of the hotel in which we meet with our clients has security cameras that are meant to make guests feel safer but that immediately remind Bashmilah of the cameras in his cell that monitored his every move. In these, and countless other ways, the impact of their enforced disappearances are ongoing and will not be stemmed until the United States provides the answers to the questions that our clients (and many others like them) deserve.

J. Wells Dixon: Redacted

Before the transfer of Majid Khan to Guantánamo in 2006, he was held in secret CIA detention as a "ghost" prisoner. The United States employed various forms of torture and then sought to keep the torture secret by classifying any mention of it by Khan or his attorneys. Below appears an unclassified portion of a declaration we filed regarding Khan's torture, after the government's redactions.

The CIA Torture Program
   The CIA detention and interrogation program that Khan and the other ghost prisoners were subjected to is called ███████████
██
██
██
██
██
██
██
██
██
██
██
██
██
████████████████████████████████████

Steven M. Watt and Ben Wizner: The Not-So-Secret Man

In November 2006, our client Khaled El-Masri traveled to the United States to observe oral arguments in his lawsuit against U.S. officials and contractors. Under normal circumstances, such a visit could hardly be more ordinary. But there was nothing ordinary about El-Masri's visit. Remarkably, El-Masri may be the only victim of the Bush administration's torture and detention regime to have been present in a U.S. courtroom to witness the argument of his case.

El-Masri, a German citizen of Lebanese descent, is among the more well-known, and ill-fated, victims of the Bush administration's warped antiterrorism policies. On a December 2003 bus trip from his home in Ulm, Germany, to Skopje, Macedonia, El-Masri was detained by Macedonian border guards, who mistakenly questioned the validity of his passport, and then turned him over to local CIA officials who thought—again, mistakenly—that they had landed a big fish. He was handcuffed, blindfolded, and beaten; his clothes were sliced from his body; he was photographed, shackled, and dressed in a diaper; and he was chained to the floor of a plane and injected with drugs. He was flown to Afghanistan, a country in which he had never set foot and with which he had no ties.

El-Masri was imprisoned in a secret CIA-run dungeon outside Kabul known as the "Salt Pit," where he remained for nearly five months—even though the CIA was soon aware that it had ensnared the wrong man. (Jane Mayer reports in her indispensable book *The Dark Side* that CIA agents on the rendition flight to Afghanistan were *already* certain that El-Masri was not a terrorist but that he was nonetheless held in brutal conditions for many months.) In May 2004—long after El-Masri's wife and children had left Germany for Lebanon, convinced they'd been abandoned—he was again blindfolded, put on a plane, and flown to Albania, where he was deposited on a mountain road.

By the time the ACLU filed suit on El-Masri's behalf against former CIA director George Tenet and others in December 2005, the details of his ordeal were known throughout the world. And his story was an important one. The public debate about the Bush administration's rendition and torture policies had been dominated by discussion of what rights "terrorists" should receive. To place an inarguably innocent victim of the administration's so-called "war on terror" before the world as the public face of the CIA's rendition program might help reframe the debate, we believed, and create more room for discussion of due process and the rule of law.

We knew, though, that the Bush administration would seek to dismiss our legal challenge by asserting the "state secrets privilege." There might never be a trial, and we might have to reach the public in other ways. So we asked El-Masri—tentatively, at first—whether he would consider traveling to the United States to tell his story. Because El-Masri had never been charged with any crime—and because he was a citizen of Germany, a close ally of the United States—we believed there should be no legal obstacle to his traveling to the United States to announce the filing of the suit.

As El-Masri himself joked, his prior experience involving the United States and planes had not exactly been a good one. But he was eager to present himself to the American people, to share his experiences, and to demand answers. We booked his flight and scheduled a news conference.

U.S. authorities had other plans. El-Masri never made it further than Immigration and Customs Enforcement. He was briefly detained by U.S. agents—"I thought they might take me to Guantánamo," he later told us—and placed on a return flight to Germany. But the administration had not silenced El-Masri. At our press conference, El-Masri appeared live by satellite, and the image of him addressing a crowd of reporters was published worldwide.

Even after such a potentially traumatic experience, and even after his suit was dismissed on the dubious ground that discussion in a U.S. court of what had been discussed throughout the world would reveal "state secrets," El-Masri was willing to try again. The Fourth Circuit had scheduled oral argument on his appeal for November 2006, and this time the State Department assured us that he would be admitted into the country. And so El-Masri himself was present in a Richmond, Virginia, courthouse as we demanded that he get his day in court. Even as the government's lawyers insisted that El-Masri's allegations could not be brought forward in court without harm to national security, his simple presence in the courtroom served as powerful rebuttal.

El-Masri was an eloquent ambassador for other victims who either remained detained or, like his fellow rendition victim Maher Arar, are still perversely barred from the United States even after being released without charge. On Capitol Hill, El-Masri spoke to members of Congress and their staffs about the brutality of his ordeal and his simple demand for acknowledgment and explanation. In New York, he met with scholars, activists, and supporters, many of whom were grateful for the chance to thank him for his courage and tenacity.

There were occasional reminders that his recovery will be a lifelong process. As we exited the Virginia courthouse, a crowd of television cameras stood waiting for comment. It was a warm day, and El-Masri had his overcoat folded over his arm. We offered to hold it for him, but he clutched it tightly, as if to create a barrier between himself and the cameras. It was impossible not to remember that less than three years earlier, the CIA had stripped him of his clothes and dignity before photographing him repeatedly.

We knew that El-Masri's presence in the United States would provide invaluable benefits to our advocacy against torture and arbitrary detention. We hoped it would provide some benefits to him as well—that he would see that many Americans were distressed by the Bush administration's policies and supported his demand for justice. In an op-ed published in the *Los Angeles Times* some months after his visit, El-Masri contrasted his hostile treatment from U.S. courts with his warm treatment from the Americans he met:

> During my visit in November, many Americans offered me their personal apologies for the brutality that had been perpetrated against me in their name. I saw in their faces the true America, an America that is not held captive by fear of unknown enemies and that understands the strength and power of justice. That is the America that, I hope, one day will see me as a human being—not a state secret.

John Sifton: Spying on the CIA

In hindsight, one of the most salient features of the Bush administration's detention and interrogation operations after September 11 was their surprising shoddiness. Almost every aspect of operations involving detention overseas, from the Guantánamo Bay saga to CIA secret prisons, was marked with amateurishness, naiveté, sloppy execution, or a combination of the same.

Consider the screening of detainees during U.S.-led operations against the Taliban in Afghanistan. In early 2002, hundreds of low-level detainees with little intelligence value began to be transferred to Guantánamo, even as many hundreds of more important Taliban fighters, who probably possessed important and useful intelligence, were released. U.S. personnel on the ground evidenced an oddly unsophisticated understanding of the Taliban or al Qaeda, for instance, appearing to think that illiterate and ill-trained foot soldiers left behind by the Taliban's leadership (Afghans) would somehow know the whereabouts of Osama bin Laden and Ayman al-Zawahiri (Arabs).

Consider also the weak excuses offered for detention. Those who were detained were held on the flimsiest of grounds: unsupported assertions by Afghan or Pakistani interpreters, informants, or intelligence personnel or poorly reasoned arguments by U.S. personnel in Afghanistan ("detainee was captured in the vicinity of an ongoing military operation"). From 2003 through 2008, hundreds of detainees in Afghanistan and at Guantánamo were put through CSRTs, in which vague, unsourced, and often incorrect information was presented as evidence of detainees' status as illegal enemy fighters. Frequent mistranslations by interpreters—either during initial interrogations or at Guantánamo—had significant effects on detainees' freedom.

Then there is the issue of the "high-level" detainees with connections to the Taliban or al Qaeda. In 2004 through 2006, dozens of these detainees were dumped into the military detention system from CIA custody, where they had been severely mistreated while under interrogation. These interrogations were not coordinated with other U.S. intelligence or law enforcement efforts; whatever "confessions" or "evidence" resulted, even if they were confirmed, could now never be used in a proper court, whether here or abroad. These mistakes and others have now severely complicated efforts to prosecute detainees for any crimes they may have actually committed.

But in some respects, the most surprising slackness in U.S. detention operations after September 11 was with the failure of military and intelligence personnel to keep their operations secret. Throughout the years after 2001, journalists, human rights investigators, and lawyers managed to obtain a surprising amount of information about U.S. detention and interrogation operations.

As early as March 2002, human rights investigators and journalists in Afghanistan began interviewing Afghan detainees who had been detained at Bagram Air Base north of Kabul or the Kandahar air base. They learned a great deal about abusive interrogations. By early 2003, accounts were emerging from former Guantánamo detainees, and human rights groups were starting to piece together facts about the CIA's highly secret rendition and detention program for higher-level detainees.

The information about these abusive operations did not emerge quickly or all at once, but emerge it did—in spades. The CIA's secret rendition and detention programs are one example. The programs were highly classified and highly secret even within the CIA. Sites of detention were unknown; even the International Committee of the Red Cross, which visits Guantánamo detainees, was not allowed to see CIA detainees. Yet, by late 2005, significant information had been revealed about these operations. How did that occur?

The exposures came from many quarters. In late 2001, Masood Anwar, a Pakistani journalist with *The News* in Islamabad, spotted one of the first CIA rendition flights out of Karachi. Anwar wrote down the tail number of the plane, N379P, which later came to be known as a CIA detainee transport plane. In 2002, human rights groups and the Red Cross started asking government officials about the whereabouts of detainees such as Abu Zubaydah, who had been arrested but whose whereabouts were still unknown. It emerged that Abu Zubaydah may have been taken to a site in Thailand. Peter Finn and Rajiv Chandrasekaran of the *Washington Post* uncovered evidence of other detainees' renditions to countries in the Middle East and North Africa. In December 2002, *Post* journalist Dana Priest reported on abuses in CIA-operated detention facilities, including in Afghanistan. Human Rights Watch started investigating in Kabul.

The contributions then poured in from everywhere. Journalists pieced together major aspects of the CIA's operations: finding and interviewing CIA officers, discovering the identities of other CIA airplanes and officers' aliases, unraveling the web of front companies used to conceal the CIA's transfer of detainees, and uncovering facts behind rendition operations from Europe to Asia.

Fredrik Laurin, a journalist with Swedish television, linked the CIA plane N379P to another CIA rendition from Stockholm to Cairo and started tracing the plane's activities. The *New York Times* and *Newsweek* obtained flight records for that plane and several others. Margot Williams at the *Times* and Julie Tate at the *Post* obtained corporate data and public records revealing a larger scope of CIA aviation operations. Seth Hettena at Associated Press obtained a Freedom of Information Act response revealing the tail numbers of all civilian planes permitted to land at overseas U.S. military bases—a list that contained many of the tail numbers of the CIA's planes, both the familiar N379P and other new finds.

Meanwhile, Priest and Tate at the *Post* and investigators at Human Rights Watch, of which I was one, focused suspicions on Poland and Romania as locations at which the CIA maintained detention operations, ultimately obtaining confirmation from government sources on the location of the sites. Brian Ross of ABC News learned that after the Eastern

European sites were exposed, prisoners were reportedly flown from those sites to Morocco (although the White House kept ABC from reporting it at the time). The Council of Europe launched an investigation into detention and rendition activities in Europe and obtained additional flight records. Later, Polish prosecutors launched a criminal investigation there.

Amnesty International, Human Rights Watch, and the *Times* found and interviewed former CIA detainees. FOIA litigation by the Associated Press, the ACLU, and the Center for Constitutional Rights produced information about former CIA detainees at Guantánamo—lower-level prisoners who had been kept short-term in CIA detention. Every piece of the story seemed to come from a different source.

The CIA made a number of major mistakes. Primary among them was sloppy tradecraft: although many CIA officers often used sophisticated aliases and covers, their operations' secrecy suffered from a number of surprising weaknesses. CIA aviation operations were handled by corporate front companies, some of which were hidden by oddly thin veneers. Pilots' aliases could be cracked by searching FAA records for real persons with characteristics matching those of the aliases. CIA officers passing through Europe also broke their aliases, for instance, by calling their homes from hotels. Police records from Italy and France, revealing these calls, could later be used to confirm officers' identities.

It also proved strangely easy for investigators to confirm that personnel were CIA: public-records searches for CIA officers would typically reveal a set of overseas State Department or U.S. military base postings and post-office-box addresses in northern Virginia near Langley.

It was also foolish of the CIA to use Eastern Europe for detention facilities—they should have known that exposure of the secret would lead to investigations by European institutions. The CIA also should have known that detainees—some of whom were released or transferred to Guantánamo as early as 2004—would remember their time in CIA custody and repeat their experiences to their lawyers and to the Red Cross.

Lawyers and human rights groups worked together, sharing "intelligence" to uncover what intelligence agencies were doing with detainees. When I was working at Human Rights Watch, I managed to piece together a good deal of information about the CIA's detention facilities in Afghanistan by collecting accounts from former CIA detainees at Guantánamo, mostly from notes provided by habeas attorneys. I called and met with numerous Guantánamo attorneys to inquire whether their clients had been in CIA custody. In several instances, attorneys I reached were not aware that their clients had been in CIA custody until I explained that their clients' own accounts matched those of other CIA detainees. In one notable example, I spoke with one of the editors of this book, Mark Denbeaux, after I came to suspect his client had been in a secret site in Afghanistan—the detainee had described one of his earlier places of detention in ways that closely matched other detainees' descriptions of a CIA site in Afghanistan. The next time Mark went to Guantánamo, he confirmed this previously secret fact with the detainee.

To be fair to the CIA, it should be noted that keeping secrets isn't easy, even if one is careful. Running covert CIA operations or any secret program presents significant obstacles in maintaining secrecy. Weak links, key activities that must be out in the open, loose lips and leaks—there are many potential holes through which secrets can escape. The only hope for the secret holder is to conduct activities as covertly as possible, limit the number of confidants, and, most important, inspire in confidants a fealty to the need for secrecy.

Therein lies the lesson for the CIA. Ultimately, the true Achilles' heel for the CIA programs was that the operations were foolish and involved serious crimes: disappearances, abuse, torture, and brazen violations of domestic laws in countries that were considered allies. As a result, many CIA personnel had little reason for respecting or honoring the secrecy surrounding these operations, since the operations themselves were so questionable. Many personnel thought the programs would ultimately do damage to the United States. In the end, personnel provided information about the programs to the media and human rights groups precisely because the operations were so ill-advised. Needless to say, the disclosures were important to the investigations. Although many facts about CIA detention and interrogation operations were discovered through investigation, much information was found or confirmed through leaks from government personnel.

The illegality of the programs also served as fuel for those who were investigating the CIA, and it served as a unifying target. After all, the efforts by the cast of characters I have described—journalists, human rights investigators, lawyers—were not coordinated. Sometimes the efforts were even at cross-purposes—in fact, journalists and human rights investigators often argued and kept secrets from one another. But almost everyone involved was motivated by a desire to expose government wrongdoing, and the motivation provided great strength. Ultimately, investigations exposed the sins of clandestine programs run by the most powerful spy agency in the world. The glue that held these efforts together was not institutional or structural—it was moral. U.S. counterterrorism officials would do well to appreciate the lesson.

Aziz Huq: The Human Cost

I came to my representation of detainees in 2005 through a series of fortuities rather than any clear plan. My first work was as part of a team representing a pair of U.S. citizens detained in Iraq. For some time, we did not have contact with the clients, who were detained in the Camp Cropper facility located adjacent to Baghdad International Airport. The military, however, at some point permitted our clients to make monthly phone calls to family or counsel. Thus, unlike many early counsel for Guantánamo detainees, we had at least some contact with our detained clients.

Yet the calls were scratchy and brief. It was hard to understand much of what was said. And it was passing odd to be conversing with a Camp Cropper detainee while watching the lower-Manhattan morning traffic. One of our clients had also been beaten and electrocuted soon after his seizure. Seeing photos of his injuries, released in the course of our habeas corpus litigation, left a deeper impression.

Legal proceedings, like those in almost all the terrorism-related detention cases, snagged on threshold procedural issues, particularly the jurisdiction of the federal courts to hear the suit, thanks to the government's obdurate strategy of resistance to any meaningful judicial inquiry. For almost three years, we litigated an obscure cluster of legal questions surrounding a terse 1949 Supreme Court opinion, *Hirota v. MacArthur*. The government relied on this opinion to claim that any U.S. detention operation with a multinational component could claim immunity from federal court oversight. It sought, in other words, a blank check from judicial review. The issue went all the way to the Supreme Court, where we won the battle but lost the war. Unanimously, the Court rejected the government's jurisdictional argument but repudiated, with narrow exceptions, our arguments that standing laws and treaties prohibited the government from holding our clients and then transferring them to far-from-fair criminal trial in Iraqi tribunals.

It is, of course, impossible to maintain emotional fever pitch across the span of three years. Family, friends, the mundane clutter of everyday life intervene. Yet some lawyers for detainees, I noticed, maintained rigorous and careful emotional engagement throughout. This was especially true for some lawyers for Guantánamo detainees who traveled frequently to meet their clients and whose clarity of commitment I came to admire.

But other lawyers, including myself, approached their detention cases with professionalism and some detachment. Physical distance and the practical difficulty of contacting or establishing human connections with detainee clients impeded close connections. And the heavily procedural nature of the litigation, with the briefing and arguments hinging on abstruse procedural and constitutional issues, meant that the litigation itself drew attention away from human issues toward legal arcana.

Although professional detachment is at least defensible as the appropriate way of managing lawyer-client relationships, public debate about Guantánamo and other detention sites has also been removed from the stories of the people who are in fact detained. Some advocates for the detainees in the not-for-profit community have used this detachment to their short-term advantage, building a consensus for closing Guantánamo that is not grounded in the stark human facts of the detentions. Rather, they have focused on how detention operations harm the United States' foreign relations and standing in the world. Although this approach has yielded important short-term success, it is far from clear that the ensuing consensus will uniformly benefit the detainees at Guantánamo and elsewhere in the end.

Despite a series of compelling stories about the treatment and fate of detainees that have appeared in the media, including the *New York Times* and the *Washington Post,* public debate around Guantánamo has not coalesced around the idea that the Cuban prison facility must be closed because of the moral tragedy of detaining innocents en masse or the continuing fact of prolonged illegal detentions. Even as the population of the Cuban detention facility dwindles, few commentators or journalists seriously question the Bush administration's claim that the remaining detainees are "dangerous" in some legally undefined way, despite the fact that analogous aspersions on the detainee population have serially collapsed in the past.

Rather, advocacy about detention policy has focused on the harm to "us" and has not lingered over the harm to "them." In advocating against Bush-era detention policies, the organization for which I worked and many organizations like it trained rhetorical fire on the symbolic cost of Guantánamo to what Harvard scholar Joseph Nye has called the United States' "soft power": its ability to use persuasion and shared norms, embodied in international law and institutions, to secure strategic aims in the geopolitical sphere that would be too costly to obtain by force alone. For example, one of the most high-profile advocacy campaigns around detention policy—albeit one focused primarily on torture rather than detention—has been Human Rights First's organizing of former generals and other retired military officers. Human Rights First's campaign was but the most extreme example of a trend of using messengers and messages framed less around human rights and hinging more on an appeal to enlightened self-interest. Key institutional funders supporting rights advocates in this field echoed and reinforced this strategy.

The resulting "soft power" arguments aligned human rights with a growing consensus in the D.C.-based foreign policy establishment decrying the strategic poverty of President Bush's foreign relations. Foreign-policy experts argued that the Bush approach rested on the plainly false assumption that the United States could routinely scare or bully other countries into agreeing to its geopolitical goals and that military force measured influence. In joining with these critics of Bush, the human rights movement assumed that political change flowed from building coalitions around perceived shared interests, rather than investing in the transformation of perceptions themselves.

The strategy worked in an immediate sense. During the 2008 presidential election campaign, both major-party candidates agreed about the need to close Guantánamo but also agreed about the reason for their commitment: deterioration of the United States' image in the world. The human cost to detainees figured only incidentally in their manifest calculus. In signing executive orders in January 2009 directing the end to sanctioned torture and aiming toward Guantánamo's shuttering, President Obama brought Human Rights First's coterie of generals to the White House for a photo opportunity to give him political cover.

Yet arguments abstracted from the felt realities of detention, and hinged on shared, non-rights-based zones of interest, quickly find limits. Although human rights advocates might agree with the foreign policy establishment on the stain of Guantánamo, their alliance unravels when it comes to the harder questions of how to handle those detainees. In particular, when it comes to proposals to create a new modality of indefinite detention somewhere else (call it Guantánamo 2.0) or to tinker with the federal courts by fashioning from whole cloth a set of new "national security courts," few voices in the public sphere decry the very notion of continuing to imprison people who have been torn from their lives, locked in cages, and brutalized for years on end.

The absence of tangible human stories and detail also opened a space for advocates for Guantánamo 2.0. Because those giving voice to the detainees have been far too few and far between, such advocates for renewing Guantánamo were able to leverage the lingering (false) impression that detainees are necessarily murderous and untrustworthy, "terrorists" and not human beings. Hence, Brookings Institute scholar Benjamin Wittes could advocate continued indefinite detention for many Guantánamo detainees based in part on his "instinct" about the detainees and his feeling that their stories "just ring false." In light of the exhaustive and increasingly large amount of powerful evidence of injustice, unnecessary suffering, and governmental arrogance or indifference, the ease with which Wittes and others disregard the human facts of detainees is breathtaking. But perhaps that ease is also the fault of lawyers such as me, who have not given adequate public voice to the experience of their clients, and who have acquiesced to a public strategy of alliance building over the direct appeal to compassion.

Moreover, the foreign-relations framing of detention advocacy drove inexorably toward a concentrated focus on detention in Guantánamo to the exclusion of detention operations in Iraq and Afghanistan. In the court hearings that I attended and participated in around my Iraq representation, one could not but be aware of the clammy pressure imposed by continuing military operations in Iraq. Absent a public consensus around the "harm" of detention operations, such as the one that developed around Guantánamo, the 20,000-plus detentions in Iraq, however brutal and unjust they might have been, simply aroused no outrage comparable to that manifested over the Cuban base. The same was true of Bagram Air Base in Afghanistan. To be fair, litigation strategy aimed at securing jurisdiction over Guantánamo before raising the harder questions posed by farther shores reinforced this tendency. But at bottom, public condemnation of Bush's detention policies hinged less on the human stuff behind those detentions than on theories about optimal deployment of U.S. influence on the geopolitical stage—a choice of foundations that decisively set limits to what could be done.

Short-term advocacy success is not always consistent with longer-term substantive goals. What foundations and prominent donors want to fund won't always (or even usually) transform public debate. As of this writing, at the dawn of the Obama administration, with a slew of executive orders about Guantánamo still sinking in, it is far from clear how well the trade-offs have been managed by those who care about detention issues.

From this perspective, it is necessary to question strategic choices, even if answers are few on the ground. Would the advocacy around detention issues, or even the results in specific cases, have been different if lawyers had grappled earlier and more publicly with the human costs of detention policy? More intimately, should I have identified and repudiated my own professional detachment earlier? Or would the differences in race, ethnicity, and religion that separate the Guantánamo detainees from the mass of the American public have rendered such a strategy nugatory and ineffective from its inception? Whether and how I and others could have done things differently will always remain a question.

Coda

Anant Raut: Paradise

It was the part of the afternoon that pops the thermometers in Guantánamo from "Sweltering" to "Broiling," yet that hardly seemed to faze the female soldier jogging past our van.

"Around here, we call it the '2-9-2,'" yelled our escort from the front, struggling to be heard over the noise of the van willing itself up the steep road to the prison camps.

"What's that?"

"Girls who are 2s on the mainland are 9s here but go back home and are 2s again."

"Fascinating." Scrub and cacti sloped down in all directions. Off in the distance, the blades of three wind turbines spun lazily, cranking out some small fraction of the base's energy needs.

"Yeah, me and a couple of buddies were thinking of printing up T-shirts that said, 'You're One Plane Flight Away From Being Ugly Again.'" He snickered and slapped the steering wheel.

"I can't think of any possible downside to that plan."

A stern look from the more senior soldier sitting behind him sobered him quickly, but laughed he had, because when you're barely twenty, twenty-one, that kind of stuff is funny. These are the boys we send to fight and die for our causes.

"You know, we don't hate all of the guards here," Abdullah had told me during our last visit.

I leaned forward in my green plastic lawn chair toward the card table that separated us in the interview trailer. "You don't?"

He shook his head. "The ones that treat us with respect, we treat with respect. They're just doing a job. We understand that."

• • •

With a grateful screech, our van pulled over to the side of the road. They were moving prisoners around in Camp Echo and needed us to stand down for about fifteen minutes.

Our translator tapped me and my colleague on the arm and gestured to a rustle of brown by the side of the road.

"Hey look," said our more senior escort. "It's Stubby."

An iguana darted out onto the roadway, stared down the van, and then walked cockily over to the other side. Where his tail should have been dragging was a stump followed by mystery and folklore. Hence the name.

I rocked back and forth on my heels, trying to generate a breeze, as the guards at the camp entrance went through my bag. I nodded at a guard standing cleverly in the shade; she nodded politely back.

"How's it going?" I called out.

"Fine, sir."

"How long you been in Paradise?"

"Too long, sir."

"Watch the Super Bowl last night?"

"I don't care for football, sir."

A glance at the Velcro patch where her name should have been, and I remembered that the guards were expressly instructed not to reveal any personal information, not to the prisoners, not even to their lawyers. Idly, I wondered how far I could take it. ("Is that the ocean?" "I can neither confirm nor deny that sir." "Does November come before December?" "Never cared much for calendars, sir." "Do the planets move in elliptical orbits?" "I don't subscribe to Keplerian motion, sir.")

"Who are you here to see?" asked the guard with the clipboard. You knew a guard was important if he was carrying a clipboard.

"Abdullah al-Anazi."

The guard looked up at me with exasperation. I knew what was coming next; I provoked it every time.

"We only go by numbers around here."

"514."

The guard began looking down his sheet once more.

"The double amputee."

•   •   •

"Yeah, Stubby's an ornery one all right!" our driver chortled.

"Look at the way he looks at you. Look at him," said the second escort, watching Stubby saunter nonchalantly across the road. "He ain't afraid of nobody."

"This one's real peaceful," the guard told us as he unlocked the door. "You won't have any problems with this one."

"Our paralegal Nicole was down at the beach one time, and one of them came right up to her and ate all of her grapes," said my colleague.

"They love sugar," said the older escort. "They can smell it. One time, I had a butterscotch in my mouth. Stubby chased me clear cross a parking lot for it."

"Can you still walk on those?"

Abdullah had hiked up the khaki legs of his prison uniform. His prosthetic legs were held together with duct tape and were showing more signs of cracking. They were the same broken pair he'd had for three years. They had never been fitted properly.

When he'd asked, he was told he could get new ones "through [his] interrogators."

"Not all the time," he said. "But I can manage. Thank Allah, they keep me in a ground-floor cell."

"We submitted the affidavit from Dr. Nicholl," I told him. After I had described to a U.K. physician the condition of Abdullah's prosthetics and confinement, he had written an extensive affidavit on his own volition, laying out the basic health and exercise requirements for new amputees, none of which were being provided to Abdullah. "Predictably, there's been no response."

Abdullah unfastened one of his prosthetics so that I could get a better look. New cracks were beginning to form around the outer lip. I was pulling it closer to my face when I felt it go rigid in my hand. I looked down. The leg shackle fastened around the plastic ankle was pulled taut.

I handed Abdullah his leg back so that he could reshackle himself. "The DOD says that you all are getting two hours of exercise a day. Is that right?"

He laughed. "It's more like two two-hour blocks every three days. And you never know when you'll get it. Sometimes they'll wake you up in the middle of the night to go exercise." He continued: "It's basically a wire mesh cage. You can walk back and forth inside of it. If you say anything to any of the guards along the way, they'll take you back to your cell. If you touch any of the wire mesh walls while you're inside the cage, they'll take you back to your cell."

"So what do you do?"

"You walk back and forth."

"For two hours?! You can't do anything else?"

"Sometimes there's a ball."

"Oh, that's nice."

"But the ball can't touch any of the wire mesh walls, or—"

"—they'll take you back to your cell. Got it. What are you supposed to do with the ball, then?"

"Look at it, I suppose?"

"So what did you do?" asked our translator.

"I gave him the butterscotch, and he went away," responded our escort. "I had to."

"You can't touch these bastards," said our driver, shaking his head in disgust. "They're a protected species." Iguanas are protected by the Fish and Wildlife Service under the Endangered Species Act, which is rigorously enforced on the base. Violations can result in criminal penalties of up to $50,000 or imprisonment for one year. "Now they're freakin' everywhere."

"Even if you accidentally run over one of them, it's still a $10,000 fine," added our driver.

We looked at the rock where Stubby was sitting. He was ugly and brown, his scales the color of aged parchment, stained with asymmetric dark blots. A long, forked tongue occasionally slithered in and out. He didn't make a sound, hardly even moved but for the rhythmic swelling of his torso, but his beady little black eyes fixed us with a look of pure malice.

"But what if you just ran over one in the middle of the night?" asked our translator. "Who's going to know?"

"No sir," countered our driver. "If you failed to report it, you'd be in even bigger trouble."

"Oh, c'mon," cajoled our translator. "How's anyone ever going to find out?"

The older soldier dismissed that thought with a violent shake of his head. "The law's the law. They take that stuff pretty seriously around here."

•   •   •

"I mean—well, in a nutshell, they're saying the new law says that you have no rights in the courts, not even the right to argue that you don't deserve to be here. And we're arguing that's unconstitutional, and so we're right back to where we were in 2004." I flipped in frustration through the stack of cases in my hand, searching for something more intelligent to say.

Overhead, the air-conditioning unit in our interview trailer droned soporifically. A cockroach scurried by my foot.

Abdullah was the first to break the silence. "Do you want to hear a joke?"

I looked up. "Sure."

"This one is very popular among the brothers right now. There's a contest, okay, between Israel, England, and the United States, to see who can go into the jungle and bring back a lion the fastest.

"England goes first. Two hours later, they come out with a lion. Israel goes next, and one hour later, they come out with a lion.

"Then it's the United States' turn. They go into the jungle. One hour passes. Two hours pass. Three hours pass. Night is beginning to fall, and the judges are getting worried. So they go in after them to find out what happened.

"Fifty meters in, they find the Americans. Two of them are holding a donkey, and the third one is beating it until it confesses that it's a lion."

"Look, I feel bad for some these guys. I really do," said the staff judge advocate, oblivious to my previous ten minutes of facts and figures. It was the previous day, eating lunch at one of the tables outside the Naval Exchange, where my colleague and I had chanced into a conversation with him as he stopped to say hello to our escort. "The guys who have been cleared to leave but whose countries won't take them back I feel bad for. But I have no sympathy for the rest of these guys. If they hadn't done something wrong, they wouldn't be here."

Abdullah was caught fighting coalition forces in the Tora Bora mountains, injured during a bombing raid, and subsequently shipped to Guantánamo. At least, that's what the government says he did, when it was forced to file some sort of allegations with our judge.

But the curious thing is, they don't have any corroborating evidence. Not one iota. All they have is the word of the warlords who picked him up off a hospital bed as he was recovering from the first of two amputations engendered while seeking refuge in a neighboring country at the wrong time, the same warlords whom the United States paid $5,000 and never saw again.

In fact, the main reason Abdullah is still there is a psychological "evaluation" by someone of unspecified qualifications, who wrote that the loss of his legs makes Abdullah an ideal candidate for suicide-bombing recruitment.

Which presents an interesting end game. Because either the United States intends to hold Abdullah for the remainder of his natural life for falling victim to a U.S. bomb, or they're waiting for his legs to grow back.

"Well," I said as we gathered our papers and collected our trash, "I'll file another motion with the magistrate judge, and follow up with the DOJ about why you're not getting new prosthetics—"

Abdullah cut me off with a wave of his hand, as if to say, "Fine. Whatever makes you feel better."

We exchanged farewells in Arabic, and then I and knocked on the door. It opened just enough for me to make out the face of the shade-favoring female soldier.

"Prisoner transfer," she said in clipped tones. "You'll have to hang out here for ten minutes." She then pulled the door closed tightly. A moment later, we heard the bolt slide back into place.

Well, this is terribly awkward, I thought. We had finished saying our goodbyes, yet there we all were again. Abdullah waved the translator over and whispered something in his ear; our translator laughed.

"What did he say?"

"He wants to know, are you being held here without charges too?"

Under intense pressure from habeas attorneys, Guantánamo officials did create a (short-lived) camp for those prisoners who they realized were not combatants but had simply been in the wrong place at the wrong time. These prisoners were given more freedoms, too; they could walk around their fenced-in yard, stare out at the ocean, and even watch movies. Rather than admit outright error, the officials kept the camp a little ways off from the other camps. That way, the inhabitants still looked like prisoners, but prisoners with considerably more privileges.

The name of the camp?

Iguana.

Timeline: Guantánamo and the "War on Terror"

2001

SEPTEMBER 11, 2001: The terrorist organization al Qaeda hijacks four commercial passenger airplanes and intentionally crashes them into targets in the United States, killing more than 3,000 people.

SEPTEMBER 14, 2001: Congress passes the Authorization for Use of Military Force. The resolution states that "the President is authorized to use all necessary and appropriate force against those nations, organizations, or persons he determines planned, authorized, committed, or aided the terrorist attacks that occurred on September, 11, 2001, or harbored such organizations or persons."

OCTOBER 7, 2001: Operation Enduring Freedom commences in Afghanistan.

NOVEMBER 13, 2001: President Bush issues an order establishing the first military commissions since World War II. The order fails to guarantee due process protections or judicial review.

DECEMBER 27, 2001: Defense Secretary Donald Rumsfeld announces that Taliban and al Qaeda suspects captured abroad will be relocated to the Guantánamo Bay Naval Base. The following day, a secret memorandum by the Justice Department's Office of Legal Counsel advises that U.S. courts have no jurisdiction to review the detention and treatment of foreign prisoners held at Guantánamo.

2002

JANUARY 11, 2002: Guantánamo receives its first twenty detainees. The detainees are housed in open-air cages at Camp X-Ray.

JANUARY 27, 2002: Vice President Cheney calls the detainees at Guantánamo "the worst of a very bad lot."

FEBRUARY 7, 2002: The White House announces that all Taliban and al Qaeda detainees are "unlawful combatants" and therefore do not qualify for any protections under the Geneva Conventions.

FEBRUARY 19, 2002: The first habeas corpus petition on behalf of a Guantánamo detainee is filed in federal court in Washington, D.C.

FEBRUARY 27, 2002: Approximately two-thirds of the detainees at Guantánamo go on a hunger strike to protest their mistreatment.

APRIL 28, 2002: Camp X-Ray is closed and replaced by Camp Delta, a more permanent detention facility. There are more than 300 detainees at Camp Delta.

MAY 8, 2002: Jose Padilla is arrested by the FBI at Chicago's O'Hare Airport. One month later, President Bush designates Padilla, an American citizen, an "enemy combatant" and transfers him to the U.S. Navy brig in South Carolina, where he is held incommunicado and without charges.

AUGUST 1, 2002: John Yoo and Jay S. Bybee of the Justice Department's Office of Legal Counsel author a memo finding that interrogation techniques do not constitute torture unless they result in "death, organ failure, or serious impairment of bodily functions." The memo also states that, as commander in chief, the president can legally authorize torture.

SEPTEMBER 2002: The CIA produces an internal report stating that many detainees held at Guantánamo are either low-level recruits of the Taliban or innocent persons captured in the fog of war.

DECEMBER 2002: Defense Secretary Rumsfeld approves a memo calling for the use of harsh interrogation techniques and military trainers travel to Guantánamo to provide instruction in the use of those techniques.

2003

MARCH 11, 2003: A federal appeals court rules that Guantánamo detainees have no right to seek habeas corpus relief in federal courts.

MARCH 19, 2003: The U.S. invasion of Iraq commences.

MAY 1, 2003: President Bush delivers the "Mission Accomplished" speech in a military flight-suit uniform aboard the USS *Abraham Lincoln*.

MAY 9, 2003: Guantánamo reaches its peak population of 680. In total, approximately 770 prisoners will be held at Guantánamo.

JUNE 23, 2003: President Bush declares Ali Saleh Kalah al-Marri an "enemy combatant." Al-Marri, a legal resident, had been in federal custody since December 2001 pending trial on criminal charges. He is the second person in the United States declared an "enemy combatant" and is transferred to the South Carolina Navy brig.

JULY 3, 2003: President Bush designates six individuals eligible for trial before military commissions.

NOVEMBER 10, 2003: The Supreme Court agrees to hear the first Guantánamo detainee case.

NOVEMBER 25, 2003: Lord Johan Steyn, one of England's top jurists, condemns Guantánamo as "a monstrous failure of justice" and "a legal black hole."

DECEMBER 3, 2003: David Hicks becomes the first Guantánamo detainee to be given a lawyer when he is assigned military counsel in his military commission proceeding.

2004

APRIL 28, 2004: The Supreme Court hears oral argument in the case of alleged "enemy combatant" Yaser Hamdi, an American citizen, who was being detained without a hearing or access to a lawyer. In response to questioning by one of the Justices, the U.S. Solicitor General assures the Court that the United States does not torture prisoners. That same evening, CBS's *60 Minutes II* breaks the Abu Ghraib prison abuse story. Photographs of the mistreatment of detainees by U.S. forces spread rapidly across the world.

MAY 11, 2004: The United States is reportedly detaining more than 9,000 prisoners in overseas facilities.

JUNE 28, 2004: The Supreme Court issues rulings in *Rasul v. Bush* and *Hamdi v. Rumsfeld*. *Rasul* holds that federal courts have jurisdiction to hear habeas corpus petitions filed on behalf of Guantánamo detainees. *Hamdi* holds that U.S. citizens must receive a meaningful opportunity to challenge the basis for their detention under the Constitution's guarantee of due process.

JULY 7, 2004: Deputy Secretary of Defense Paul Wolfowitz issues an order establishing the Combatant Status Review Tribunal (CSRT) at Guantánamo. Purportedly created to determine whether detainees are "enemy combatants," the CSRT is designed to subvert habeas corpus review through sham proceedings.

AUGUST 24, 2004: First military commission at Guantánamo begins.

AUGUST 31, 2004: Gitanjali Gutierrez becomes the first civilian lawyer to meet with a Guantánamo detainee.

OCTOBER 11, 2004: The Bush administration returns Yaser Hamdi to Saudi Arabia rather than try to defend his detention before a federal judge.

NOVEMBER 8, 2004: Federal District Judge James Robertson declares in *Hamdan v. Rumsfeld* the Guantánamo military commissions invalid and enjoins the Pentagon from proceeding with the trial against Yemini citizen Salim Hamdan.

DECEMBER 1, 2004: A Department of Justice attorney tells District Judge Joyce Hens Green that the president can detain as an "enemy combatant" even a "little old lady in Switzerland" who sends a check to an orphanage in Afghanistan if, unbeknownst to her, some of her donation is passed to al Qaeda terrorists.

2005

JANUARY 25, 2005: Guantánamo detainee Mamdouh Habib is returned to his home country (Australia) when his attorneys were on the verge of presenting evidence in court of his illegal rendition and torture.

JANUARY 31, 2005: Judge Green rules that the CSRT violates due process.

FEBRUARY 14, 2005: Alberto Gonzales replaces John Ashcroft as the U.S. attorney general.

MARCH 29, 2005: The CSRT process is completed. Almost ninety-five percent of the detainees are determined to be "enemy combatants." Even the small percentage of detainees who are declared "no longer enemy combatants" remain imprisoned at Guantánamo.

MAY 2005: Riots break out at Guantánamo in response to intentional abuse of the Quran.

JUNE 24, 2005: Vice President Cheney's jet is used to fly a group of retired military analysts to Guantánamo for public relations tours of the base.

JULY 15, 2005: The D.C. Circuit Court of Appeals overturns Judge Robertson's ruling in *Hamdan*.

SEPTEMBER 2005: A hunger strike at Guantánamo protesting mistreatment and denial of due process grows to almost 200 detainees.

NOVEMBER 2005: There are 14,500 detainees held in overseas prisons by the United States. The Department of Defense has detained more than 80,000 persons in total.

NOVEMBER 2, 2005: The *Washington Post* reports that the CIA has been secretly detaining and interrogating alleged al Qaeda suspects at a Soviet-era compound in Eastern Europe.

NOVEMBER 22, 2005: The Bush administration announces criminal charges against Jose Padilla and seeks his return to civilian custody after three and a half years of military detention and just two days before it must defend that detention before the Supreme Court.

DECEMBER 30, 2005: President Bush signs the Detainee Treatment Act (DTA), which prohibits any U.S. personnel from engaging in "cruel, inhuman and degrading treatment." The DTA, however, also eliminates habeas corpus for detainees at Guantánamo.

2006

FEBRUARY 15, 2006: The United Nations recommends closure of Guantánamo.

APRIL 19, 2006: The Defense Department releases the names of 558 people who have been held at some point at Guantánamo.

MAY 10, 2006: Attorney General of England and Wales, Lord Peter Goldsmith, says that Guantánamo's existence "remains unacceptable."

JUNE 10, 2006: Three Guantánamo prisoners commit suicide.

JUNE 30, 2006: The Supreme Court issues *Hamdan v. Rumsfeld*, invalidating the military commissions at Guantánamo and finding that no prisoner is without protection under the Geneva Conventions. The Court also rejects the government's argument that the DTA eliminated review over pending habeas corpus cases.

SEPTEMBER 6, 2006: President Bush confirms on national television that the CIA has been operating a network of secret prisons, or "black sites," where so-called enhanced interrogation techniques have been used. Bush also announces that fourteen so-called high-value detainees—all of whom were reportedly tortured—would be transferred to Guantánamo.

SEPTEMBER 26, 2006: The International Committee for the Red Cross sends a delegation to Guantánamo to meet with the fourteen newly transferred detainees.

OCTOBER 17, 2006: President Bush signs the Military Commissions Act of 2006 (MCA), re-creating military commissions at Guantánamo. The MCA also eliminates habeas corpus not only for Guantánamo detainees but also for other foreign nationals held elsewhere as "enemy combatants."

NOVEMBER 17, 2006: The Pentagon announces a plan to build a new compound at Guantánamo to hold military commission trials.

2007

FEBRUARY 20, 2007: The D.C. Circuit Court of Appeals rejects a legal challenge to the MCA brought by Guantánamo detainees.

MARCH 26, 2007: David Hicks pleads guilty to one charge of providing material support for terrorism in the first military commission trial, which is widely condemned as a circus and a sham. Hicks returns to Australia the following month to serve the remaining nine months of a suspended seven-year sentence.

JUNE 10, 2007: Former secretary of state Colin Powell calls for the immediate closure of the Guantánamo detention center.

JUNE 29, 2007: The Supreme Court reverses its initial decision and grants review over the Guantánamo detainees' challenge to the MCA.

NOVEMBER 8, 2007: Michael Mukasey is confirmed as attorney general, replacing Alberto Gonzales. During his confirmation hearings, Mukasey refuses to state whether waterboarding is torture.

2008

FEBRUARY 13, 2008: The Senate passes legislation banning waterboarding and several other interrogation methods used by the CIA. President Bush vetoes the legislation.

JUNE 12, 2008: The Supreme Court issues *Boumediene v. Bush*, striking down the court-stripping provisions of the MCA and confirming that Guantánamo detainees have a constitutional right to habeas corpus. The Court also rejects the government's argument that the executive can evade habeas corpus simply by holding prisoners outside the United States.

AUGUST 6, 2008: Salim Hamdan is convicted by a military commission and sentenced by a military jury to five and a half years of imprisonment; he is credited with five years toward service of the sentence. In November 2008, Hamdan is transferred to Yemen to serve out the remainder of his sentence. He is released on January 8, 2009.

OCTOBER 7, 2008: Federal District Judge Ricardo M. Urbina orders the immediate release of seventeen Chinese Muslim Uighurs held at Guantánamo. The seventeen men had been detained since 2002 but were since cleared of all charges. Judge Urbina's order suggests that the detainees should be released to the U.S. mainland.

NOVEMBER 20, 2008: District Judge Richard J. Leon orders the release of five out of six Guantánamo detainees after the first habeas corpus hearing since prisoners were brought to Guantánamo in January 2002.

2009

JANUARY 20, 2009: Barack Hussein Obama is inaugurated as the forty-fourth president of the United States.

JANUARY 21, 2009: On President Obama's first day in office, he signs an order to close Guantánamo within a year. He also orders the closure of any remaining CIA prisons and requires the CIA to follow the interrogation methods contained in the Army Field Manual in order to prevent torture and other abuse.

FEBRUARY 18, 2009: The D.C. Circuit Court of Appeals overturns Judge Urbina's order to release the seventeen Chinese Muslim Uighurs held at Guantánamo.

FEBRUARY 27, 2009: The government announces criminal charges against Ali al-Marri and seeks his return to civilian custody after more than five and a half years of military detention and less than two months before the U.S. Supreme Court is scheduled to hear arguments in his case.

MARCH 15, 2009: According to an article published by journalist Mark Danner, an internal 2006 report by the International Committee of the Red Cross concluded that the CIA's program of "enhanced interrogation techniques," which was applied to the fourteen "high value detainees" in the agency's custody prior to their transfer to Guantánamo, amounted to torture.

APRIL 16, 2009: The Justice Department releases detailed memos describing brutal interrogation methods employed by the CIA. The methods were approved starting in 2002 and were used as late as 2005 against detainees held in CIA secret prisons.

APRIL 19, 2009: The *New York Times* reports, based on the recently released CIA interrogation memos, that two detainees, Abu Zubaydah and Khalid Sheikh Mohammed, were waterboarded 266 times.

APRIL 28, 2009: The Ninth Circuit Court of Appeals rejects the government's sweeping use of the "state secrets privilege" and refuses to dismiss a civil suit by five victims of the CIA's extraordinary rendition and torture program.

MAY 14, 2009: The Obama administration announcies that it will restart Bush-era military commissions to try some Guantánamo detainees.

JUNE 23, 2009: District Judge Ricardo J. Leon orders the release of Guantánamo detainee Abdul Rahim Abdul Razak al-Janko, finding that the government's legal rationale for detaining him "defies common sense." With this decision, the government had lost 26 of the 31 habeas hearings that had taken place since *Boumediene.*

Prepared by ADAM DEUTSCH

Contributors

STEPHEN E. ABRAHAM is an associate of Fink & Abraham LLP in Newport Beach, California.

MUNEER I. AHMAD is a clinical professor of law at Yale Law School.

BAHER AZMY is a professor of law at Seton Hall University School of Law in Newark, New Jersey.

JESSICA BAEN has worked as a paralegal with the Guantánamo Global Justice Initiative at the Center for Constitutional Rights since 2006.

SCOTT BARKER is a 1970 Air Force Academy graduate who served on active duty for eight years before resigning his commission to pursue a career as a trial lawyer in Denver, Colorado.

AMAL BOUHABIB was a member of the International Justice Clinic at Fordham Law School in New York City.

LT. COL. YVONNE R. BRADLEY, a twenty-plus-year member of the U.S. Air Force and U.S. Air Force Reserve, was appointed in November 2005 as military defense counsel to represent Binyam Mohamed in the military commissions at Guantánamo.

BRIGADIER GENERAL DAVID BRAHMS, USMC (RET.) has a private practice in Carlsbad, California.

PATRICIA A. BRONTE practices civil rights law at Stowell & Friedman, Ltd. in Chicago. She is a former partner of Jenner & Block LLP.

CHARLES H. CARPENTER is a partner at Pepper Hamilton LLP in Washington, D.C.

ANNE CASTLE has practiced law in Colorado for twenty-seven years, specializing in water law, and is involved in several organizations whose goal is to provide legal assistance to people who cannot afford to pay.

JOHN A. CHANDLER is a partner at King & Spalding LLP.

CHRISTOPHER CHANG is a Guantánamo Team Investigator at the U.K.-based legal action charity Reprieve.

CHRISTI CHARPENTIER works in the Federal Community Defender Office for the Eastern District of Pennsylvania.

GEORGE M. CLARKE III is a partner with Miller & Chevalier chartered in Washington, D.C.

JERRY COHEN is a partner at Burns & Levinson LLP in Boston, Massachusetts.

JOSHUA COLANGELO-BRYAN is a senior attorney at Dorsey & Whitney in New York City.

JOHN CONNOLLY is a member of Murphy & Shaffer LLC, a small law firm in Baltimore, Maryland.

BRANT S. COPELAND is the pastor of First Presbyterian Church, Tallahassee, Florida.

CORI CRIDER is a staff attorney for Reprieve.

MAYA D. CURTIS currently manages her own immigration law firm, Maya Curtis Law LLC, and represented over fifteen prisoners in Guantánamo while working for Jenner & Block.

DAVID J. CYNAMON is a partner in the Washington, D.C., office of Pillsbury Winthrop Shaw Pittman LLP.

GEORGE DALY is a retired civil rights lawyer in Charlotte, North Carolina.

MATTHEW DARBY is currently practicing criminal law in Houston, Texas.

JEFFREY DAVIS has a private practice in Charlotte, North Carolina.

JOSHUA W. DENBEAUX is a partner at the firm of Denbeaux & Denbeaux.

MARK P. DENBEAUX is a professor of law at Seton Hall Law School and director of the Center for Policy and Research. He is also of counsel to the firm Denbeaux & Denbeaux.

ADAM DEUTSCH is a research fellow with Seton Hall Law School's Center for Policy and Research.

REBECCA DICK formerly in private practice, is now a staff attorney at the Federal Trade Commission. The views she expresses are her own and do not reflect the views of the FTC or any individual Commissioner.

J. WELLS DIXON is a senior staff attorney at the Center for Constitutional Rights in New York.

BERNHARD DOCKE is currently a partner at Dr. Heinrich Hannover & Partner, Bremen, Germany.

JOSHUA L. DRATEL is an attorney and founder of Joshua L. Dratel PC in New York City.

BUZ EISENBERG is of counsel to Weinberg & Garber.

MARC D. FALKOFF is a professor at Northern Illinois University College of Law in DeKalb, Illinois.

MARK C. FLEMING is a partner at WilmerHale in Boston, Massachusetts.

MURRAY FOGLER is a trial lawyer and partner with Beck, Redden & Secrest in Houston, Texas.

TINA MONSHIPOUR FOSTER is the Executive Director of the International Justice Network.

DAVID FRAKT is a lawyer for the Air Force Reserve and a professor at Western State University College of Law in Fullerton, California.

ERIC M. FREEDMAN is the Maurice A. Deane Distinguished Professor of Constitutional Law at Hofstra Law School.

AGNIESZKA FRYSZMAN is a partner at Cohen Milstein Sellers & Toll; she represents four men who have been detained by the United States at Guantánamo Bay.

JOHN J. GIBBONS is the founder of the John J. Gibbons Fellowship in Public Interest and Constitutional Law at Gibbons PC in Newark, New Jersey, and a director at the firm. He is the former chief judge of the U.S. Court of Appeals for the Third Circuit.

ELIZABETH GILSON is a sole practitioner in New Haven, Connecticut, concentrating on environmental law.

H. CANDACE GORMAN is a solo-practitioner in Chicago, Illinois, who concentrates in civil rights and human rights law.

ELDON V.C. GREENBERG is a partner at Garvey Schubert Barer in Washington, D.C.

RICHARD GRIGG is a partner at Spivey & Grigg in Austin, Texas.

DAVID GROSSMAN is a staff attorney with the ABA Death Penalty Representation Project.

JONATHAN HAFETZ is an attorney with the National Security Project of the American Civil Liberties Union and has litigated numerous post-9/11 detention cases.

MASUD HASNAIN is an Arabic interpreter and translator for lawyers at Guantánamo and lives in Virginia.

SARAH HAVENS is an associate at Allen & Overy in New York City.

MELISSA HOFFER is Vice President of the Conservation Law Foundation. She represented Guantánamo detainees while a junior partner at WilmerHale.

JOHN ROBERT HOLLAND and ANNA CAYTON HOLLAND-EDWARDS are a father and daughter practicing together. Erica Grossman is also a member of our firm and involved in our Guantánamo cases.

JONATHAN HOROWITZ is Research Director of One World Research in New York City.

SUSAN HU is a law student at New York University School of Law. She worked at the Center for Constitutional Rights as a paralegal on the Guantánamo Global Justice Initiative from 2006–2008.

JAYNE C. HUCKERBY is Research Director of the Center for Human Rights and Global Justice and Adjunct Assistant Professor of Clinical Law at New York University Law School.

GAILLARD T. HUNT has a private practice in Silver Spring, Maryland.

AZIZ HUQ is an assistant professor of law at the University of Chicago Law School.

KRISTINE A. HUSKEY is a clinical professor and co-director of the National Security Clinic at the University of Texas School of Law.

GARY A. ISAAC is Counsel at the Chicago office of Mayer Brown.

GEREMY KAMENS is First Assistant Federal Public Defender for the Eastern District of Virginia.

RAMZI KASSEM is Lecturer in Law at Yale Law School.

JAN K. KITCHEL is a partner at Schwabe, Williamson & Wyatt in Portland, Oregon.

DENNY LEBOEUF is the director of the John Adams Project of the American Civil Liberties Union providing attorneys and resources in defense of Guantánamo capital cases.

ALLISON M. LEFRAK is an associate at Reed Smith in Washington, D.C.

SARAH H. LORR is a student at Fordham Law School in New York City.

ELLEN LUBELL is a principal of the firm Tennant Lubell LLC in Newton, Massachusetts.

TRIP MACKINTOSH currently practices in the areas of white-collar criminal defense and export controls compliance and defense in Denver, Colorado.

HANNA F. MADBAK is an associate at Baker Hostetler in New York City.

EMI MACLEAN was a staff attorney at the Center for Constitutional Rights from 2006 to 2009.

HOWARD J. MANCHEL is a partner at Manchel, Wiggins, Kaye LLP.

DAVID MARSHALL has a private practice in Seattle, Washington.

JULIA TARVER MASON is a partner at Paul, Weiss, Rifkind, Wharton & Garrison LLP in New York City.

DAVID MCCOLGIN is a Supervisory Assistant Federal Defender in charge of the Appeals Unit for the Federal Community Defender Office in Philadelphia, Pennsylvania.

JOE MCMILLAN is a partner at Perkins Coie in Seattle, Washington.

GEORGE BRENT MICKUM VI is a partner at Spriggs & Hollingsworth in Washington, D.C.

MAJOR MICHAEL D. MORI, U.S. Marine Corps, served as military defense counsel for Guantánamo detainee David Hicks. The views expressed are his personally and do not represent the views of the United States Marine Corps or the Department of Defense.

SAHR MUHAMMEDALLY is a senior associate in the Law and Security Program at Human Rights First.

MARK MUOIO received his J.D. from Seton Hall University School of Law School in 2009 and has been a fellow at the Center for Policy and Research since 2007.

DONNA R. NEWMAN is a partner at Buttermore Newman Delanney & Foltz in New York City.

MARI NEWMAN is a partner at Killmer, Lane & Newman LLP in Denver, where she practices civil rights and employment law.

JIM NICKOVICH practices law in San Francisco.

SHAWN NOLAN works in the Federal Community Defender Office for the Eastern District of Pennsylvania.

MATTHEW O'HARA is a partner of Reed Smith LLP in Chicago.

ANDREW G. PATEL has a private practice in New York City.

CHUCK PATTERSON is a partner at Morrison & Foerster in Los Angeles.

WESLEY R. POWELL is a partner at Hunton & Williams in New York City.

ANDREA J. PRASOW is a defense attorney in the Office of the Chief Defense Counsel, Office of Military Commissions.

JANA RAMSEY is an associate at Paul, Weiss, Rifkind, Wharton and Garrison LLP.

MICHAEL RATNER is an attorney and the president of the Center for Constitutional Rights. With CCR he is the author of *The Trial of Donald Rumsfeld: A Prosecution by Book.*

ANANT RAUT is Counsel to the Committee on the Judiciary of the United States House of Representatives. He formerly represented Guantánamo detainees while an associate at Weil, Gotshal & Manges LLP.

DAVID H. REMES is Legal Director of Appeal for Justice, a nonprofit human rights and civil liberties litigation firm. Before founding Appeal for Justice in 2008, he was a partner at Covington & Burling LLP in Washington, D.C.

MARGARET L. SATTERTHWAITE is Faculty Director of the Center for Human Rights and Global Justice and Associate Professor of Clinical Law at New York University School of Law.

JOHN SIFTON is an attorney, private investigator, and writer. He has worked for Human Rights Watch and One World Research.

AMRIT SINGH is a staff attorney at the Immigrants' Rights Project of the American Civil Liberties Union. She is coauthor (with Jameel Jaffer) of *Administration of Torture, A Documentary Record from Washington to Abu Ghraib and Beyond.*

MARJORIE M. SMITH has her own practice in Piermont, New York, where she specializes in federal criminal appeals and habeas corpus.

KENT SPRIGGS is the practitioner of Spriggs Law Firm in Tallahassee, Florida.

CLIVE STAFFORD SMITH is Founder and Director of Reprieve in London, England.

JEFFREY M. STRAUSS has practiced law at Mayer Brown in Chicago for 28 years, focusing on complex litigation and corporate transactions. He has also been involved in pro bono work on behalf of Guantánamo detainees.

COLONEL DWIGHT SULLIVAN, United States Marine Corps Reserve, served as Chief Defense Counsel in the Office of Military Commissions from 2005 to 2007.

THOMAS P. SULLIVAN is a partner at Jenner Block in Chicago, Illinois.

ALAN SUSSMAN was a partner in the law firm Ricken, Goldman, Sussman & Blythe, Kingston, New York, and is currently an adjunct professor at Bard College.

DORIS TENNANT is an attorney of Tennant Lubell LLC in Newton, Massachusetts.

HANNAH TENNANT-MOORE is an award-winning freelance writer who has covered the Guantánamo litigation extensively.

STEVEN M. WATT is senior staff attorney with the Human Rights Program of the American Civil Liberties Union.

CAROLYN M. WELSHHANS represented prisoners at Guantánamo, and wrote the piece in this volume, while employed at Dechert LLP. Ms. Welshhans has since joined the staff of the United States Securities and Exchange Commission. (The Commission disclaims responsibility for any private publication or statement of any SEC employee or Commissioner. Ms. Welshhans's piece in this volume expresses the views of Ms. Welshhans and does not necessarily reflect those of the Commission, the Commissioners, or members of the staff.)

P. SABIN WILLETT is a partner at Bingham McCutchen in Boston, Massachusetts.

THOMAS B. WILNER is of counsel at Shearman & Sterling LLP in Washington, D.C.

ELIZABETH WILSON is Assistant Professor of Human Rights Law at the John C. Whitehead School of Diplomacy and International Relations at Seton Hall University.

MARK WILSON is Senior Trial Counsel at the Federal Community Defender for the Eastern District of Pennsylvania.

RICHARD WILSON is a professor of law and Director of the International Human Rights Law Clinic at American University Washington College of Law in Washington, D.C.

PAUL M. WINKE is a counsel of WilmerHale in New York City.

BEN WIZNER has been a staff attorney at the American Civil Liberties Union since 2001.

GORDON S. WOODWARD is a partner with the law firm of Schnader Harrison Segal & Lewis LLP.

YASMIN ZAINULBHAI is a student at Fordham Law School in New York City.

NOV - 6 2009

CENTRAL ISLIP PUBLIC LIBRARY

3 1800 00265 3547

2653547

343.   The Guantánamo Lawyers
7301
GUA

$24.95

Central Islip Public Library
33 Hawthorne Avenue
central Islip, NY 11722-2496

GAYLORD M